Game Development with Godot 4

Godot is a rapidly growing free and open-source game engine for creating 2D and 3D games, and interactive applications on many platforms, including desktop and mobile. There has been intense interest in this engine among game developers worldwide. This tutorial book offers an accessible, easy-to-follow and fun introduction to Godot Engine 4 for game developers, both complete newcomers and migrators from alternative game engines, like Unity and Unreal. This book practically explores the process of setting up the Godot software for the first time, creating 2D and 3D scenes with interactive elements, and using the GDScript language to create common gameplay elements, like first-person controls. Overall, this technical book offers a structured and friendly introduction to many of Godot's impressive features to help you get started at making games as an indie game developer. This book explores nodes, scenes, hierarchies, import workflows, scripting, animations, user interfaces, working with resources, and creating gameplay elements, among others.

Alan Thorn is a game developer, author, and educator. Alan has written 34 books, presented 30 online courses, and created 33 games, including the award-winning adventure, Baron Wittard. Alan is dedicated to helping creative people make high-impact experiences. He was Studio Director at Wax Lyrical Games, and now he is course leader for 'Indie Games Development' at the BAFTA-winning National Film and Television School, an incubation space for breakthrough gaming talent.

Game Development with Godot 4
A Complete Introduction

Alan Thorn

CRC Press
Taylor & Francis Group
Boca Raton London New York

CRC Press is an imprint of the
Taylor & Francis Group, an **Informa** business

Designed cover image: Shutterstock

First edition published 2026
by CRC Press
2385 NW Executive Center Drive, Suite 320, Boca Raton FL
33431

and by CRC Press
4 Park Square, Milton Park, Abingdon, Oxon, OX14 4RN

CRC Press is an imprint of Taylor & Francis Group, LLC

© 2026 Alan Thorn

ISBN: 978-1-032-77728-3 (hbk)
ISBN: 978-1-032-75924-1 (pbk)
ISBN: 978-1-003-48452-3 (ebk)

DOI: 10.1201/9781003484523

Access the Support Material: www.routledge.com/9781032759241

Typeset in Minion
by SPi Technologies India Pvt Ltd (Straive)

Contents

Introduction

THE GAMES INDUSTRY ALWAYS seems to be in a kind of chaos: a tumultuous swirl of creation and destruction. In this fast-moving and high-risk context, many brave people decide to become independent game developers. These people choose to make their own games, in their own time, and in their own way, using a variety of powerful tools. An increasingly popular tool of choice for indies is the Godot game engine. This is a free, open-source, and dedicated program for building games, interactive applications, VR, mobile games, and more. This program is an alternative to the many well-known engines out there, such as Unreal, Unity, and GameMaker. This book is a dedicated introduction to Godot for the indie developer, an introduction that shows Godot as a viable alternative to many well-established engines. So, thank you for choosing this book. I hope it helps you along in your exciting journey.

WHAT IS GODOT?

Godot is a computer software called a *Game Engine*. The rest of this book is dedicated to the larger question of what exactly Godot is and can do. But, in summary, Godot is designed to be a complete suite of tools for building video games that run on a wide variety of platforms. Godot is notable for being a cross-platform tool for making cross-platform games. Godot can not only make games for desktop, mobile, and consoles, but the engine itself can also run on Windows, Linux, and Mac. This allows you to develop games on your chosen operating system, so you can use the tools and UIs that you prefer. As we'll see, Godot is free, cross-platform, open-source, and community-driven. It has been in development for many years now and remains actively developed by the core team.

WHO IS THIS BOOK FOR?

There are many ways and approaches to learning Godot. This book is one of them. If most of the following applies to you, then this book is probably a good match:

1. You're completely new to Godot. You've heard about it and now want to learn more.

2. Maybe you've explored other engines, such as Unity or Unreal. Maybe you've used them before and now want to relate your knowledge to Godot.

3. You enjoy learning from books. Sure, there are many ways to learn game development, from video tutorials to in-person courses. But a book offers you an offline way to consume and enjoy learning at your own pace.

4. You want to learn enough of Godot to feel confident in the basics, be able to build your first game, and be prepared to easily learn more for the future.

HOW SHOULD I READ THIS BOOK?

If you're completely new to Godot, then this book should be read from cover to cover, chapter by chapter, in the order you encounter them. I recommend reading the book through first without being at the software and then going back and following along in the software on the second reading, completing the projects and exercises step by step. If you have some prior experience with game engines, Godot or otherwise, you may find it more useful to skip ahead to specific chapters of interest.

WHAT OUTCOMES CAN I EXPECT FROM THIS BOOK?

By reading this book, you will explore an overview of the Godot engine as a game development tool. The book is written for newcomers to the engine and doesn't require any specific pre-knowledge. Chapter 4 on Programming introduces the Scripting Language, GDScript, and assumes a basic understanding of programming concepts, such as variables, functions, and loops. You can get this knowledge by learning languages like Python, JavaScript, or C#. However, you may also be able to pick up these concepts as you work through the chapters here. Apart from code, I approach each chapter as an introduction to a specific feature, or set of features, in Godot. This foundational knowledge will allow you to start using Godot with a new confidence and fluency that will let you build games. There will always be more to learn, as with any tool, but the knowledge here can act as a skeleton, or framework, to which new ideas and new learning can be attached with greater understanding.

CAN'T I JUST LEARN ALL THIS STUFF FROM YOUTUBE ANYWAY?

Yes, you can. That shouldn't be surprising in a fast-paced, tech-driven industry where people share knowledge with each other all the time. There is no 'secret body' of game development knowledge that unlocks the secrets of professional game development. Being a professional game developer is about practicing your skills over time and seeing a game engine as a problem-solving tool. What this book does, which is sometimes harder to achieve on YouTube, is package the beginner knowledge into a structured learning pathway, where different subjects are introduced in a logical order that allows you to get the most from your learning, saving you time.

DOES THIS BOOK FEATURE COMPANION FILES?

Yes. Many of the exercises presented in the book feature companion files. However, I try to keep the projects as empty of assets as possible, so you can focus on the concepts and ideas themselves. For this reason, I try to introduce projects in such a way that you don't need the files, even though they are available.

ISN'T THIS BOOK OUT OF DATE ALREADY?

Well, that depends on when you're reading this. But, in a fast-paced industry that changes almost daily, almost every book, article, video, or resource is in some way out of date. Nonetheless, this book features so many foundational concepts, which – despite surface changes – have remained the same in Godot and in game development for a long time. For this reason, depending on when you read this, the latest version of Godot may feature UI changes and buttons in slightly different places, but many of the concepts will be the same. For best results, I recommend using Godot 4.4.

CHAPTER 1

Introducing Godot

Getting to Know the Engine

W ELCOME TO THE BUSTLING world of game development, and con-
gratulations on choosing Godot for making your games. Godot is
simply an amazing piece of software from which you can build nearly any
game imaginable. You're probably here because you want to make video
games professionally, either as an employee working at an established
games company or as a self-employed independent developer making
your own games in your own way for a niche audience. Either way, this
chapter cuts to the chase about what Godot is in general terms. It further
explores the many excellent reasons to choose Godot for your next game,
as well as some important limitations to be aware of. Making games is a
highly technical and time-consuming process. For this reason, it's essential to weigh many broader technical points before investing your valuable
time into creating any games using Godot, or any engine, to ensure that
you're making the right decisions for the right reasons within the very
busy world that we all live in. I'm very excited to show you the amazing
Godot. So, let's get started.

1.1 WHAT EXACTLY IS GODOT?

Godot is a game engine. This software is specifically designed to help you
make games, both 2D and 3D. Its features and toolset are purpose-built to
support technically aware people to assemble games in a convenient and

DOI: 10.1201/9781003484523-1

flexible way, striking a fragile balance between ease of use and technical power. Godot is *not* an artificial intelligence (AI) for generating games automatically at the click of a button, nor is it a no-code environment where cookie-cutter games are customized entirely using the mouse in a drag-and-drop way, requiring no previous game development knowledge. Godot aspires to neither of these. Rather, Godot assumes some basic, technical expertise from the user – such as familiarity with 2D and 3D concepts – and it offers them a hugely powerful and convenient suite of tools for making professional-grade games through an easy-to-use interface, known as an Integrated Development Environment (IDE). To learn and use Godot effectively, you don't need to have previously used any other engine or to have taken any classes in game development. However, a basic awareness of computer programming (in any popular language) and a foundational grasp of 3D (such as a coordinate system measured in X, Y, and Z) are assumed by both Godot as an engine and by the rest of this book too (Figure 1.1).

Godot's comprehensive feature set, like that of almost every other game engine, is designed to support the creation of a game throughout *most* of its lifetime. Godot does a superb job of this. Specifically, a 'typical' game developer who is making a 'typical' game will use Godot in all the following four major ways, taken sequentially.

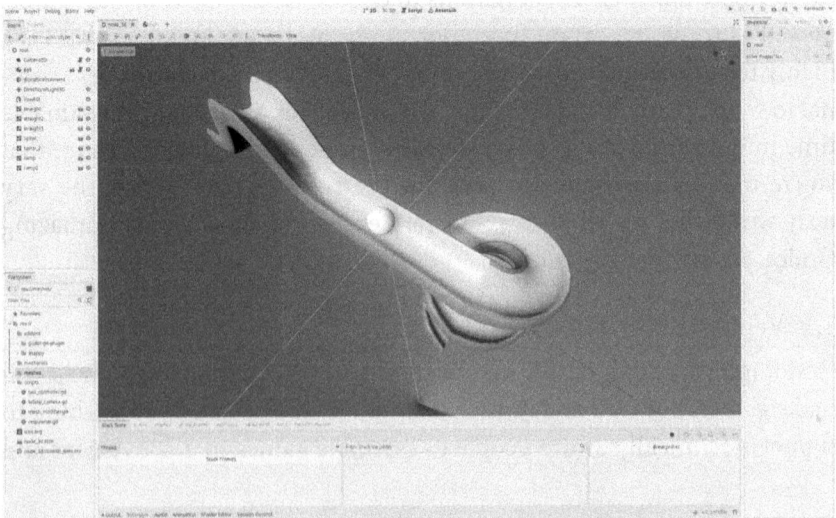

FIGURE 1.1   Godot being used to create a marble runner game.

1. **Asset Importing**. The starting point for building a game inside Godot is to import ready-made props into Godot. This includes meshes – like characters, weapons, rocks, and trees – and also music and sound, and some but not all animations. This represents your full menu of content, which can be included within the game world. Note that Godot *assumes* you have all these things *ready-made* and also in a format and medium that it can accept optimally. Godot is *not* a content creation tool, like Blender, Maya, or 3DS Max. Content creation tools are used by artists to begin with nothing and then to sculpt meshes, draw textures, create rigging, and create other data as a collection of assets. Those assets themselves are exported from the content creation tool in a specific format and can be fed into Godot for use inside a game. Godot therefore supports the import process according to a specific set of rules, allowing developers to import their assets from content creation software into the engine, where the assets can finally be used *as-is* within a game. If a developer later changes their mind about the fundamental structure of any imported asset – such as wanting to change a pine tree into a willow tree instead – then the artist must *return* to the content creation software and make the changes there prior to re-exporting the new version again back into Godot. Later chapters of this book will explore the import process in more depth in the context of using Blender as a content creation tool.

2. **Scene Construction**. Importing assets is about getting content into Godot in a form that is accessible and usable. Once the import process is completed, developers may then *use* the imported content. Most notably, this happens through level design or scene construction. Godot offers extensive level design tools, allowing you to place meshes meaningfully within a 3D space to build both interior and exterior worlds, from forests to space stations, depending on your assets. Additionally, Godot offers tools for configuring imported characters – such as humanoid characters – to behave as intended and tools for customizing how the surface of meshes are rendered, as well as many other tools that ultimately affect how the stage is dressed, made, and behaves. The full breadth of tools offered here is truly staggering, powerful, and in constant flux in each new release. No exhaustive list would be possible or even useful. Rather, these tools collectively are used for building worlds from the ready-made assets you import. It is also these tools that most readily come to

mind when most people think of a game engine and its value. We will cover a substantial number of these tools throughout the book.

3. **Coding and Testing**. After a developer has created at least the basic template of a world from imported assets, they are ready to make things come alive by using programming. This includes making the player character move around and jump in response to player input and making non-player characters (NPCs) behave with intelligence and reason. It also includes applying the rules and forces of the game, such as recognizing physical collisions when they occur, creating gravity and physical forces that pull objects downwards, and creating a win-and-loss condition that allows the player to progress from level to level. In Godot, such gameplay behavior may be created by a programmer using one of two languages, namely GDScript or C#. C# has the widest industry traction generally as a language, but surprisingly, it is GDScript that is most commonly used in Godot. More on this subject is discussed later. Unlike many other popular engines, Godot comes with a complete code editor that lets you write and debug code directly from the Godot interface, with no external software required.

4. **Exporting**. The final tools that developers normally use in Godot are the export tools. These allow developers at the end of the development process to take a fully made game inside the engine and to convert it automatically into a standalone, executable form, which people can play independently. This exported version of a game is standalone insofar as it doesn't require players to have the Godot engine installed themselves to play the game. The game can simply be played as a self-contained entity on the player's computer, like any other application. The export process is presented to developers through only a limited set of 'simple looking' windows inside Godot, but it is actually a complicated process in many cases. By default, Godot can export games for the PC platform, mobile, web, and consoles too. That sounds exciting. However, each of these export options is attached to many conditions, limitations, and technical minutiae, some of which we will visit later in this book. As with most engines, there is a world of difference between the advertised platforms that you can, technically, export to and the platforms that, in practice, you will feasibly be able to export to. This can be a

painful area where creative aspiration can meet the cold, hard reality of limitations – with cost, time, expertise, law, and regulation being important factors.

NOTE. Before proceeding further, check out some of the excellent work from the talented Godot community being created by using the engine here: https://godotengine.org/showcase/

1.2 THE POWER OF GODOT – REASONS TO USE THE ENGINE

Godot is an incredibly powerful and desirable engine. It unquestionably holds its own in a fast-paced world where many excellent engines exist. Developers today are simply spoiled for choice when it comes to game engines. A quick search online reveals that Unity, Unreal, GameMaker, RPG Maker, GDevelop, Construct, Stride, and many other engines exist to help developers turn their dreams into games. And, rest assured, all these engines are excellent choices. That is why all of them are still being used today and all have survived for long periods of time, and some through especially difficult times too. The question as to which engine one should use for their next game is best met not by finding fault with the competition, but by understanding the many highlights and strengths of each engine to see how it connects with your purpose. That is, by understanding the many different ways that an engine will add value to what you plan to do. Godot is certainly not alone in being amazing and in having many wonderful characteristics that we can all enjoy and celebrate as developers. But this section highlights some key strengths of the Godot engine. It looks at important ways in which Godot, as an engine choice, can benefit you, your business, and your games immensely. In short, it looks at some of the underlying ways in which Godot is so powerful, and why it makes a great choice in the contemporary world of game development. It is important to at least understand these reasons, even if not all of them apply to your case or are especially important to you. By understanding the strengths and benefits it brings, we can also plan better for the future.

1.2.1 Godot Is Open Source

Open source is basically the idea that a program's source code is 'made public' such that absolutely anybody (including you) can fully inspect the code, view it, learn from it, and, potentially, even modify or enhance it for their own purposes or to contribute back to the community. Being able to read and understand the source code necessarily requires a certain level of technical knowledge, but the idea of open source is that any interested person can access the code of a program at any time. Godot is a fully open-source engine in this sense. You can view its complete source code here: https://github.com/godotengine/godot. An open-source engine is especially valuable to a game developer because it means that a developer can see how their engine is made under the hood, feel confident about what it does, and be able to amend or enhance the engine to suit their needs if necessary, including to fix bugs or to add features.

Most comparable engines are not open source. And even if some others are open source, it's not usually under the same generous terms as Godot. Instead, most engines are *proprietary*, and their source code cannot be viewed or modified by anybody but the engine developers themselves or anybody else they grant permission to view. The code is therefore locked up inside a black box, metaphorically. Such cases mean that you, as a *game* developer and a *user* of the engine, must necessarily trust the vendor (the engine creator) to fix any substantive bugs that may be found in the engine, to responsibly maintain the engine code, and to periodically release new features – including security features – to keep pace with industry developments, cybersecurity, and general change. Given that the game engine will be at the core of your business if you choose to use it for game development, closed-source engines therefore require you to put a lot of trust into a single engine vendor whose interests may or may not align with your own. If they do align with your own, it's possibly only coincidentally so. It's worth reflecting on. Now, this kind of implicit trust may be a trust that you are *willing* to give to an engine developer for the sake of making games. After all, we put our trust into many different companies simply to do our jobs on a daily basis in many areas of life. However, in a bustling world where high-quality open-source engines are easily available for game development, it is not a trust that you *must* give. Nor is it a trust that engine developers are entitled to. Consequently, open source as a model helps developers feel like an integral part of the engine development community, even if they don't actually modify an engine or even if they simply use it 'as is' to make games. It still gives them a level of scrutiny and input into the engine, and it helps them to understand the engine more deeply.

1.2.2 Godot Is Free Software

Godot is free software, and that's truly marvelous news for everybody. However, 'free software' is more of a movement than a price issue. Although Godot is indeed free of any price to download and use, even for commercial purposes, this is not actually what is meant when it's said to be 'free software'. Software is classed as 'free' by the Free Software Foundation (FSF) when it supports four basic *freedoms* for users (https://www.gnu.org/philosophy/ free-sw.en.html#four-freedoms). Namely, the freedom to run the program for any purpose, the freedom to view the source code, the freedom to redistribute copies of the original program, and the freedom to redistribute any modified versions of the program. With Godot, you get all those freedoms, and it's free in the common sense of the word too. It literally costs nothing. You can find out more about how Godot is free software by viewing the following license page on the Godot website: https://godotengine.org/ license/. Knowing that an engine is free software is empowering for a developer, because it shifts an important kind of control from engine developers to users of engines, allowing developers not only access to the source code, as already mentioned, but also the ability to run the engine unencumbered by various other restrictions and limitations in law.

> NOTE. You may wonder: if Godot truly is free of charge, then how does it make money and support itself? After all, there must surely be costs even in making the engine available to download. One way is by support from the community in donations. You can find out more and donate to this excellent community by visiting the following donations page here: https://fund.godotengine.org/

1.2.3 Godot Is Cross-Platform

Godot stands apart as one of the most cross-platform engines available today. This is not about the different platforms that you can eventually export your games to, such as mobile and consoles. That is important, but that's not what is meant in this section. Rather, it's about the different platforms that Godot, as an engine, *can run on during development*, allowing you to develop and work on different types of computers. Godot runs on Windows, Mac, and Linux. Additionally, there is also a Web Editor version (https://editor.godotengine.org/releases/latest/), which is Godot running inside a web browser. Within the world of Linux, Godot can run on many different flavors, including Ubuntu (https://ubuntu.com/), PopOS (https://pop.system76.com/), and Mint (https://linuxmint.com/).

Impressively, Godot is not substantially feature-limited on any platform, and so it looks, feels, and behaves the same on all supported platforms in most respects. This book does not assume that you're using any particular platform. You can use Windows, Mac, or Linux and follow along with the book successfully. It is, however, worth mentioning that some export options – such as exporting to iOS or to consoles – do make platform requirements due to how those platforms work, rather than from any limitations of Godot. This does not apply to any projects created in the book but is worth remembering for your own projects in the future. For example, you may need an iMac to export for iOS platforms or a special Development Hardware Version of a console (such as a Nintendo Switch) to successfully build for those platforms.

1.2.4 Godot Is for 2D and 3D

Godot is a general-purpose game engine and resolutely doesn't, by design, attach itself to any one style or genre of game, as some other engines may elect to do, for better or worse. Rather, Godot follows a similar and praiseworthy line to both Unity and, to some extent, Unreal by offering an extensive feature set for creating *both* 2D and 3D games, as well as allowing interesting hybrids anywhere between. This is reflected in the naming conventions used throughout the engine, as we will see later, such as in class names and object names, where many items are post-fixed with a 2D or a 3D designation. In addition, Godot also supports AR and VR development and can also include live-action videos. In short, Godot abstracts game development to its widest practicable extent and supports the maximum kind of creative freedom, allowing developers to build games in any genre, in any style, and on almost any platform. In theory, this offers you significant creative freedom at the design stages. As with all engines, each design choice necessarily comes with its technical limitations at the implementation stage, often constrained by the hardware on which the game runs, as well as by your development budget. This marks the collision point where ideas meet reality. There will always be limits to the number of polygons renderable on any single frame, the number of objects shown to any one camera, the maximum size of textures, the capacity of music or audio that can be played, the totality of post-processing that can be applied, and so on. These limitations are almost always context-sensitive, and they happen because computer power is finite and precious and because our pockets are not bottomless. But all these technical limitations largely determine only how deep one may go, and not how wide. And that's empowering.

In terms of width, indeed, Godot allows both 2D and 3D, AR, and VR, and this is among the widest of all possible widths. We will see later how to create content in Godot in both 2D and 3D, as well as a mixed medium.

1.2.5 Godot Is Tried and Tested

A not-unimportant question to ask when choosing any engine is, has the engine been used previously by anybody to actually make any real, playable, and finished games? This question is relevant because its answer, if positive, may give us some reassurance that the engine is battle-tested and ready to be of service. If the answer is no, you may be dealing with either a very new engine or a deeply problematic one. This alone need not stop you from using the engine. After all, the very first game for any new engine *must* be made by *someone*. But it should lead you to ask further probing questions about *why* before taking the important leap. Certainly, if you are very new to game development, I would strongly discourage you from choosing a brand new, untested, and poorly documented game engine. Doing so is usually the starting point for a project that ends badly, assuming it doesn't get abandoned beforehand. However, with Godot, the entire issue is muted because the answer here is firmly 'yes'. Yes, Godot has now been used by many different developers to power many excellent games in many genres on nearly every contemporary platform. The Godot showcase page, with its list of commercially created Godot-powered games, stands as an impressive testament to the clear momentum that Godot is gaining industry-wide as its successful adoption increases. This can be both a cause of optimism and excitement in making the choice to use Godot. It is also an indication that community support – such as technical support – for the engine is sufficiently robust. It's certainly robust enough to create the unquestionable climate that we now have where a steady stream of Godot releases is always flowing.

1.2.6 Godot Is Supported

The concept of 'support' in the world of computing is a truly messy one indeed. Almost no program is released today without 'support', and no sensible company or developer wants to declare their software is 'totally unsupported', even for a lower price. Support as a concept is a 'warm blanket' and a 'feel good' word. It feels like the kind of thing that every program should have. Whenever you choose software, it certainly feels good knowing that there's 'support' around if you wake up one day and find yourself unfortunate enough to need it. But what does it *really* amount to in practice? What does 'support' really look like, especially for a free and open-source game engine like Godot?

For some, the ideal support option is the corporate dream: a premium and shiny package that you pay a company handsomely to deliver to get access to a direct hotline linking you instantly to someone incredibly knowledgeable with solid answers readily available on demand. Of course, the reality of that scenario might simply be you asking questions endlessly to an obtuse chatbot that fails to grasp even the fundamentals before you scream out for a human who truly isn't there. But in any case, none of these methods is normally how support works in free and open-source software for game developers. It's simply not what support means, and often this is for the better. For Godot, support takes two major forms. That is, the act of getting help to use the software effectively will lead you to one of two places, and maybe both.

1. **Community**

   Godot, as an engine, is supported by an amazing community of talented, knowledgeable, and very kind-hearted people who spend a lot of time online simply helping other developers use the Godot engine to make games. These people are not employees or paid support workers. Rather, they are other members of the community who also use Godot and want it to succeed, and they choose to go online and share their knowledge to help. The community is a great place for asking questions, sharing problems, and generally hearing about upcoming features in the engine. The community is spread across multiple social channels, which you can access freely here: https://godotengine.org/community/

2. **Documentation**

   Godot is a well-documented engine. It features a comprehensive online library of resources to both learn and use the engine, ranging from how-to tutorials targeted at newcomers to more in-depth reference documentation for experienced users, such as class API documentation. During this book and during your career as a Godot game developer, the documentation will inevitably be your constant companion and friend. It will help you reference important information, so you'll probably have it open and accessible always. Please don't fall into the dangerous trap of believing that support is only for newcomers, as though experienced developers somehow reach such a point of inward know-how that the documentation becomes super-fluous for them. This isn't true. Godot is so wide and deep that you'll always have a need to look up things. Thankfully, in addition to the online library, Godot also has an offline built-in version of the reference documentation directly in the editor. This will be covered later.

1.2.7 Godot Is Interoperable

Interoperability is an engine's ability to play nicely with other related software. In this respect, Godot does an unquestionably great job. Godot can import lots of different types of data from external sources. As we'll see, you can import images as textures in most common formats, such as PNG and TIFF; you can import audio and sounds as OGG or WAV; you can import fonts from standard font files like OTF; and you can import 3D meshes as FBX or GLTF files. If some of those file types are unfamiliar to you, don't worry. We'll cover them later in the book. For now, it is sufficient to note that Godot can import many media types and can output to many different platforms. It should be mentioned that one of the historical reasons why interoperability is so crucially important for a game engine – including Godot – is because game engines are *not*, strictly speaking, content creation tools. As mentioned earlier, Godot is *not* used by artists to create 3D models or by composers to make soundtracks. These kinds of assets are created *ex nihilo* and externally, in other software such as Blender or Audacity. Eventually, they are exported from these programs in particular file formats and then imported into Godot, ready-made and ready to use. Without this pipeline of interoperability, therefore, Godot would essentially be near unusable because you couldn't otherwise import anything.

> NOTE. Although you *can* import meshes into Godot, that doesn't mean that Godot supports *every* feature of your content creation software. Depending on which program you use to make your 3D models and which features within that program you use, some data may export as intended and others not. This can lead to models looking or behaving slightly differently in Godot compared to the content creation software. We will discuss this important issue again later in the book.

1.3 GODOT – ITS BENEFITS AND LIMITATIONS

There is a true and meaningful sense in which Godot – and any game engine generally – may be said to have 'unlimited potential'. Indeed, a game engine can be used to make almost anything imaginable, whether that's Unity,

Godot, Unreal, or any engine. This is true enough. Nonetheless, we find ourselves in a world of many practical constraints – including hardware and time and budget. We must usually make compromises in our work-flow to accommodate these limits. We take shortcuts and avoid expensive plans. This is not due to the limitations of software but because we need to get things done in the shortest time possible and within the lowest budget possible. Thus, different engines meet our needs in different ways. Different engines shine for different purposes and applications. This is because of their development history, where features are added to serve various kinds of users over time. And so, there are some types of games for which Godot is *ideally suited*, simply *because* of the features it has, the documentation available, and the way those features are implemented currently. But conversely, and for the same reasons, some games are more inconvenient to make in Godot than in other engines, even though they are not impossible to make. This is true for all engines, and Godot is no exception. This section therefore takes some time to explore the general limitations of Godot to help you set your expectations before starting projects.

1. **Assets and Libraries**

   Assets are props. They include all the ready-made models, textures, animations, and music that you can simply drop into your game to assemble a scene. This includes weapons, characters, architectural elements, trees and foliage, special effects, and whole behavior systems. Now, you can make your own custom assets from scratch using additional software, or you can source ready-made assets (free and commercial) from third parties over online marketplaces. The Unity and Unreal engines both have truly enormous online marketplaces filled with assets that you download or buy. This is great because you can assemble good-looking games quickly by using them, whether they are production-grade games or early prototypes. The main creative downside to using these non-exclusive assets is that many other developers may have used them many times before you, so your game could end up appearing like a lot of others. But that said, there are still many ways you could tweak or adjust assets to appear meaningfully unique. This is about striking an artistic balance and depends on good judgment more than good software. Godot, however, doesn't yet have an equivalent asset store, as we will see. There is a growing and expanding Asset Library in Godot, which we will explore, and it contains interesting and useful assets. And there are other sites too, seeking to become an asset library for Godot. However, these places do not offer a similar level of choice or sophistication when compared to some other engines. For this reason, Godot users don't have the same immediate access to as big a library of ready-made content as Unreal or Unity. This is not necessarily a problem if you're making your own assets or are happy with the more limited choice from the Asset Library. However, if you're hoping for a massive library of Godot-specific, production-grade, ready-made materials, then you could end up disappointed.

NOTE. There are also third-party sites that offer general-purpose assets for multiple engines, like Godot, such as https://kenney.nl/assets.

2. **Third-Party Integrations**
   Some popular third-party tools in game development, like *FMOD* and *wWise* – which are used extensively for sound design – have varied support for Godot. There are many other tools and libraries too, such as MongoDB, Firebase, and hardware integrations like Arduino. Here, the support situation is rapidly changing for many tools as Godot gains wider adoption. However, in several instances, some tools are simply not built with Godot compatibility out of the box yet. There may be hacks or workarounds to build this compatibility manually. That's one of the great benefits of open source, but it can be time-consuming, especially if you're a solo developer. In other cases, some tools may have either full or partial support, and this may be all that is needed. Godot is a growing and establishing engine. As such, industry-wide acceptance is growing, and so is third-party support. It's important to recognize and research this issue upfront because, if you're coming to Godot from another engine like Unity or Unreal, where third-party support is wider, you may have expectations around third-party integrations. Particularly if you're migrating from another engine and have a project that uses such integrations already. If these integrations are crucial to you and your team, please do research about their compatibility with Godot before starting your next project or migrating an existing one to avoid any unpleasant (or pleasant) surprises!

3. **Language Support**
   Most engines support a programming language. This language is used by programmers to code gameplay instructions, which define how a

game should behave when played. For example, how many weapons can a player collect? Which button makes a character jump? Should enemies chase you? These are the kinds of questions, among many others, that are answered with coded solutions. Godot supports two languages, namely GDScript and C#. You don't need to know or use both languages. Typically, you choose just one and use it consistently throughout a single project. Godot primarily supports GDScript, and this book features code only in that language. Although C# is supported, it has sometimes lagged behind in feature support. GDScript is like, but still distinct from, Python. If you already code in Python, you'll probably feel at home with GDScript. It's a great language. I detail it further later in the book. But it does pose a potential limitation. Many engines and tools use other general-purpose languages, which exist in many industries. GDScript, by contrast, is domain-specific. You're only likely to find it in Godot. So, it has a narrow application.

4. **Rendering, Realism, and Performance**

Godot features an intricate, versatile, and powerful render engine. The renderer is the internal engine component responsible for presenting 2D and 3D imagery to the screen in a performant way across devices. Using the Godot renderer, you can express complete 3D worlds with detailed lighting, animation, surface details, and much more. It's truly amazing indeed. However, in comparison to Unity and Unreal, the Godot renderer still trails behind in terms of feature parity. There are still some things that a Unity or an Unreal renderer can do, or do better, that the Godot renderer cannot do. This is not a criticism of Godot, but rather an important technical point of difference worth noting. In practice, this probably means that you'll find it easier to make a photorealistic Triple-A game in Unreal or Unity compared to Godot. But not everybody wants to make such a game. For cartoon styles, retro styles, illustrated styles, 2D comic styles, and more, you'll find plenty of great options in Godot.

5. **Console Exports**

The dream of 'build once and deploy everywhere' still exists in the game development community. It's an exciting idea. It's what most engines seem to aspire to. It's the thought of using a game engine to build your game only once and then using the supplied engine tools to output that game as a standalone entity, one that runs smoothly and the same on as many platforms as possible – such as PC, mobile, and consoles. Unfortunately, the ugly reality with every engine is that platform-specific work by the developer must happen to make a game run and run well, on different platforms. And sometimes that work will be substantial. This is no different in Godot. Godot can, in theory, export your game to many platforms, including consoles. However, to achieve that *in practice*, a lot of work is needed. For consoles, you'll probably need to apply for a license with the console manufacturer, you'll need to understand how its game controllers work, and you'll need to meet various content guidelines and legal requirements. This can get pretty complicated quickly for a lone developer. And if you don't get a handle on those things, then no amount of theory will deliver your game to those platforms. In sum, therefore, if you've never made a game before or have never worked with Godot before, I strongly recommend you pick one or two easily accessible platforms for newcomers and stick with those initially for your first title. This includes PC, web, and mobile platforms.

6. **Career Potential**

Throughout the rest of this book, I assume that you've chosen Godot as an engine because you want to make your own games or to work with friends and colleagues on building a game together of your own design. Godot is an amazing tool for that. It's perfect for indies. I think you'll love it! But sometimes, people don't choose to learn an engine for this end. They don't choose an engine to make their *own* games. Instead, they choose to learn an engine for *getting a job* at an established games studio to work in the industry on potentially bigger-budget games designed and led by other people. In this case, these people learn an engine to add value to their curriculum vitae or resume, and there's nothing wrong with that. However, I do not recommend Godot currently for this purpose. If you scan the job ads worldwide for most game studios today, they often seek people with experience in Unity or Unreal. This is largely because studios have been using those tools for a prolonged period. Godot is very new by comparison. It truly has lots to offer but has not yet established itself within the mainstream of game development. That may happen in the future. Nobody knows. But it's not being used by big studios yet day to day, and so there are consequently fewer job opportunities available for Godot. So, if resume building is your aim, I recommend

Unreal, Unity, or both. But, if making your own games in your own way in your own time as an indie is your aim, then Godot is great!

1.4 DOWNLOADING AND INSTALLING GODOT

It's now finally time to move away from introduction, theory, and potential. By reaching this point, you've decided that Godot is the right choice for you, and you probably have a wealth of excellent game ideas in mind. So, it's time to move forward, using Godot itself in practice. This is the fun part. The startup process will span several steps in sequence: preparation, download, installation, and configuration. Let's get started.

1.4.1 Preparation

Installing development software, like a game engine, is an important step. Game engines are complex pieces of software that can potentially access many files and change many settings. For this reason, you should take important preparation steps.

1. **Decide which operating system you will be developing on** throughout the project: Windows, Mac, or Linux. Godot supports them all. If you're working in a team, I recommend that all members use the same operating system throughout the entirety of the project. That's not essential, of course. You *can* have different team members on different operating systems, and you *can* even change your operating system during development if you really want to. However, the choice of operating system is within your power from the outset, and by keeping all these factors *constant* during development (by not changing them), you are reducing your confounding variables in the event of any problems. You will be making your life simpler. So, I recommend it.

2. **Backup your system and your data**. Your data and time are precious. Time is non-refundable. Once you've spent it, you cannot get it back. So please invest some time now in backing up your computer prior to installing any software to have peace of mind. Game development is complicated. It typically relies on heavy software, lots of files, lots of revisions and versions, and lots of configuration changes. It's easy to make mistakes and for things to go wrong. I can't tell you how many good things I've lost due to bad backup practices. So, it's important that you backup and make copies of all your data and software rigorously to ensure you don't lose anything important along the way.

This includes both personal and professional files. And remember, if you share your computer with others – such as team members or family members – then be sure their data gets backed up too. Furthermore, as you progress with this book and game development more generally, be sure to make regular backups of your work and data as you go. Build data backup and storage into your habitual working practice. You will be glad that you did. There are many options for backing up data. Your operating system will have some built-in options, and there are many cloud storage products too for retaining backups and portable hard drives. Be sure to save your data securely. If you're using cloud storage, then use a secure username, passphrase, and multi-factor authentication. If you're using portable hard drives, be sure to keep them in a safe location – such as a home safe or a separate location – and encrypt your data where possible. You can get free encryption tools with Gnu Privacy Guard (GPG) https://gnupg.org/.

3. **Secure your computer with security software**. As game developers, we're going to be downloading software from the internet and working with third-party files quite often. Further, some of these assets contain code. So, it's very important that your computer is properly secured with a firewall, antivirus, and general security software prior to working in games. And further, you adopt good working practices generally that respect your system security and privacy. Each operating system has different security suites that you can download or buy, and I recommend researching these carefully to find the package that best meets your needs. The UK government has issued some accessible and friendly guidelines to general security practices online that you may find helpful. Here: https://www.ncsc.gov.uk/collection/top-tips-for-staying-secure-online.

1.4.2 Installing Godot

1. **Download Godot**. Godot is a free, open-source game engine, and there are at least three ways to download it. First, you can visit the official Godot website here (https://godotengine.org/), click 'Download', and choose the relevant build for your operating system (*Windows, Linux, or Mac*). From the official website, you have the option to download two versions of Godot: the *Standard Edition* and the *.NET Edition*. For this book, you should use the Standard Edition. The .NET Edition is for users who want to code with C#, as opposed to GDScript.

You can also download Godot from Steam here: https://store.steam powered.com/app/404790/Godot_Engine/ and from Itch.io here: https:// godotengine.itch.io/godot.

I do not recommend downloading Godot from any location or source other than any of the three methods mentioned above.

NOTE. You can download earlier versions of Godot from the Godot archive here: https://godotengine.org/download/archive/. This archive stretches back to the very first release of Godot in 2014.

NOTE. Projects in this book were made with Godot 4.3, but they should also work in Godot 4.4. This book was written at the change point between 4.3 and 4.4, and so the material is relevant to both versions. I recommend using Godot 4.4. You can download a copy of either (or both) versions from the Godot download archive. You can have multiple versions of Godot on your computer. If you use a different version, some of the projects in the associated book files may not open or behave correctly, although much of the information and knowledge from the chapters will still be relevant. In the world of game development, don't assume that all later engine versions are fully backward compatible with earlier ones. Often, your projects break if you try to open them in later versions of the engine. You should always stick with the engine version that you used to create a project unless you have a very good reason not to.

2. **Unpack Godot**. Godot is packaged in a compressed archive, which can be extracted onto your computer in a local folder, such as / *MyDocuments/Godot*. You'll need to extract all files and folders contained in the archive. Unusually, compared to most engines, Godot doesn't feature any automated installer. So, you'll need to manually create a desktop shortcut on your computer if you want quick access to the Godot executable. For MacOS, Godot is code-signed and notarized, which means it should run without issues. However, there is a troubleshooting guide on the Godot website for all platforms, which addresses common issues: https://docs.godotengine.org/en/ stable/tutorials/troubleshooting.html.

3. **Run Godot for the first time**. Double-click the Godot icon to run the program on your desktop or laptop computer. The first screen to appear is featured in Figure 1.2. The project list contains a list of recently opened or used projects. If this is the first time you're running Godot, your project list will be empty.

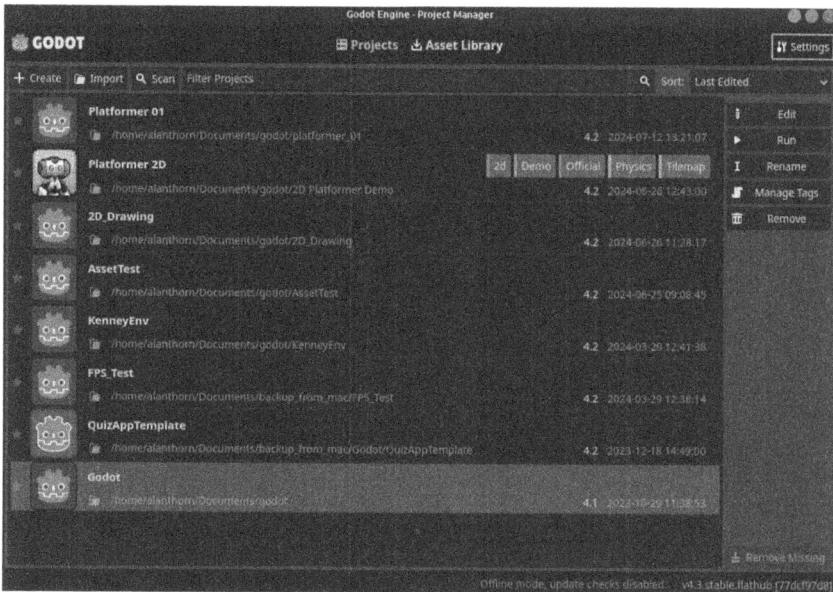

FIGURE 1.2   Startup screen for Godot.

1.5 CONFIGURING GODOT

So, you've now installed Godot successfully on your computer and started the launcher. You can check out your Godot version number from the bottom right-hand side of the launcher window. Most important is the full version number, for example, 4.3. This may be followed by other data, depending on your operating system. From my screenshot, for example, you can see that I am using Linux because of the postfix string 'stable.flathub'. A Windows or Mac installation would appear differently (see Figure 1.3).

> NOTE. Always make a note of your Godot version if you move between computers and prior to opening your projects. Remember that it's important for every team member to use the same version and for you to retain the same Godot version throughout your project unless there is an overriding reason not to.

Most of the configuration settings for Godot are embedded deeper within the software, which we will see in the next chapter. However, from the launcher, we can adjust important settings that people often miss in their eagerness to jump into the software immediately. In the top right-hand corner of the Launcher window, there is a *Settings* button (see Figure 1.4).

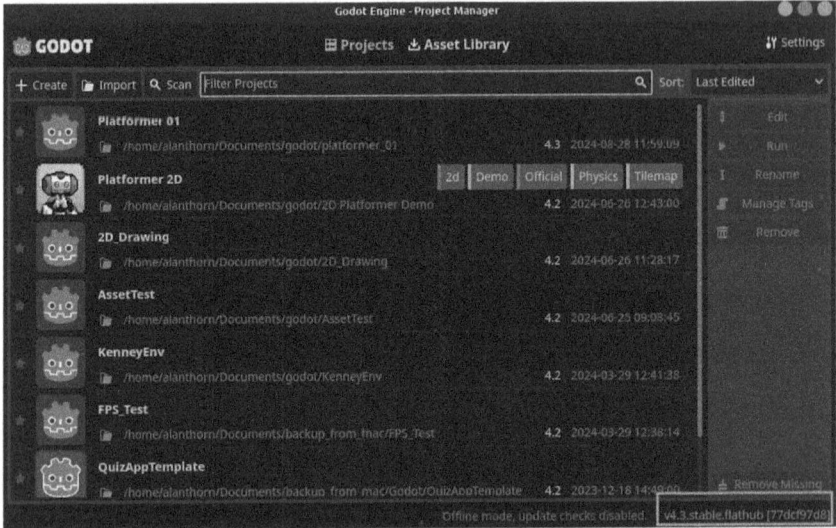

FIGURE 1.3   Checking your Godot version.

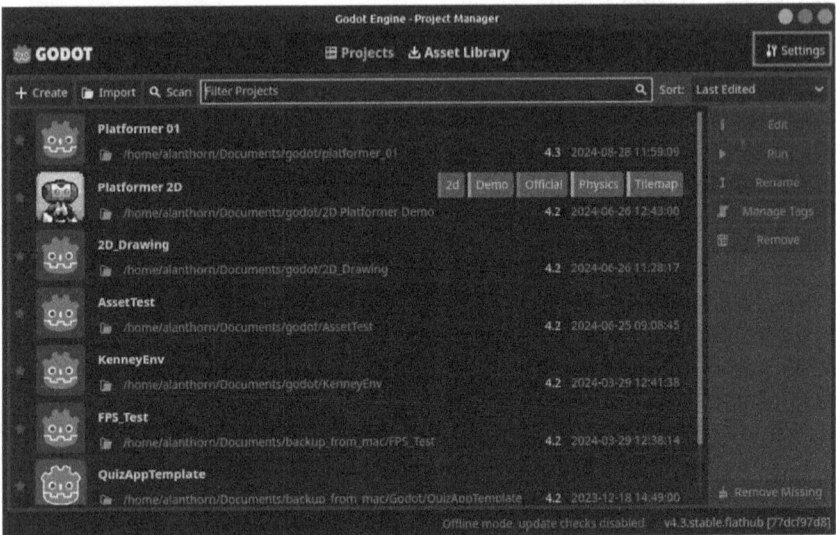

FIGURE 1.4   Accessing Godot quick settings.

Let's consider some of these settings further, as shown in Figure 1.5.

Especially important settings here are the top three: *Language*, *Interface Theme*, and *Display Scale*. Godot supports many languages, and the **Language** setting determines how menu options are shown, etc. Be sure to change this to whichever language you are most comfortable using.

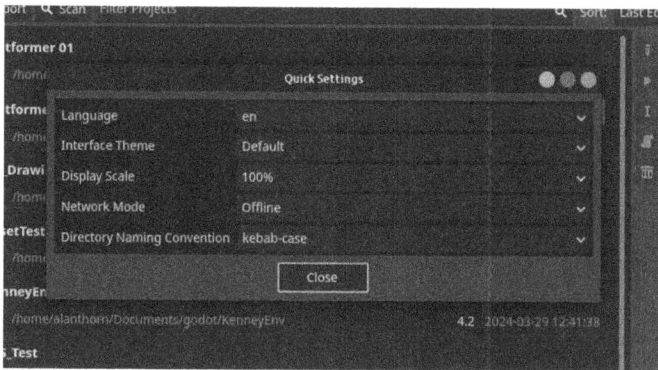

FIGURE 1.5   Godot quick settings.

However, this setting affects the Godot Editor interface for the developer rather than the language of your game for the end user. Localization of a game is an entirely different subject.

Second, the Interface Theme setting controls the color scheme for the interface. Again, this is a matter of preference. Normally, I keep to the default because it keeps the interface dark, making it easier on my eyes for longer periods and making it easier to focus on the content of the game. However, not everybody responds to darker themes in this way. I will, however, be using the **Light** theme throughout this book because it makes screenshots, especially in printed form, easier to see and read for a tutorial book like this.

Third, the *Display Scale* setting is especially useful to change if you're developing on a large screen or an unconventional display – such as a TV. In this instance, you may want to adjust this setting higher or lower to make the interface more readable and pleasant to view. Changing this value requires a restart of the software.

1.6 CONCLUSION

This chapter introduced the Godot engine within the broader context of the games industry. As a game engine, among many game engines, it represents a truly excellent choice for indie developers, industry newcomers, and those seeking to change game engines. As we will see, Godot is a versatile and powerful tool, capable of building many games in many genres. It is already a widely used tool, and its user base is growing. In reaching this far, you now have Godot installed on your computer, which is ready to use. The next chapter focuses on getting started.

CHAPTER 2

Getting Started with Godot

Your First Project

Y OU'VE NOW INSTALLED GODOT on your computer, and you could be using Windows, Mac, or Linux as an operating system. This chapter explores how to setup your first project in Godot, and any future projects, as well as how to customize the Godot editor to best suit your development needs. At almost every step of the way, Godot will present you with options – sometimes complicated-sounding options. Often, you can simply settle for the defaults, but it's important to understand when and why you should move away from them. So, we'll investigate that carefully. This chapter also explores how to create a scene within a Godot project, which will let you start building levels. It will also explore using free and open-source *Version Control software* so that you can effectively manage and keep track of your projects over time. Let's get started.

2.1 STARTING A GODOT PROJECT

Like almost every game engine today, Godot is a *project-based application.* This simply distinguishes it from file-based applications like Photoshop, GIMP, Word, Excel, Inkscape, and others. File-based applications operate on single files, like an image or spreadsheet, which can be opened and saved as a single unit. Godot, by contrast, operates on a folder and its manifold contents, which could include many files and other folders and

DOI: 10.1201/9781003484523-2

subfolders, all being treated as a hierarchical collection held together as part of a single project. This is important to know because, when backing up your projects or sharing them with others, you can't simply work with a single file; you'll need to work with many files and subfolders.

For our purposes in Godot, one *Project* is one *Game*. Therefore, you create a new game by creating a new project. That project will contain all the data needed for the game throughout its lifetime. If you intend to make multiple games at the same time, jumping from the development of one to the other, you'd then create one project *per game*. Creating a project in Godot is straightforward. From the Project Creation window, simply hit the *Create* button, as shown in Figure 2.1. You can also use the keyboard shortcut *Ctrl+N* on Windows or Linux or *Cmd + N* on a Mac.

The options from the Project Creation screen are important for many reasons. First, you should choose a suitable directory location on your computer where all project files will be stored and maintained. Although this can easily be changed later at any time, get into the habit of choosing meaningful and well-organized locations from the start to prevent your files from getting messy quickly. Poor folder organization can make your work difficult with generic folder names, hard-to-find folders, and inappropriately named files.

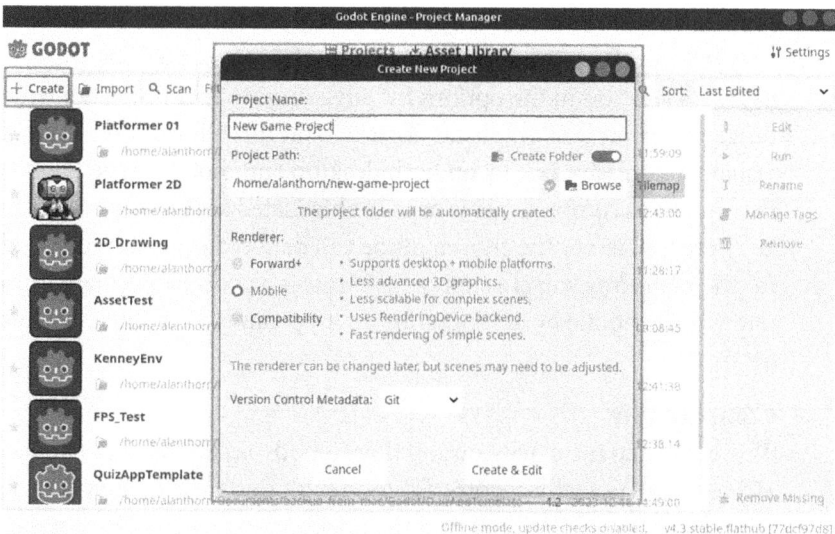

FIGURE 2.1   Creating a new project from the Project Creation Window.

2.1.1 Choosing the Renderer

Most significant here, however, is the *Renderer* option. This relates to the engine component responsible for drawing pixels to the screen. There are three choices with slightly mysterious names: *Forward+*, *Mobile*, and *Compatibility*. The default for Godot 4.3 is *Mobile*. For your first projects, you'll probably want to leave this setting as *Mobile*. However, here I discuss some of the practical differences, although the Godot creation window does a good job of explaining the options in an easy-to-understand way.

- **Forward+**
  This is the renderer to choose when you want the best and highest quality graphical performance from Godot, that is, the more sophisticated graphics often found on desktop PCs and consoles. Choosing this option unlocks a range of useful settings and features in Godot and internally affects how Godot behaves to deliver high-performance graphics. This option gives you the best quality visuals at the cost of compatibility. It doesn't work well, or at all in some cases, on older hardware, mobile devices, or in a web browser. So, you don't want to choose this option if your game is supposed to run on a mobile phone, for example.

- **Mobile**
  This is a middle-ground option between *Forward+* and *Compatibility*, as its location in the options list suggests. Mobile supports a wide range of performant graphical features, and this allows you to create visually impressive results on both desktop and mobile. True, *Mobile* may not be as comprehensive or as sophisticated as *Forward+*, but the key here is whether the chosen mode can deliver the results you need for the platforms you are supporting. This is a good choice for games that will be mobile by design or for desktop games that you later port for mobile.

- **Compatibility**
  This looks like the smelly option that nobody is supposed to choose. However, it's actually a powerful mode. It's designed to support the widest number of platforms and the greatest range of hardware possible so that your game runs on almost anything, old or new hardware. It comes at the cost of graphical quality or sophistication, but it's important to remember that even the most technically primitive games

can look beautiful under skillful art direction. So, it might seem that you're cutting off a load of features if you choose this mode, but you might just be choosing the simplest option. You should choose this mode if you're making games for web browsers, mobile devices, low-end devices, or really old computers.

NOTE. Although you can technically change the renderer settings *after* project creation, it becomes exponentially harder to change the further you progress in development. For example, you may eventually create a material, shader, or texture that works on desktop but not on mobile. If you afterward change platforms from desktop to mobile, you'd need to recreate this entire asset to keep it working. So, the bottom line is: get the renderer setting correct as early as possible. That's why you chose this setting at the project creation stage! Decide early on which platforms your game is intended for: desktop, console, mobile, web, etc. Now, if you decide that you want multiple platforms, such as desktop and mobile, *but also* want to take advantage of the desktop-only features for the desktop version, then you may need to create two different projects, one for each version of your game.

NOTE. You can find more information about the Godot renderer online here: https://docs.godotengine.org/en/stable/contributing/development/core_and_modules/internal_rendering_architecture.html.

2.1.2 Choosing Version Control

The Project Creation window features a *Version Control* setting. Later in this chapter, we'll consider version control in more depth. The default setting is *Git*, and you'll almost always leave this setting as-is, even if you're not using any version control. Don't switch it to *None*. That's not going to be very helpful. You should only do that if you either intend to use a version control system other than Git – such as *Perforce* – or if you know that you'll never, ever be using version control at all for the project, either now or later.

2.2 EXPLORING THE INTERFACE

After creating a new project, you'll be directed to the main editor interface of Godot, where you'll spend most of your development time. The interface is not unlike *Unity, Unreal,* or most other contemporary game engines. So, if you're familiar with one or more of those, you'll probably already feel familiar with the surroundings here. However, if you're new to game development entirely, then we should certainly dig deeper into the interface layout to help you understand what you're seeing. Don't skip this section. Feeling at home in-engine is very important for your enjoyable use of the software. See Figure 2.2 for the Godot interface. The interface can be broken down into Sections 1 to 4, as discussed below.

1. Section 1 of the interface, at the top-left side, is called the *Scene Dock*. When you first launch Godot with an empty project, it'll have only a very limited set of buttons, as shown in Figure 2.2. The Scene Dock is related to Section 3, the Scene View, which occupies most of the screen. The Scene Dock updates to show a list of everything that exists in the active scene (that is, the scene that you are currently viewing). If you're opening a newly created project, as we are, then you don't yet have any scenes in the project to view. In this case, the Scene Dock shows you only buttons that are used to create a new scene, as shown here.

2. The *FileSystem Dock* is, basically, an embedded *Explorer* or *Finder* interface that shows you all the files contained within the Godot project folder, as well as all subfolders and their contents. The contents of this Dock are functionally different from the other Docks.

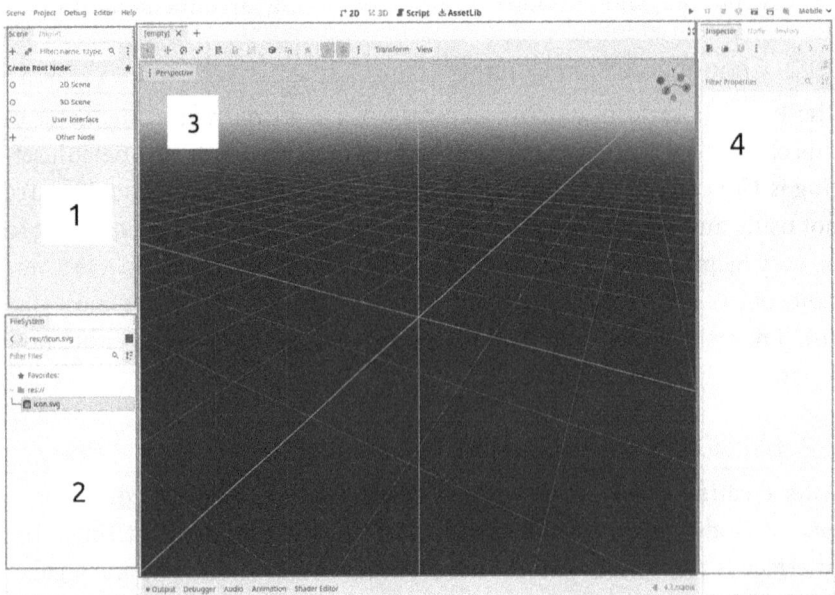

FIGURE 2.2   The main Godot interface.

The other Docks focus on content that you make *inside Godot,* such as scenes, player characters, weapons, and enemies. That is, the other docks operate within the realm of *your fiction.* The FileSystem Dock, by contrast, shows you all the files available to your project, such as meshes, textures, animations, and code. This dock is grounded in the *reality* of your computer, and it can be used to rename, move, add, and delete actual files to and from your project, and, as we'll see later, it can be used to build connections in your game between elements that rely on the files and their content.

3. The Scene View is unquestionably the largest region of space in the Godot Editor. It can display different types of data, including a complete Code Editor. However, normally, it shows the contents of the active scene, that is, the current level or space of your game inside which you're working. You'll be spending plenty of time here, building 2D and 3D worlds. Now, when you first start Godot with a new project, the Scene View is deceptive. It initially appears to show a 3D world with a grid, a skyline, and distance fog. It appears as though content already exists. But, in fact, this is just what Godot shows you by default whenever no scene is open or available for viewing. It's a strange indeterminate state, waiting for you to provide further instructions.

4. The Inspector Dock is one of the most important. In short, when you select elements in your project, such as the player character or a weapon inside a scene, the Inspector will always update its contents to show key, editable properties for the selected object, such as its position, size, orientation, name, and much more. Through this tool, we're able to change the details of objects. We'll be using this tool a lot.

2.2.1 Creating Your First Scene

We could jump into the application settings and start tweaking preferences. This is important to do. However, let's first jump into creating a new scene instead and finally get Godot out of its indeterminate state of emptiness. You'll probably find yourself doing this with many projects, as every game needs at least one scene. It's not essential to do this first, of course, but it'll offer us a clearer picture of how Godot works sooner rather than later. We'll explore Scenes in more depth later in the book. There is much to know about them. Scenes in Godot have a special importance that is not found in other engines. In short, a Scene is a single Euclidean space inside which objects exist. Scenes begin as empty spaces, and you need to populate them with the furniture of the world. Scenes can be 2D, having an X and Y dimension only, horizontal and vertical. Or they can be 3D, having an X, Y, and Z dimension. You cannot have a 4D scene. Now, in the practice of game development, a scene would *normally be a single level* – as it would be in a platformer game, like Mario or Sonic. Thus, a game with many levels often has many scenes experienced in sequence: level 1, level 2, and so on. There is no strict right or wrong about how to use scenes. They logically divide the space within a game world into more manageable chunks for the developer, and you must choose wisely how they do this. In an open-world style game, with no concept of distinct levels, as we find in platformers, you may use Scenes differently. In such a case, for example, a single town exterior might be one scene, and the interior of each building within the town might be defined in its own scene, one per building. And if the buildings were large, like a castle, you may even subdivide that interior space further into multiple scenes, one for the banquet hall and one for the dungeon, and so on. So now, let's create a new 3D scene. We're not making any particular game in this chapter; we're just exploring the interface for the first time by making a scene and taking note of important features. To create a new scene, click the *3D scene* button (see Figure 2.3).

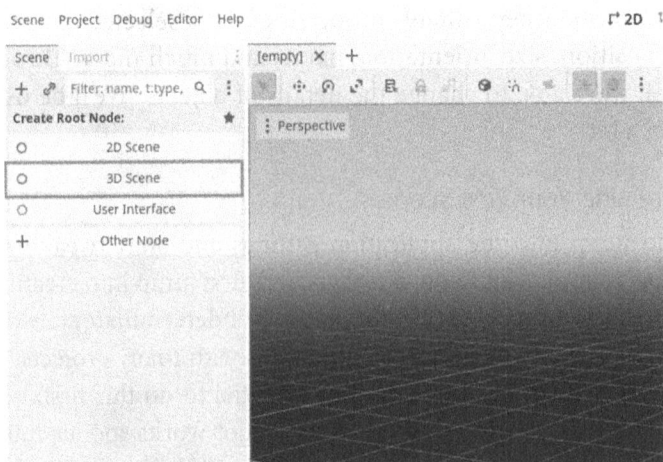

FIGURE 2.3   Create a new 3D scene.

NOTE. At this point, you may reasonably ask: if a project is only one game, then why have *multiple* scenes in a project at all? Why subdivide the game world into smaller vacuums of unintuitive and artificial space? Why not just create one massive scene to contain the world and all its belongings and all its spaces and all its people? Surely, such a monolithic structure of one scene more closely matches the real world, in which everything exists in a single contiguous space? Doing this surely makes things a lot simpler for us too, working with only one scene rather than multiple separate ones. As we'll see later in the book, there are many excellent developmental reasons to contradict common sense by dividing the world across multiple scenes, even though the scenes may not be experienced by the player as separate. There is an important gap between the appearance of the game world *to the player*, on the one hand, and how the game is actually made from scenes on the other.

Once a new scene is created, the Godot interface enters its more 'normal' and common mode, where most options are now available to you. You'll notice that the *Scene* Dock immediately shows a *Node3D* object in the list. This lists the full contents of the new scene, of which *Node3D* is the only inhabitant and is also the currently selected object by default. The perspective view at the center of the interface shows the selected object in 3D space. The object looks invisible except for three arrows connected to it in red (X), green (Y), and blue (Z). The right-hand Inspector Dock shows many properties for the currently selected object, which are divided into groups for easier access and organization (see Figure 2.4).

The final step of creating a new scene should be to save it so that Godot understands it as a bona fide asset that belongs to the project, as opposed to a temporary space. This is easy to achieve; you can choose *Scene > Save Scene* or *Scene > Save Scene As* from the menu (Figure 2.5).

2.2.2 Setting Editor Preferences

The previous section explored how to create a new 3D scene. There are other scene types, such as 2D scenes and user interfaces, and these are created in a very similar way to 3D. Before we examine scene development and navigation in more detail, let's ensure the Godot control scheme and preferences are suited to your needs. This is especially important if you're using Godot on a laptop or multi-monitor configuration because some of the settings covered here can make a major difference to how

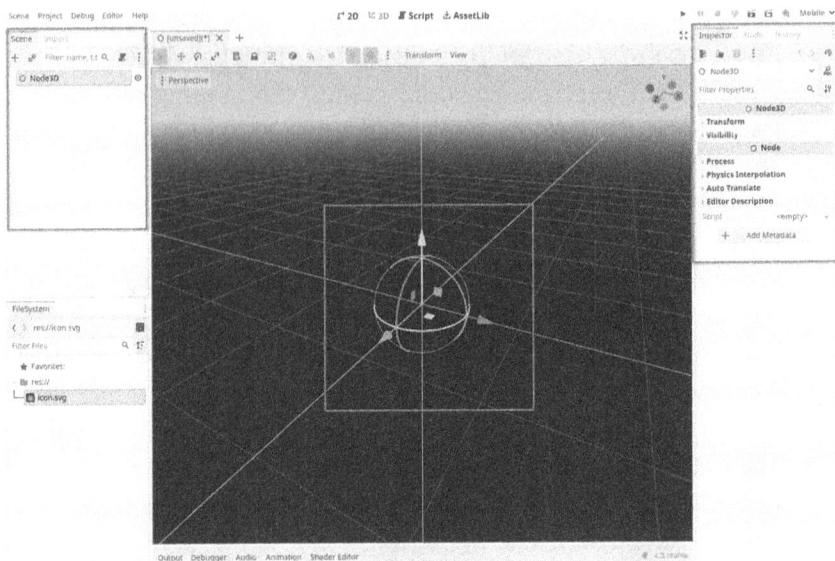

FIGURE 2.4   A new scene with a single object.

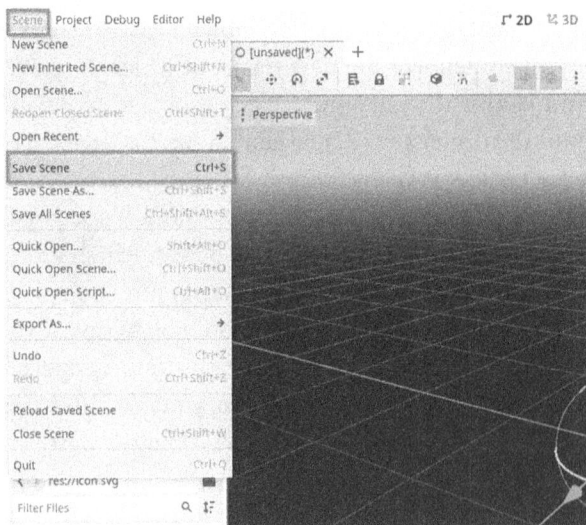

FIGURE 2.5   Saving a new scene.

you use Godot. Let's see. Start by choosing *Editor > Editor* Settings from the menu to show the Editor Settings. These settings are specific to the *Godot application* on your computer, as opposed to your currently open project. They do not affect the game that you are making directly. Rather, they affect the editor tool itself. See Figure 2.6.

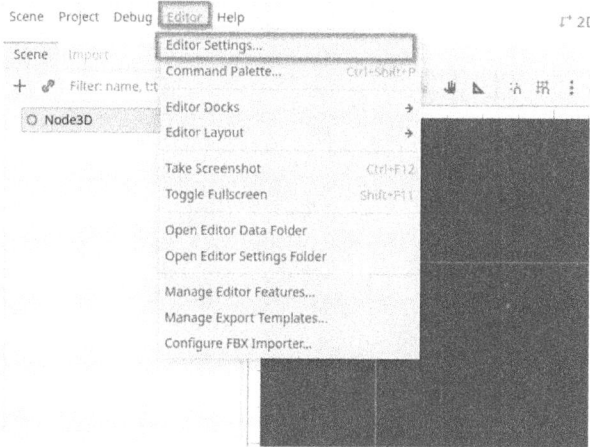

FIGURE 2.6   Accessing the editor settings.

From the Editor Settings Window, choose *Editor* from the left-hand menu. From here, there are some high-level interface settings that are useful. First, *Dock Tab Style* lets you choose whether to show icons, text, or text and icons in the titles of interface tabs, such as the Inspector tab. *Icon only* can save on-screen space, *Text only* keeps the interface feeling minimalist, and *Both (Text and Icon)* are great for larger screens. I usually choose both (see Figure 2.7).

Another useful setting here is the *Editor Screen* and the *Project Manager Screen* option, which appear on the same page. These let you control which monitor the interface appears in by default if you have multiple monitors connected. The default setting is *Primary Screen*. And you should leave it as is unless you want to display the interface on a different monitor. A further option to review is *Save Each Scene on Quit*, which should be enabled by default. If it's not, I recommend enabling it. This ensures that any open scene is automatically saved when you close it either because you are closing the editor entirely or because you're opening a different scene for viewing. Finally, another useful setting to enable is *Multi-Window* (see Figure 2.8). This is enabled by default, so you shouldn't need to activate it. It allows you to detach some windows from the interface and move them around separately. As we'll see soon, this is useful for multi-monitor set-ups where you want to display different editor features (such as a Code Editor) on different monitors.

Later chapters demonstrate how Godot can interface with other software, such as Blender, for importing content like 3D models and assets

General   Shortcuts

Filter Settings   Q

∨ **Interface**	Editor Language	en	∨
— Editor	Localize Settings	☑ On	
Inspector	Dock Tab Style	Text Only	∨
Theme			
Touchscreen	UI Layout Direction	○ Text Only on Locale	∨
Scene Tabs	Display Scale	◉ Icon Only	∨
Multi Window	Custom Display Scale	○ Text and Icon	
Editors	Editor Screen	Primary Screen	∨
∨ **Network**	Project Manager Screen	Primary Screen	∨
Connection	Use Embedded Menu	▣ On	
HTTP Proxy	Use Native File Dialogs	▣ On	
TLS	Expand to Title	☑ On	
Debug	Main Font Size	14	↕
Debug Adapter	Code Font Size	14	↕
Language Server	Code Font Contextual Ligatures	Disable Contextual Alternates (Coding Ligatur	∨
∨ **FileSystem**	Code Font Custom OpenType Features		
External Programs	Code Font Custom Variations		
Directories			
On Save	Font Antialiasing	Grayscale	∨
File Dialog			

Close

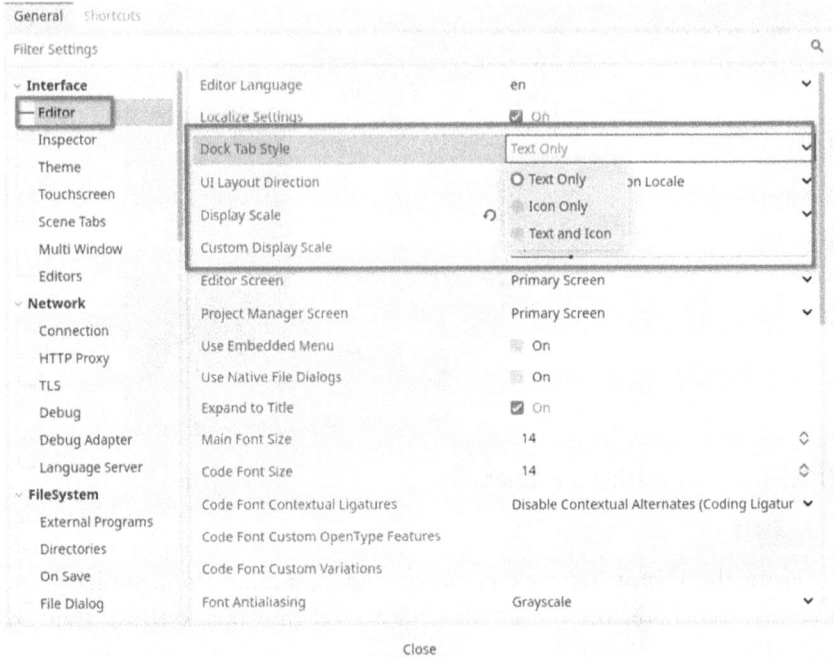

FIGURE 2.7   Tweaking tabular display.

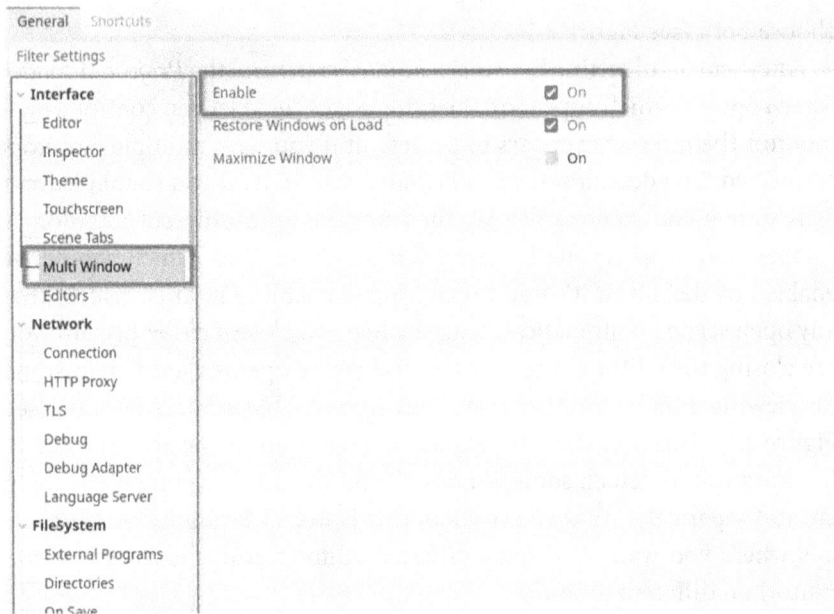

General   Shortcuts

Filter Settings

∨ **Interface**	Enable	☑ On
Editor	Restore Windows on Load	☑ On
Inspector	Maximize Window	▢ On
Theme		
Touchscreen		
Scene Tabs		
— Multi Window		
Editors		
∨ **Network**		
Connection		
HTTP Proxy		
TLS		
Debug		
Debug Adapter		
Language Server		
∨ **FileSystem**		
External Programs		
Directories		
On Save		

FIGURE 2.8   Enabling multi-window.

directly into 3D scenes. If you check out the *FileSystem* > *External Programs* option from the *Editor Settings* menu, you can specify other, related programs on your computer to Godot. You can choose their file location. By doing this, Godot will launch the relevant application whenever you try to open an unsupported file in the FileSystem dock, which Godot cannot edit directly, such as images and 3D models. As we'll see, Godot can *use* images and 3D models inside Scenes, but it cannot *edit* the original data. This is why it's useful to specify the locations of other software, in case you ever need to quickly edit the originals while working inside Godot (Figure 2.9).

NOTE. Common applications that you would choose here are *Photoshop*, *GIMP*, or *LibreSprite* for *Raster Image Editor*; *Illustrator* or *Inkscape* for *Vector Image Editor*; *Audacity* for *Audio Editor*; and *Blender* or *Maya* for *3D Model Editor*.

Next, we'll configure the behavior of 3D scenes from the *Editor Settings* dialog. To do this, select *Editors* > *3D* from the left-hand menu. This section features quite a few options. First, under the *Navigation Scheme*, you can choose the keyboard shortcuts and control style for moving around inside 3D scenes. We'll see soon how to navigate 3D scenes. If you're familiar with other engines like *Unreal* or *Unity* or 3D software like *Maya*, then you'll probably want to set this as *Maya*. I'll be using this Maya convention

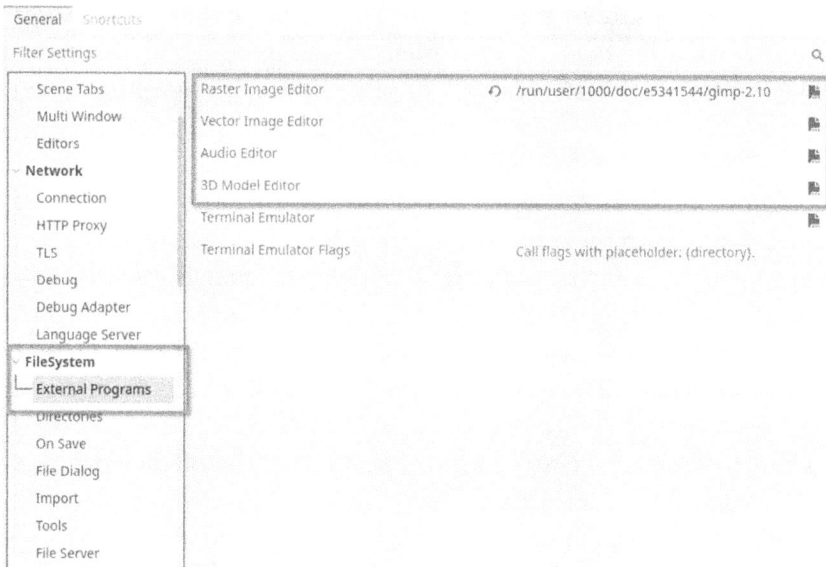

FIGURE 2.9   Specifying application paths.

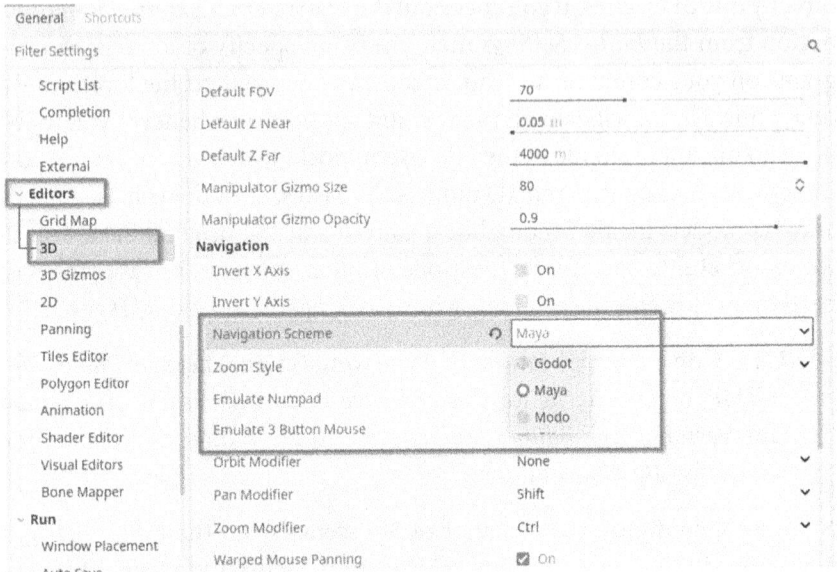

FIGURE 2.10   Updating the control scheme.

throughout the book because it's widely used in the industry. So, let's change the setting here (see Figure 2.10).

Finally, if you're using Godot on a laptop with a trackpad rather than a mouse, then be sure to enable *Emulate Numpad* (if your laptop doesn't have one) and *Emulate 3 Button* Mouse (see Figure 2.11). This ensures Godot offers you the full range of navigation features on a laptop.

2.2.3   Hierarchies and 3D Scenes – Adding an Object

Let's create our first 3D object in a 3D scene. Well, actually, we already have a 3D object in the scene we created earlier! This was added by default when the scene was first made: a *Node3D*. By default, every scene must have at least one object. That's not a necessary, philosophical requirement. That's just the way Godot works practically. This is called the root **Node**. In fact, in Godot, all 'objects' are called 'nodes'. I'll refer to them as such from hereon. If you're coming to Godot from the Unreal Engine, objects are called **Actors**. If you're from Unity, objects are called **GameObjects**. In Godot, each object (or each separate *thing*) is a Node. So, every scene has a *root Node*. You can't delete this node without also destroying the scene itself. The default Node3D, which was added automatically, is a 'thing' that lives in the scene, but it's an invisible thing. The player will never see it.

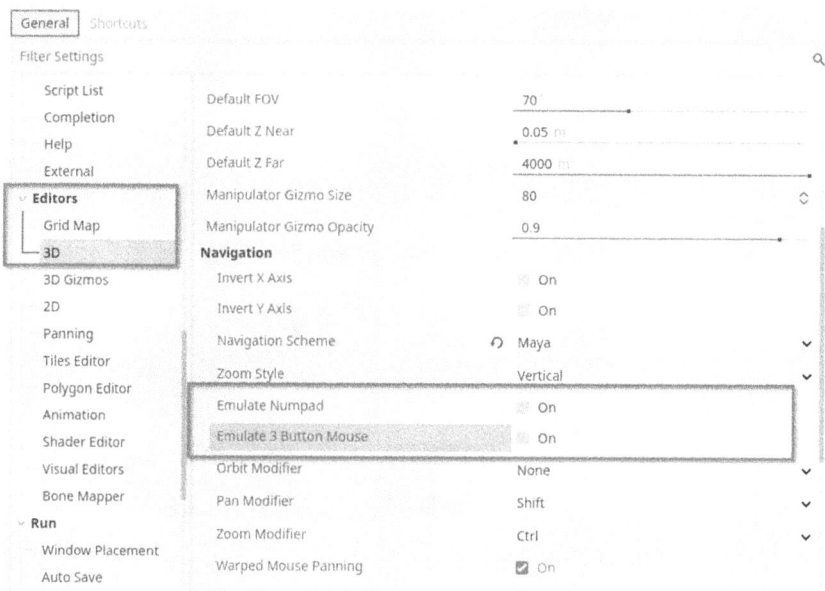

FIGURE 2.11   Enabling a 3-button mouse for laptops.

Now, although this node is 3D insofar as it lives within a 3D scene at a 3D position, it doesn't have any bulk or dimensionality. It has neither width nor height nor depth. It is simply an 'empty' or a 'point', located at the scene's origin. It will essentially act as a folder, or a container, for all other nodes that we may add in future. Therefore, this object is formal, structural, and entirely conventional. So now let's add a cube. Let's add something that a player could actually see and notice if they lived inside our scene. To do this, right-click your mouse over the extant *Node3D* object from the *Scene Dock*, and choose *Add Child Node* from the context menu (Figure 2.12).

When you select this option, Godot presents a *Create New Node* Window (see Figure 2.13). We want to add a cube. However, like many occasions in Godot, you can't simply jump straight to the thing you want to add. There's no option for it. There is no 'Generate Box' button. You need to 'build' the box from the simpler parts that are on offer. This makes Godot powerful and flexible because you can build complexity. However, it also means that creating simple objects quickly, like cubes, involves more steps than you may think necessary or intuitive. To start, we need to add a **MeshInstance3D**. Start to type this into the *Search* Field of the dialog. Godot will make a match and present it as an option for you to

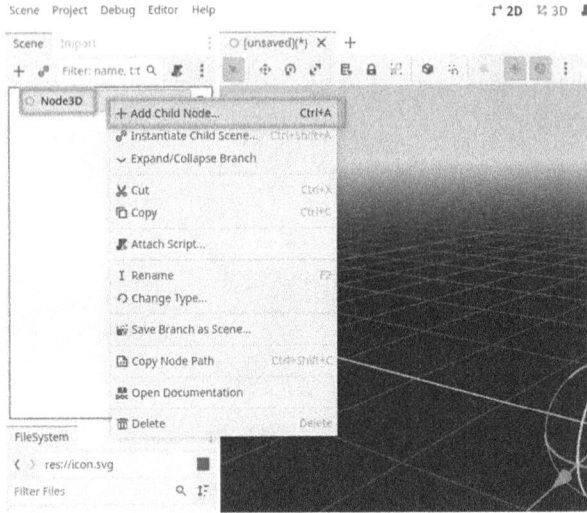

FIGURE 2.12   Adding a child object.

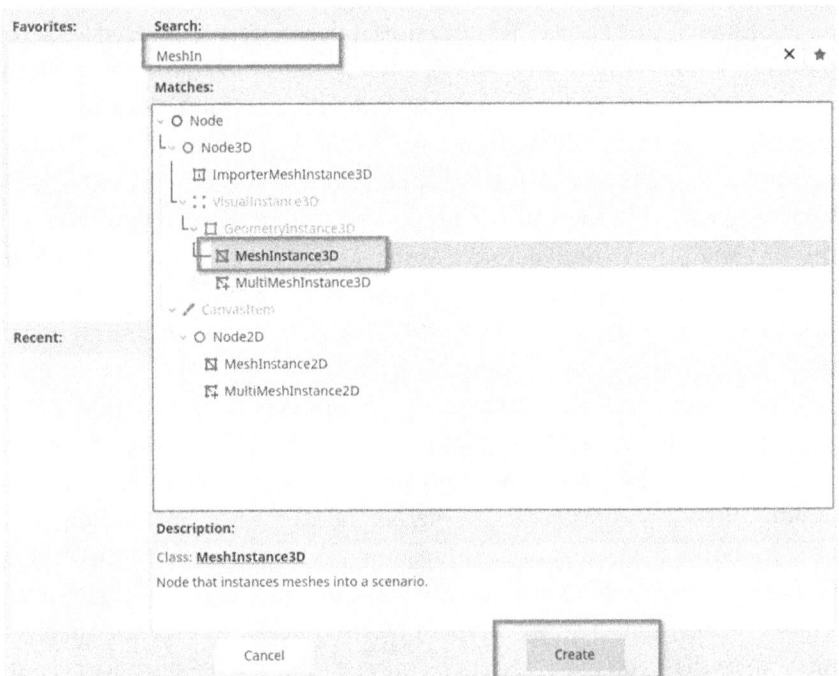

FIGURE 2.13   Creating a Mesh Instance as the starting point for a cube.

choose from the list below the search field. A MeshInstance3D is simply the basis, or starting point, for any 3D model of any complexity: cubes, spheres, cylinders, etc. Go ahead and select it, and then choose *Select* or hit the Enter key to accept it.

After the *MeshInstance3D* is added to the scene, you'll notice that the Scene dock changes substantially. It now shows the *MeshInstance3D* in the list, and it is *indented* beneath the *Node3D* object above. The indentation expresses a hierarchical relationship that exists between the *Node3D* and the *MeshInstance3D*. In being added to the scene, the *MeshInstance3D* is a *Child Node* of the *Node3D*, and the *Node3D* is a *Parent Node* of the *MeshInstance3D*. This has practical implications. Specifically, if you delete a parent from the scene, then you delete all its children too. If you move, rotate, or resize a parent in 3D space, then the same effects will cascade downward to all children. That is, children *move with* their parents, they rotate with their parents, and they scale with their parents. However, if you move a child, it will move independently of its parent. Changes to children do not cascade upward to parents. This hierarchical (top-down) relationship can be found everywhere in games. It's powerful. It may seem a mere formality right now if you've not encountered it before, but we'll see examples later of this relationship in action and how it can save us lots of work further down the line (see Figure 2.14).

The newly created *MeshInstance3D* is created in an empty state, without any dimension or bulk – just like the *Node3D*. However, from the *Inspector*, we can change how this object is configured. From the *MeshInstance3D* tab in the Inspector, we can select *BoxMesh* from the *Mesh* drop-down list (see Figure 2.15).

Choosing the *BoxMesh* preset will fire an internal Godot system to generate a procedural box (that is, a box mesh based on numerical inputs). We can even use the Inspector to tweak those inputs after creation if we want to, such as the *height*, *depth*, and *width*. And that's it! We've made a box in just a few steps. You might have noticed that the *Mesh* drop-down offered other Euclidean solids too; spheres and cylinders, for example (Figure 2.16).

> NOTE. Not everything is as it seems with our newly generated box. If you were a player who could walk around that scene, for example, you'd find that you could easily walk straight through the box as though it were only an apparition – a ghostly box in appearance only. We'll see how to fix that kind of issue in a later chapter.

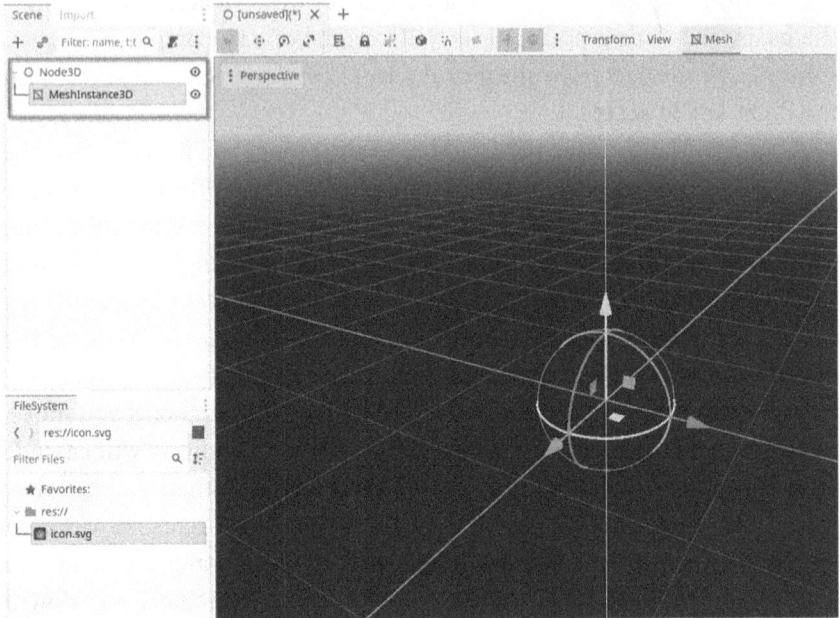

FIGURE 2.14   Adding a MeshInstance3D to the scene.

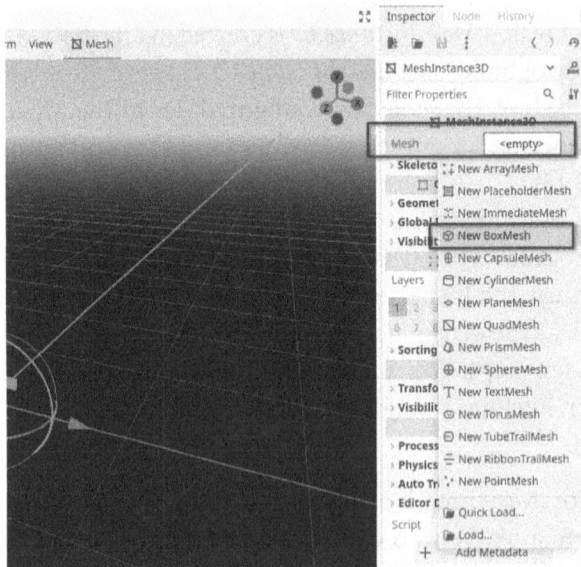

FIGURE 2.15   Choosing a Mesh preset.

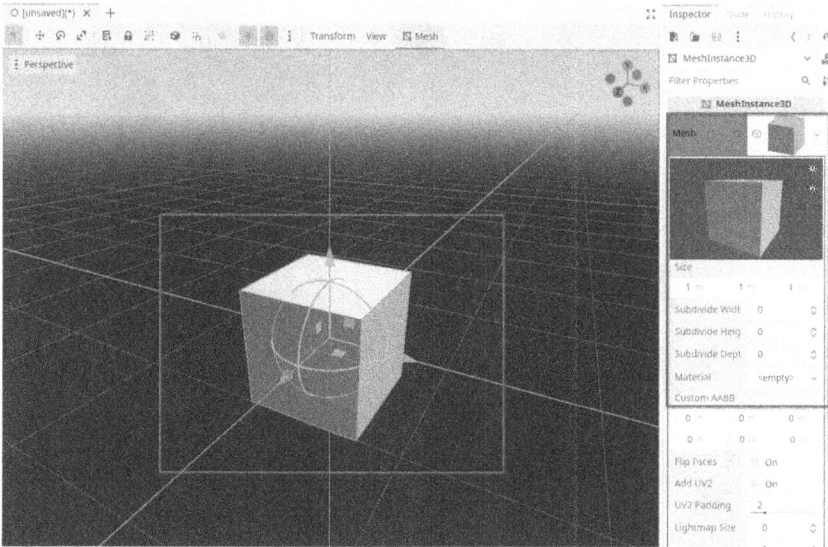

FIGURE 2.16 Generating a procedural box.

2.2.4 Viewport Navigation – Exploring a Scene

We've now made a cube in a 3D scene. That was simple. If we wanted to build a scene more sophisticated than this, we'd eventually need the ability to navigate around the 3D viewport and look around the scene to make better-informed judgments on what to do, and we'd also need the ability to transform objects in 3D space: move, rotate, and scale them into new configurations according to our designs. Let's start with understanding navigation controls. That is, let's get familiar with moving the viewport camera around the scene. These controls will need to be habitual to you for effective use of the engine. First, let's be clear about what we're doing: the scene view, as shown in Figure 2.17, is our *director's eye* view of the scene. It's *not*, however, what the *player* would necessarily see if they played the game right now. They could potentially see the same scene but from a totally different camera angle, perspective, etc. Here, I'm referring only to our developer view of the scene, as presented in the Godot interface, so that we – as creators – can move around as users to build our world effectively. Thus, by changing the angle, view, and location of the *perspective camera*, we *do not* affect what the player would see at all. That's controlled differently.

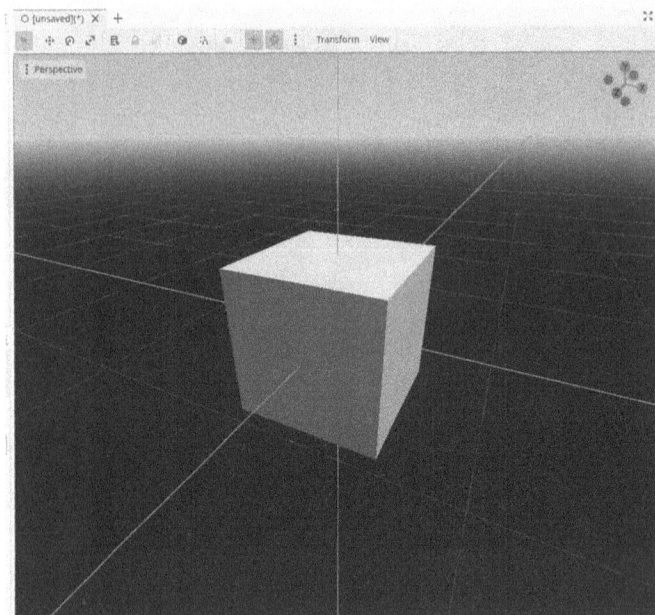

FIGURE 2.17   Navigating a Godot scene.

First, you can **'dolly'** the camera forward or backward toward the view-port center by rolling the middle mouse wheel or by rolling the vertical line on your laptop trackpad. This scrolls your camera forward or back-ward along an imaginary line in the direction that the camera is looking. The movement is quite smooth. Some people would describe this action as a *Zoom*, but that's not technically what is going on. Zoom implies that the camera is held stationary while its lens is adjusted to bring further objects closer to its view. But here we are actually *moving* the camera toward our focal point. If you don't have a mouse wheel, you can also dolly by pressing *Ctrl +* or *Ctrl –* on your keyboard to move forward or backward, respec-tively (see Figure 2.18).

You can also **Pan** the viewport camera up, down, left, and right. This essentially slides the camera around a plane without any rotation. It's like a sidestep, but also includes an 'up-step' and 'down-step'. To do this, hold down the *Shift* key on the keyboard, hold down the *middle mouse* button, and then, with both held down, move your mouse around to control the pan direction. Pan is very useful for previewing a scene from a distance.

You can also **Orbit** the viewport camera around a specified target, or focal point. This effectively lets you rotate the camera *around* a target.

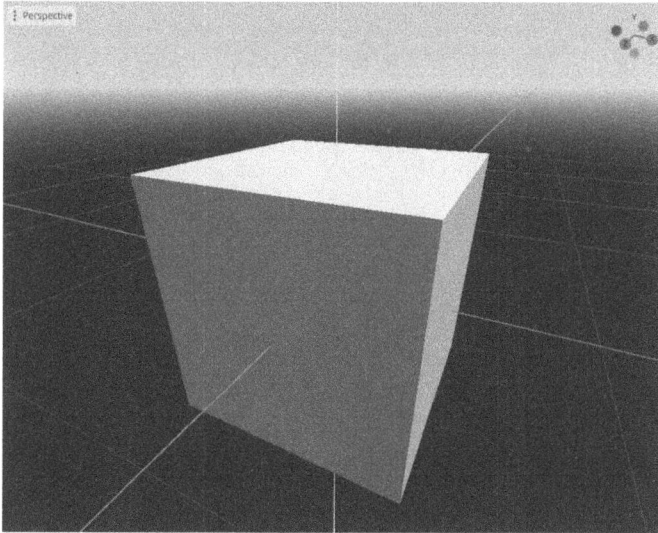

FIGURE 2.18   Dolly forward and backward.

And combined with the Dolly feature, as mentioned, you can easily move closer to and away from selected objects. To Orbit, first, select the object that should be at your center of rotation by clicking on it with the mouse. In the example scene used here, we only have a cube. You select it by left-clicking on it inside the viewport using the mouse, or you can click on it by name from the Scene dock. Once selected, press the *F* key on the keyboard. F stands for *Frame*. When you press this, the viewport camera automatically centers on the selected object in response. Now, by holding the *Alt* key on the keyboard, you can *left-click* and drag your mouse in any direction to rotate around the selected object. Make sure to hold down the *Alt* key as you do this. You can complete a 360-degree Orbit in this mode. It's a powerful feature that lets you easily inspect objects in the scene. See Figure 2.19 for an Orbit in action.

Finally, you can adopt a **6DOF** (Degrees of Freedom) style first-person camera that lets you float around the level and inspect anything. This is especially useful when working with big scenes that have many interior spaces. To access this mode, hold down the *right mouse button*. With the button held down, you can use the *WASD* keyboard keys. *W* walks forward, *S* walks back, *A* side steps left, and *D* side steps right. And you can also move the mouse around to control the orientation of your head.

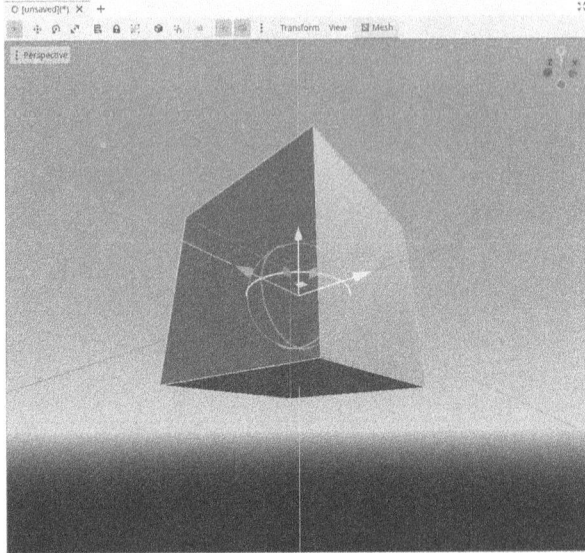

FIGURE 2.19   Entering Orbit mode.

2.2.5 Object Transformations – Building a Scene

Let's build a simple room: namely, four walls and a floor. You might think that we already have those with the cube we made earlier. After all, if you step *inside* the cube, walking through its outer shell into its interior space, you already have walls and a floor. Voila! But, if you try that for yourself, you'll notice immediately that the cube turns invisible when your camera steps inside it. Even though the cube continues to exist, it ceases to be visible so long as you remain inside. Here, you're experiencing a feature of game engine renderers called *Backface Culling*. Game engines make objects one-sided by default. This began as an optimization strategy so that an engine doesn't waste time drawing surfaces that shouldn't or couldn't, be seen, like the other side of a brick wall that the player can never reach anyway. Now, in our case, we could try adjusting the single box that we have to make both sides of it visible. But we won't. It's more hassle than it's worth to do that. Instead, we'll assume that one cube can be resized to make the floor, and then we'll add more cubes to make the walls. That approach is easier, and it's also the most common approach in game development.

First, position your viewport to get a comfortable view of the space (see Figure 2.20). To build a room, don't work too closely to your objects; a good isometric-style shot works well, elevated above your subject.

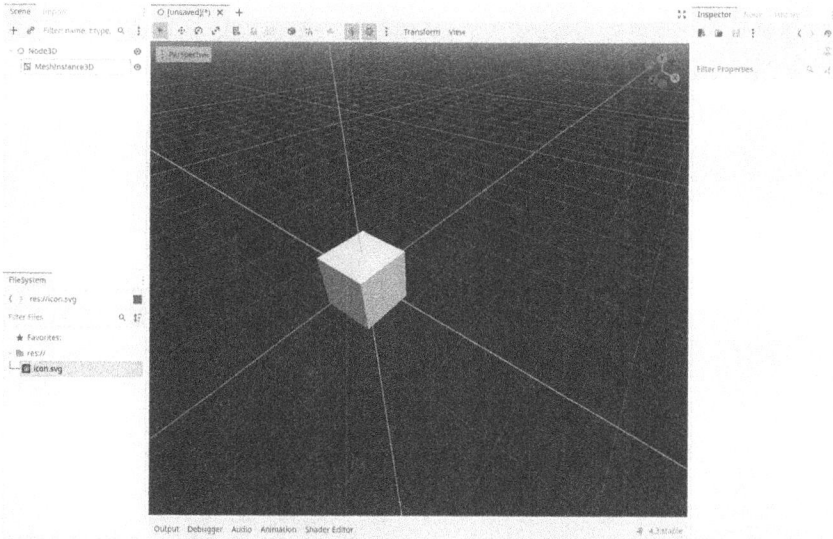

FIGURE 2.20   Preparing to make a room.

Next, select the box mesh. From the *Scene* dock, right-click on the mesh and choose *Rename* from the context menu, or press *F2*, or you can double-click the object to rename it too. Enter the name *Floor* and press *Enter* (see Figure 2.21). It's good working practice to name all your objects appropriately so that you can easily determine their function simply by their name. When you work with scenes full of objects, it can become difficult to select them in the viewport, as it's so easy to mis-select something else very close by. For this reason, selecting objects from the Scene Dock by name is important.

Our box is too tall for a floor. We need to flatten it considerably. Given that we created this box parametrically by using a *MeshInstance3D* node, as opposed to importing a mesh from Blender, for example, we have the luxury of being able to tweak its original height using the Inspector, where we can change the *Size* properties (see Figure 2.22). I entered a value of *0.1m* for the height.

Most meshes in games will not be of the procedural kind where you have direct access to the dimensions, as we had with the cube above. They will be imported as-is from content creation software, like Blender, and you will have no easy way to type in new values for properties like dimensions. In this case, you can modify the size of an object by using a **Transform**. Transform refers to a collection of three properties grouped

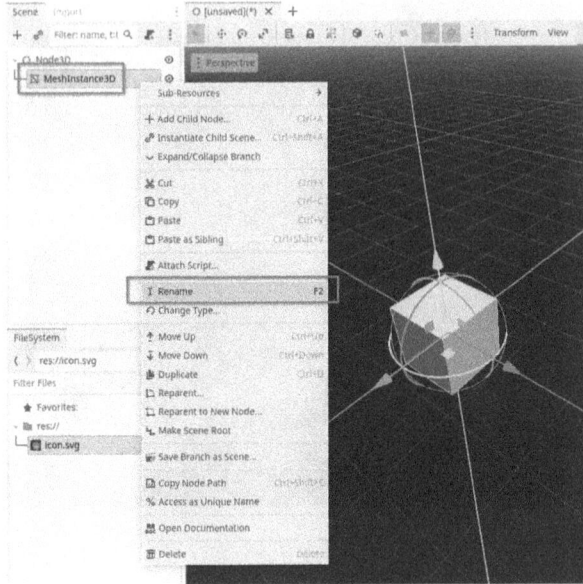

FIGURE 2.21 Renaming nodes from the Scene Dock.

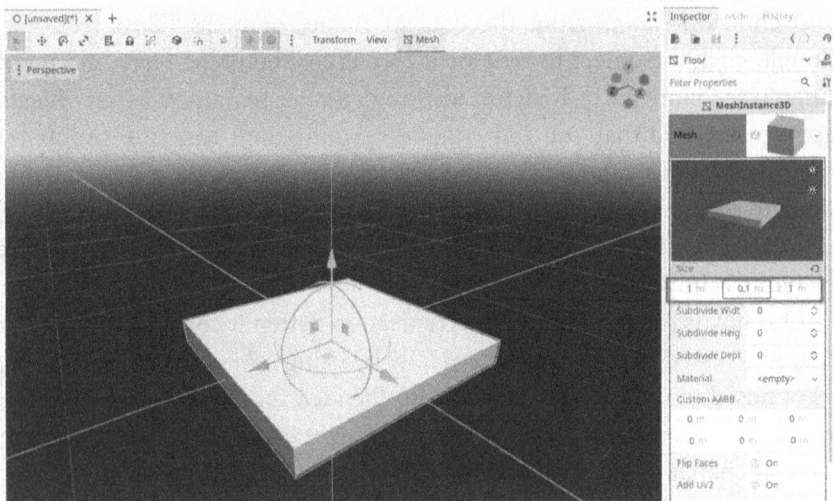

FIGURE 2.22 Resizing the box to be a floor.

together in a single package of data: **Position** to define the location of an object in 3D space in terms of X, Y, and Z. **Rotation** to define the orientation of an object in 3D in terms of *Pitch*, *Roll*, and *Yaw*. And finally, **Scale**, to define a scaling factor by which an object should be enlarged or shrunk. A scale factor of 2 means that an object should be stretched to twice the size.

A scale factor of 3 means three times the size, and a value of 1 means the object should be left unchanged. That makes sense because $N x 1 = N$. A value of 0.5 means the object should shrink to half size. A value of 0 means the object will be compressed to nothing, since $N x 0 = 0$. Objects with a 0 scale cannot be seen. And finally, negative values (such as –2) will enlarge the object but also mirror it (flipping it horizontally or vertically around its center). You can access the Transform for a node via the *Transform* rollout in the Inspector when the node is selected (see Figure 2.23). To change an object's scale, you can type in new values. By default, the scale values are 1.

> NOTE. You can specify unique values for each dimension of scale if needed. An object with the same scale for X, Y, and Z is affected by the *Uniform Scale*. You can, however, vary the scale in each axis, leading to a *Non-Uniform Scale*. For the floor, a non-uniform scale is appropriate. You would leave the width (X) and depth (Z) unchanged but reduce the scale in Y to shrink the height of the cube.

> NOTE. It's important to remember that scaling does not technically change the internal size or dimensions of an object. Scale is a force applied to an object. For example, an object that is *10m* in width remains *10m* even with a Scale Factor of 2. The Scale Factor

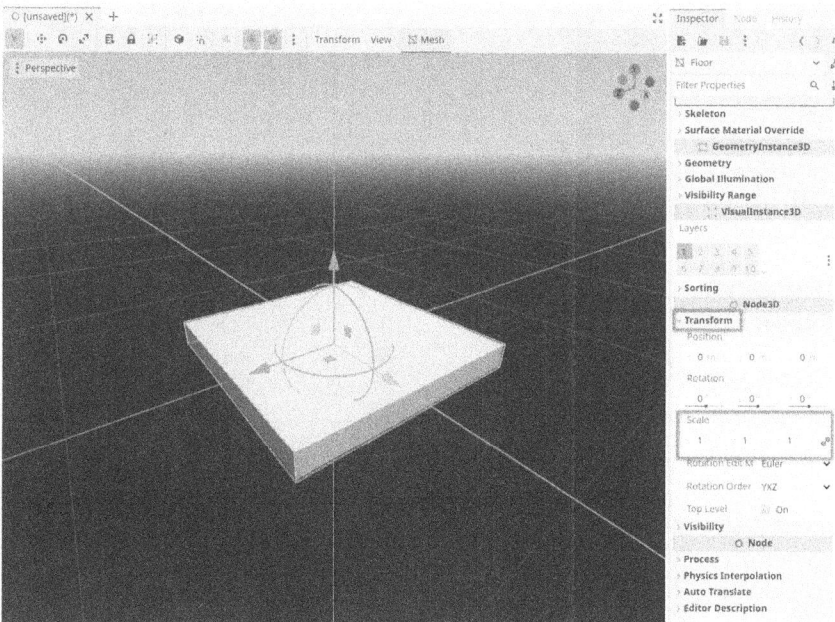

FIGURE 2.23   Setting an object's scale.

is *multiplied* by the native width to enlarge the object to the doubled size that is seen. The visible size is a function of those properties. This means that an object's visible size is determined by two properties: its actual dimensions *combined* with its scale. However, the properties themselves remain independent variables. This may seem a dry technical point. But, as we'll see, it can cause practical confusion because it means that an object's visible size cannot be determined only by its dimensions.

Next, let's ensure the newly scaled floor object is positioned as we'd like it to be in the scene. You can easily change the position of any object. Select the floor and press the *W* key to access the *Translate* tool. Or, you can select the *Translate* tool via its button in the viewport toolbar. However, since you'll be using the *Translate* tool very, very often, it makes sense to learn its very easy keyboard shortcut (see Figure 2.24).

Once the *Translate* tools are activated, you can interactively move the selected object around the scene using the viewport **Gizmo**. This appears as three arrows centered on the selected object. These do not appear for the gamer in *Play* mode. They are for your reference only. The red arrow indicates the X axis, the green is Y, and the blue is Z. By clicking and then

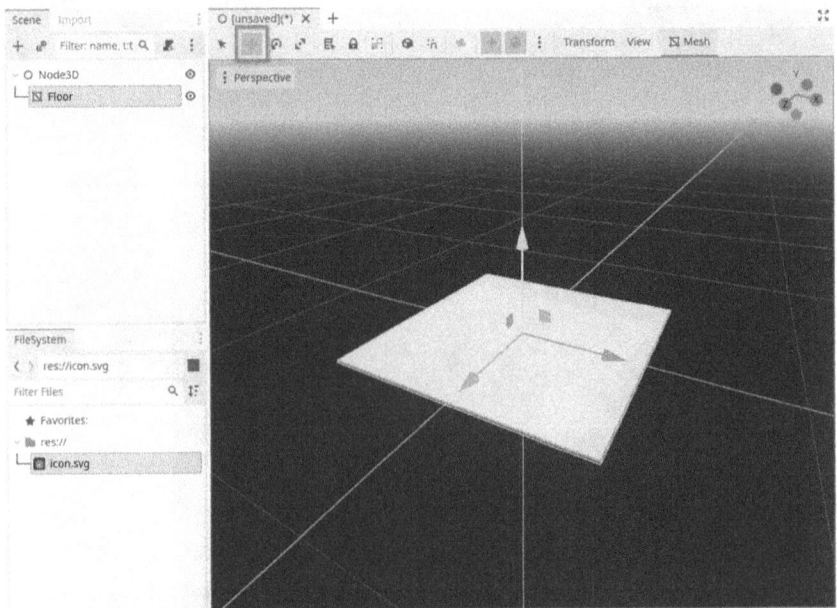

FIGURE 2.24   Accessing the Translate tool.

dragging *on an axis*, you will move the object as you move your mouse, and you will constrain the object's movement to only the chosen axis. This is useful for making precise transformations. Similarly, you'll also notice smaller red, green, and blue squares close to the intersection of the Gizmo arrows. By clicking and dragging on these squares instead, you'll move the object but constrained to two dimensions instead of one (see Figure 2.25).

For our example floor, surrounded by four walls, I'm fine with the object being positioned at the world origin. So, I'll leave it where it is without using the Transform gizmo. If it's not there already, you can use the Gizmo to move the floor to the origin, and you can also precisely position the floor from the Inspector by moving to the Transform rollout and typing in a new position. For the world origin, the location of (0, 0, 0) is correct (see Figure 2.26).

Now that we've made the floor, let's create the four walls. Godot makes this easy. Select the floor object and press *Ctrl + D* to duplicate the object, or you can alternatively right-click on the floor from the *Scene* dock and select *Duplicate* from the context menu. As with translating objects, I strongly advise you to remember this keyboard shortcut. You'll use it often when level designing. By choosing *Duplicate*, you'll create a second, clone

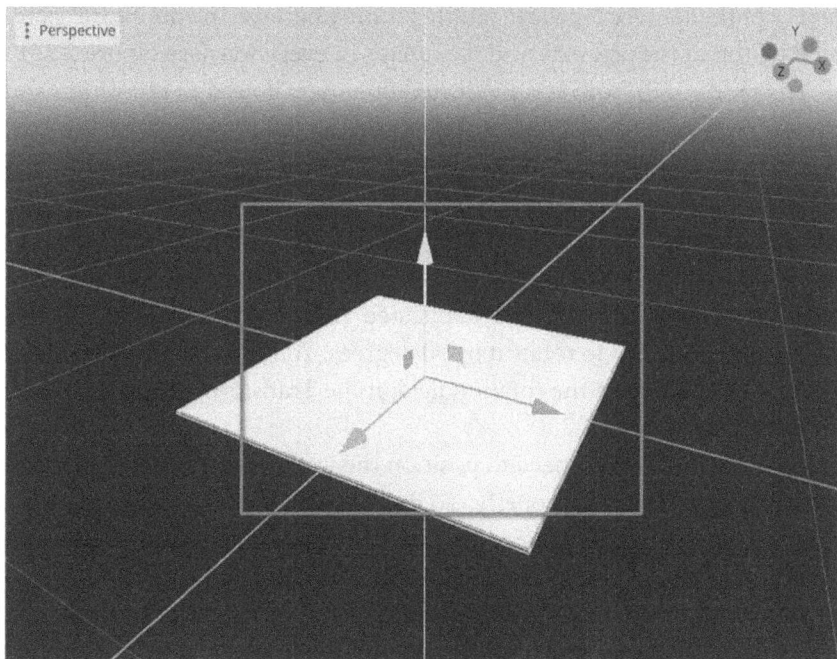

FIGURE 2.25   Translating an object with the Gizmo.

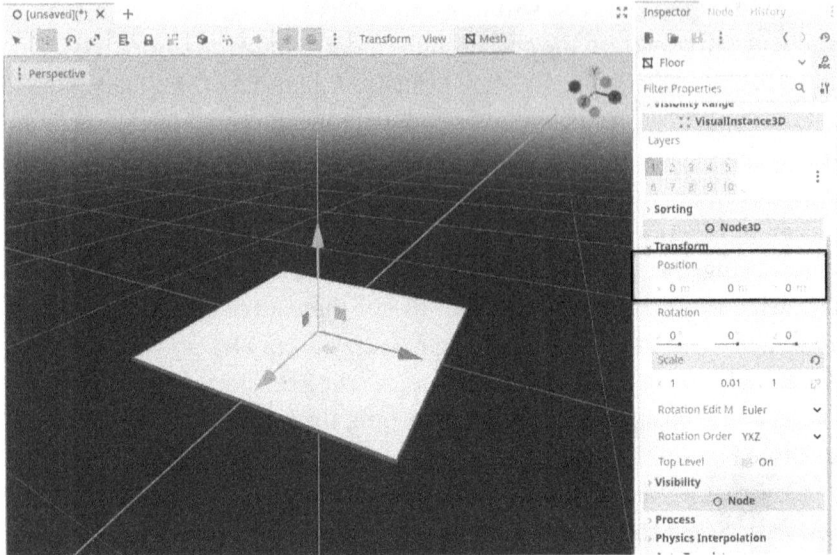

FIGURE 2.26   Specifying the object position to the world origin.

mesh of the original. This is a separate and independent object. It'll be listed in the *Scene* dock as a new object too. You may not initially see the object in the *Perspective* view, but this is only because the duplicate is created on top of the original, and it overlaps in every way (see Figure 2.27).

To make a wall from the duplicated floor, you'll need to reposition and rotate the floor. You can access the Rotate tool by pressing *E* on the keyboard or by choosing the *Rotate* mode from the perspective view toolbar. As with Translate, the Rotate Gizmo presents you with three axes that form a **Gimbal**: red (X), green (Y), and blue (Z). These are presented as circles, showing you the three different axes of rotation. You can click and drag any circle to rotate the duplicated floor into a wall orientation. Effectively, you need to rotate it by 90 degrees. You can also achieve this by typing the rotation in the rotation field of the Transform group inside the Inspector (see Figure 2.28).

After rotation, you'll need to position the wall in the correct location to stand against the floor properly. To do this, you can use the Translation tool to position the new piece, or you can type in new values. But here you'll run into a problem. By default, the Translate tool lets you move an object around continuously, with position values potentially running into many decimal places. The result is that you can never be fully certain that your object is positioned exactly where it needs to be unless you avoid the

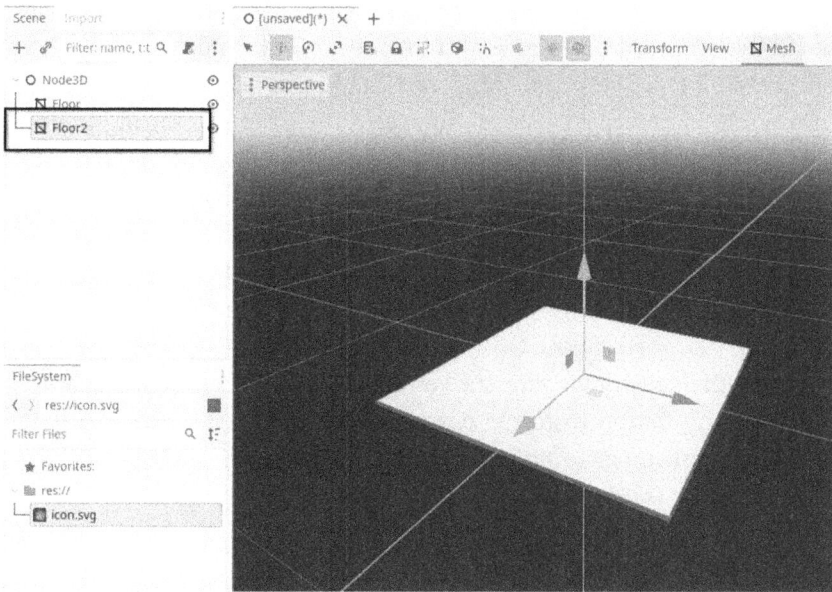

FIGURE 2.27   Duplicating an object.

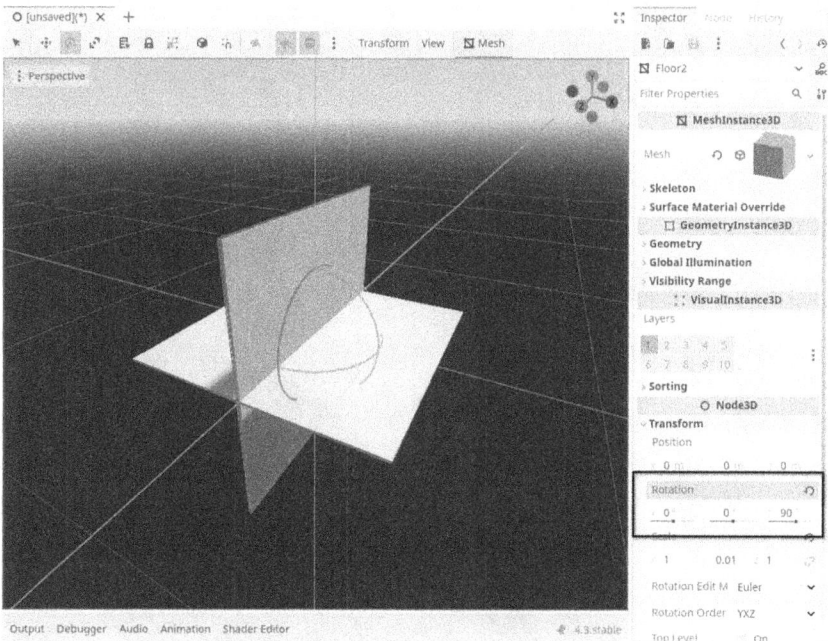

FIGURE 2.28   Rotating the wall into correct orientation.

Translate tool and simply type in values instead. Or unless you don't care! To solve this precision issue and to make Translate more precise, Godot offers the *Snapping* feature. This forces the Translate tool to move objects in discrete increments or steps. To access the *Snapping* settings, choose *Transform > Configure Snap* from the viewport settings (see Figure 2.29).

From the Snap Dialog, the default value for Translate is 1. This means that, when *Snapping* is enabled, the *Translate* tool will lock all movement into steps of 1 unit (that is, 1 meter). In many cases, this value works fine. For our wall scenario, however, let's get more precision. Let's change this from *1* to *0.5*. Then choose OK (see Figure 2.30).

Next, Enable *Snapping* for the settings to take effect. To do this, click the Snapping button from the perspective view toolbar. This is a toggle button, so remember to press the button again later when you no longer need snapping (see Figure 2.31).

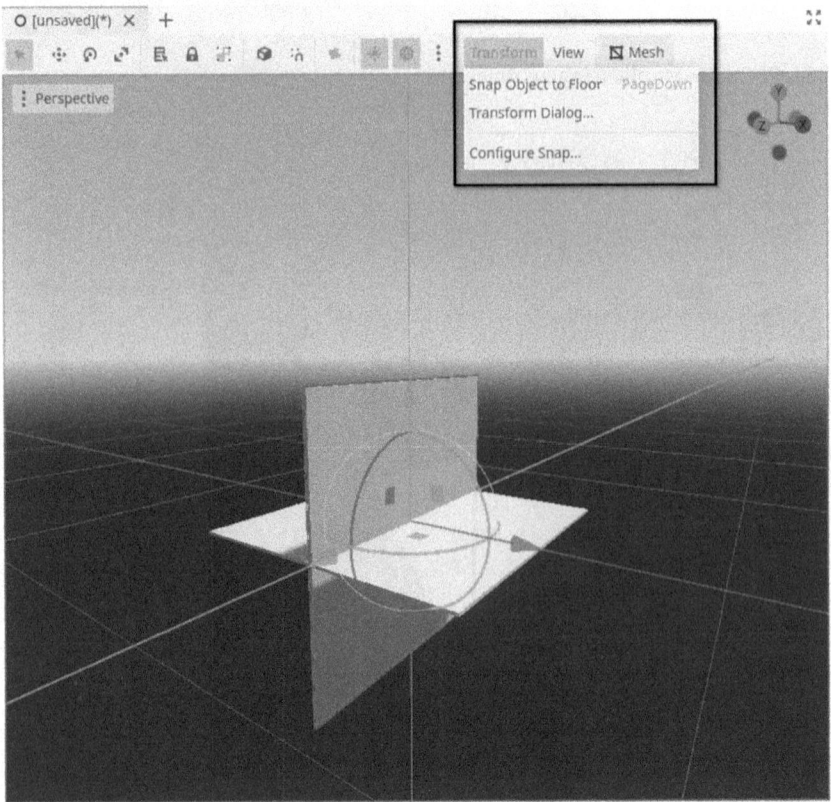

FIGURE 2.29   Rotating the wall into correct orientation.

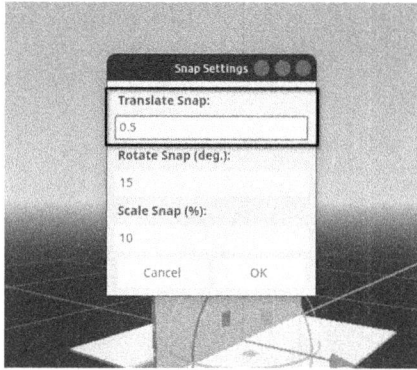

FIGURE 2.30   Configure translate snapping.

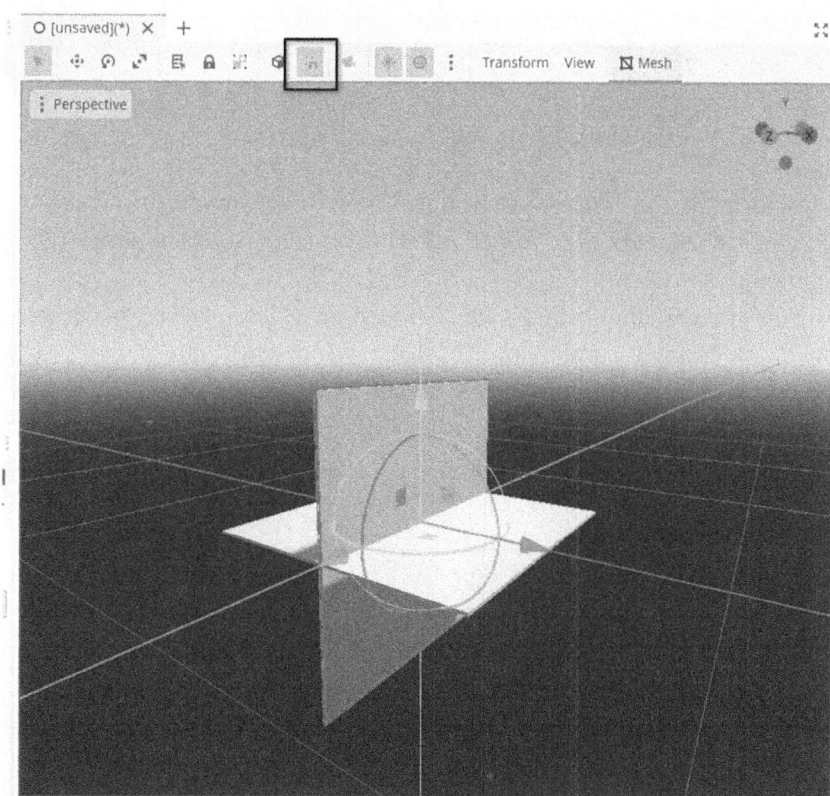

FIGURE 2.31   Toggling Snap on and off to control the Translate tool.

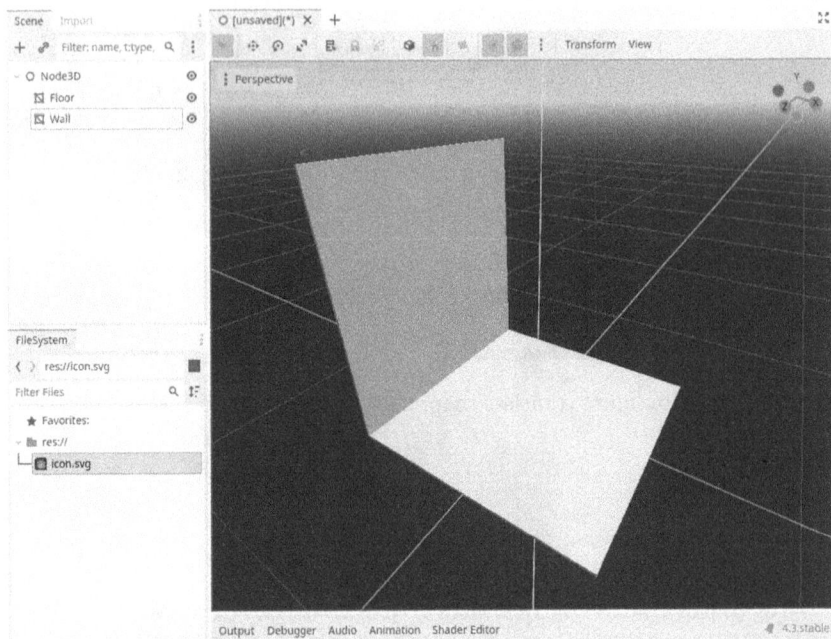

FIGURE 2.32   Positioning the wall at the correct location.

With snapping enabled for the Translate tool, you can now use the Gizmo to click and drag the wall into the correct, and exact, position (see Figure 2.32).

Now you can duplicate the wall piece three times to create the remaining walls. Using a combination of Rotate, Translate, and Snapping, you can move them all into place to create a box room. Four walls and a floor. See Figure 2.33 to see the result.

2.3 VERTEX SNAPPING – INSTALLING AN ADD-ON FROM ASSETLIB

In Godot, you'll normally work with many meshes, from power-ups and weapons to wall segments and statues. It could number in the hundreds or even thousands. Many of these assets may come from artists in your team, made to a known specification. But also, they may come from third-party sources, such as contractors or online asset stores. Perhaps they were made a long time ago. In these cases, you may not know the exact dimensions of a mesh, and this can be problematic. You'll simply be left to drag and drop the mesh into Godot and start working with it in a scene, however it is made. However, you'll also need to align meshes of different sizes and

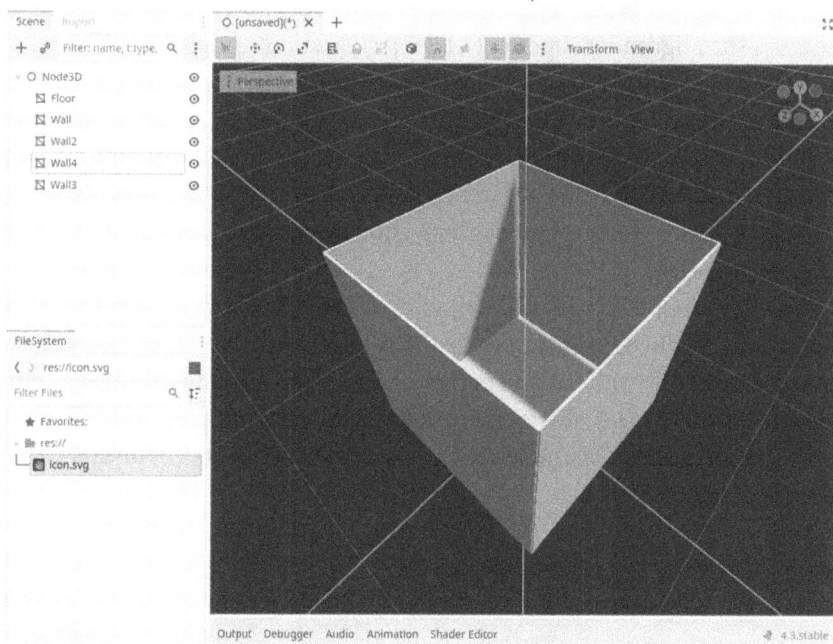

FIGURE 2.33   Completing the box room.

types together to form a complete world. This can be difficult to do when they are different shapes and sizes. A common case is aligning together two or more repeatable wall sections, like building blocks, to form a longer section and make it look seamless and whole. Hallways and space stations commonly employ this technique, recombining many smaller elements into larger patterns to create an expansive world. This approach depends on your being able to precisely line up meshes so that gaps and overlaps don't happen, spoiling the effect of continuity. We've seen earlier how Grid Snapping and typing in values can solve this, in theory. But both methods are tedious when you have many meshes. For Grid Snapping, for example, you need to assume that all meshes have a size that conforms to the same base increment, and for type-ins, you must be prepared to type in the position for every single mesh involved. That's painful.

Thankfully, another good solution is available in the form of *Vertex Snapping*. Users coming from Unity will likely already be familiar with this feature. Vertex Snapping lets you automatically move a complete mesh such that any vertex (point) on the selected mesh will be perfectly overlapped with a vertex on another mesh. Normally, you use Vertex Snapping to align corners with corners and edges with edges. Vertex Snapping ensures the alignment is perfect and exact, and not simply 'roughly right'. Now, Vertex Snapping is good news! But it's not a native feature of Godot. To access it, we'll need to install an add-on. But it's free, open source, and is built into the Godot editor. Let's see how we can install this add-on, and thereby many others that are available too. Consider the following scene in Figure 2.34. It features two simple cube mesh instances that need to be aligned together.

To start importing an add-on, click on the *AssetLib* button from the top-center of the Godot interface. This links to an online, community-maintained collection of assets that you can download and import into Godot. Some of the assets are intended to be imported into existing projects, and some of the assets are complete projects themselves (see Figure 2.35).

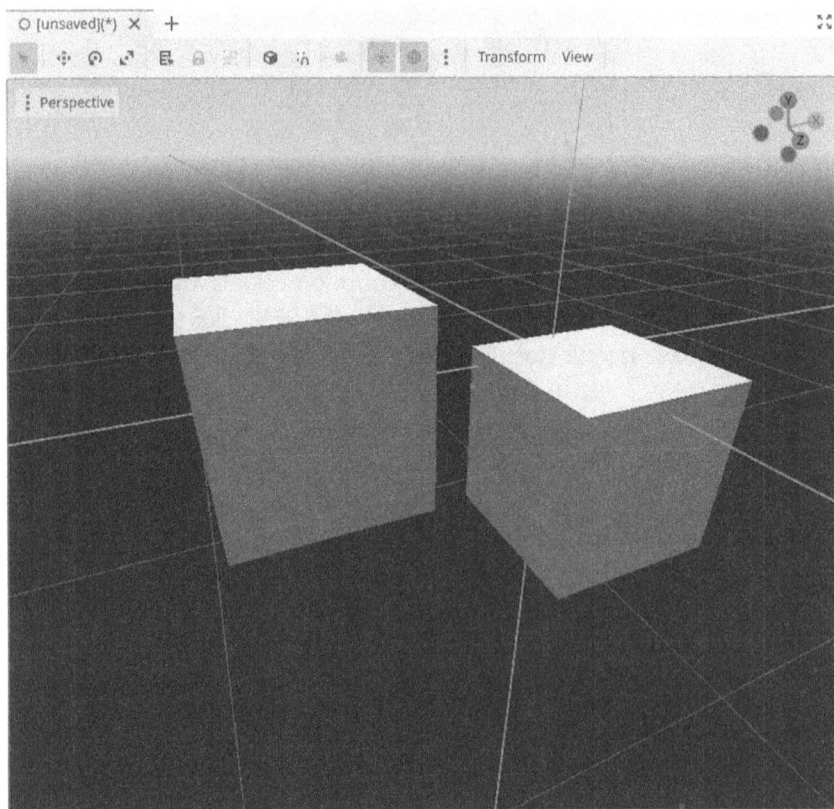

FIGURE 2.34   Two cube meshes in need of alignment.

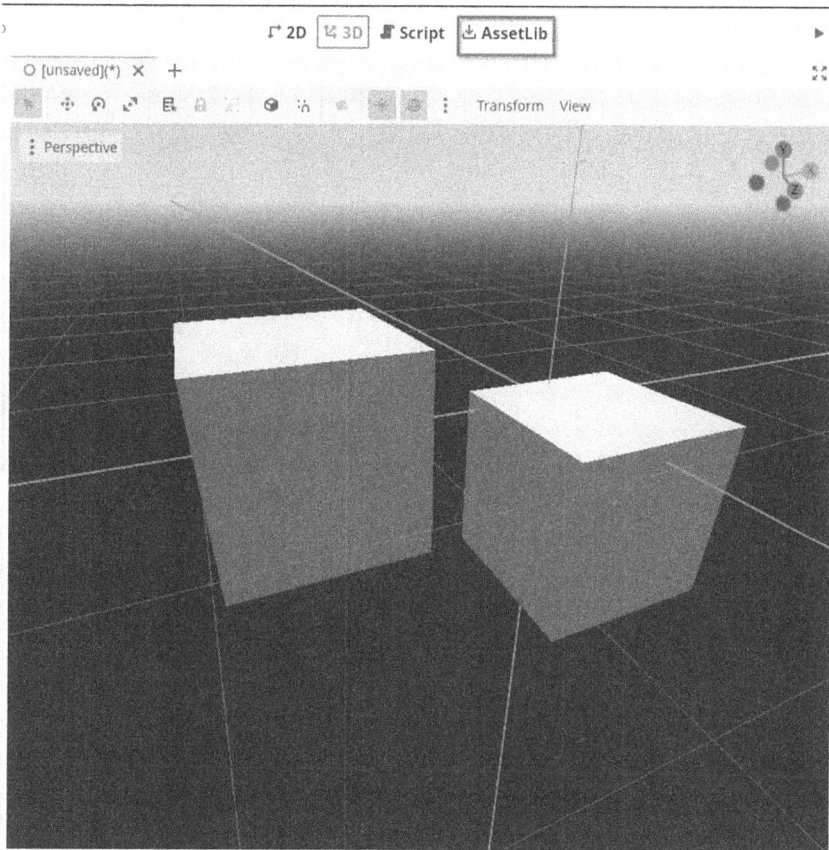

FIGURE 2.35   Accessing the Godot Asset Library.

From the AssetLib, search for *Snappy*, listed by jgillich. Use the search term *Snappy*, and make sure the *Category* is specified as *All*. When you do this, Snappy will appear as an installable option in the list (see Figure 2.36).

Double-clicking the Snappy option presents you with a confirmation dialog. Choose the button Download to install Snappy to your computer locally within the project. It's important to note that this download is *project-specific*. The add-on will live in your currently open project. You'll need to download it again for other projects if you intend to use it there (Figure 2.37).

Godot may prompt you with a further confirmation dialog, outlining the location within your project where the newly downloaded files will be installed. You can change this by clicking the *Change Install Folder*

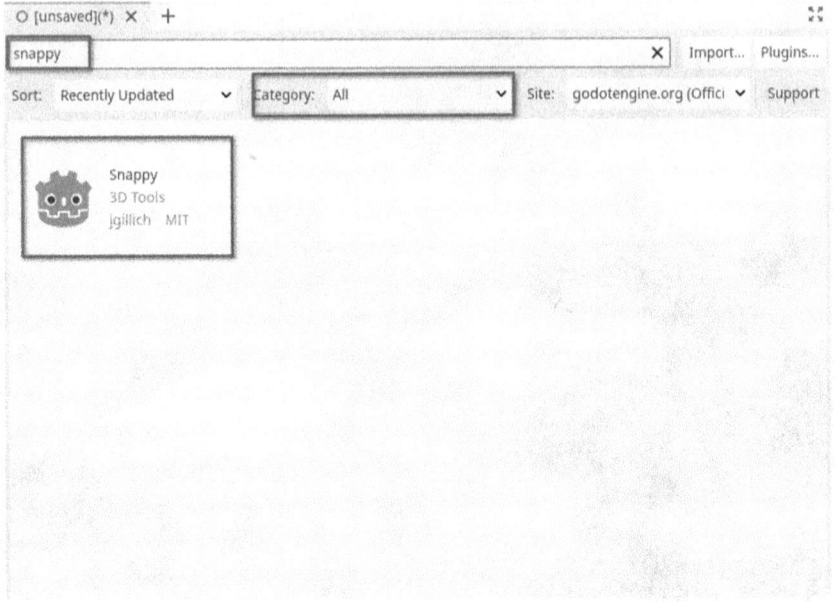

FIGURE 2.36   Downloading Snappy from the Godot Asset Library.

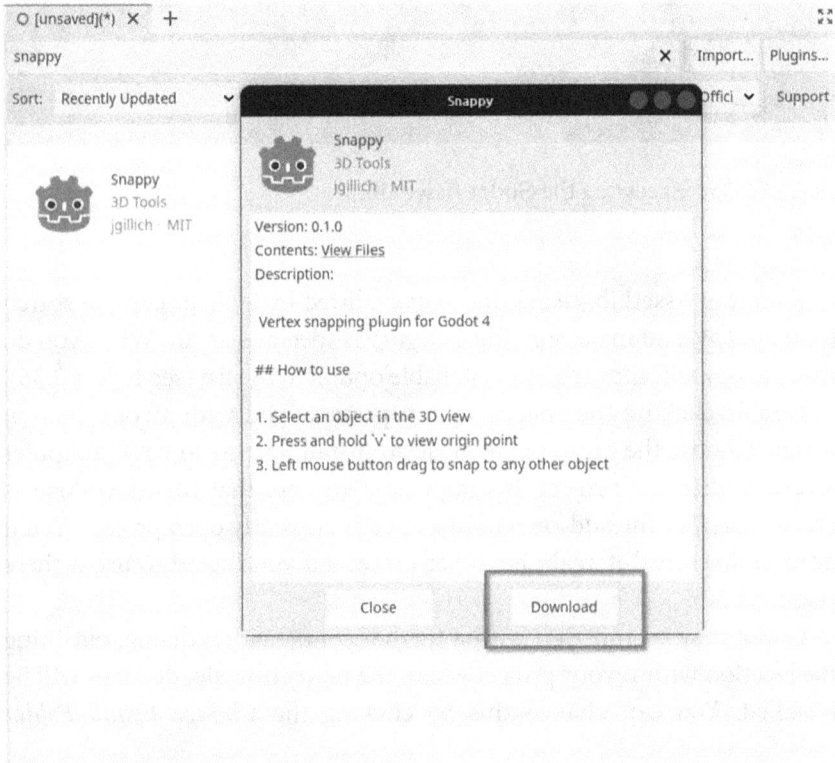

FIGURE 2.37   Downloading Snappy.

button, but for this example, I will accept the defaults. You can accept by clicking the *Install* button (Figure 2.38).

After installation, you can confirm success by viewing the *FileSystem Dock*. You should see an addons folder and newly installed files inside. This will reflect the location shown in the previous step (see Figure 2.39).

If the files are present, then the plugin is *almost* ready. If you try to use it now, by moving objects in the scene, it still won't work. There is a final activation switch that you need to press. It's buried in the *Project Settings* window. Choose *Project > Project Settings* from the application menu, and this displays the Project Settings window (see Figure 2.40).

NOTE. The Project Settings Window is quite comprehensive. We'll have reason to return there later to change many other settings.

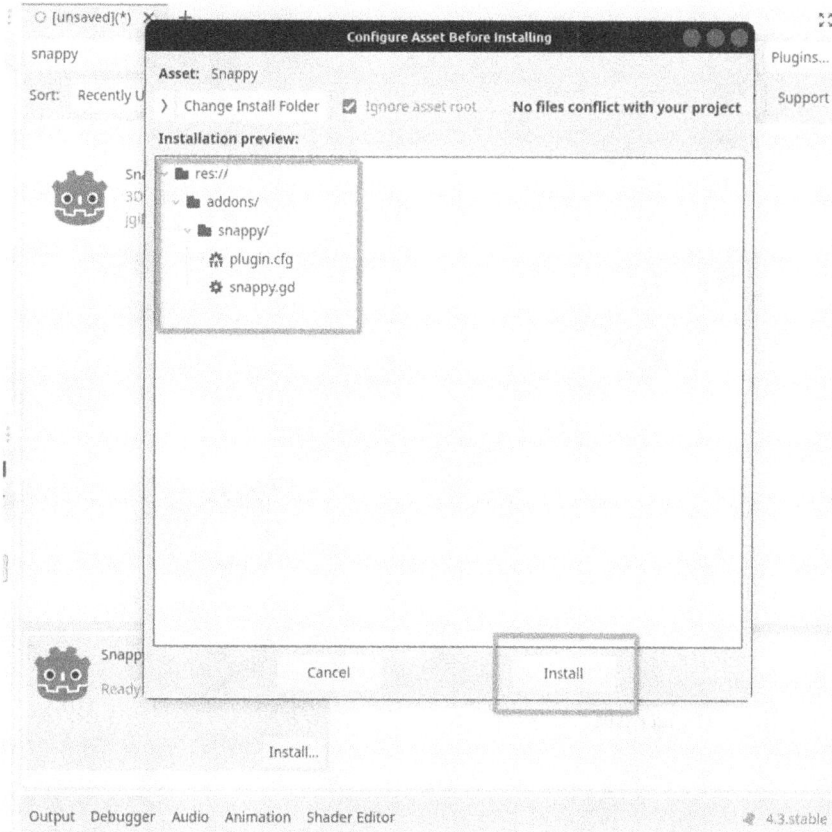

FIGURE 2.38   Choosing the Download destination.

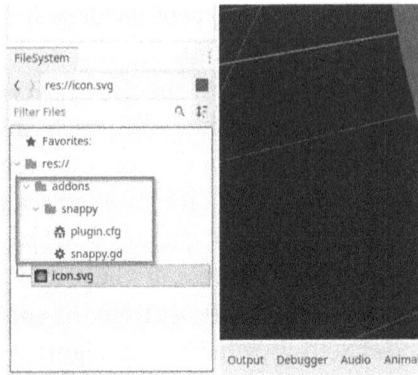

FIGURE 2.39 Confirming the installation folder for Snappy.

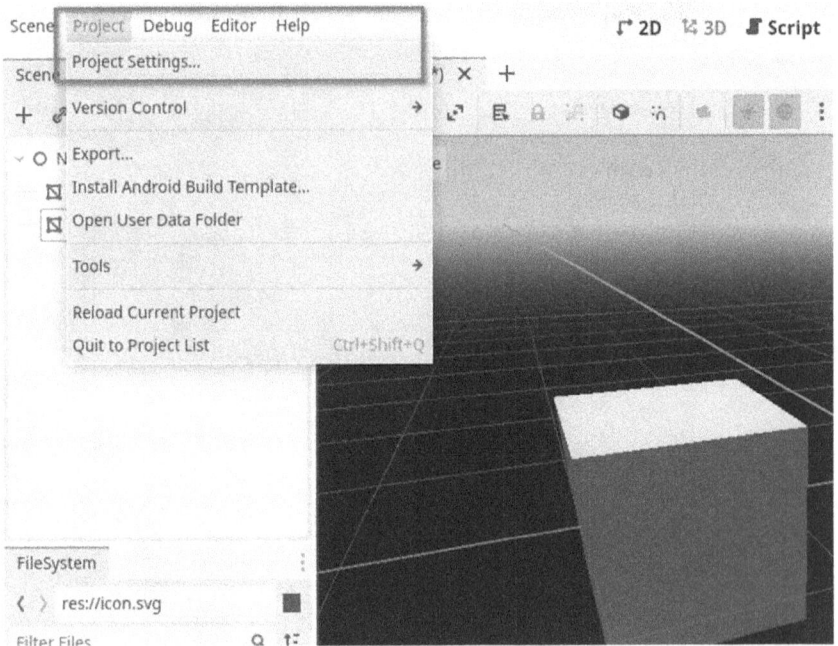

FIGURE 2.40 Accessing Project Settings.

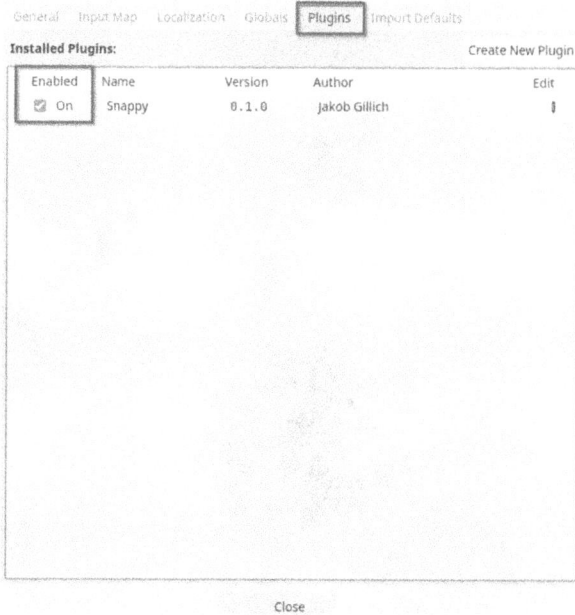

Installed Plugins: Create New Plugin

Enabled	Name	Version	Author	Edit
☑ On	Snappy	0.1.0	Jakob Gillich	┇

Close

FIGURE 2.41   Enabling the Snappy Plugin.

From the Project Settings Window, choose the Plugin tab. Then insert a checkmark in the Enabled box in the left-hand column. This finally enables the Snappy plugin. Next, we'll use it to snap together two cube objects (see Figure 2.41).

To use Vertex Snapping, return to the perspective viewport and frame the view to include both cubes. Select a cube and then hold down the V key on the keyboard to engage Vertex Snapping mode. With the V key held down, move your cursor over different vertices of the model. As you do this, you'll notice a yellow dot, or ball, latch onto the nearest vertex (see Figure 2.42).

Hover your mouse over the corner vertex of the selected cube – the vertex nearest the opposite cube. Then, with V still held down, click and drag this from this vertex to the nearest corner vertex of the opposing cube, and then release your mouse and the V key. This will align the selected cube over to the opposite cube, with the corner vertices touching (see Figure 2.43).

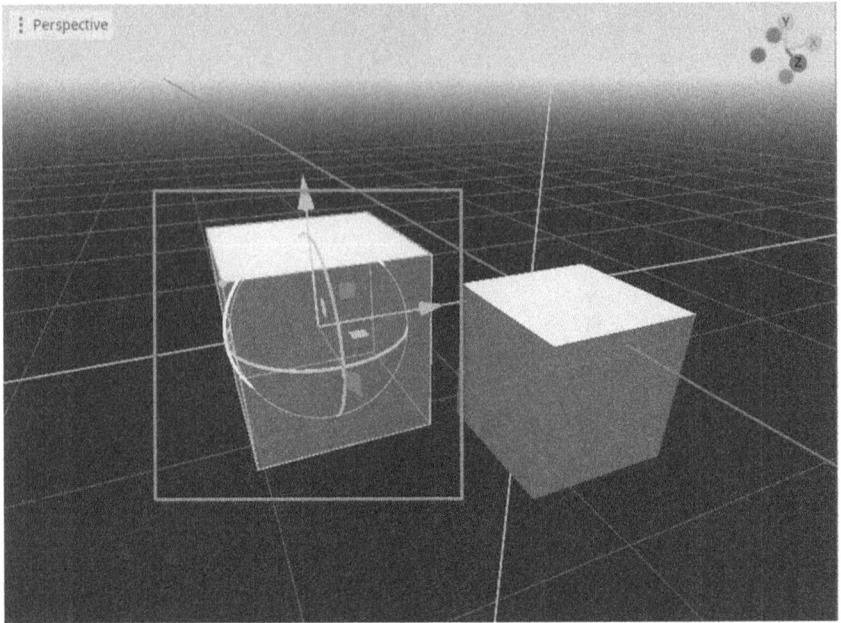

FIGURE 2.42   Engaging Vertex Snap.

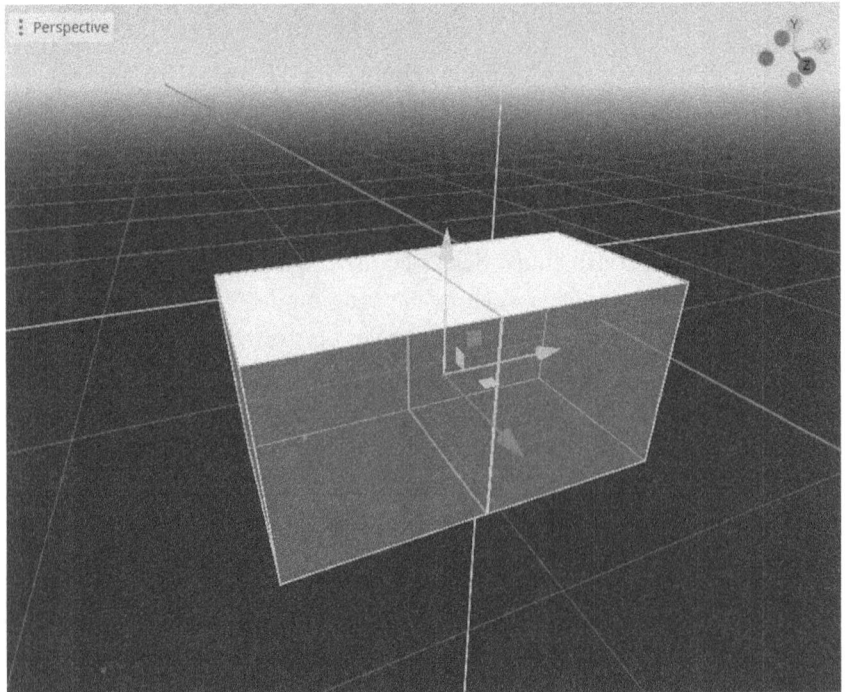

FIGURE 2.43   Snapping together two cubes.

2.4 FILESYSTEM DOCK – UNDERSTANDING THE PROJECT FOLDER

Godot is a project-based application. You create a new project to build a new game, and all data and files related to that game are stored together inside a single folder named the *project folder*. The contents of this folder, and its subfolders, are viewable directly in the editor from the *FileSystem* dock. The contents are significant because any files that you add to this folder, whether it's via the Godot editor or through Explorer or Finder, essentially become part of the Godot project (see Figure 2.44).

The project folder corresponds to a real folder located somewhere on your computer. You may forget where this is or be unsure how to navigate there. You can easily find your way directly to this folder where needed. Hover your cursor anywhere over empty space inside the *FileSystem Dock* and then right-click your mouse, choosing Open in *FileManager* from the context menu. Selecting this will open your operating system's file browser at this location (see Figure 2.45).

NOTE. To prevent any confusion, errors, or conflicts, I recommend avoiding any edits to files in this folder while directly using Explorer when the Godot project is open. Always go through the Godot interface when making changes to this folder. The FileSystem dock lets

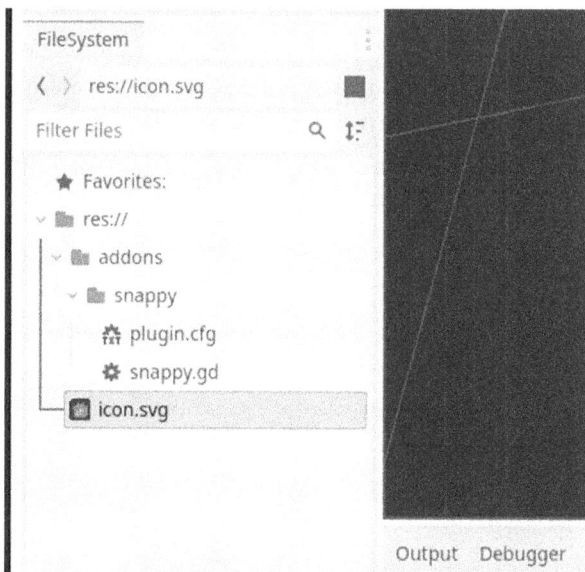

FIGURE 2.44   Viewing the project folder from the Godot Interface.

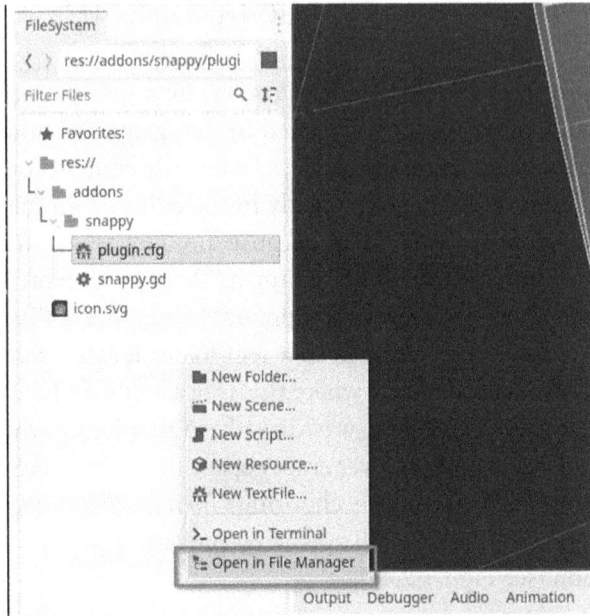

FIGURE 2.45   Viewing the project folder from the Godot interface.

you create folders, drag and drop files, rename files, and delete files. This ensures that Godot understands what changes are being made.

Let's take a brief look at the contents of our project folder when a project is newly created. You'll notice that it includes a default Godot icon file in SVG format, some Git version control files (*.gitignore* and *.gitattributes*), and a project.godot file. The latter is a high-level, text-based configuration file that Godot generates to summarize the project. The file looks like this:

```
; Engine configuration file.
; It's best edited using the editor UI and not
directly,
; since the parameters that go here are not all
obvious.
;
; Format:
; [section] ; section goes between []
; param=value ; assign values to parameters

config_version=5
```

```
[application]

config/name="PlatformGame_Book"
config/features=PackedStringArray("4.3", "Mobile")
config/icon="res://icon.svg"

[editor_plugins]

enabled=PackedStringArray("res://addons/snappy/plugin.
cfg")

[rendering]

renderer/rendering_method="mobile"
```

NOTE. These settings define which renderer we are using (*Mobile*), and they also list any add-ons or plugins that the project is using (*Snappy*).

If you ever want to backup your project or to share your project with someone else, then you should certainly make a copy of the entire project folder and all its contents, and not simply specific files within the folder. They are not supposed to be separated. They function as a single package. One way to archive everything together in a convenient package is to use a compression program, such as *7-Zip. Before copying or archiving the folder,* you should close Godot in case it has any changes to make to metafiles within the project folder. Remember not to store your compressed archives inside the project folder; otherwise, they'll be classified as being part of the project themselves too. So, store your archives elsewhere (see Figure 2.46).

Let's turn now to an interesting note about file systems. If you right-click on a file inside the *FileSystem Dock* and then choose *Copy Absolute Path*, paste the result into a text editor and see what you get. You'll get a fully qualified system path to the selected file. For example, this is what I see when I copy the Absolute Path for the Godot icon SVG.

```
/home/alanthorn/platformgame _ book/icon.svg
```

This may not be surprising. But now, right-click the same file and choose *Copy Path* instead. The result should be very different. Here is what I got for the same file:

```
res://icon.svg
```

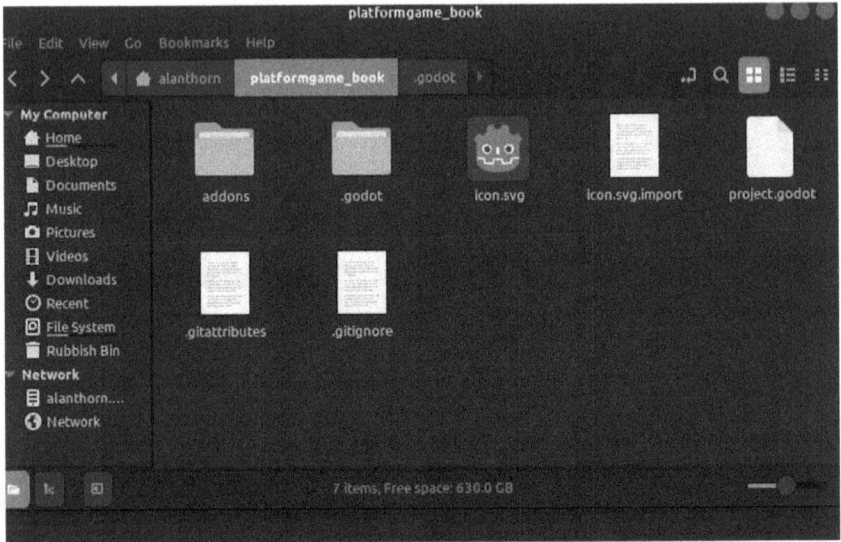

FIGURE 2.46   The Godot project folder.

As you can see, Godot is creating a mapping between **two different file-systems**. The Absolute Path refers to the file location that is given by the operating system (e.g., C:\My Documents\Document01.pdf). This path can vary from operating system to operating system. It's a useful path to know for locating a file *on your local computer*. The regular path of Godot, however, is an internal naming system used by Godot to uniquely identify files internally. This is useful to reference a file within the Godot project, independently of any name or path an operating system may have assigned to the file. It will remain consistent across all operating systems. Godot uses the term **resource** to refer to a *file* within its system. Some engines use the term *asset* to mean the same thing. An image file is a texture resource, a 3D model is a mesh resource, and so on. More will be said of this path system later in the book. You can also find more information about it at the Godot documentation online here: https://docs.godotengine.org/en/stable/tutorials/scripting/filesystem.html

2.5 GIT – VERSION CONTROL FOR GODOT PROJECTS

Game development requires plenty of iteration and refinement in your workflow. This necessarily means that you'll be changing, updating, and editing your project a lot; trying out new ideas, adding in new meshes or levels, and so on. Some of these changes will remain and become part of the final game because they worked well, and yet other changes will be abandoned because they didn't work at all or simply proved unfeasible within the constraints that you have, technical or budgetary, for example. In this case, and to work tidily, it'd be useful if we could achieve the following things in our workflow:

1. The ability to share the latest version of our project systematically with all team members, wherever they are

2. The ability for everybody to work on, and contribute to, the same project and files, but without creating conflicts or without team members disrupting other people's work accidentally

3. The ability to keep track of what files have changed in a project and who is responsible for those changes

4. The ability to test out new ideas and take the project in new directions, without compromising our existing work, especially if our new ideas don't work out

5. The ability to rewind our project to earlier states if needed; to restore older versions if the newer changes are taking us further from where we want to be

Sounds good, right? Well, you can already achieve this by just being incredibly organized and systematic with backups through cloud storage, like *OneDrive, DropBox, Proton Drive*, or *Google Drive*. But that method will get tedious, time-consuming, and thereby very expensive, very quickly. You'll end up spending lots of your time managing files and team member contributions to ensure that nothing breaks, instead of building a game. For this reason, we need a better method for managing projects, and version control can offer this if we embrace it and use it properly. Obviously, if you don't embrace it and don't use it properly, it can become your worst nightmare too! This is not a reason to avoid it but a reason to learn it. So, we can learn **Git** version control to keep track of our Godot projects. Let's get started.

> NOTE. This section is *optional*. You can skip it and move to the next chapter. You don't *need* to install or use Git to work with Godot. You can create Godot projects and make games without Git or, indeed, any version control at all. This is all true. However, Git can make your workflow easier and more efficient, and it works on all operating

systems and is free. For this reason, it's a useful skill to know. I recommend using it.

2.5.1 Installing Git

Installing Git is straightforward, but the steps vary significantly from operating system to operating system. So, rather than cover the installation steps for every scenario in this book, I will direct you to the download page where instructions can be found for your computer. The download page is here: https://git-scm.com/downloads

> NOTE. The download page sometimes talks about a *Git Client*. This is usually an optional mouse-driven visual interface that sits atop Git, allowing you to use Git without resorting to command-line or terminal instructions. Examples of Git Clients are *GitHub Client*, *GitKraken*, and *SourceTree*. More can be found here: *https://git-scm. com/downloads/guis*. For this book, I recommend using the Git command line. When starting out using Git, it is helpful to understand its core commands and how it works. Later, if you prefer visual tools, you can use a Git client, or you may prefer to continue with the command line. So, you don't need to download and install a separate Git client.

When using Git for game development, it's also useful to use a Git add-on called *Large File Storage* (LFS). This add-on optimizes the workflow when working with large, binary files, such as image files, mesh files, and music, as opposed to text files like code. To download and install this add-on, you should visit this page: https://git-lfs.com/.

2.5.2 Getting Started with Git

The best way to learn Git is probably by using it to track a folder with some basic files, like text files, and seeing how it works in practice. This knowledge can then be extrapolated to manage a Godot project folder. So, let's do that. Start by creating a new, empty folder on your computer (outside of your Godot project), and which can be easily deleted when you're done practicing. I've created a folder called *test-git* (see Figure 2.47).

To start using Git to track files inside a folder, you need to create a new **Repository**. Sometimes abbreviated to **Repo**. This is, essentially, a database that Git creates to keep track of all changes to files within the folder, and over time the repo will grow larger and contain more data as your project progresses. The database is stored inside the project folder itself as a hidden file. This means that you will delete the repo if you delete the folder.

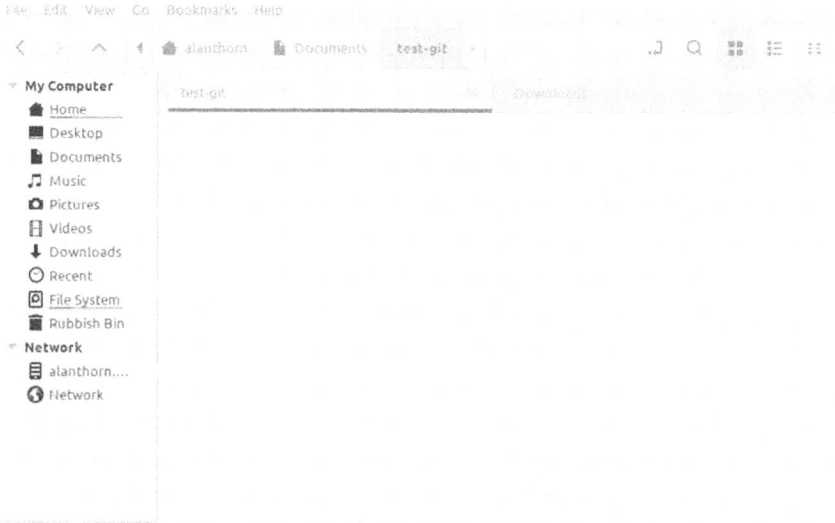

FIGURE 2.47   Creating a new folder.

You need to create a new *Git Repo* for each project that you want to put into version control. So, you normally create one Git Repo for each Godot project, and therefore, one Repo per game. To create a new Repo, you should first navigate the command line (terminal) to the newly created folder to ensure that all following terminal commands apply to the selected working directory. For example, on a Linux command line, this would be as below. You may need to use a different path and folder name, depending on where you placed your new folder.

```
cd Documents/test-git
```

> NOTE. For this example, make sure that you create a new Git repo in a new, empty folder as I have done. Don't create it in a directory full of existing files. And don't store any valuable data in our newly made folder. This will be a 'throw away' example. We're going to be using Git by example here to go back and forth in history, which will lead to file changes and maybe even deletions of data in this folder and its subfolders.

To create a new Repo for the working directory, enter the following command into the terminal and press Enter. Make sure you do this inside the Working folder (the directory that you created for working with Git):

```
git init
```

My terminal replies with:

```
Initialised empty Git repository in /home/alanthorn/
Documents/test-git/.git/
```

If you return to the project folder and view hidden files, you'll notice a new, special folder. It's called *.git*, and it contains all the data needed by Git to maintain a Repo. If you were to delete this folder, you'd end up deleting the entire Repo (see Figure 2.48).

During the Git download and installation phase, we also downloaded an add-on called LFS. Git is normally intended to work with text-based code files and small binaries so that developers can share work easily. However, game developers often work with potentially large files that change a lot over time, such as meshes, animations, videos, textures, and other media. If you don't use the LFS add-on, Git will effectively make whole copies of these files for every change, and this can end up creating large repositories that take a long time to download, requiring lots of cloud storage to maintain and entailing high bandwidth use. All these things are bad. So, to optimize your Repo for storing large files, you can enable the LFS add-on. You need to do this for each Repo you make. To activate LFS for the current Repo, enter the following command at the terminal and press *Enter*.

```
git lfs install
```

My terminal replies with:

```
Updated git hooks.
Git LFS initialized.
```

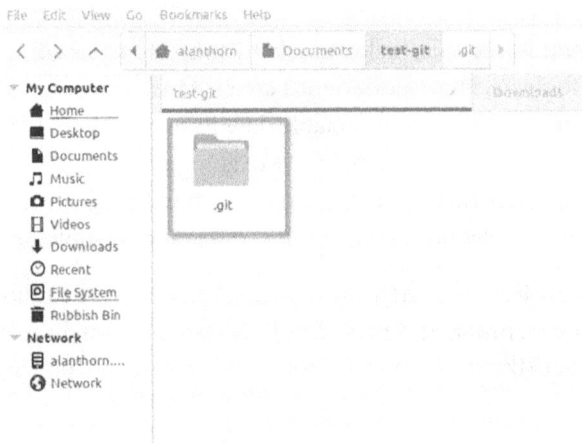

FIGURE 2.48   The *.git* folder contains all repo data.

Finally, you can check up on the status of Git to ensure things are good. To do this, enter the following command at the Terminal and press Enter:

```
git status
```

The reply should be something like below:

```
On branch master

No commits yet

nothing to commit (create/copy files and use "git add"
to track)
```

If so, you're good to move to the next step.

2.5.3 Tracking Changes to a File with Commits

Let's see what happens now in our Git repository if we add a text file to our newly created folder. Git uses the term **working tree** to simply describe the contents of your folder. It is the folder itself and everything inside it. It is the current state of your project on your computer. The working tree does not include any data in the *.git* subfolder. That is the **Repository** and its associated metadata. Go ahead and create a new .txt file (called *mytext.txt*) in the *working tree* with the following text inside, as below. Also see Figure 2.49.

```
This is the original text file!
```

After saving the file, enter the following command in the Terminal and press *Enter.*

```
git status
```

This time, the response from the terminal is different because Git has detected a change within the working tree. The message reads:

```
On branch master

No commits yet
```

Untracked files :
(use "git add <file>…" to include in what will be committed)
mytext.txt

```
nothing added to commit but untracked files present
(use "git add" to track)
```

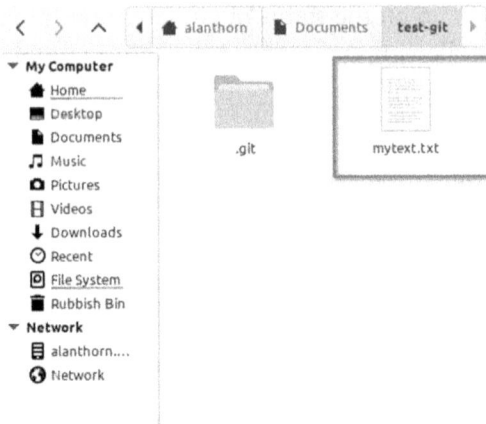

FIGURE 2.49   Creating a new text file in the working tree.

When a change is made to a file (or a new file is added), Git detects the fact but will not automatically take any action. You must then explicitly tell Git which files you want it to track. That is, which files it should record. The next step here is to effectively build a *snapshot of the contents of the working tree* so that later, potentially, it could be restored to this point, as you have recorded it. You build this snapshot in two steps. You must first add all files 'to be recorded' into an index, which Git calls the **staging area**. You can add or remove files to and from the staging area without affecting the repository. It's an intermediary space. The reason it exists is because, when working with lots of different files, you may want to group sets of related files together and add them to the repository in separate units. You can add files to the staging area individually by name, but more commonly you will add files by type or perhaps add everything in the working tree that has changed. Let's add every changed file in the folder to the staging area. In this case, we only added one file.

```
git add *
```

NOTE. If you ran the *git status* command now, you'd see the new file highlighted in green rather than red, indicating that the change has been added to the staging area.

NOTE. If you add a file to the staging area and then afterward decide to remove it again, you can do so with the command *git rm –cached <filename>*.

Next, the file changes have been added to the staging area. If you're happy to track these files, you should *commit* them to the Git Repo. This will add an entry into the Git database, affecting the taking of a snapshot of the staged files. To do this, you can write the following command.

```
git commit -m "first commit"
```

> NOTE. The **commit** command accepts an *–m* parameter, which means 'message'. For each commit you make, you should write a descriptive message. This normally describes what changes you made or introduced. Commit messages should be short but descriptive. In this example, our message is 'first commit'.

Now run *git status*; it will now show that there are no changes detected, as follows:

```
On branch master
nothing to commit, working tree clean
```

Let's modify the text file by appending a second line and saving it. It now reads:

```
This is the original text file!
```
This is a second line

With the file modified, let's run another *git status* command. It shows the following:

```
On branch master
Changes not staged for commit:
(use "git add <file>..." to update what will be
committed)
(use "git restore <file>..." to discard changes in
working directory)
modified: mytext.txt

no changes added to commit (use "git add" and/or "git
commit -a")
```

And so, we should now stage and commit these changes. As follows:

```
git add *
git commit -m 'added second line'
```

We have now made two separate commits. Now try running the following command:

```
git log --oneline
```

The output will be:

```
e3b418f (HEAD -> master) added second line
2ad3714 first commit
```

You will see that each commit is listed in reverse order, with the most recent at the top. Each line shows a separate commit in your **Commit History**. The text *HEAD -> master* means that your working tree shows the contents for the most recent data. The most recent commit is normally located at the *HEAD*.

Now go ahead and practice by making some more commits, simply by modifying the text file several times and then committing each time.

> NOTE. If you're working with many files, your project changes not only by the *addition* of new files or by the *amendment* of existing files – as we have seen – but by the *deletion* of files, that is, the entire removal of one or more files from your project. Git will capture deletions, as with additions and amendments. However, the *git add* command will not 'add' such deletions to the staging area by default, making it hard to commit deletions in the project history. You fix this by using *git add –a **. The *–a* option means 'capture **all** changes'.

2.5.4 Undoing Commits with Revert

Obviously, one of the reasons to version control your work at all is to allow for the possibility of rewinds. That is, to return your working tree back to an earlier state. This may be because you want to review or find something from a while ago, or perhaps because you don't like the most recent direction of your project, and you simply want to backstep entirely and ignore more recent edits. Git offers many ways to 'rewind' your work. One way is the **revert** command. This allows you to undo one *or* more commits in your history. Let's continue from the previous example. I'll assume you made some additional commits of your own, as I have. If I type git *log – oneline*, you can see my commits. There are four in total.

```
b847e07 (HEAD -> master) fourth
5c0a3f5 third
```

```
e3b418f added second line
2ad3714 first commit
```

Now, if you want to 'undo' all changes in the *most recent* commit (fourth), returning your project back to the *previous* state (third), you can use the command *git revert HEAD*.

You might think that running *git revert HEAD* multiple times like this in succession will successively undo more commits going further back in history. Essentially, you rewind the project commit by commit until eventually you end up back at the very first commit, beyond which you cannot revert anymore. However, this understanding of a stepped rewind approach is actually wrong. It's not how Git behaves. Each *revert* action undoes a commit, but it also *creates a new commit* in the history, which becomes the new HEAD. The new commit *keeps track of the fact that you reverted to an earlier commit*. Your revert becomes part of the project history. See the output of my log command here:

```
f32a562 (HEAD -> master) Revert "fourth"
b847e07 fourth
5c0a3f5 third
e3b418f added second line
2ad3714 first commit
```

This means that running *git revert HEAD* multiple times repeatedly just *reverts the previous revert*. It undoes the undo. It would be a loop of undo, redo, etc., for as far as you wanted to go. Your project history would build up with successive commits, keeping track of the reversion history. Sounds like a nightmare loop.

If you want to actually rewind across *multiple* commits, returning the project back to an earlier state before the most recent or previous state, then you must first use *git log –oneline*. Let's say that I want to return back to the first state of the project, 'first commit'. That's quite a radical reversion, but it can be done, nonetheless. You can see that this first commit has an ID of *2ad3714*. For you, the ID will probably be different because the IDs are dynamically generated by Git. Make a note of the ID for the commit that you intend to return to. You'll need it. You can use the revert command to undo a range of commits, not just one commit. The range operator is (..). Take a look at the following example, which, for me, reverts the head *back to* the first commit.

```
git revert -n 2ad3714..HEAD
```

After the revert, the original files are restored but are counted as 'staged changes' in need of committing. So, you'll need to Commit them with *git commit*, e.g.,:

```
git commit -m 'back to first'
```

Now the log history appears as:

```
c7eb212 (HEAD -> master) back to first
f32a562 Revert "fourth"
b847e07 fourth
5c0a3f5 third
e3b418f added second line
2ad3714 first commit
```

And the contents of my text file are:

```
This is the original text file!
```

Voila! We can now restore a Git repo backward and forward to any arbitrary commit. You now have a time machine, effectively. Obviously, there's more to learn about Git, such as *branches*. These let Git sidestep in the project timeline to alternative histories, rather than just forward-step or backstep as we've been doing in this example. However, here we have enough information to start version controlling a Godot project.

> NOTE. For more information on using Git in-depth, I recommend the free online book Pro Git, written by Scott Chacon and published by Apress here: https://git-scm.com/book/en/v2.

2.5.5 Using Remote Repositories

Git is a Distributed Version Control system. It *can* run just fine on only one computer if necessary, keeping track of your work fully locally. *But* when you combine Git with a server, such as a cloud service like *GitHub, GitLab*, or *BitBucket*, then you can create a **Remote Repository**. This is, essentially, a separate 'Repo in the Cloud'. There are two major advantages to this. First, your project files are stored at a separate location, in addition to your own computer, acting as a form of backup. Second, multiple people (such as team members) can now collaborate, synchronizing their changes together across multiple computers and locations through a single remote repo, which acts as a single source of truth. In this section, we'll setup a remote repo that works with GitHub, a well-known Git hosting provider.

I don't have any connection or interest in GitHub as a company; I simply chose this platform because it is accessible for this example. Please check out the many options available to you when deciding on a place to host Git. An alternative way to host is by using your own VPS (Virtual Private Server), such as Ubuntu Server. The details of self-hosting are beyond the scope of this book. To access GitHub, you'll need to sign up for a free account at https://github.com/.

In this example, we'll upload our existing Repo on our local computer, as created in previous sections to manage a text file, to GitHub. To do this, create a new Repo on GitHub from your web browser. From the Dashboard, click *New*. This presents you with the *New Repo* screen. Fill that in with some basic details, such as the Repo Name (see Figure 2.50; Press *Create*).

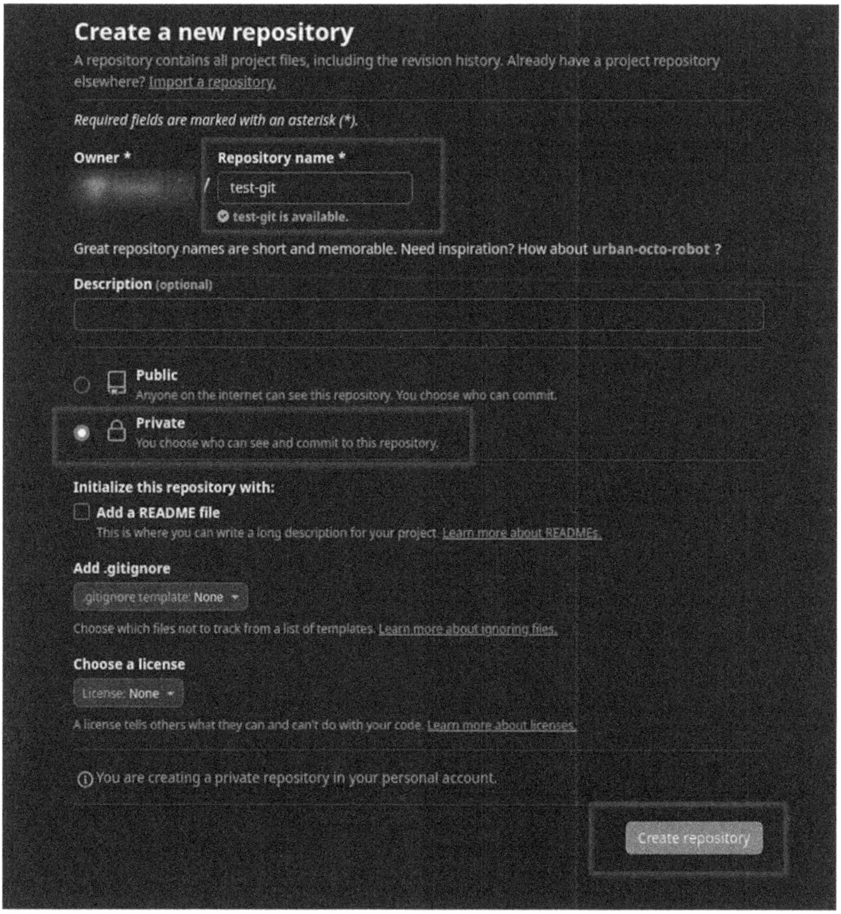

FIGURE 2.50   Creating a new repo at GitHub.

After the Repo is created, it will be empty and awaiting contributions from you. GitHub will also help you by listing how you can access the Repo remotely to add or change content. The Repo welcome page at GitHub shows the address for your Repo. It will probably be in the following structure: https://github.com/<username>/<reponame>.git.

> NOTE. *Username* should be replaced by your GitHub username, and the *Repo Name* should be replaced by the name given to your repository. Remember, the full path to your repo will be listed on the repo welcome page, where you will be directed after its creation.

Next, run the following command locally for your repo to configure the remote repo as a destination.

```
git remote add origin https://github.
com/<username>/<reponame>.git
git branch -M main
```

Finally, to push your changes from the local to the remote, you can run the following command:

```
git push -u origin main
```

> NOTE. You should run this command every time you make a local change and need to update the remote repository.

Since the *Push* command writes changes to the Remote Repo, Git will ask you for your credentials for authentication to protect your Repo from unauthorized access. You can use your GitHub username and password, but it may also expect a User Access Token in place of the password. If this is the first time that you're using GitHub, you probably won't have a User Access token. You can find more information on how to generate one here: https://docs.github.com/en/authentication/keeping-your-account-and-data-secure/managing-your-personal-access-tokens.

After successfully pushing your branch to the remote, you can return to GitHub and confirm that this was successful. You will now see your files uploaded there. You can now download your project and any changes using the command:

```
git pull origin
```

2.5.6 Ignoring Files with GitIgnore

We've seen how to version control a simple project with only one text file. Your Godot projects will contain many files. Some of those files are system-specific, such as user preferences, keyboard shortcuts, crash logs, and other kinds of metadata that should not really be shared across multiple users, especially when they have different preferences. This kind of data, therefore, does not affect the content of the project or the game. Rather, it affects only how the Editor behaves for a single user, and this should vary for each user. For this reason, we don't want this data being uploaded to the Repo because it is system-specific. To instruct Git to ignore specific files, you should use a **.gitignore** file. This file should be placed in the root folder of the project (not the *.git* folder). The developer community has kindly created an excellent database online of many .gitignore files for common applications, including Godot. This file contains the common files that Godot creates, which can be safely ignored by Git. You can download this file and place it inside your folder for any Godot project that you want to version control using Git. Here: https://github.com/github/gitignore/blob/main/Godot.gitignore (see Figure 2.51).

> NOTE. You don't need to stage or commit this file. Simply by its existing in the project folder, Git will use this file to determine automatically which files to ignore.

2.5.7 Managing Large Files with LFS

Git is normally intended to version control code or text-based files. It can manage other file types – namely, binary files – but large binary files, such as images, can start to slow down a repository over time. This can also become problematic if you're using cloud storage that has very specific

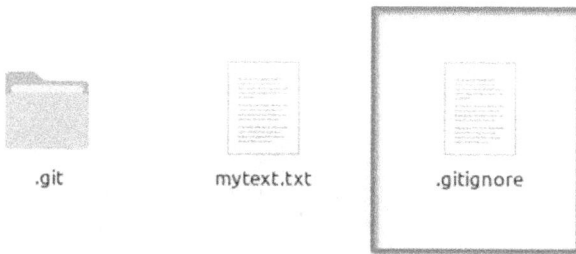

.git   mytext.txt   .gitignore

FIGURE 2.51   Adding a Godot GitIgnore file.

limits on the total size of your repository and your bandwidth. You could use a *.gitignore* file to simply have Git ignore all images and meshes, but that represents a lot of important content for games, so you'll end up excluding lots of valuable data. Instead, we can use Git LFS, which effectively stores all images in a separate sub-repository and handles them differently and optimally. To use LFS, you'll first need to create a text file inside the project folder alongside *.gitignore*, called *.gitattributes*, which lists all files to be managed by Git LFS. You'll need to write the lines using a special syntax. For Godot, the following .gitattributes file is pretty comprehensive, as it includes images, meshes, and more:

```
## git-lfs for Godot##
*.gif filter=lfs diff=lfs merge=lfs -text
*.psd filter=lfs diff=lfs merge=lfs -text
*.ai filter=lfs diff=lfs merge=lfs -text
*.jpg filter=lfs diff=lfs merge=lfs -text
*.jpeg filter=lfs diff=lfs merge=lfs -text
*.png filter=lfs diff=lfs merge=lfs -text
*.ico filter=lfs diff=lfs merge=lfs -text
*.ttf filter=lfs diff=lfs merge=lfs -text
*.bmp filter=lfs diff=lfs merge=lfs -text
*.pdf filter=lfs diff=lfs merge=lfs -text
*.docx filter=lfs diff=lfs merge=lfs -text
*.mov filter=lfs diff=lfs merge=lfs -text
*.avi filter=lfs diff=lfs merge=lfs -text
*.mkv filter=lfs diff=lfs merge=lfs -text
*.zip filter=lfs diff=lfs merge=lfs -text
*.rar filter=lfs diff=lfs merge=lfs -text
*.tar filter=lfs diff=lfs merge=lfs -text
*.exe filter=lfs diff=lfs merge=lfs -text
*.dll filter=lfs diff=lfs merge=lfs -text
*.doc filter=lfs diff=lfs merge=lfs -text
*.xls filter=lfs diff=lfs merge=lfs -text
*.fbx filter=lfs diff=lfs merge=lfs -text
*.blend filter=lfs diff=lfs merge=lfs -text
*.obj filter=lfs diff=lfs merge=lfs -text
*.xlsx filter=lfs diff=lfs merge=lfs -text
*.ase filter=lfs diff=lfs merge=lfs -text
*.aseprite filter=lfs diff=lfs merge=lfs -text
*.flc filter=lfs diff=lfs merge=lfs -text
*.tga filter=lfs diff=lfs merge=lfs -text
```

```
*.xcf filter=lfs diff=lfs merge=lfs -text
*.mp3 filter=lfs diff=lfs merge=lfs -text
*.wav filter=lfs diff=lfs merge=lfs -text
*.ogg filter=lfs diff=lfs merge=lfs -text
*.mp4 filter=lfs diff=lfs merge=lfs -text
*.ogv filter=lfs diff=lfs merge=lfs -text
*.otf filter=lfs diff=lfs merge=lfs -text
*.tif filter=lfs diff=lfs merge=lfs -text
*.svg filter=lfs diff=lfs merge=lfs -text
*.gltf filter=lfs diff=lfs merge=lfs -text
*.glb filter=lfs diff=lfs merge=lfs -text
*.dae filter=lfs diff=lfs merge=lfs -text
*.exr filter=lfs diff=lfs merge=lfs -text
```

After you've created this file, you can add any files of these types to your project. Just use the regular Git commands of *git add* and *git commit*. You can also use the command *git lfs ls-files* to show a list of all files in the Repo being managed by Git LFS. And that's it! Git will manage the rest and ensure your Repo behaves properly using your binary files too. Excellent.

2.6 CONCLUSION

This chapter focused on getting to know Godot, some of its features, basic scene design, and finally version control generally to keep track of your projects. Together, these fundamentals represent a solid foundation for building Godot games.

CHAPTER 3

Resources

Textures, Meshes, and More

THIS CHAPTER EXPLORES THE 'life blood', or essence, of any game or interactive project made in Godot; namely, the *resource*. Many engines use the term 'Asset' instead, but we'll adopt Godot's lesser-used terminology throughout this book. In simple terms, resources collectively refer to all the files and content on which your project depends, such as images, sounds, code files, meshes, animations, videos, text files, and more. Each file is a separate resource, and all of them together constitute the resources of your project. Most resources, like meshes, are typically made in an external application (such as Blender) and then imported into Godot for incorporation into a scene. However, some resources, like Scenes, are made directly inside Godot using the built-in Editor tools. Resources are not always standalone and separate from each other, as it may initially seem. There is a dependency and a hierarchy that holds between them. Although any two meshes (e.g., the player character and a weapon mesh) live independently of each other in separate files, some resources depend on and link to each other by their very nature. For example, a Scene is a resource, but it *depends* upon all the other resources, such as meshes and sounds, that are included within that scene. As a resource, it has connections that reach out to other resources. This weblike interdependency between resources is important, as we'll see, because it means that deleting a resource from the project, or even changing a resource after import, can have important implications for other, dependent resources. In the

DOI: 10.1201/9781003484523-3

worst case, deleting a resource can even break or invalidate another resource where a dependency exists. So, you need to be very careful when working with resources. This chapter explores that workflow for resources and considers useful tips and techniques along the way.

3.1 IMPORTING YOUR FIRST RESOURCE (TEXTURES)

Let's start by importing an image file into Godot as a resource. One of the simplest resources to import is the texture, which is a 2D image file in any traditional image format. Godot can import images from many different formats, such as JPG, BMP, and TGA. Technically, the original file itself is not the resource. Rather, by importing the file into Godot, Godot will accept the file, add some configuration settings, and apply optimizations to it, and the *result* is a *resource*. The result is an adaptation of the originally imported file, adapted to be more digestible for a real-time game engine. Importing an image file is straightforward enough. You just drag and drop the file (or even multiple files) from your file explorer and into the Godot Filesystem Dock. On releasing your mouse over the dock, the files will be imported automatically. Depending on how many files you import and the size of those files, it may take some time (see Figure 3.1). All files used in this chapter are also included in the book companion files, in the *Chapter 03* folder.

> NOTE. A lot of technical information on importing images into Godot as texture resources can be found at the Godot official documentation here: https://docs.godotengine.org/en/stable/tutorials/assets_pipeline/importing_images.html

> NOTE. If you're looking for some great and free software to create 2D textures and images, consider the following applications: *GIMP* for editing photos and generating tile sets (https://www.gimp.org/), *Krita* for painting illustrations and concept art (https://krita.org/en/), *Inkscape* for creating logos, icons, and menu items (https://inkscape.org/), and *LibreSprite* for creating retro-style pixel art (https://libresprite.github.io/).

3.1.1 Exploring Import Files for Textures

After importing your texture file into Godot, let's check out what's really happening under the hood, inside the project file system. Right-click on your newly imported texture from the Godot dock and choose *Show in*

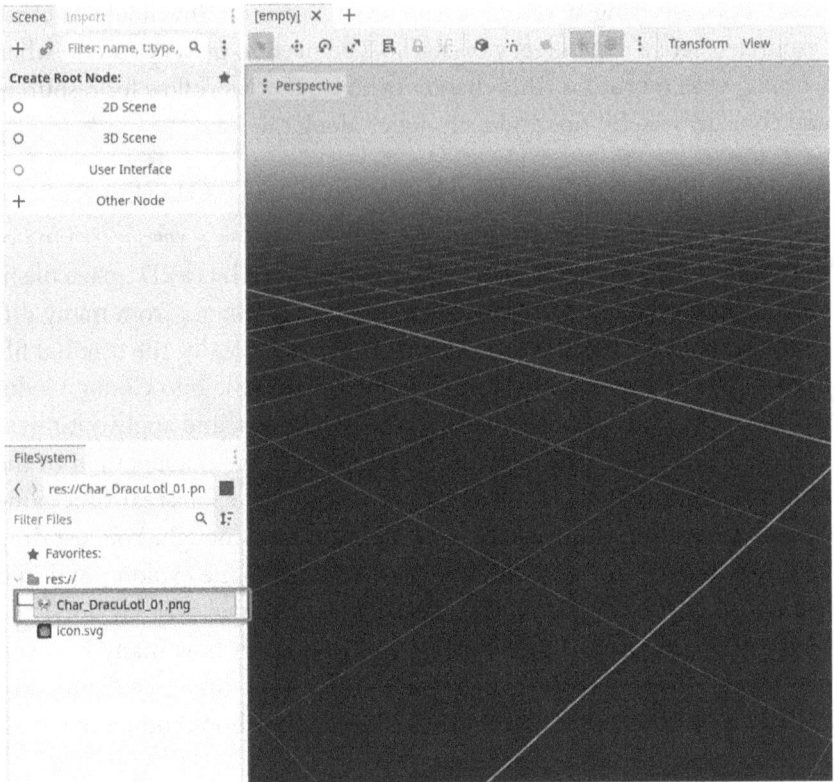

FIGURE 3.1   Importing a Resource into Godot.

File Manager. This displays the files that form part of your project (see Figure 3.2).

Notice that, in addition to your originally imported texture file, Godot has created an additional file with a matching name and a '.import' extension (see Figure 3.3). This companion file is a text-based configuration file, which describes to Godot how the image *should* be imported and configured.

Import files can be opened, viewed, and even edited inside any standard text file editor. This makes it easy to version control, compare, and track changes. Here is an example import file, as shown in Code Sample 3.1.

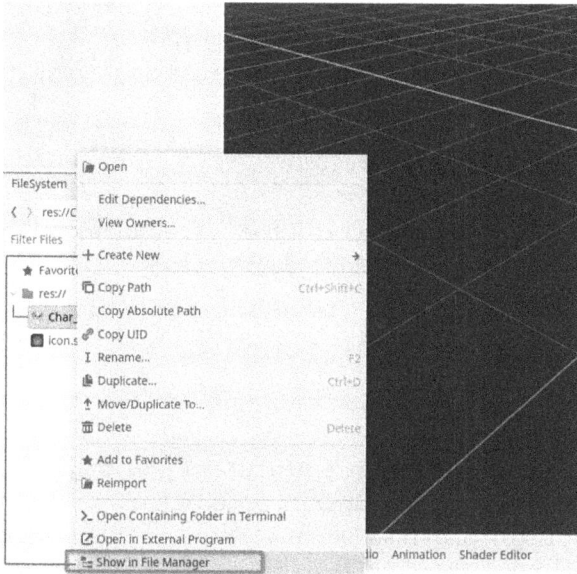

FIGURE 3.2 Accessing the texture resource from the file system.

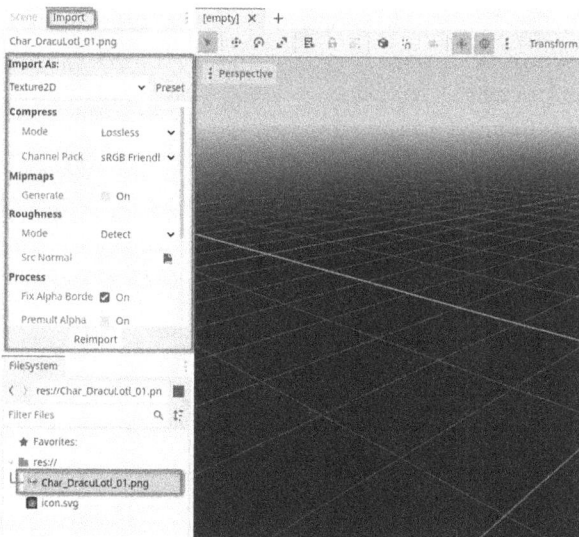

FIGURE 3.3 Viewing the resource import files.

CODE SAMPLE 3.1

```
[remap]
importer="texture"
type="CompressedTexture2D"
uid="uid://chnt06bevrrf4"
path="res://.godot/imported/Char _ DracuLotl _ 01.png-
186e20dcdba243ece080719d246d39f9.ctex"
metadata={
"vram _ texture": false
}

[deps]
source _ file="res://Char _ DracuLotl _ 01.png"
dest _ files=["res://.godot/imported/Char _
DracuLotl _ 01.png-186e20dcdba243ece080719d246d39f9.
ctex"]

[params]
compress/mode=0
compress/high _ quality=false
compress/lossy _ quality=0.7
compress/hdr _ compression=1
compress/normal _ map=0
compress/channel _ pack=0
mipmaps/generate=false
mipmaps/limit=-1
roughness/mode=0
roughness/src _ normal=""
process/fix _ alpha _ border=true
process/premult _ alpha=false
process/normal _ map _ invert _ y=false
process/hdr _ as _ srgb=false
process/hdr _ clamp _ exposure=false
process/size _ limit=0
detect _ 3d/compress _ to=1
```

NOTE. Although you can edit an import file inside a text editor, I don't recommend doing so because the Godot editor offers you a visual and validated way of doing so. We'll consider this in the next section.

3.1.2 Editing Texture Import Options

After importing a file into Godot, you can tweak its import settings. Adjusting these settings will effectively create a reimport of the file, and it will change how the resource behaves. Each file type has different and domain-specific import settings, from images and meshes to audio and video. You can access the import settings for any resource by first selecting it inside the *FileSystem* dock and then switching to the *Import* Dock. The settings displayed here will reflect the settings featured in the associated import file, as shown in Code Sample 3.1 in the previous section (see Figure 3.4).

Let's consider some of the key Import Options for textures. The first option is *Compression Mode*, of which there are many choices. This option can affect the visible quality of the texture; that is, the amount of artifacting that can appear on the texture during gameplay. The first option is *Lossless*, which is the highest and most preserving level of quality. This would normally be used for 2D games, loading-screen backgrounds, user interfaces, and icon elements. Now, you might wonder why anybody would ever choose an option other than Lossless, especially if this truly offers the best quality. After all, who doesn't want their textures shown at the best quality possible? The answer is *Nobody*. So, the reason for other options is less about quality and more about technical necessity and balance. Games often feature lots of large images and textures. That's a huge amount of

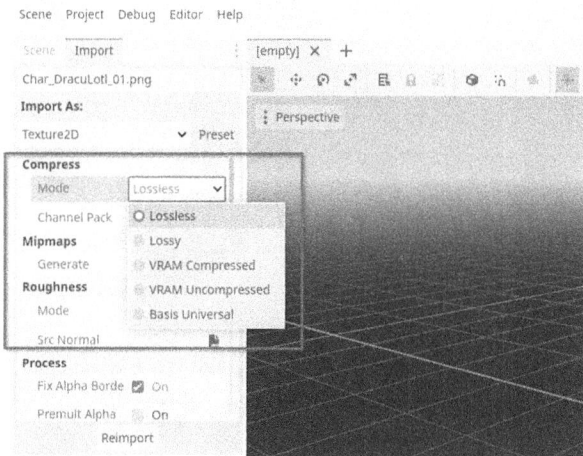

FIGURE 3.4 Editing the import settings for a resource.

data with many choices. This option can affect the visible quality of the texture; that is, the amount of artifacting that can appear on the texture during gameplay. The first option is Lossless, which is the highest and most preserving level of quality. This would normally be used for 2D games, loading-screen backgrounds, user interfaces, and icon elements. Now, you might wonder why anybody would ever choose an option other than Lossless, especially if this truly offers the best quality. After all, who doesn't want their textures shown at the best quality possible? The answer is Nobody. So, the reason for other options is less about quality and more about technical necessity, more about balance. Games often feature lots of large images and textures. That's a huge amount of data when considered in totality. Processing it in real-time, as games do, can significantly impact performance, especially when run on older hardware. One way to optimize performance in this complex balancing act of resource usage is to strategically accept some degradation in the quality of textures. For this reason, other choices for the *Compression* option become incredibly important for resource-heavy games, which includes most games! Lossy is useful for 2D games with many large textures, such as Hidden Object games or an epic side-scrolling platformer game. And there is *VRAM Compressed*, which is useful for 3D games, like first-person shooters, with lots of textured meshes. See Figure 3.5 for the Compression Import options.

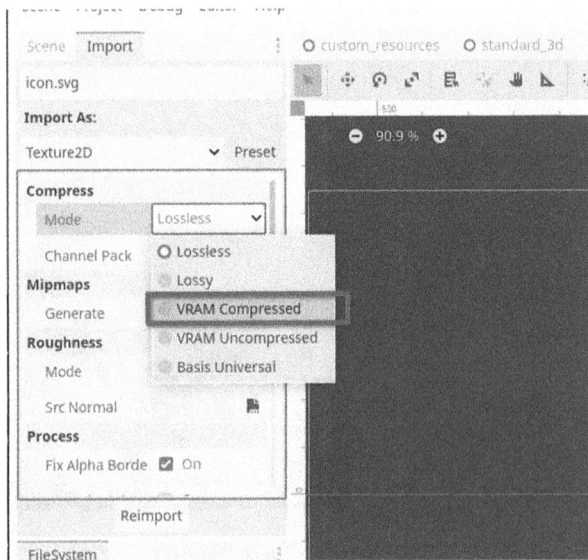

FIGURE 3.5 Compression import options.

Another option is whether to *Generate Mipmaps*. This is a Boolean, true or false, option. This option is not something you would normally activate for 2D games. It's mostly for 3D games, and especially 3D games like first-person shooters, where the same texture (like a brick wall) will be viewed at many different angles and distances by the player during gameplay. By enabling Mipmaps, Godot automatically generates multiple and different-sized versions of the texture at incrementally smaller sizes from the original. This happens at the time of import. Godot will then dynamically choose which version of the texture to use during gameplay, depending on the camera angle and distance to the texture. This ensures that the best-sized texture is chosen to minimize artifacting and boost performance. In short, you should enable this option for 3D games that feature moving cameras and then disable it for other types of games (see Figure 3.6).

3.1.3 Textures, Materials, and 2D Scenes

Standard textures, on their own, only represent image data – namely, pixels. Usually, lots of them. The Import Options that accompany textures, as we saw previously, give Godot more information on how textures should be used practically within a Godot project. However, none of this pixel data actually displays the texture of an object in a scene, such as on a 2D Sprite or a 3D mesh. For this step to happen, an *additional* resource type is

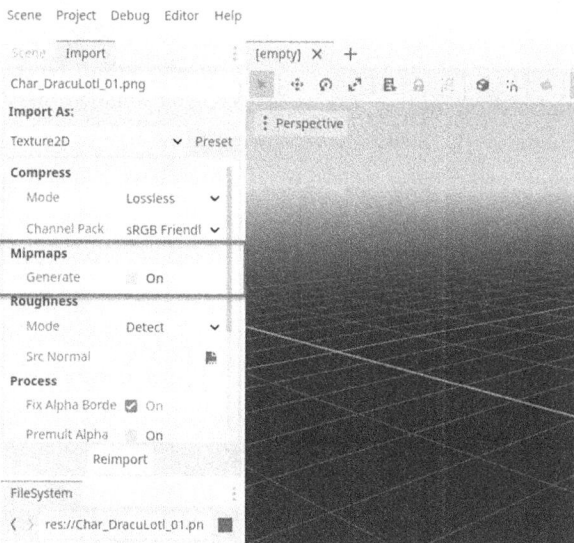

FIGURE 3.6   Enabling Mipmaps.

necessary, namely the **material**. The material resource defines an object's surface (either 2D or 3D), including how shiny and smooth or how dull and rough a surface is. It also defines how textures relate to that surface, as we'll see. It defines whether the pixels are a skin for the object, wrapping around its surface, or whether they define its bumpiness, among other things. Materials, therefore, are a connecting resource in that it is *through* materials that textures can be shown on in-game objects at all. Textures represent a *source* of data, and materials define a *destination* for that data. For this reason, materials are attached to objects in a scene and can, in theory, differ on a per-object basis – one material per object; for example, different materials for different 3D characters. Although, in practice, many different objects share the same material, such as collectible power-ups in a platformer game. In this section, we'll see how to create a material resource and then how to apply it to a 2D object.

> NOTE. The basic principle of recycling is critical to optimization. For this reason, you should try to use as few materials and textures as possible. Reuse and share these resources wherever it is appropriate to do so.

Let's explore how textures relate to 2D scenes and objects. Let's create a new 2D scene, which uses the same principles we saw in the previous chapter for creating 3D scenes (Section 2.2.3). From the *Scene* Dock, choose *2D Scene* (see Figure 3.7).

Now, the easiest and fastest way to get a texture into a scene is simply by dragging and dropping the texture from the *FileSystem* Dock into the *2D Scene* view. When you do this, Godot makes some assumptions about your use case. It creates a 2D Sprite object named after the texture and then configures that object to display the texture, which you dragged and dropped. In many cases, these Godot assumptions will be appropriate (see Figure 3.8).

Although the drag-and-drop method is certainly convenient, we surely want to understand how things work under the hood. Let's delete the newly created Sprite and try this process again the manual way. This will be more revealing about how Godot works. To do this, create a new, empty 2D scene. Select the root node, and then right-click and choose *Add Child Node* from the context menu (see Figure 3.9). This displays the Node creation menu.

From the *Create New Node* menu, choose *Sprite2D* and then hit the *Create* button. A Sprite2D is a Node dedicated to showing a single image

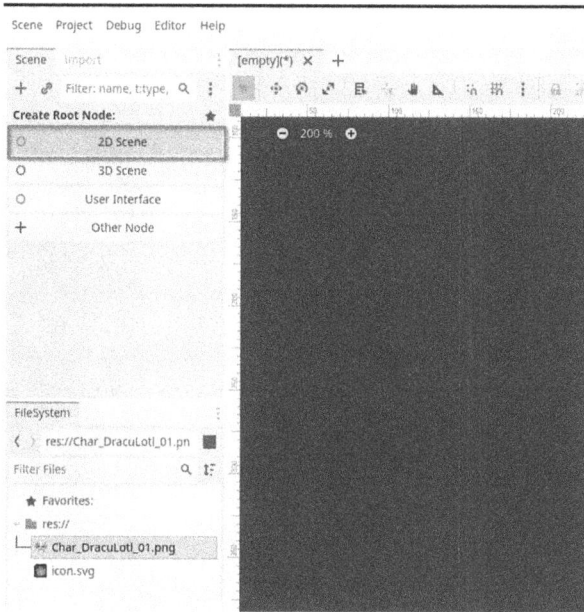

FIGURE 3.7   Creating 2D scenes.

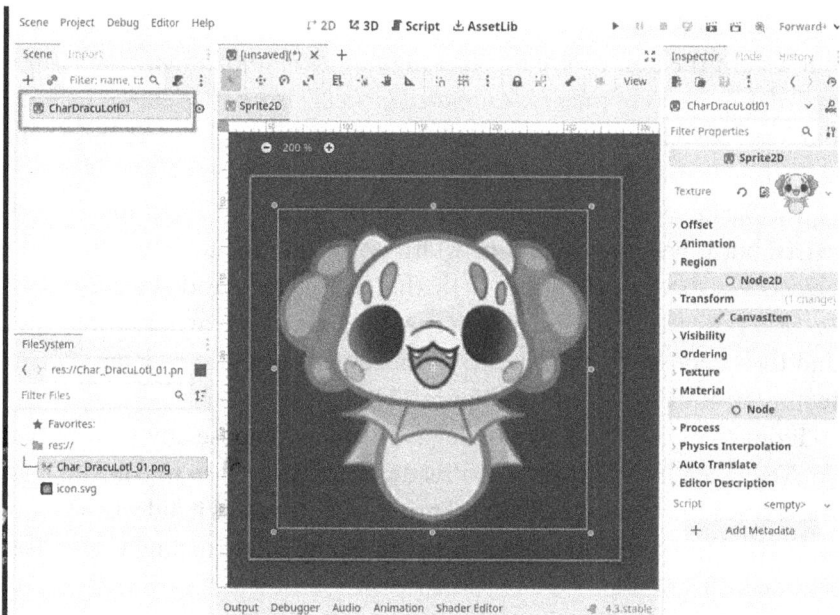

FIGURE 3.8   Creating 2D Sprites from a Drag and Drop.

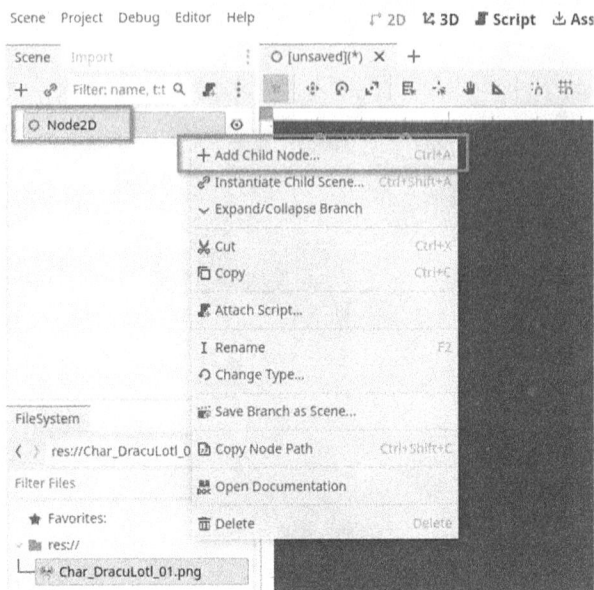

FIGURE 3.9   Creating a new 2D node.

texture within a 2D scene. Like most Game Objects, it can be procedurally moved, scaled, and rotated to create animated transformations in code. But it's not the best choice for showing *frames of animation*. That is, animated sequences of images. *AnimatedSprite2D* is a better choice for that. But here, we'll focus on the single frame, *Sprite2D*. So, let's add this to the scene (see Figure 3.10).

The Sprite Node is created in the scene as an empty object insofar as it exists, but it has no visibility or width or height. To add a texture to the object, we should first select it in the *Scene* Dock and then from the *Inspector* use the *Texture* field. Click on the drop-down arrow for this field and then choose *Quick Load* from the context menu to pick an existing texture inside the project (see Figure 3.11).

From the *Quick Selection* dialog, you should choose any texture that you've loaded into your project already. Then click *Open* to confirm, and the texture will be assigned to the Sprite, looking just as it did when Godot auto-configured the object for us by dragging and dropping earlier (see Figure 3.12).

In reaching this far, we've managed to display a texture in the scene using a Sprite without any reference to a material resource. And yet, despite

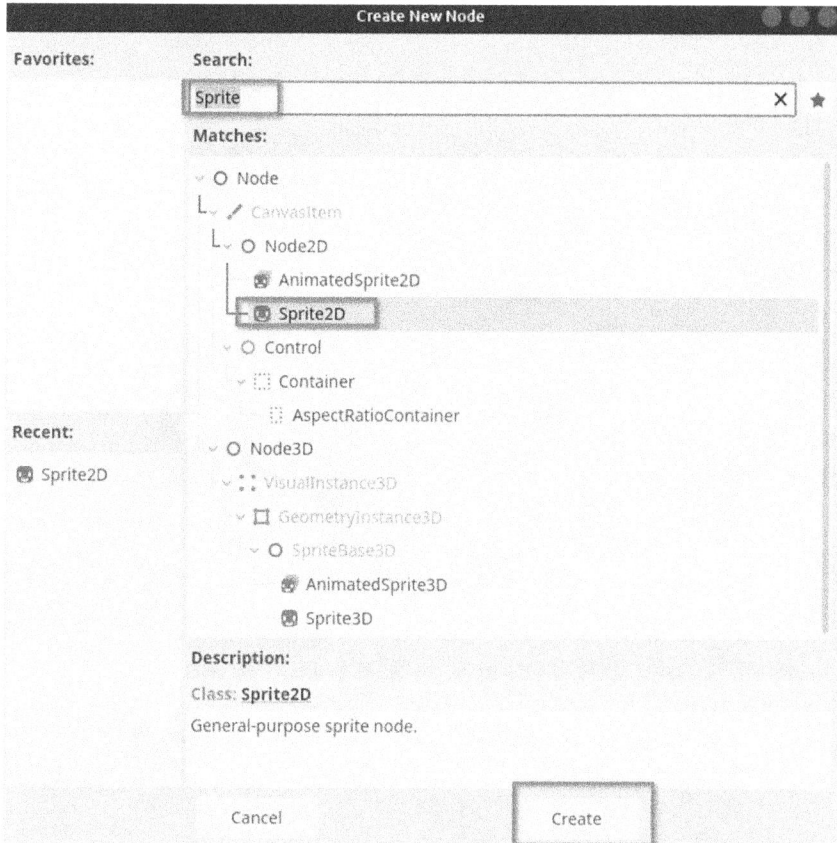

FIGURE 3.10   Creating a Sprite2D node.

appearances, a material is being used. Godot has created an internal, default material that it's now using to show the texture in the Sprite. But we can still see that materials are relevant here by selecting the Sprite in the scene and then scrolling down inside the Inspector to the *Material* section. Expand this section to reveal a variety of adjustable properties (see Figure 3.13).

Let's create our own new, material resource. To do this, find the material field in the Inspector and click on the drop-down arrow next to '<empty>'. From here, choose New *CanvasItemMaterial*. This is a material dedicated to 2D objects (see Figure 3.14).

When you do this, some interesting things happen. First, the Sprite's appearance in the scene remains completely unchanged. That is, it looks just as it did before. Second, the material field now becomes populated with a completely new value – specifically, a new material resource. It's no

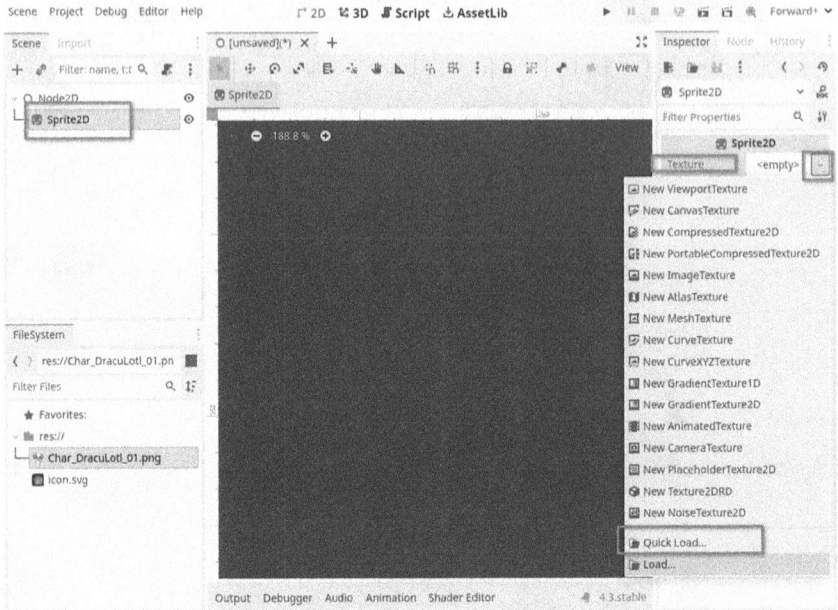

FIGURE 3.11   Configuring the texture field for a Sprite object.

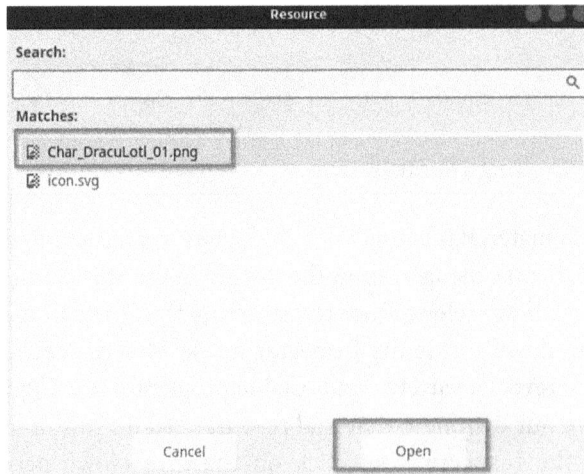

FIGURE 3.12   Selecting a texture to assign onto the Sprite.

longer empty, as it was. And third, you can view more information and properties for this material by clicking on the material field itself (see Figure 3.15).

To confirm that this material influences the Sprite, let's change some of its values and see what it does. Click the drop-down for the *Blend Mode*

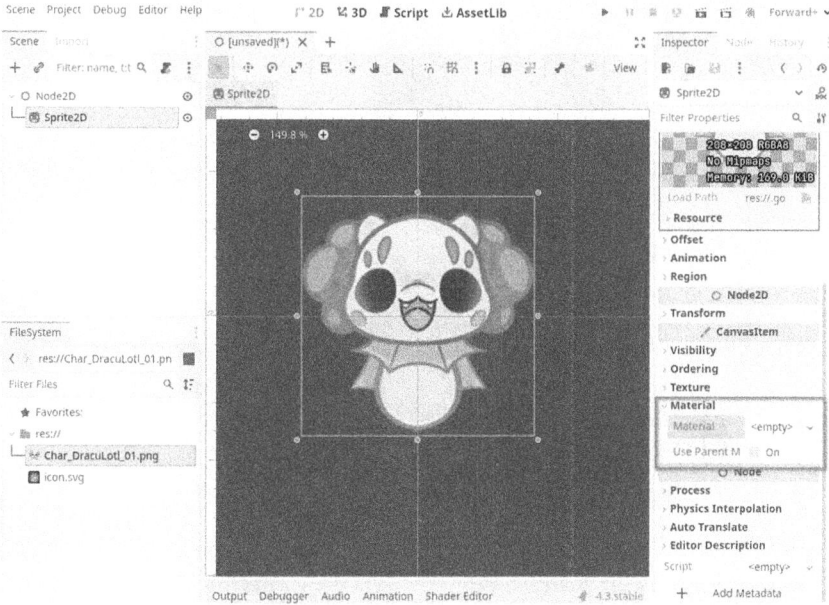

FIGURE 3.13   Exploring material properties for a Sprite.

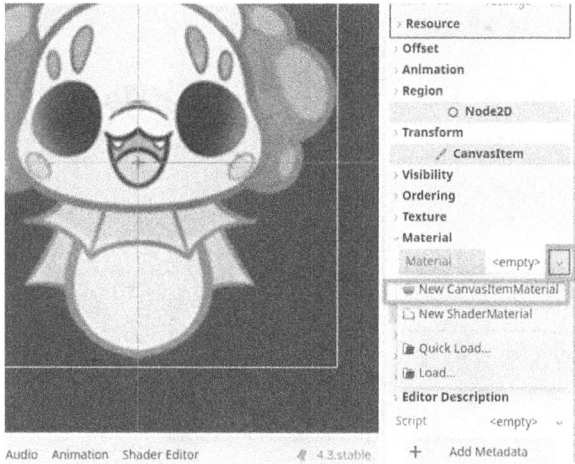

FIGURE 3.14   Creating a new material from the Inspector.

field and change from *Mix* to *Add*. This radically changes how the Sprite appears in the scene, seeming to be much brighter. You can try the other values too. These changes confirm that the material does indeed control how the Sprite is rendered (see Figure 3.16). In the next section, we'll continue to explore this resource type to see what else we can learn.

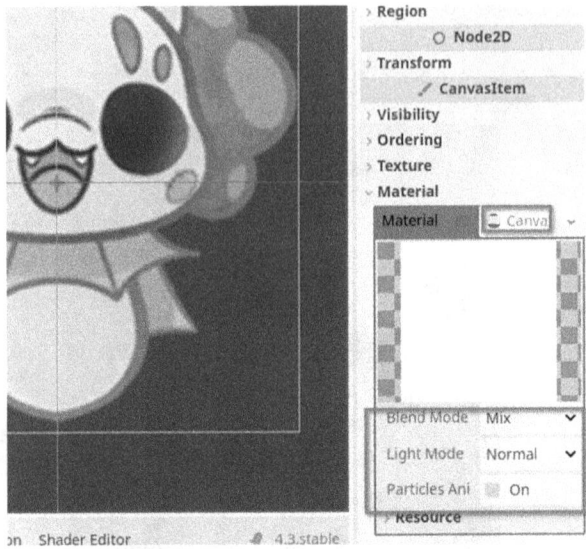

FIGURE 3.15 Viewing material properties via the Inspector.

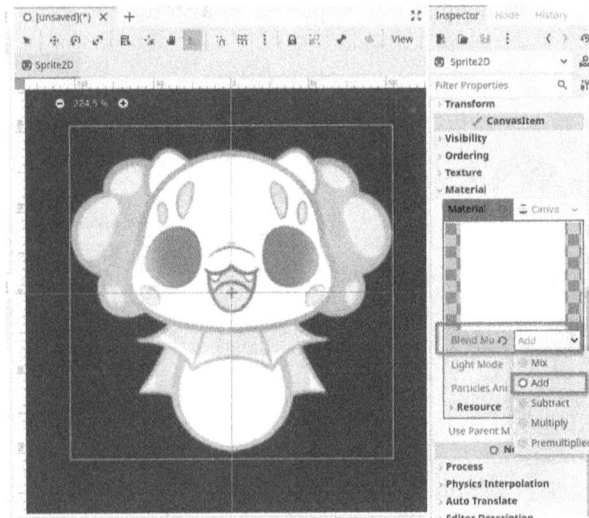

FIGURE 3.16 Changing a Sprite Blend Mode.

3.1.4 External and Built-In Resources

This section continues from the previous in exploring the material resource specifically, but in so doing we'll also examine a distinction that Godot makes generally across all resources, including materials. Let's select the Sprite object that we created previously and duplicate it to create a second, identical version. This will be revealing. To do this, select the object in the *Scene* Dock and press *Ctrl + D* on the keyboard, or else right-click the object and choose *Duplicate* from the context menu (see Figure 3.17).

At first sight, you may not notice that two Sprite objects exist from the duplication, because they'll initially both be stacked atop each other in the scene, in the same location. You can simply use the transform tool, however (covered in Chapter 2, Section 2.2.5), to move one of them beside the other. Now, with both objects side by side for a visual comparison, select *any* one of them in the scene and change its material *Blend* mode back from *Add* to *Mix* by using the Inspector (see Figure 3.18).

When you change *one* of the materials on *one* of the Sprites, you'll notice that *both* Sprites change in appearance simultaneously. This is not because the Sprite themselves are connected in some unseen way, but because they both *share* the *same* material. This may seem strange and counterintuitive initially. After all, you were previously able to change the position of one Sprite without it affecting the position of the other when you moved them side by side. The reason this doesn't apply to the material is because materials are resources, and a resource is a separate object or file. You used the

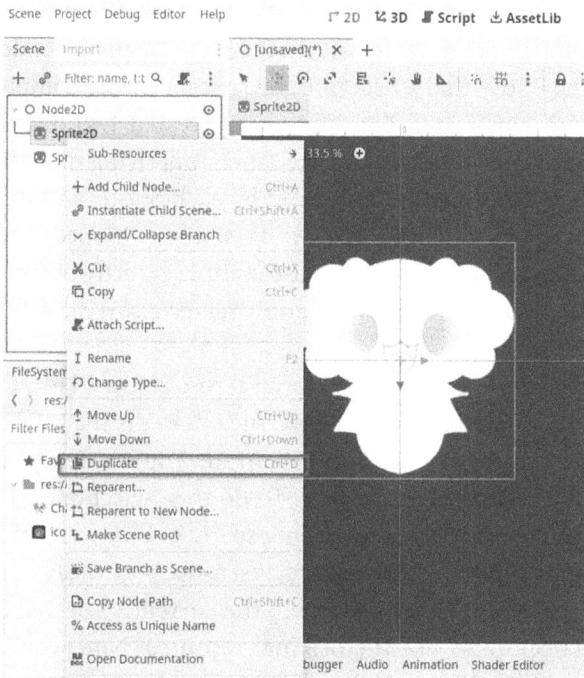

FIGURE 3.17   Duplicating a Sprite.

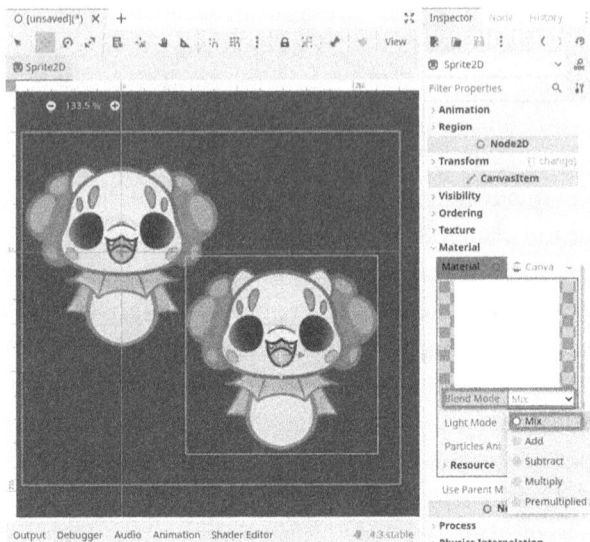

FIGURE 3.18   Changing the material for a single instance.

Inspector in Section 3.1.3 to create a new material resource. This resource is an independent entity, separate from the Sprite. The resource is not a node and doesn't exist spatially within the scene as an object does, but it is a free-floating entity that exists nowhere except in the computer's memory. When you duplicated the Sprite, you created two different objects (two different Sprites) that link to the same underlying material resource. The resource itself is merely referenced by each Sprite, and neither Sprite contains nor owns the resource or its settings. Hence, changing the resource will impact all objects that use it either directly or indirectly. This applies to all resources in Godot, not only materials. We'll see other examples later.

OK. So, how *can* you vary the material across objects? How can I change it for one Sprite, but not for the other? The answer is that, for two Sprites, you'll need two materials. One for each Sprite. You can easily make a separate material resource from the first. To do this, select one of the Sprites, and from the material drop-down, choose *Make Unique* from the context menu. This will duplicate the resource, just as we previously duplicated the Sprites, and assign the new duplicate to the currently selected Sprite, leaving the other Sprite to use the original resource. Now, you can change them separately (see Figure 3.19).

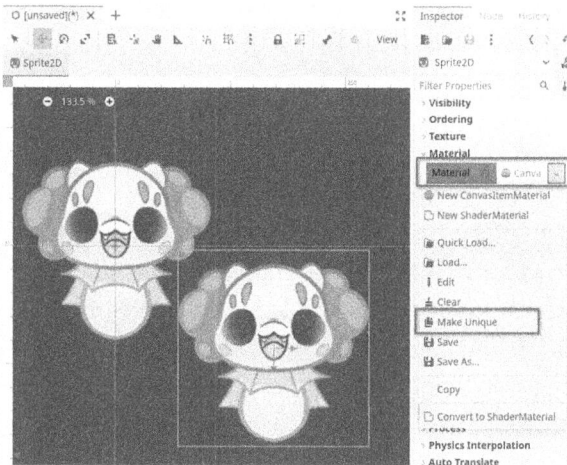

FIGURE 3.19 Duplicating a resource.

At this point, you may reasonably wonder about our manually created material resource in comparison to the imported texture resource imported earlier. Specifically, our texture resource exists outside of any scene, within the *FileSystem* Dock, and it can easily be selected separately from any Node within any scene. But the material resource is different, it seems. Unlike the texture, the material doesn't appear in *FileSystem* as a selectable thing at all. It can only be edited by first selecting an object in a specific scene (such as a Sprite object) and using the designated Inspector fields. And it's hard to see how such a resource, made in this way, could be used or accessed in other scenes or even transferred to other Godot projects. It's therefore a lot more inconvenient for sharing and reusing. Thankfully, we can easily 'fix' this. In so doing, it marks the conceptual distinction that Godot makes between *built-in* resources and *external* resources.

The imported texture is an *external resource* because it exists explicitly as a unique file in FileSystem and can be used in any scene or project. The recently created material, by contrast, is an example of a *built-in resource* because we created it in a very specific, local way through an object and through the Inspector inside a specific scene. Although it still exists as a resource for the active scene and can be shared by multiple objects in that scene, it nonetheless doesn't feature as a file alongside other resources in the FileSystem. The advantage of this kind of 'local' resource is that your game may contain many of them, and they don't clutter your FileSystem view. But, if you want to share the resource across scenes and across projects, then you'll want to make the resource an external one. To do that, select one of the Sprite objects, and from the *Material* section in the Inspector, expand the *Resource* section within (see Figure 3.20).

By checking the *Path* field within the *Resource* Group, you'll notice that it appears empty. This means the resource is a built-in resource. To convert the resource into an external resource, click the drop-down arrow from the *Material* section and choose *Save* from the context menu (see Figure 3.21). Then name your file and save.

After saving, you'll notice the material is saved to the FileSystem in the *TRES* format, which is a text file that can be read, edited, and version-controlled easily. You can also double-click this file from the FileSystem to view its properties independently in the Inspector, outside of any scene or object. If you change the properties here, in this global space, any dependent objects using this resource will also change. For example, changing the *Blend* mode from *Add* to *Mix* will affect any Sprites using this material (see Figure 3.22).

Finally, if we wanted to configure our second Sprite object or any additional Sprite object to use our external resource as a material, we do that by first selecting the object and moving to the *material* roll-out in the Inspector.

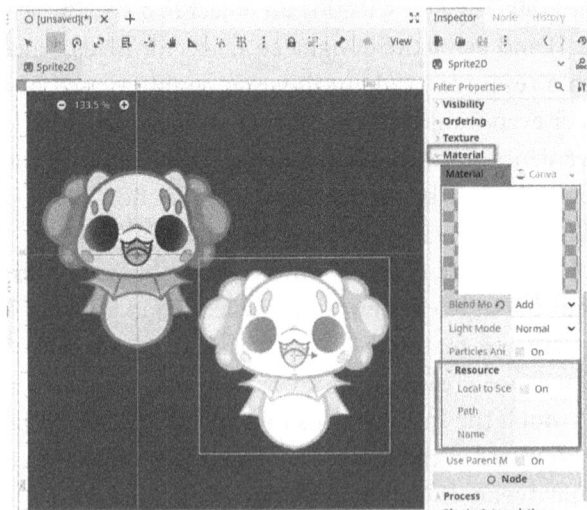

FIGURE 3.20   Viewing resource information.

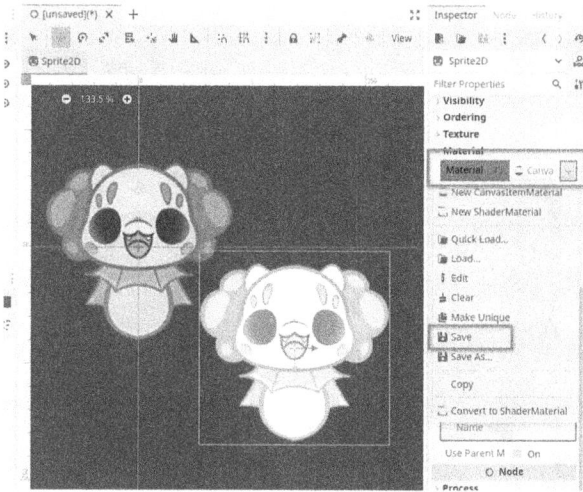

FIGURE 3.21   Saving to an external resource.

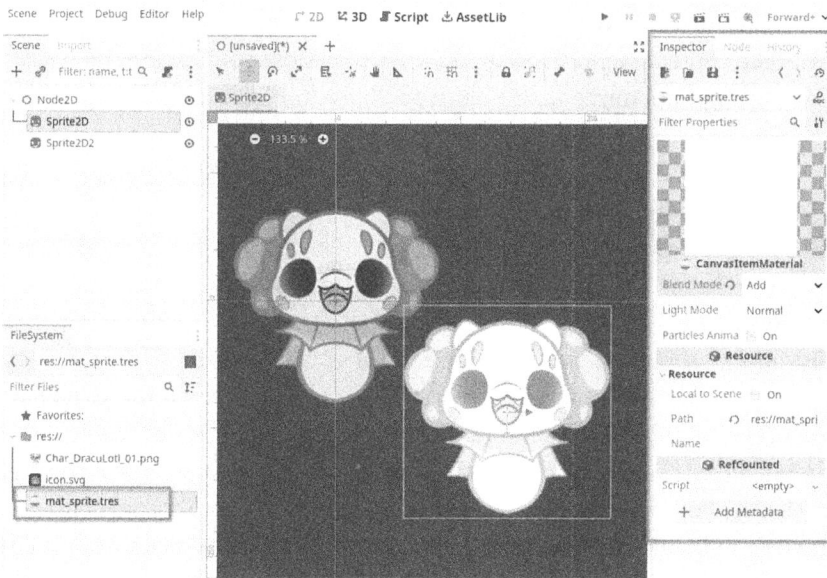

FIGURE 3.22   Applying changes to an external resource.

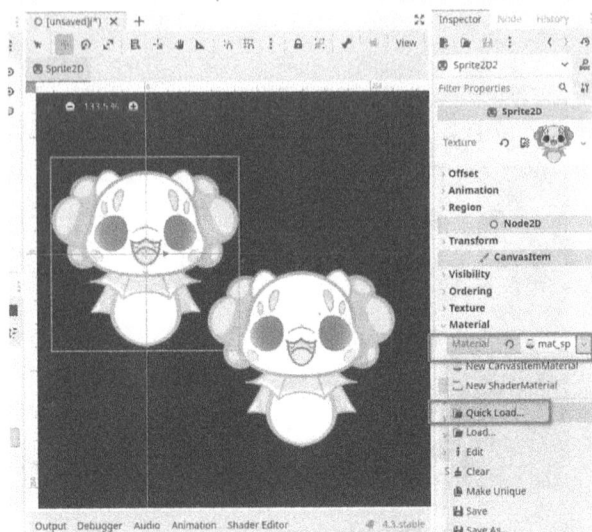

FIGURE 3.23   Sharing a single external material across multiple Sprites.

Click the material drop-down, as seen before, and choose Quick Load from the context menu. From here, you can choose your external resource. Easy, though not immediately obvious! Refer to Figure 3.23.

3.2 TEXTURES FOR 3D OBJECTS, HANDS-ON

We'll now move into the vibrant world of textures for 3D scenes and objects, such as primitives and meshes. These textures in 3D work much like they do for 2D, but with additional options, details, and complexities. Before moving forward, please ensure that you've read the previous section in full about textures and 2D, even if you do not intend to make 2D games. This section relies on important knowledge covered there. As with the previous section, I'll assume that you've already imported a single texture of any size or format that you want to apply to a single 3D object in a 3D scene. For this example, we'll use a cube object. More complex meshes are covered later in this chapter. In practice, meshes and scenes normally rely on multiple textures rather than only one, but the process for importing and using one texture or multiple is the same. So, we'll work with one texture for simplicity and clarity (see Figure 3.24). For this texture, ensure the *Generate Mipmap* setting is enabled, as it should be for most 3D objects that will be seen from different angles and distances.

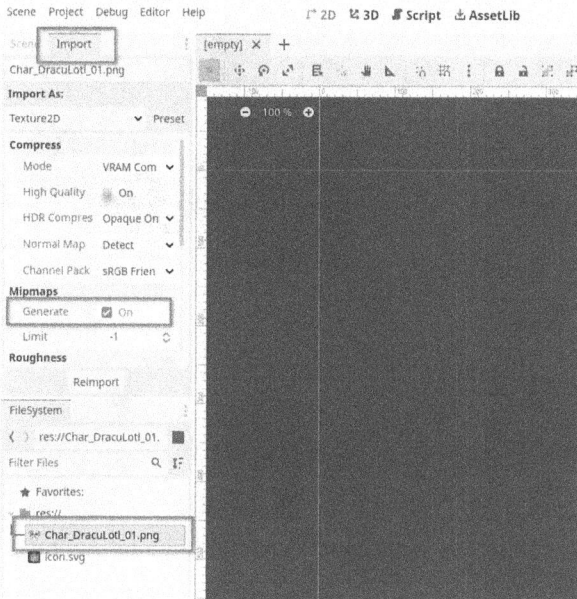

FIGURE 3.24   Importing a texture for 3D use.

3.2.1 Creating Materials for 3D Objects

Materials for 3D objects in 3D scenes can be both external and built-in, as with 2D scenes and workflows. Let's start by creating an external material, which will be used shortly to apply our imported texture across the surface of a 3D model, such as a cube. The advantage of an external material is that it can be easily shared across multiple objects, scenes, and even projects. To create an external material resource, move to the *FileSystem* Dock and right-click on the root node 'res://'. This root represents the topmost folder of your Godot project's internal file system for assets. After right-clicking, choose *Create New > Resource* from the context menu (see Figure 3.25). This displays the resource creation menu.

Next, create a *StandardMaterial3D* resource. Select it from the *Matches* list and then press the *Create* button. There are many different material types in Godot for different purposes and use cases. The *StandardMaterial3D* is the most common type for 3D scenes. You'll be asked to assign the material a unique filename. I chose 'standard_3d', but you can use any suitable name for your games (see Figure 3.26). As with all standard resources, this is saved inside a text-based *TRES* file.

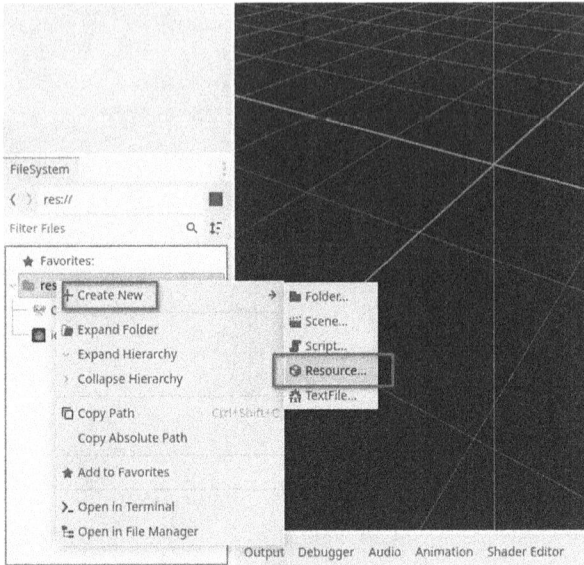

FIGURE 3.25   Creating a new material resource.

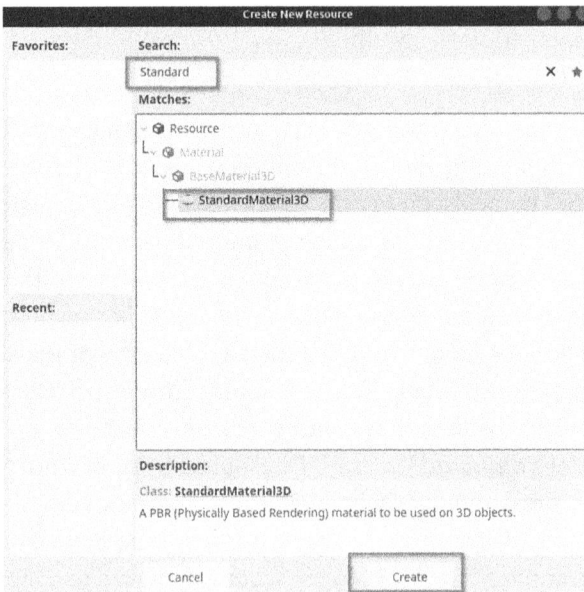

FIGURE 3.26   Creating a standard 3D material resource.

NOTE. The TRES file is similar to, but different from, the IMPORT file. Both are text-based, human-readable, and editable. TRES, however, represents the native properties of a Godot-created resource. IMPORT, by contrast, saves the import settings used to convert an imported file into a resource.

To configure and edit the newly created material, double-click on it from the *FileSystem*. This displays the material properties in the Inspector. From here, expand the *Albedo* field. This field controls a surface's color under normal lighting conditions. It's what we call, in common sense terms, the *color of an object* (see Figure 3.27).

From the *Albedo* rollout, click the drop-down arrow in the *Texture* field, and choose *Quick Load* from the context menu. Then select the texture that you imported into the FileSystem earlier. When you do this, a connection is immediately made between the material and the selected texture. The texture is not copied or duplicated. It still retains its independence from the material, which means that future changes to the texture, if any, will automatically be reflected in the material. The Inspector features a preview pane, where you can see a live version of your material on a sample 3D object (see Figure 3.28).

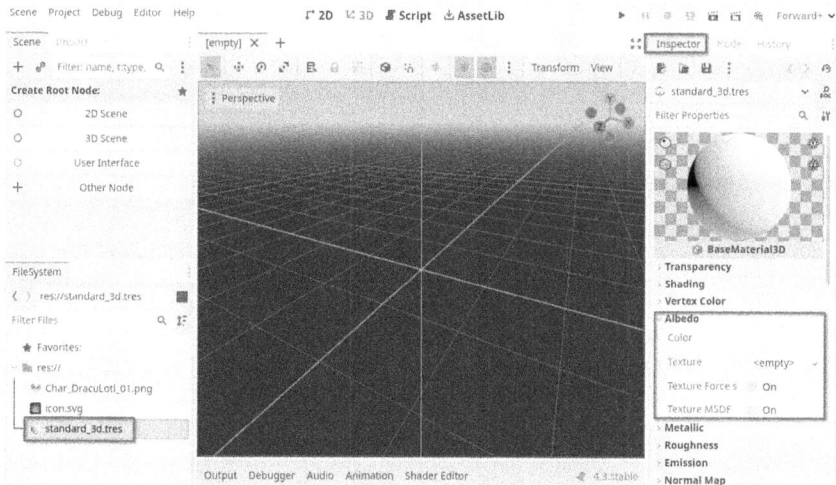

FIGURE 3.27 Defining the color of an object's material.

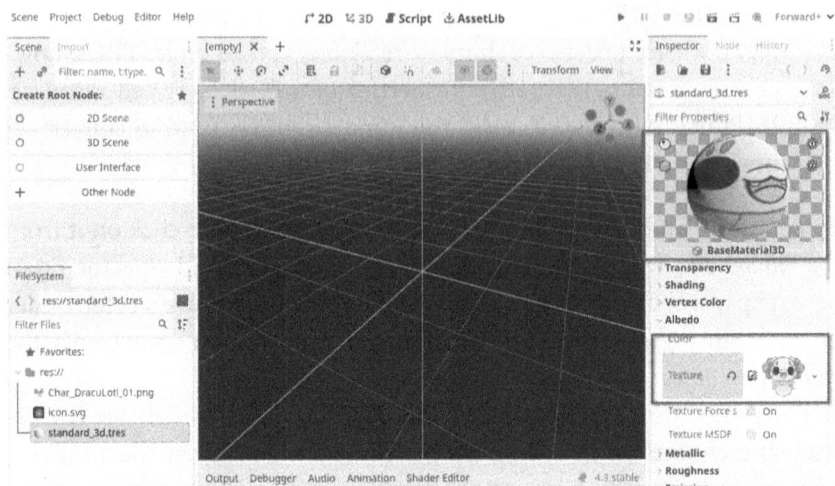

FIGURE 3.28   Updating a material's Albedo texture.

3.2.2   Assigning Materials to 3D Objects

The previous section focused on material creation as an external resource. The created material is currently a stand-alone resource that is not attached to any in-game instance, such as a mesh or a Sprite. That is, the material currently exists *in theory* but not *in reality*. As a potentiality rather than an actuality. Let's now assign the material to a 3D object. To do that, create a new 3D Scene. Refer to the previous chapter, Section 2.2.3, on creating a 3D scene with a cube object. We'll begin with a plain, blank cube, as shown in Figure 3.29.

There are different ways to assign a material to a 3D object in Godot. The quickest and most straightforward way is to expand the *Surface Material Override* field from the Inspector, with the *MeshInstance3D* selected, and then from the *0* slot, click the drop-down arrow and choose *Quick Load* from the context menu, selecting the newly created material (see Figure 3.30).

> NOTE. Each *Surface Material Override* may have more slots than simply 0, as we have here. There may be an additional 1, 2, 3, or even more slots. Each slot represents a connection to a single material. Normally, if a single mesh uses only one material, there will be only a 0 slot. But some more complex meshes may have different materials for different parts (such as a material for the character's skin, another for hair, and another for clothes).

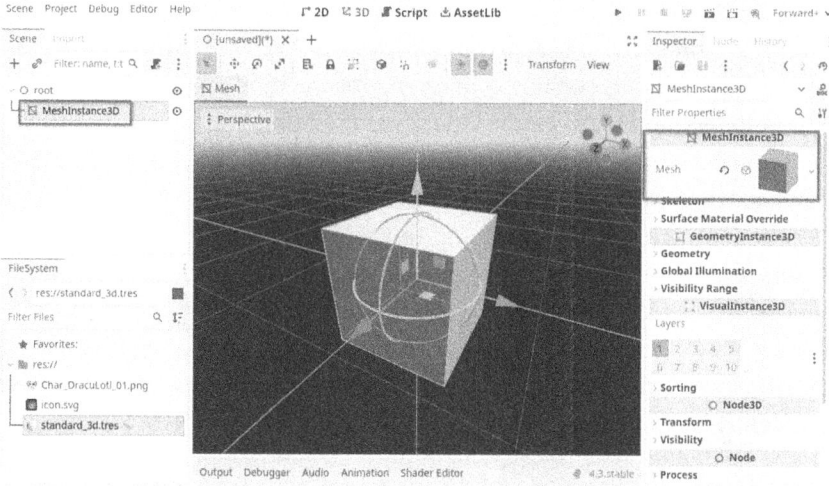

FIGURE 3.29   A 3D scene with a newly created cube mesh.

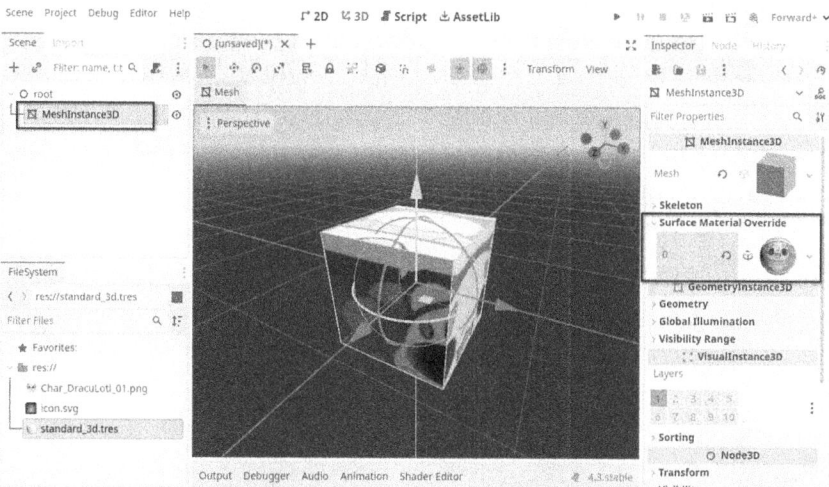

FIGURE 3.30   Assigning a material to a 3D object.

As the material is assigned to the 3D object, its surface will immediately change, which updates the viewport. You should see your selected texture wrapped around the object's surface. It may not appear at the scale, orientation, or location that you expect. The scale, orientation, and location of a texture on a surface are defined by an object's *UV Mapping*. This mapping is a specialized coordinate system and is part of the mesh and not part of the material. You cannot normally change the mapping through the material. Typically, if you don't like how a texture is being wrapped around a model, you'll need to jump back into the 3D modeling software – such as Blender – to tweak the mapping for the model and then reimport it back to Godot. However, the Godot material offers some very basic controls that can change how a texture is wrapped in a limited way. You'll find these controls inside the properties for your material resource, under the *UV1* rollout. A mesh may have up to two UV channels: UV1 and UV2. Again, these are defined inside a 3D modeling program, as we'll see in later sections. Each channel defines how the surface of an object unwraps flat onto a 2D image. Most objects, however, use only one channel and therefore can unwrap in only one way. From the UV1 rollout, you have two controls: *Scale* and *Offset*. We'll explore these further (see Figure 3.31).

The *Scale* Property behaves as follows: values less than 1, such as 0.5, will seem to stretch parts of the texture across the whole surface of the model. Values higher than 1 will tile and repeat the texture across the surface (see Figure 3.32).

> NOTE. The Scale field features a lock icon at the far right-hand side of the field. By default, this locks the uniformity of scale. In other words, if you enter a value of 6 for the X field, then Godot will automatically enter 6 for Y and Z. If you click the lock icon to break the connection, then you can enter different values for each field and change the tiling in different directions.

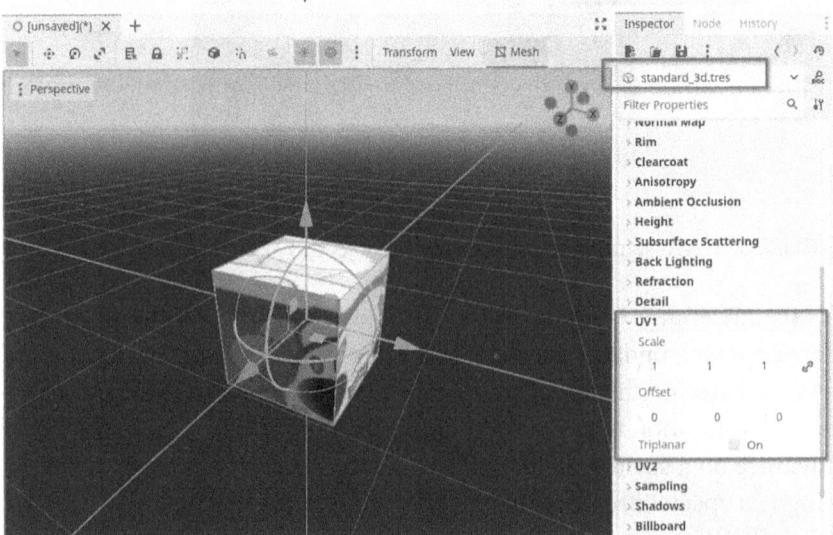

FIGURE 3.31   Accessing the scale and offset properties for a material.

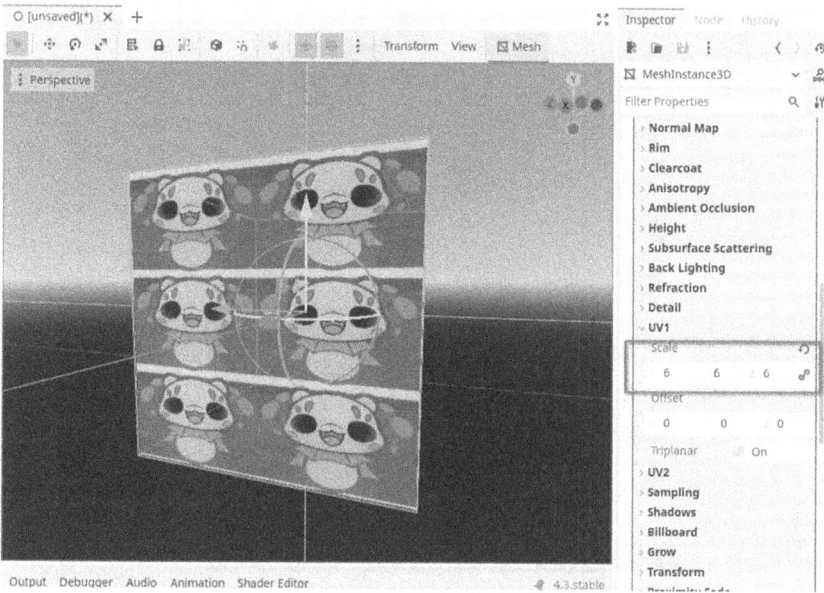

FIGURE 3.32   Using scale to stretch and tile a texture.

The *Offset* property is fun and behaves as follows: By changing X, for example, you will slide the texture along a local X axis, changing its starting point on the mesh surface. A great use of animating this value is for sliding a water texture along a flat plane to create the illusion of running water, a popular technique in retro-style games (Figure 3.33).

3.3 MESH RESOURCES: THE EXPORT AND IMPORT PROCESS

Mesh resources are a truly complex subject because there are many parts to them, such as geometry, mapping, textures and materials, and rigging and animation. A mesh can be a simple static prop, such as a crate or a weapon. It can be an architectural element, such as a wall or a door. It can be an animated character, such as the player or an NPC. Meshes can be created in different visual styles too, from cartoon to photoreal, and they can be assembled in different programs with different features, such as Maya or Blender. At their most basic, however, all meshes are structurally made from three basic ingredients. These are vertices, edges, and faces. Now, there are other programs and disciplines out there that conceive of meshes in different terms from these three elements (such as hypersurfaces and splines), but these do not normally apply to Godot or

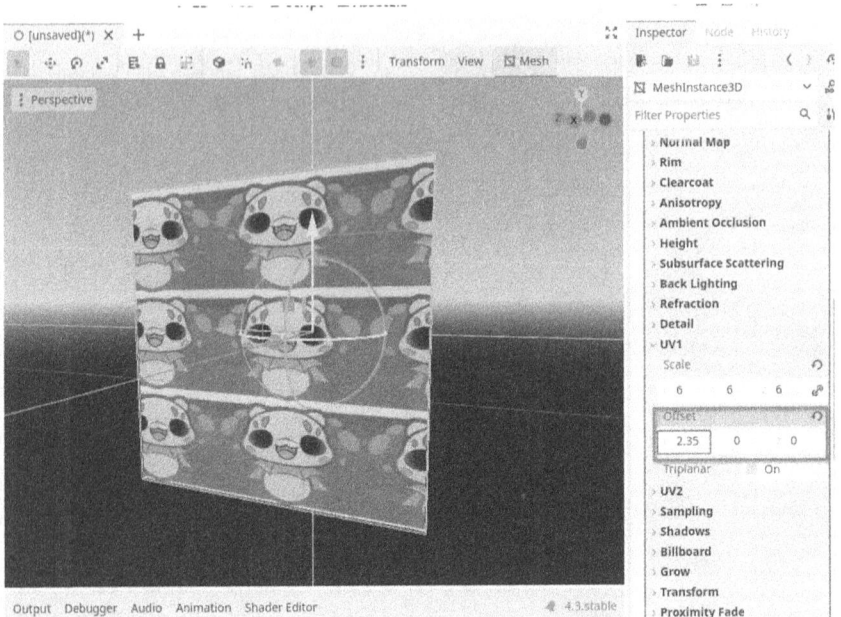

FIGURE 3.33 Sliding a texture along a cube surface using the offset field.

game development. For our purposes, we have the vertex (plural: vertices), which defines a corner point; the edge, which is a straight line connecting any two vertices; and the face (or polygon), which is a surface created whenever a series of edges forms an enclosed loop – such as when the three edges of a triangle loop back around to their starting point. Of these, the face is special because it's the only element that a player can see during gameplay. The player cannot see vertices or edges unless the developer is using a special kind of material.

This section explores the 3D modelling software, *Blender*. It examines how to export a static prop mesh from that software to be import-ready for Godot. Each 3D modeling application will have a different process for exporting a mesh – Blender has one approach, and Maya another. In this section, we will not consider animated characters but rather meshes that do not move by deformations. This includes walls, floors, windows, statues, pillars, weapons, and many others, for example. Although Blender is a different program from Godot (and this book is about Godot), Blender is nonetheless an excellent starting point for our exploration of meshes. This is because, through Blender, we can see meshes in action prior to their being imported. Specifically, we'll create a quick mesh together inside

Blender (don't worry, you don't need art skills!), and then we'll go through the process of exporting that mesh from Blender and into Godot, step by step. Along the way, we'll consider many interesting subjects that can enhance our workflow exponentially. Blender is a free and open-source application that can run on Windows, Linux, and Mac, and can be downloaded from https://www.blender.org/. If you don't use Blender, or use a different program, then you don't need to follow along with this section step by step, but I still recommend reading it, especially if you're new to working with meshes in game development. It will feature some useful concepts and ideas that transfer valuably across many different programs, including Godot.

3.3.1 Creating a Mesh in Blender

Let's create a mesh together inside Blender. If you don't want to follow this process, you can still learn a lot about meshes by reading this section, and our final exported mesh is also included in the book companion files (in the Chapter 3 folder) for your convenience. To start, load up the Blender software (I am using Version 4.3.2). You'll end up with an almost empty scene, which includes only a cube at the world's origin (see Figure 3.34).

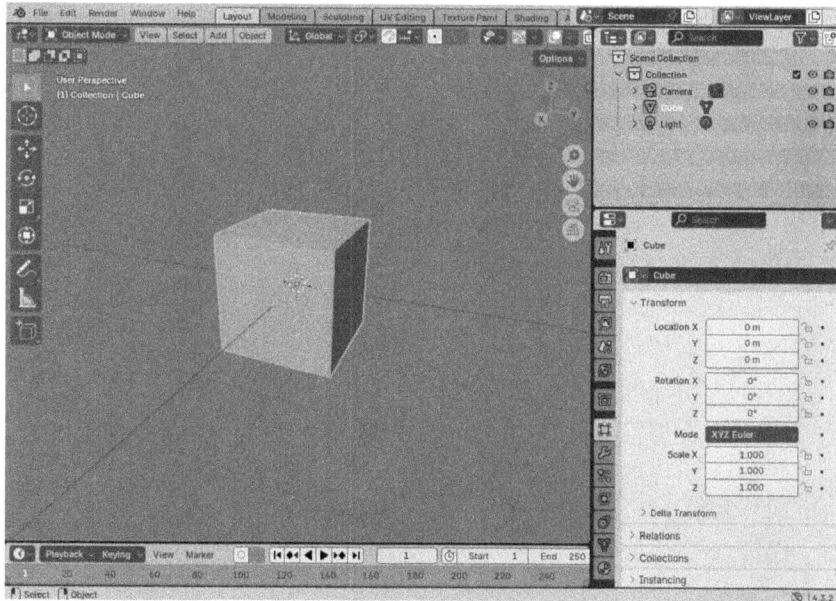

FIGURE 3.34 Blender startup file.

We don't need the auto-created cube made by Blender. After all, we can easily make one of those ourselves in Godot using the *MeshInstance3D* node. So, select the cube by clicking on it, and then hit the *Delete* button on the keyboard to remove it from the scene. This returns us to an *almost* empty scene. Although we have no rendered, visible items remaining in the scene, there are still non-visible items there. Specifically, a camera and a light. You can see this from the Blender *Hierarchy* Panel, which works a lot like the Godot Scene Tree, listing all items in the scene. This is important to know because, as we export content later, we don't want to accidentally export non-visible items like cameras and lights (see Figure 3.35).

Now let's create a more complex mesh to export from Blender. To create this, choose *Add > Mesh > Monkey* from the creation menu at the top of the viewport. Suzanne is Blender's test model, equivalent to the Utah Teapot found in many other modeling applications. It's a quickly generated 3D model. When you select this option, a 3D head mesh is created at the world origin (0, 0, 0) immediately. The location of the model is important when exporting, as we'll see soon (see Figure 3.36).

3.3.2 Exporting a Mesh from Blender Using GLTF

After completing our mesh in Blender, let's export it now to Godot. For more complex meshes, you don't need to wait until the mesh is fully completed to export it. You can export multiple times during development

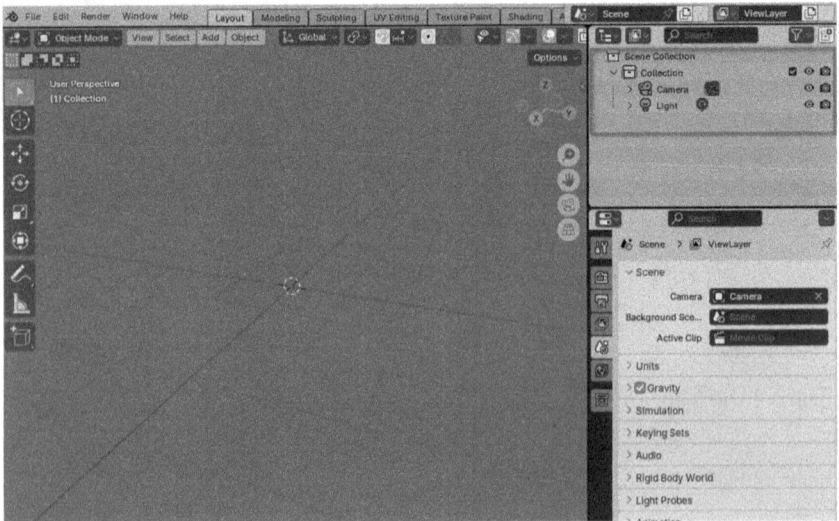

FIGURE 3.35 Viewing scene contents from the hierarchy.

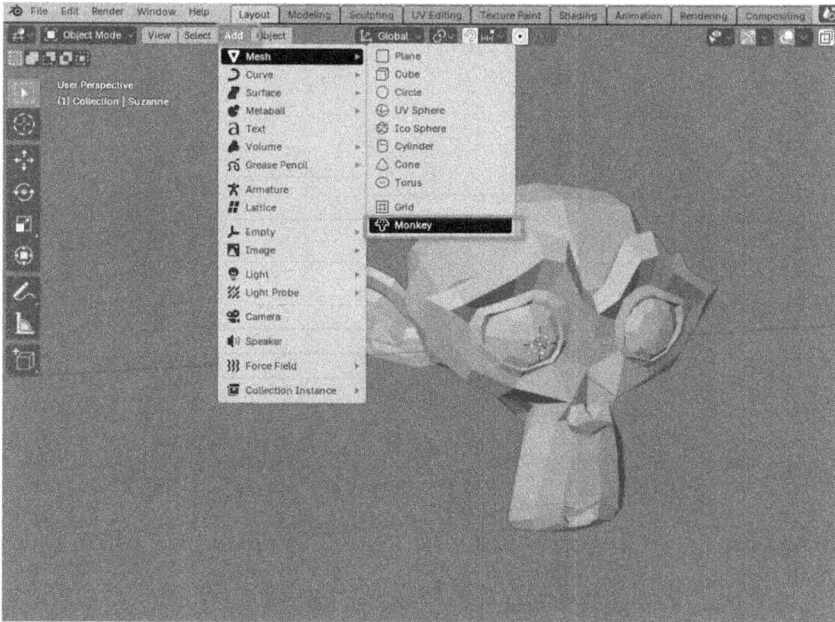

FIGURE 3.36   Creating a mesh in Blender.

and jump back and forth between Blender and Godot to visualize your mesh as it gets refined. The export process can sometimes be involved and complicated because, ideally, we don't want anything to be lost in translation, so we need to take care of how we export. The goal is for our mesh in Godot to appear identical to its Blender counterpart. That sounds simple, but sometimes it's not always possible. To start, select the mesh in the viewport by clicking on it. Selected meshes in Blender have a bold, solid-color border surrounding them (see Figure 3.37).

Next, provided the selected mesh looks good to you, let's see the top-level properties for it: namely, its position, rotation, and scale. We normally want these to be at their identities, that is, a position of (0,0,0), a rotation of (0,0,0), and a scale of (1,1,1). Otherwise, the meshes will display at unintended offsets and locations when imported into Godot. To do this, click the Object Properties tab from the Inspector and view its properties (see Figure 3.38).

If these values are set differently from the identities, then you have two options. One: you could type in (0,0,0) for the location, (0,0,0) for rotation, and (1,1,1) for scale, *but* doing so may change the model in ways you do not want. For example, it may orient the model away from how it *should* look.

FIGURE 3.37   **Preparing to export.**

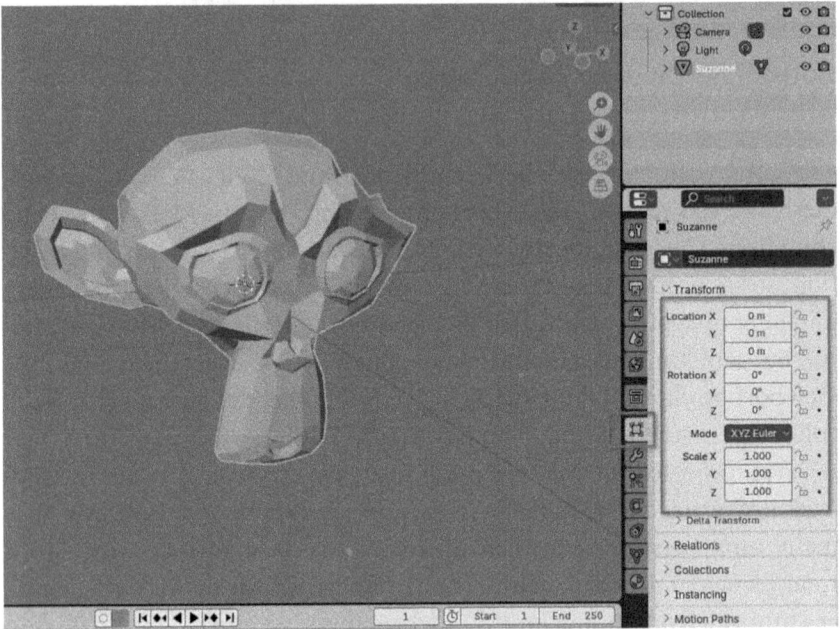

FIGURE 3.38   Checking a mesh's position, rotation and scale.

The alternative, which leaves the model unchanged, is to *Apply All Transforms*. This keeps the current position, rotation, and scale of the model and accepts its current state as the identity state. This is the more common method. To achieve this, select *Object > Apply > All Transforms* from the object menu (see Figure 3.39).

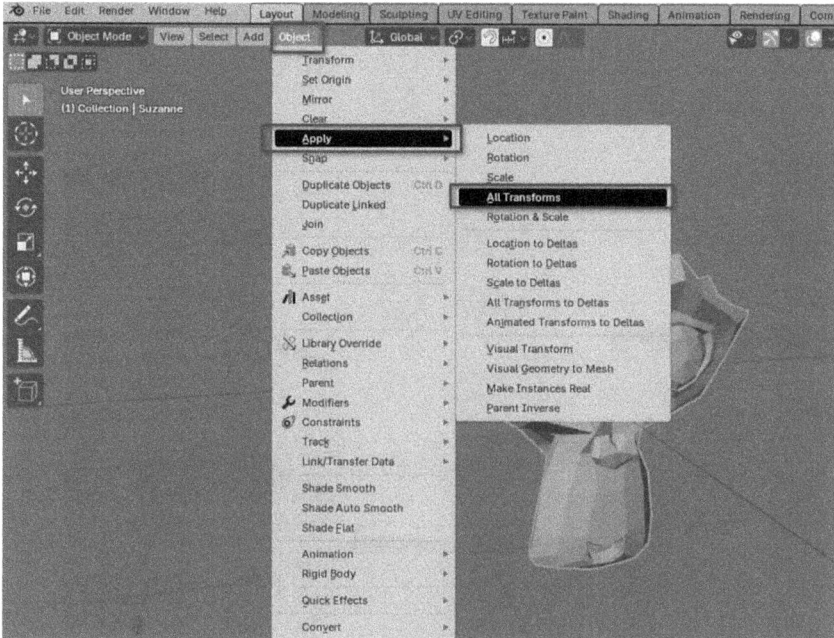

FIGURE 3.39   Applying all transforms for a selected mesh.

Now we're ready to export our selected mesh. Godot accepts meshes in either the FBX format, which is commonly used by Maya, and the GLTF format. We'll use the latter since it is well-supported in all modern Godot versions. To do this, select *File > Export > glTF 2.0* from the file menu. This displays the export menu where you can customize export options (see Figure 3.40).

The GLTF Exporter has many options. First, ensure the *Format* field is appropriate. The two options are either GLB (binary) or GLTF. The default GLB is the faster-performing and simpler option and should be preferred. There is an additional and optional *Copyright* field where you can enter authorship details for the asset you are exporting (see Figure 3.41).

Next, expand the *include* field. This lets you refine what objects are exported. By default, everything in the scene will be exported – both visible and non-visible objects – regardless of what meshes you may have selected in the viewport. However, let's enable the *Selected Objects* option to ensure that only selected objects will be exported (see Figure 3.42).

The include section allows you to filter the export by object, such as selected objects or visible objects. The data section allows you to narrow your export further by selecting which properties of the exported objects should be retained, such as materials and rigging. It's tempting perhaps to

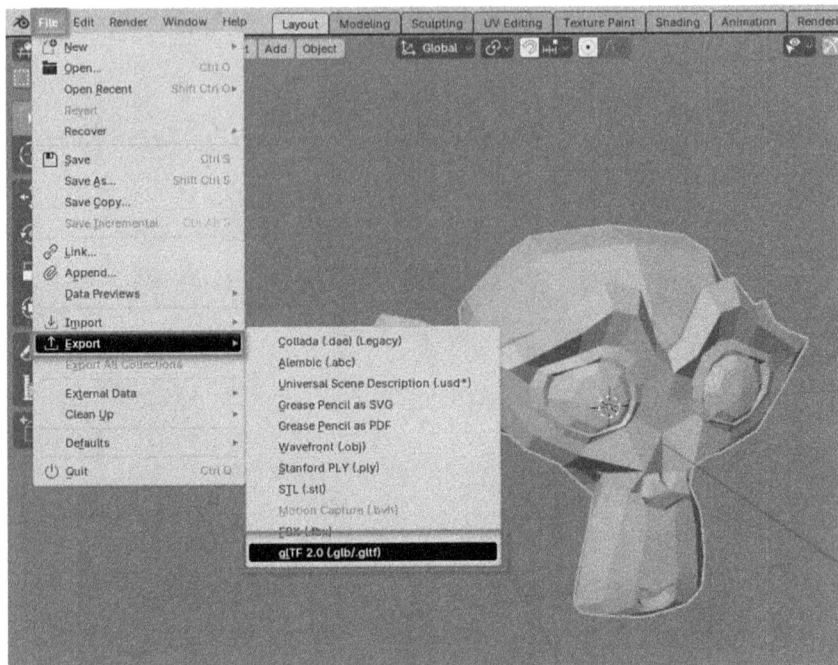

FIGURE 3.40 Accessing the glTF export tool in Blender.

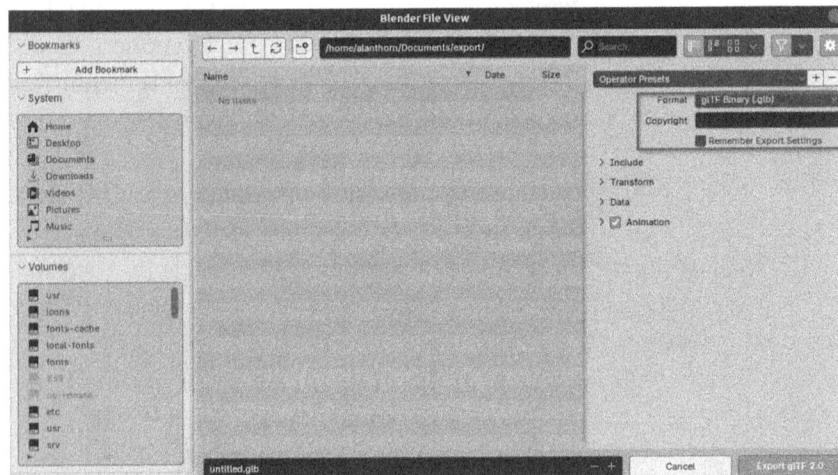

FIGURE 3.41 Setting the GLTF format.

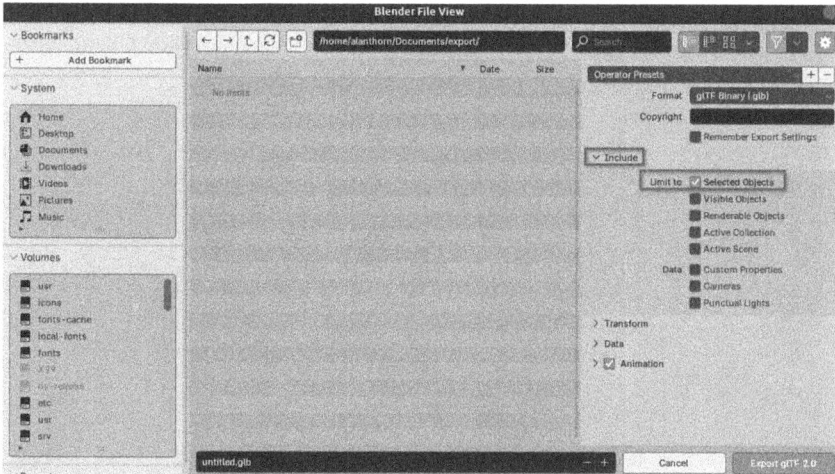

FIGURE 3.42   Limiting the export to selected objects.

enable everything here, reasoning that this would be the best approach for importing your mesh as faithfully as possible. However, you should export the minimal amount needed for your mesh to work and behave as needed in Godot. This keeps your file size to a minimum and reduces the amount of data that Godot needs to process. For our Suzanne mesh, I have left everything at their defaults for this section, except I have disabled both *skinning* and *animation*. The mesh is not animated (see Figure 3.43).

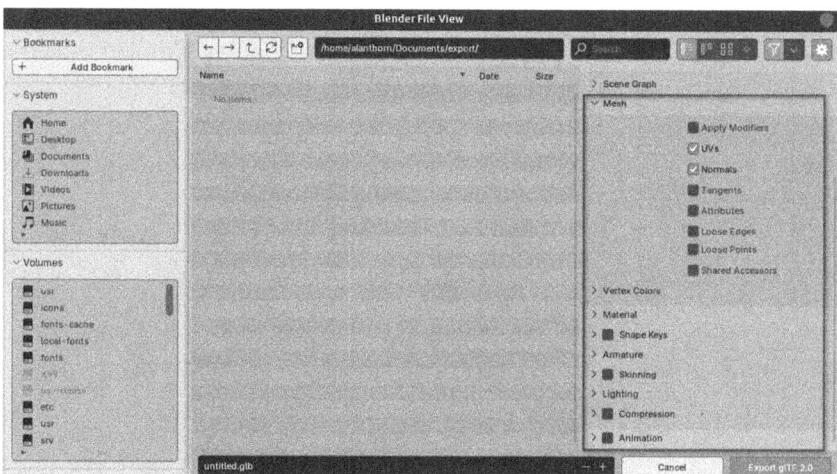

FIGURE 3.43   Filtering exported data.

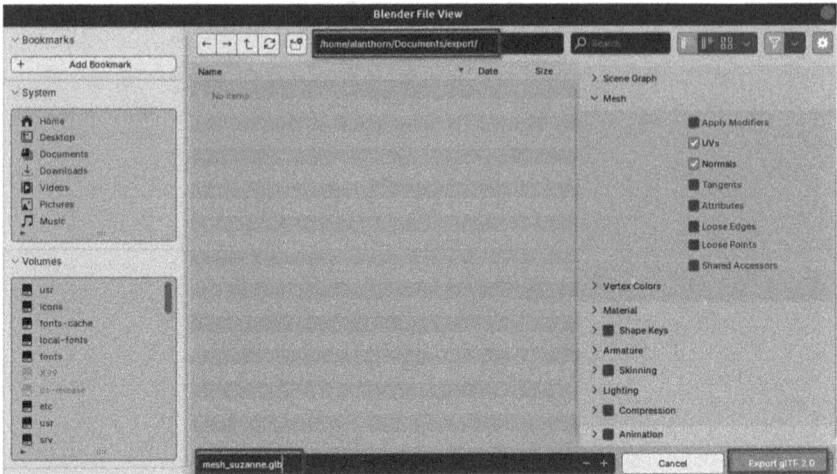

FIGURE 3.44 Exporting to a GLB file.

Finally, name your mesh appropriately, select a destination folder on your computer, and then choose *Export*. This will create a new GLB file on your hard drive (see Figure 3.44).

3.3.3 Importing a Mesh to Godot from GLTF

Meshes for game development are commonly found in the FBX and GLTF formats. FBX is the most common for Unity and Unreal. The GLTF format is more common in the Godot world, and it comes in two forms, namely *GLTF* and *GLB*. The mesh exported in the previous section, which is included in the book companion files in the Chapter 3 folder, is in the GLB format. This is the most common form. It is a mesh of the Suzanne Monkey, exported from Blender 4.3.2. Importing a mesh like this into Godot is much like importing an image texture in the initial stages. You simply drag and drop your mesh file from your file browser and into the *FileSystem* dock in the Godot editor. When you do this, the mesh is added to your project automatically as a resource (see Figure 3.45).

> NOTE. More technical information on importing meshes in Godot can be found in the official Godot documentation here: https://docs.godotengine.org/en/4.1/tutorials/assets_pipeline/importing_scenes.html

Great! So, Godot has now imported your *mesh*. Or has it? Let's see. Start by creating a new 3D scene and then drag and drop the GLB resource into the 3D viewport. You'll notice that a new object is created, and it looks just like your mesh (see Figure 3.46).

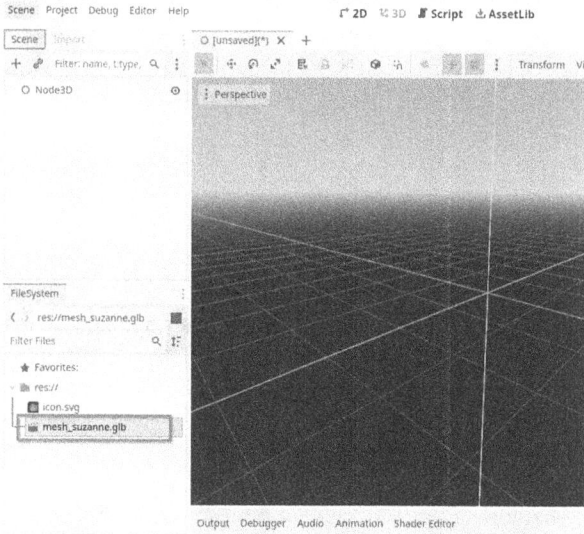

FIGURE 3.45   Importing a GLB file into Godot.

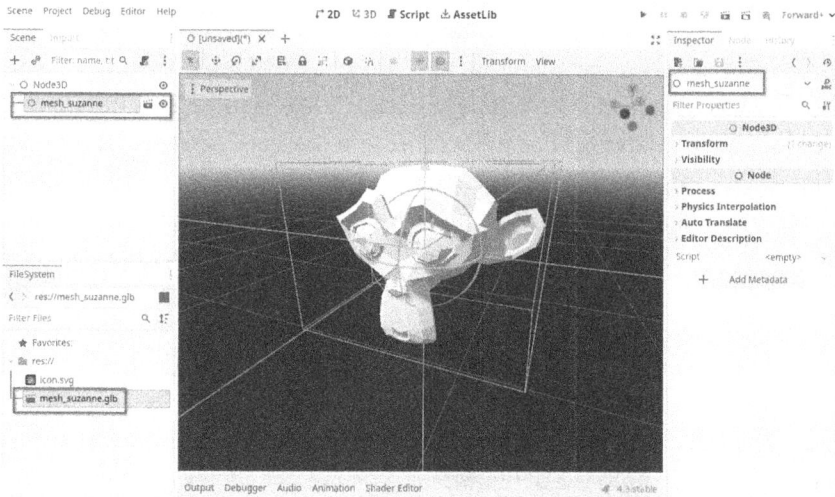

FIGURE 3.46   A new mesh is created based on the imported resource

Things look good, at least at first sight. But there are some interesting points to note, which are likely to cause confusion, especially if you're approaching Godot coming from either Unity or Unreal. First, notice that there is an unusual clapboard icon next to the object name in the *Scene* Dock. This doesn't appear on any of the objects we created previously.

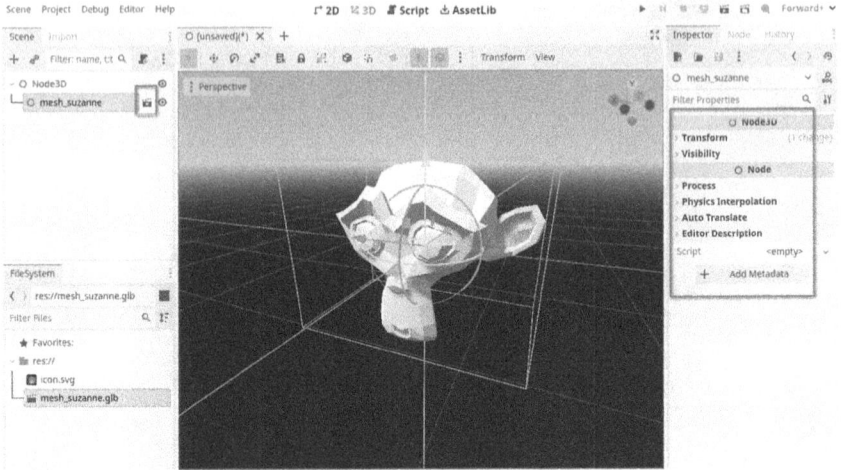

FIGURE 3.47   Exploring the imported GLB mesh inside a scene.

And second, even when the object is selected in the scene, there seems to be no way to change its material override from the Inspector, as we did with the cube mesh created earlier. We cannot seem to change any mesh properties, like texture, material, and shaders (see Figure 3.47).

So, what's going on here exactly? Seems strange, right? Here's the answer: Godot understands GLTF and FBX files to represent 3D *scenes* rather than *meshes*. A single GLTF file doesn't represent a single mesh but rather a scene that *could* contain one or more meshes. You may be working in the tradition of a single file representing a single mesh. It makes sense and feels nice and neat. But that tradition is a convention rather than a requirement of the file format itself. So, by importing GLTF files, you are technically importing a 3D scene (such as a Scene from Blender) which is a three-dimensional space containing one or more meshes *as child nodes*. For this reason, when you drag and drop our Suzanne file from the *FileSystem* Dock into the 3D viewport, you are not actually instantiating a single mesh. Rather, you're instantiating a complete scene that contains a mesh. That is why, when selecting our object in the Scene Dock, you don't see a bunch of properties for a single mesh inside the Inspector; because you are really selecting a higher-order root object that represents a scene, inside which the mesh lives as a separate child object. You can confirm that this is indeed the case by clicking once on the clapboard icon beside the Suzanne object from the Scene Dock. When you click this, it asks a technical question about scenes. For now, choose *Open Anyway* (see Figure 3.48).

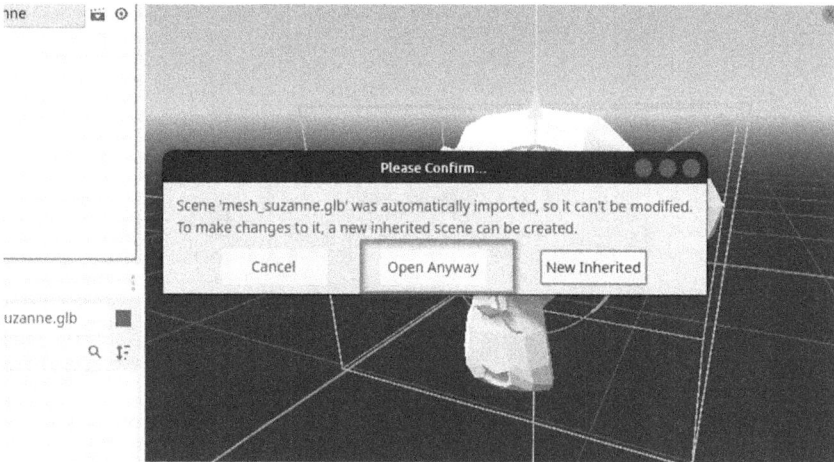

FIGURE 3.48   Opening up the GLTF scene.

Choosing this option will open a new Scene tab beside the original scene and display the full contents of the imported scene – the Suzanne scene. Doing so, our imported object (Suzanne) finally reveals itself to be a scene and not simply a mesh. And because we previously dragged and dropped an instance of Suzanne into our original, empty 3D scene, that instance is actually a scene *embedded* in a scene. This concept of scenes within scenes (embedded scenes) is an incredibly powerful idea that forms a core part of the Godot workflow, and we will revisit it later in this chapter and throughout this book. It's analogous to Prefabs in Unity and Unreal.

OK. So, let's keep exploring. If we now examine the Suzanne mesh scene in its own scene resource, you'll see that it features two nodes in the hierarchy, namely a root node and a Suzanne node. If you select the Suzanne node, you'll see all the expected mesh properties in the Inspector, such as material and surface overrides. Therefore, this is the mesh node. Now, our scene here features two nodes, but naturally different scenes will have different nodes and configurations, and this complexity varies depending on your exported data (see Figure 3.49).

Good. Now, what about changing the mesh properties? For example, we might want to create two versions of the same imported mesh, one with a red material and one with a blue material. This is certainly common in the retro platform games where multiple enemies in a level are often repeated but with different materials and colors to indicate their strength. Surely, we don't need to create the variations in Blender or Maya and then export each variation separately as different meshes? Thankfully, Godot offers us

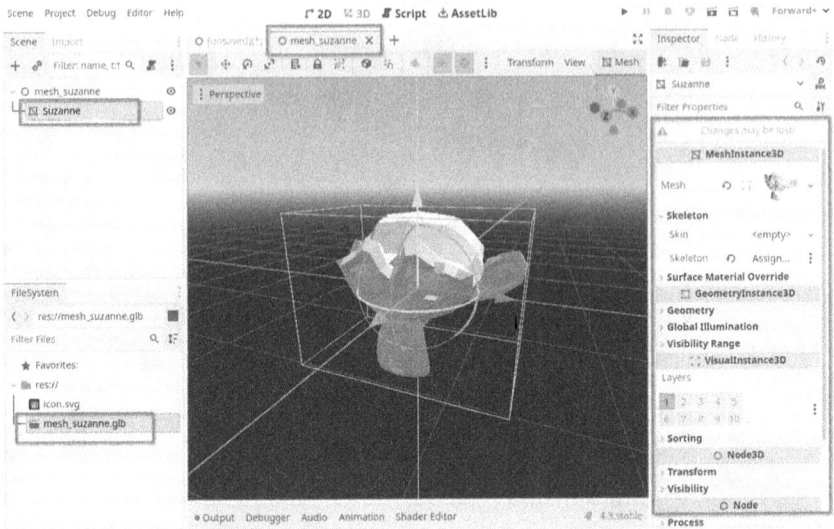

FIGURE 3.49   Selecting the mesh node inside a GLTF resource.

a range of features for varying our imported meshes and assets. However, the originally imported GLTF file that we are now viewing in the scene editor is read-only. Back when we clicked on the clapboard icon to view the scene and chose 'Open Anyway', we were effectively being warned there by Godot that by opening the original scene, we could only view its contents and not modify them. So, let's close the Suzanne mesh scene since we cannot change it and find another way. To do that, we click the *Close* button. It may, absurdly, ask us if we want to save any changes made (see Figure 3.50).

3.3.4 Modifying an Imported Mesh with Inherited Scenes

We've seen now how we can import any number of meshes from Blender, using GLTF, and display them effectively inside a regular Godot 3D scene. You simply drag and drop the scene (which contains a mesh) resource from the FileSystem dock into the scene viewport, and this method will work well. That is, provided you don't need to modify the mesh, or meshes, in any way. If you want to change a mesh's material, re-scale the mesh, or add additional data such as colliders or weapons, then you'll certainly need a method for modifying the imported meshes. By default, the imported scene resources are read-only and cannot be changed, as we've seen. There are different approaches to get around this problem. This section considers one of them, which works well for any type of mesh, whether it's a prop,

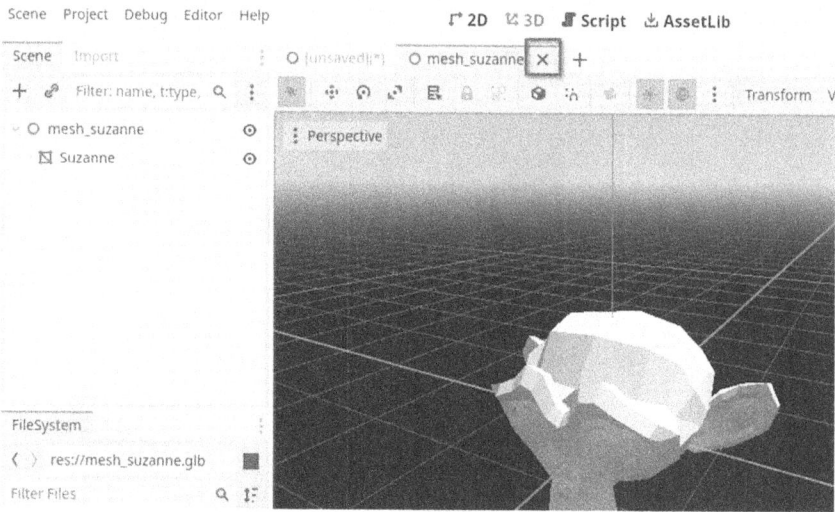

FIGURE 3.50   Closing the imported GLTF scene.

architectural element, or character. To get started, drag and drop your imported mesh into an open scene, as we already did in an earlier section (see Figure 3.51).

The newly added mesh has a clapboard icon next to its name in the Scene Dock, which means it's an embedded scene. That is, although it appears as one node in the hierarchy, it could represent many more child nodes. Click on the clapboard icon and choose *New Inherited* from the context menu (see Figure 3.52). This focuses on the scene in a new tab.

Let's make one version of the mesh red and the other blue. Let's make blue first. Select the mesh node (the child node) in the newly opened scene. From the Inspector, expand the *Surface Material Override* and create a new *StandardMaterial3D*. Then expand the *Albedo* slot and assign a blue color to it. The mesh will immediately change to blue in the viewport (see Figure 3.53).

Now Save this scene with *Ctrl + S* and use a different filename (such as *Mesh_Blue*). The saved variation will now appear in the *FileSystem* Dock as a separate scene (see Figure 3.54).

Now go back to our previous scene and again select the clapboard icon for the original Suzanne mesh. Then repeat the process of creating a new, inherited scene for the red variation. Be sure to save the scene meaningfully, for example, *mesh_red*. You'll now end up with a FileSystem dock containing a total of three scenes: the original Suzanne scene and two other scenes, which are variations that derive from the original (see Figure 3.55).

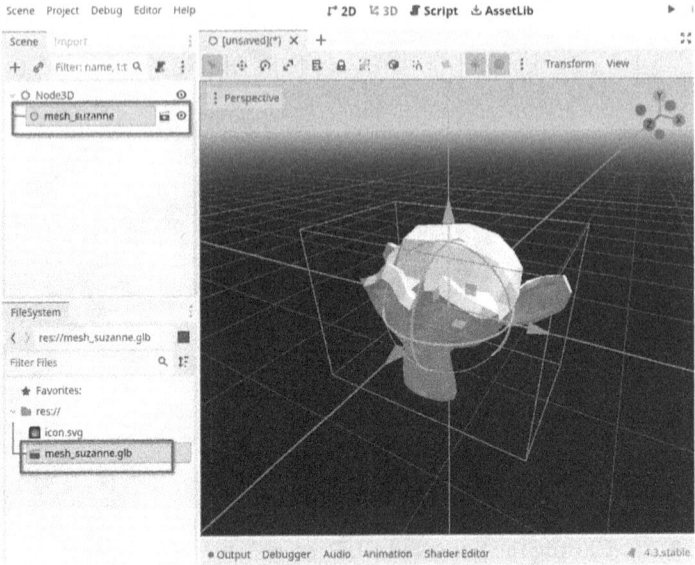

FIGURE 3.51 Closing the imported GLTF scene.

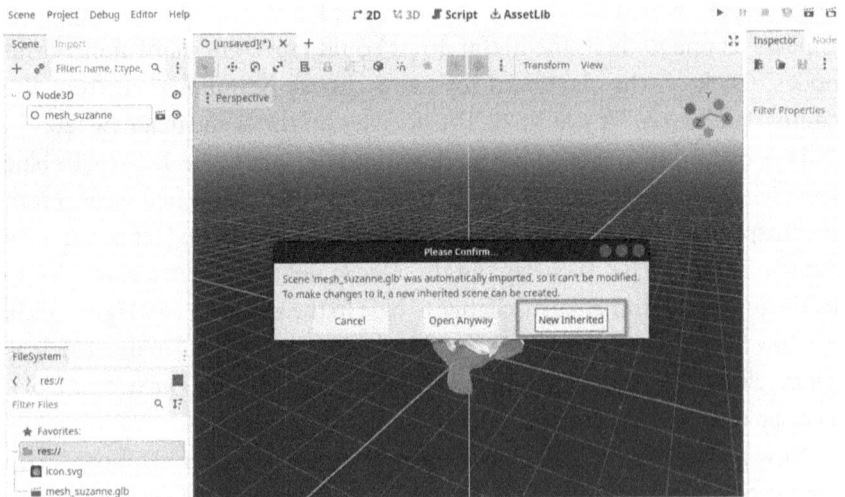

FIGURE 3.52 Creating an inherited scene for making mesh changes.

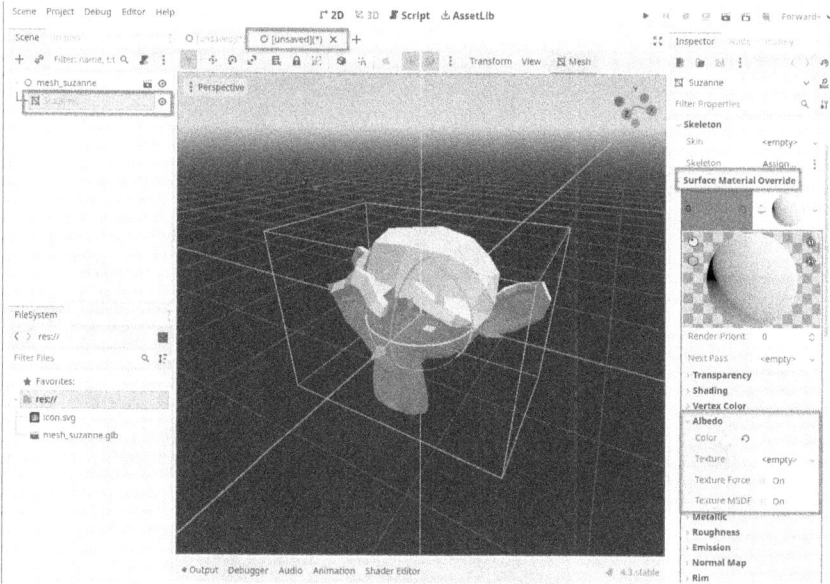

FIGURE 3.53   Updating the mesh material to blue.

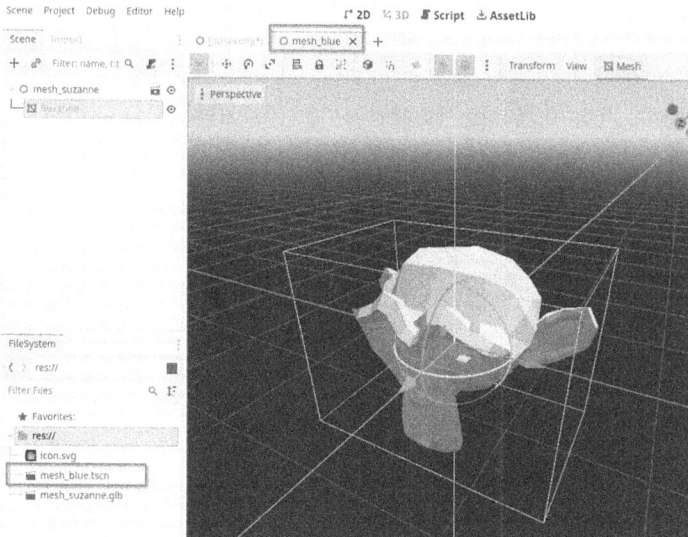

FIGURE 3.54   Saving a blue mesh variation.

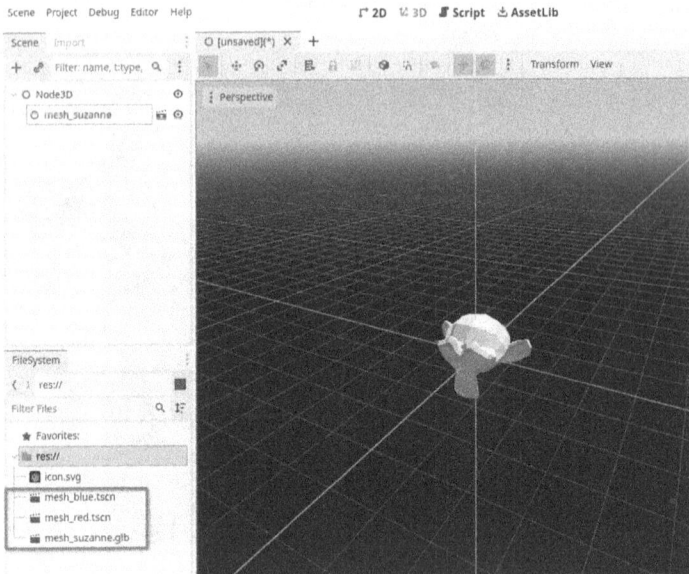

FIGURE 3.55 Creating blue and red variants of an imported scene.

Excellent! You can now drag and drop the variations into the active scene, placing them side by side in a lineup. You have now imported a mesh and varied its properties in an efficient and accessible way (see Figure 3.56). Unlike the original Suzanne mesh, which will always be read-only, you can always open up and edit the variations. And, if your variations are instantiated in multiple places and multiple scenes, then all instances will instantly update to reflect any changes you make upon saving.

3.4 BLENDER AND GODOT LIVE LINK EDITING

Godot integrates well with Blender. This integration has now reached an impressive stage such that, in addition to importing meshes into Godot from *GLTF* files, as we've seen, we can also connect to Blender through its native file type, .*blend* files. That is, Godot can open .*Blend* files. This seamless 'live link' approach practically means that we can save a file in Blender, import that directly into Godot, and then return to Blender, where any saved changes to that file are automatically updated live in Godot. In this way, there is a continuous, one-to-one correspondence between the two applications when they share the same blend file. This workflow is especially appealing because, in theory, it removes the need to tediously 'export' any meshes via an exporter tool – like FBX or GLTF. Plus, it retains a live connection between the two applications, making it

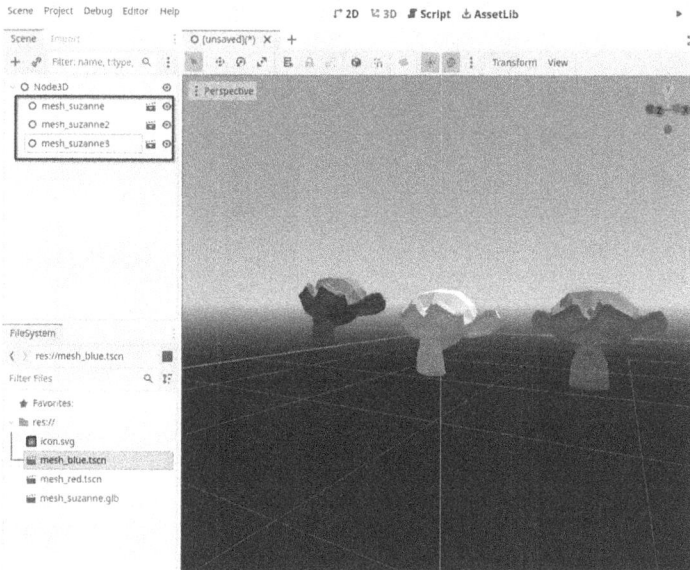

FIGURE 3.56 Adding mesh variations to a scene.

frictionless to change your work whenever needed. This section explores how to set up the live link connection between Blender and Godot, and we also examine the limitations and technical risks of this solution if you rely on it entirely.

3.4.1 Creating a Connection between Godot and Blender

The first step to seamless integration between Godot and Blender is to make Godot aware of the location of Blender on your computer. That sounds straightforward, but it can actually be trickier than it first appears. To achieve this, start by choosing *Editor > Editor Settings* from the Godot application menu (see Figure 3.57).

From the *Editor Settings* dialog, choose *FileSystem > Import*, and from there enter a valid and fully qualified path to the Blender executable on your computer, using the *Blender Path* field (see Figure 3.58). On Windows operating systems, this will likely be straightforward, as you can easily choose the install location of Blender. On Mac and Linux, this is potentially more complicated. For Linux users especially – such as the popular *Linux Mint* Distro – you may even need to download and extract Blender manually from the official Blender website, as opposed to using a pre-packaged version from the system package manager, like *Flatpak*. After changing this, you'll need to restart the Godot Editor.

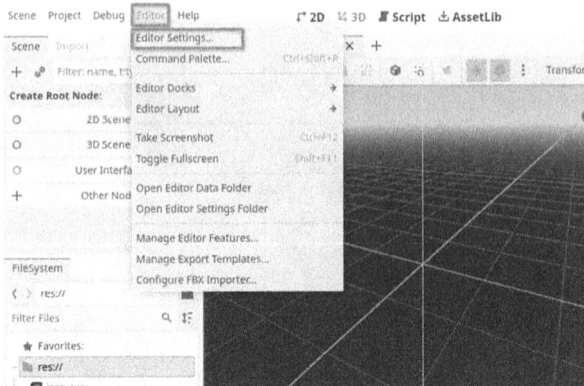

FIGURE 3.57   Accessing the Godot Editor Settings.

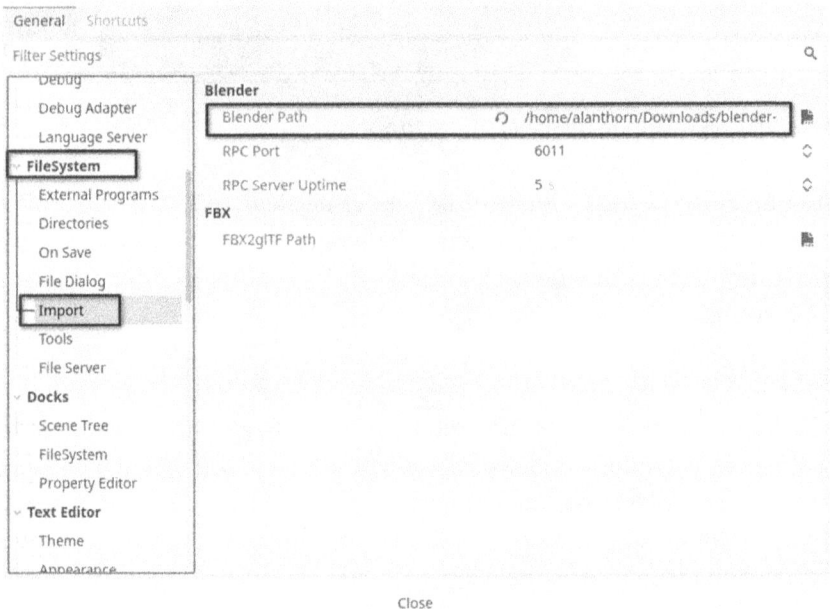

FIGURE 3.58   Specifying the install location of Blender.

After restarting Godot, or at some later point in the process, you'll see an error message if you got the Blender location wrong or if there was an issue accessing Blender at the specified location. If and when this happens, Godot may disable Blender connectivity entirely to prevent any future error messages from showing while using Godot. However, if you later return to the *Editor Settings* and enter a new and correct path to Blender, Godot will still have deactivated Blender connectivity. To re-enable this option, start by choosing *Project > Project Settings* from the application menu (see Figure 3.59).

From the Project Settings menu, enable *Advanced Settings* in the top-right-hand corner. This reveals a selection of more advanced and less commonly used options (see Figure 3.60).

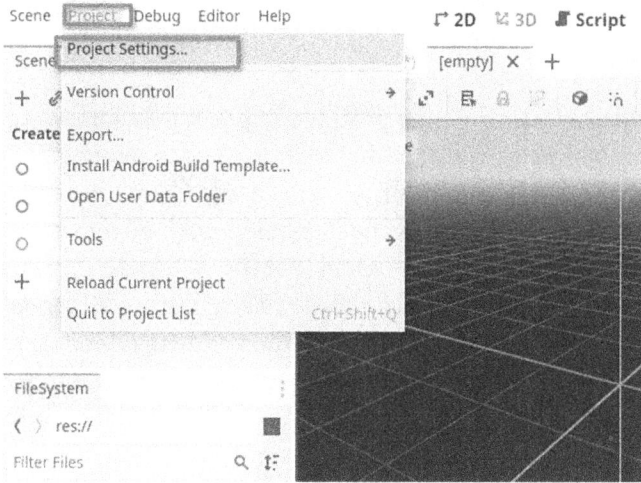

FIGURE 3.59   Accessing Project Settings in Godot.

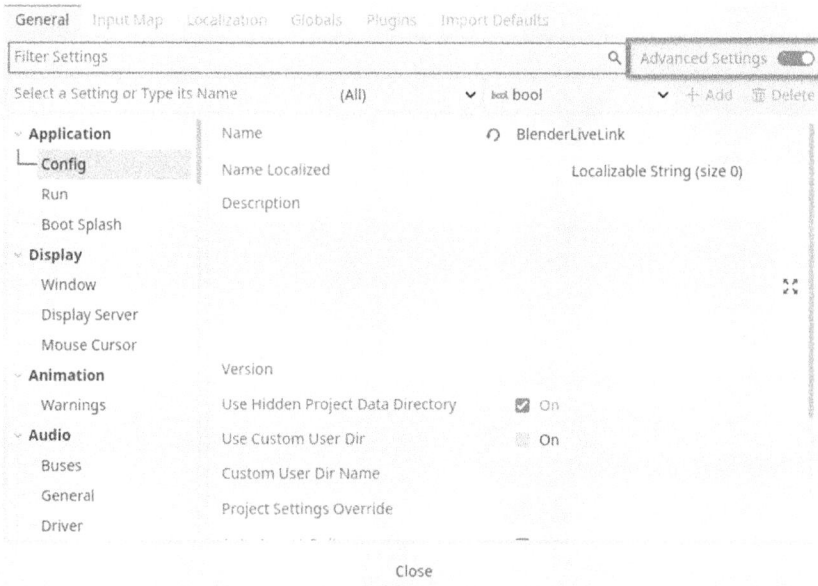

FIGURE 3.60   Enabling advanced options from the Project Settings dialog.

Next, view *FileSystem > Import* options, and be sure to enable the Blender field (see Figure 3.61). That's it. Blender import will be re-enabled again. Note that Godot may disable this field again if an error occurs connecting to Blender at the new path.

3.4.2 Creating a Shared Blend Scene

Next, let's switch over to Blender and create a new scene featuring Suzanne Mesh, as we created earlier. We'll eventually connect this to Godot (see Figure 3.62).

Now, return to your Godot project and select the topmost node in the FileSystem hierarchy, which is the 'res://' node, the topmost folder in the file system. Right-click on this node and choose Copy Absolute Path from the context menu. This copies the FileSystem path of your Godot project to the clipboard, which will be pasted later inside Blender (see Figure 3.63).

Now, return to Blender and choose *File > Save* from the application menu to access the file-saving features. Then paste the *Absolute Path* of the Godot project, copied previously, to save the Blender file into your Godot file system directly. Give your Blend file a suitable, unique, and meaningful name, as this name will display in Godot too (see Figure 3.64).

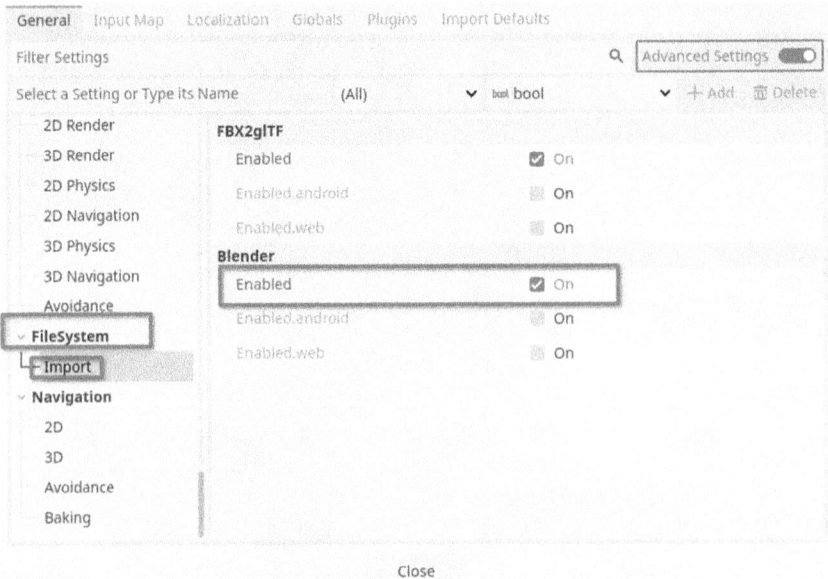

FIGURE 3.61   Re-enabling Blender importing.

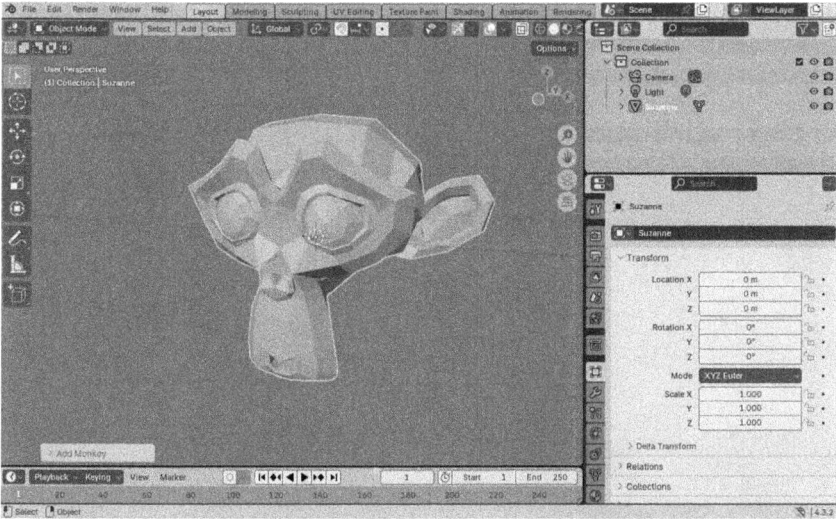

FIGURE 3.62   Create an empty Blender scene with a Suzanne mesh.

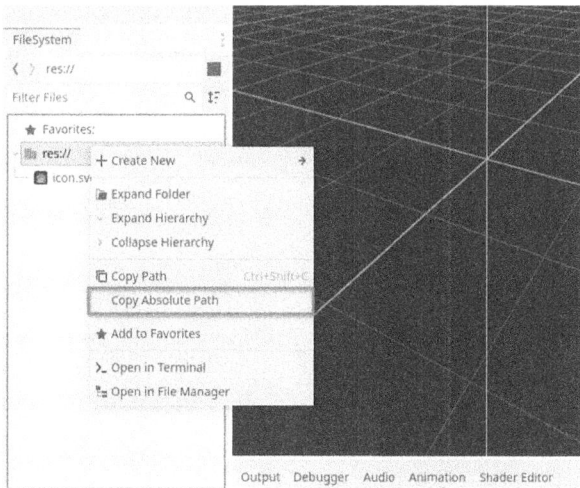

FIGURE 3.63   Copying the Absolute Path of a folder location.

Return to Godot, and you'll automatically see your Blend file appear in the *FileSystem*. Next, create a new 3D Scene and drag and drop the Blender file into the 3D viewport. You'll immediately see the contents of your Blender scene. However, the scene may not appear as you expected because all objects in the Blender scene, including any lights, were also imported into Godot (see Figure 3.65).

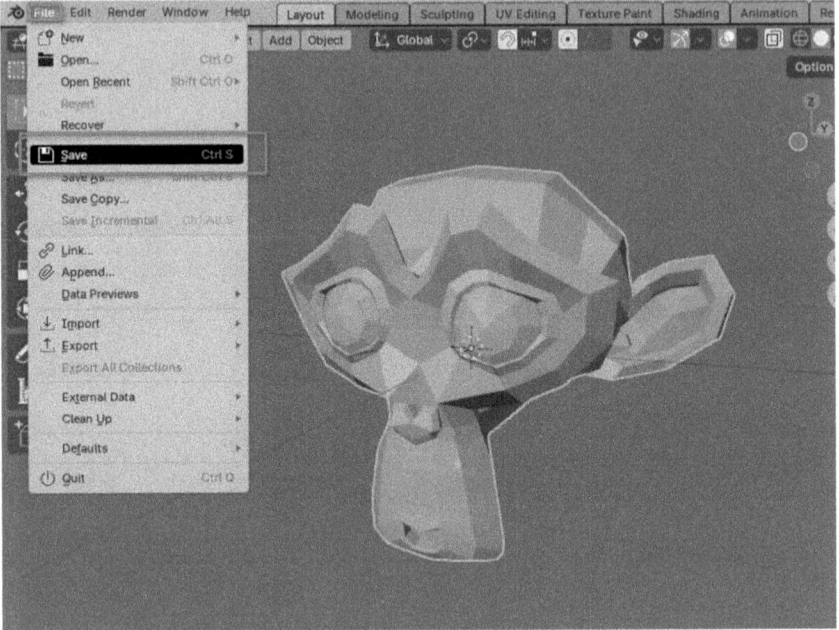

FIGURE 3.64 Saving a Blend File into a Godot project.

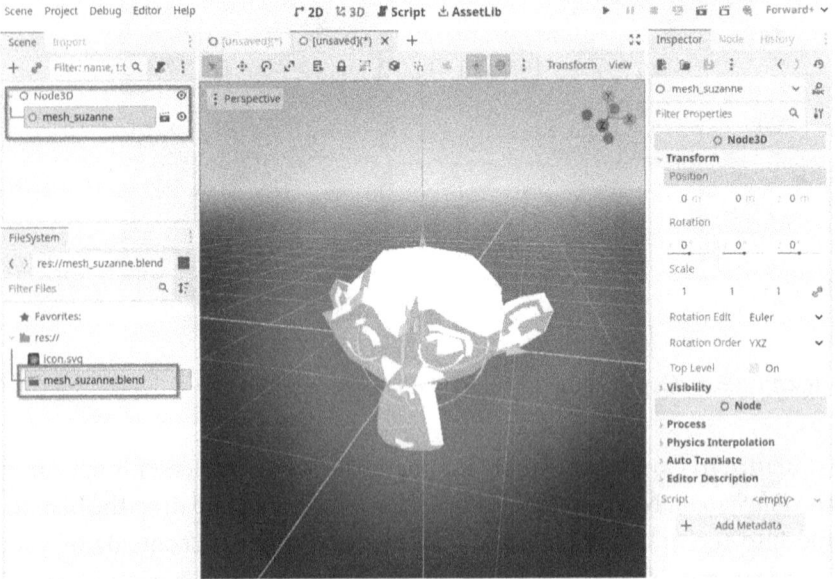

FIGURE 3.65 Establishing a connection to a Blender Scene.

If you see your Blender scene in the Godot viewport, then that's great news. You can now easily jump back to Blender, make any changes, and then re-save. Godot will automatically detect the saved changes and update the scene with your latest changes. Amazing! No need for an export, and no need for any dragging and dropping files.

3.4.3 Mesh Name Suffixes

Previously, we successfully established a live connection to a Blender scene between Godot and Blender. This offers us many technical and logistical advantages. However, you'll notice from Figure 3.65 that everything in the Blender scene, including lights and cameras, is imported directly into Godot, regardless of whether we want them or whether they are useful. If we wanted to exclude some items – such as the cameras and lights – one solution would be simply to delete them manually inside Godot. However, those unwanted items would, of course, return every time we re-saved the Blender file, and Godot updated the scene in response. Another solution would be to delete the items from the Blender scene itself, using Blender. But this is problematic too because we might want to keep those items in Blender, usually because they are useful there. So, an alternative solution that Godot offers us is *mesh name suffixes*. These are special letters that we attach to the end of object names in Blender. These change how Godot behaves during the import process. When Godot encounters a reserved combination of letters at the end of an object name, it responds in a specific way to that object on an object-by-object basis. Let's consider the case of excluding specific objects from being imported from a Blender scene. For this, the suffix of *–noimp* (meaning: No Import) can be appended to the name of any object that Godot should ignore at import time, acting as though it didn't exist. For our example Blender scene, created in the previous section, there is a camera and a light object that I'd like Godot to ignore specifically. Consider Figure 3.66.

After applying naming suffixes to the lights and cameras and then re-saving the scene in Blender, Godot will automatically reimport the file and exclude the specified objects. This allows us to keep the objects in Blender and remove them in Godot. Nice feature. It should be noted that this feature also works for the GLTF Export workflow and not only the live link.

> NOTE. For more details on other supported Godot suffixes, check out the official documentation here: https://docs.godotengine.org/en/stable/tutorials/assets_pipeline/importing_3d_scenes/node_type_customization.html.

FIGURE 3.66 Godot ignores objects with the naming suffix -noimp.

3.4.4 Advantages and Disadvantages of Live Linking

It's worth closing this section with a brief discussion on the pros and cons of Blender to Godot live-link editing. I'll divide these into 'reasons for' and then 'reasons against', and you can make a judgment for your own needs. In short, there is no right or wrong approach. If you choose to avoid Live Linking, then your alternative for importing meshes from Blender is the GLTF export workflow above. If you instead use Maya, you can export as GLTF or FBX.

Reasons for:

1. **No need for Exporting**
   Perhaps the strongest reason to choose Live Linking is that it avoids the tedium of exporting meshes separately and of having to choose the right settings and configure everything in the correct way. It takes some of the intricate and annoying work away from you, and that's tempting!

2. **Fast and Interactive**
   Another great reason is simplicity and speed. With Live Linking, you can jump almost seamlessly back and forth between Godot and Blender and make changes that update as soon as you push save in Blender. This interactivity is impressive.

Reasons against:

1. **Software Lock-In**

   Blender to Godot Live Linking only works between those two applications. Although many applications export to GLTF and import from it, only Godot supports Live Linking with Blender in this way. This means your team is tied into using Blender for 3D modeling if they are to take proper advantage of Live Linking.

2. **Easy to break**

   Each machine in your team needs both Godot and Blender installed and to be configured correctly in order to live link. This depends on users understanding how to set things up, having the correct permissions, and knowing their way around the file system properly.

3. **Version Invalidation**

   If you upgrade your software often, such as always using the latest Godot or Blender, then please remember that code changes and feature additions can impact how these applications work with each other. There is the potential for breaks to happen.

3.5 THE MESH ADVANCED IMPORTER

Whether you're importing *FBX*, *GLTF*, or *Blend* files, Godot features a general-purpose *Advanced Import* tool for meshes. This is useful in many situations, as we'll see. You access this tool simply by double-clicking the mesh file from the *FileSystem* dock or by right-clicking the file and, strangely, choosing *Open Scene* from the context menu (see Figure 3.67).

The tool contains a combination of preview features, optimization settings for meshes, and even a series of batch process features. The tool will open in the *Scene* tab (see Figure 3.68).

3.5.1 Setting the Mesh Scale

Rather than scan through every feature of this tool, let's explore at least two key reasons during development why you would use it and how it can achieve those core purposes. First, your imported mesh may appear too large or too small in the scene compared to everything else. This is especially important when the player characters, or enemy characters, need to be a specific size to fit through doorways, tunnels, and other spaces. You commonly find this problem when working with different assets by

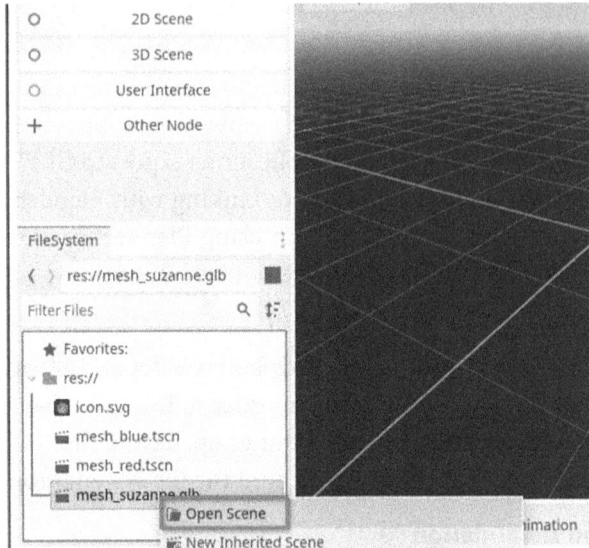

FIGURE 3.67 Accessing the Advanced Mesh Import tool.

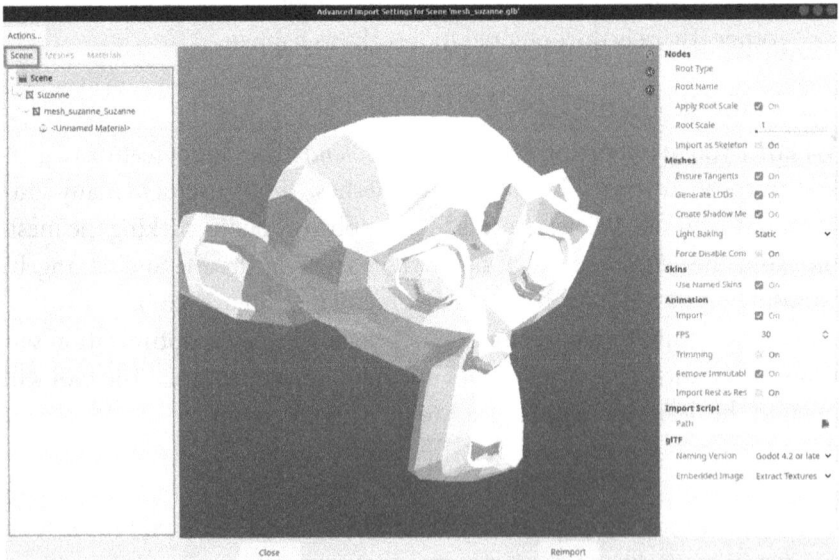

FIGURE 3.68 Viewing the advanced mesh import tool.

different artists, made for different games or purposes. In any case, one way to solve this is by returning to Blender and fixing the size there at the source, or you could simply change the individual scale of every instance of the mesh in every scene. The latter is tedious if you're using many instances of the imported mesh, such as many enemies repeated throughout the scene.

To solve this more effectively in Godot, you can use the Root Scale setting. When set, the mesh is uniformly scaled by the specified scale factor (1 means default size, 2 means double-size, and 0.5 means half-size, etc.), and this becomes its default size whenever the mesh is added to a scene. If you change this value, or any value in the Advanced Mesh Importer, it will also affect all existing instances of the mesh that already exist in any scenes you have, if any (see Figure 3.69).

3.5.2 Separating Meshes

Another important feature of the Advanced Importer is mesh separation. Your imported file is technically a scene, which contains many meshes and other objects in a single 3D space. If there are many objects, they will be treated as a single scene unit by Godot because they are contained within the same scene. The meshes within can be moved and transformed separately when edited using the scene editor, but they all still constitute part of a larger scene, which is taken in its entirety when embedded into another scene. For this reason, it's often convenient to separate the meshes from the imported scene file, saving them separately not as smaller scenes, but as mesh resources that can be added to scenes on their own. This has advantages and disadvantages, as we'll see. To start separating a mesh, click on the *Mesh* tab from the Importer tool and select the mesh to separate (see Figure 3.70).

Next, enable *Save to File* from the tool Inspector, and then select a valid path in the project. Then finally choose *Reimport*. This reimports the mesh

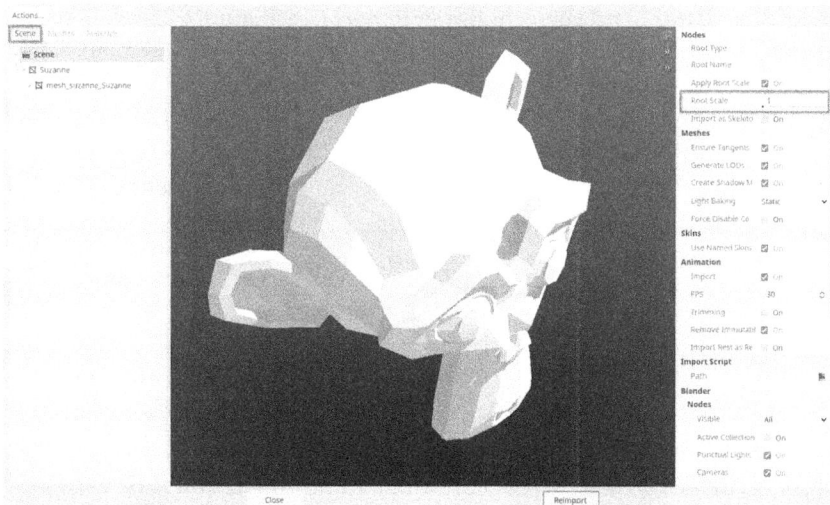

FIGURE 3.69   Setting the root or Mesh scale.

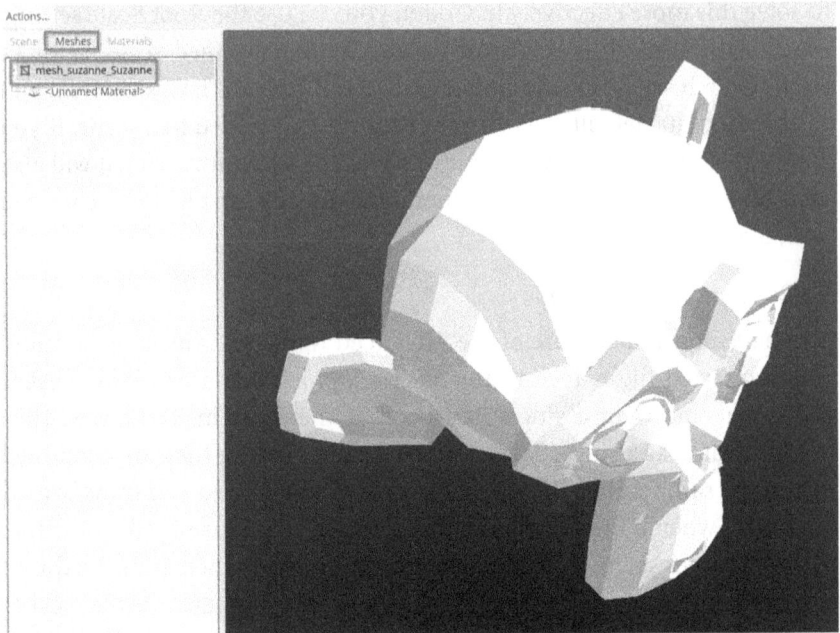

FIGURE 3.70   Choosing a Mesh for separation.

into Godot and applies all saved meshes, creating separate mesh resources for them (see Figure 3.71).

If you're extracting many meshes from a file, and not simply one or two, then you can use the Batch tool to set a save path for multiple meshes at once. This tool is available from the *Actions* Menu. Choose *Actions* > *Set Mesh Save Paths*. And then choose *Reimport* (see Figure 3.72).

> NOTE. When a mesh is saved from an imported scene file as a mesh asset and a separate resource, it becomes separated from its attendant material and collision information. The former defines how the mesh surface should appear under lighting, and the latter defines whether the mesh is a solid object. You can easily but manually configure these again for each instance of the mesh.

3.5.3 Separating Materials

Finally, you may want to externalize mesh materials to separate material resources that you can edit separately from the *FileSystem*, or even through code, as we saw earlier in Section 3.2. This gives you easier control over an object's surface. You will probably want to do this if you'll be assigning

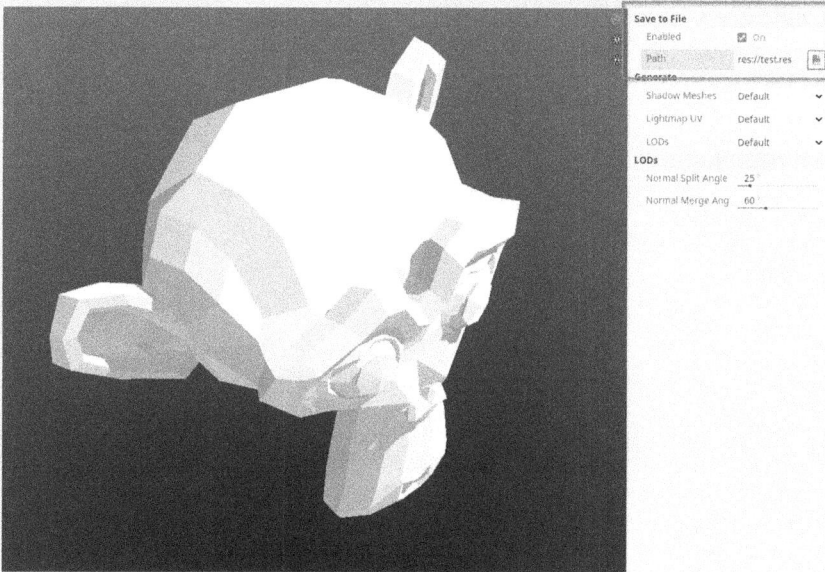

FIGURE 3.71   Choosing a Save Destination.

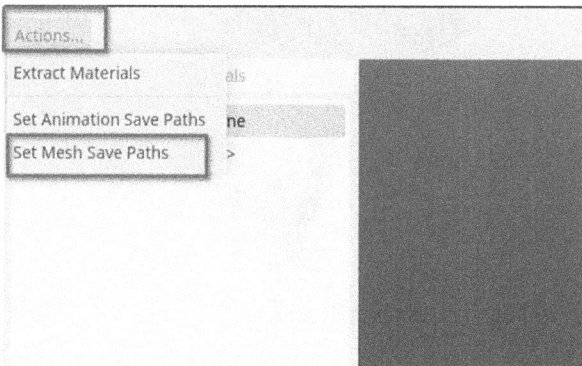

FIGURE 3.72   Setting multiple save paths.

different materials to the same mesh, if you're changing a material, or if you want to access the material from code. You probably won't do this if you're happy with the mesh material as it is and have no need to make any changes. To start, select the *Materials* tab from the tool and then choose a material to save (see Figure 3.73).

From the Inspector, choose *Enabled* under the *Use External* category, then select a valid path (see Figure 3.74).

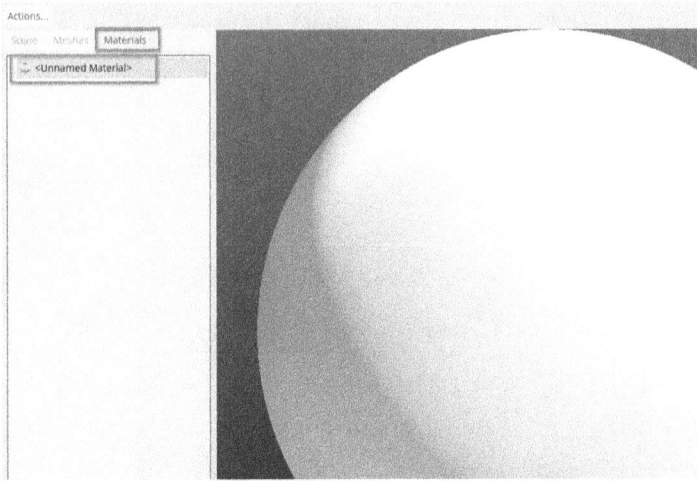

FIGURE 3.73   Extracting materials.

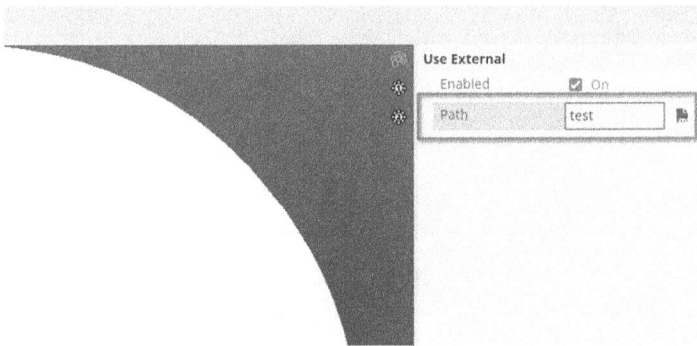

FIGURE 3.74   Enabling external materials.

As with meshes in the previous section, you can export many materials at once using a batch process tool. This is especially convenient with materials, as even one mesh can contain many materials. To export multiple, choose *Actions > Extract Materials*. This exports and externalizes all materials in the imported file (see Figure 3.75).

3.6 CONCLUSION

This chapter explored how to work with the most common and fundamental resources in Godot, namely *textures*, *materials*, and *meshes*. Together, these represent the building blocks of nearly every game and

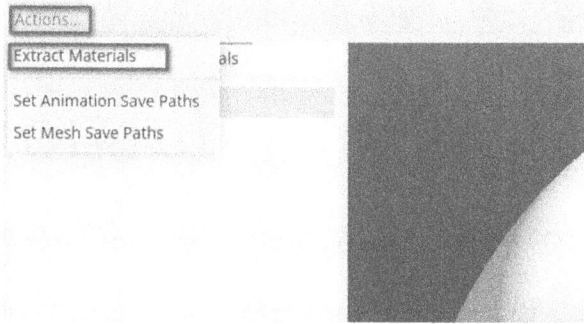

FIGURE 3.75   Extracting all materials.

interactive media. We'll see later that there are many other resource types, and we'll explore some of them in greater depth as we encounter them in our work, such as *TileMaps* and *GridMaps*. Overall, this chapter is critically important to anybody working in Godot for any purpose. Having now covered these essentials, we can move on to code, functionality, and the general structure of a Godot program.

CHAPTER 4

GDScript Introduction

Programming Games

T HIS CHAPTER EXPLORES THE fundamentals of game programming in Godot using the *GDScript* language. Programming for games is essentially about creating the DNA of a game world – the constituent ingredients that bring otherwise lifeless assets, such as meshes and textures, to life. Code, or programming, is what essentially makes 'stuff' happen *inside* a game. You push a button on the gamepad, and the player character jumps *in response*; you shoot an enemy, and they die in response; and you reach the end of a level, and the game responds by progressing to the next one. These are examples, perhaps crude examples, of code in action and they exemplify why code is so critically important. This chapter assumes you have a basic familiarity with programming in any standard language – such as *C++* or *C#* or *Python* or *JavaScript* – as well as the core concepts common to all languages – such as variables, functions, loops, and conditionals. But I assume you are new to GDScript and its application in Godot. As such, this chapter is more of a quick-start guide for a literate programmer seeking an accessible orientation point for coding in Godot in the fastest and most effective way. We'll consider how to get started at coding in Godot and how to create basic functionality, and we'll make some comparisons to other, relevant engines – such as Unity – which will be especially helpful if you're approaching Godot from that engine. This chapter is not, however, intended for readers who have never explored programming in any language. If that's your case, then you can still read through

DOI: 10.1201/9781003484523-4

this chapter and learn a lot, but I recommend complementing the materials here with a more comprehensive and dedicated introduction to coding to help you consolidate all the essential principles.

4.1 FIRST STEPS – WHICH LANGUAGE?

Before coding in Godot, you'll need to decide on which language to use, and this is not an unimportant decision. Godot natively supports two languages for gameplay scripting, namely C# and GDScript, and sound arguments can certainly be made for choosing either language. For example, C# offers industry-wide acceptance and plenty of tutorial resources for learning the language, and it has applications outside of Godot. GDScript, which is similar to Python, is a domain-specific language (you'll only encounter it inside Godot), but it's arguably simpler to learn and use, and it definitely gives you access to the greatest range of Godot features across every supported platform, from desktop to mobile. So, this book will focus on GDScript.

> NOTE. Whichever language you choose, stick to that one for the entirety of your project. I strongly discourage mixing languages. This results in additional confusion and will be most unhelpful to your projects.

> NOTE. If you choose C# as a language, you'll need to download a special build of Godot. The .NET version. This is available from the Godot homepage here: https://godotengine.org/download/.

4.2 MAKING A HELLO WORLD PROGRAM WITH GDSCRIPT

The first program that any coder should learn to create is 'Hello World'. Indeed, this is a useful program to make, so that's what we'll do here. This program essentially prints the message 'Hello World' to the debug panel (*Output*) of Godot when the program first runs; that is, every time that *Play Mode* is activated. This section assumes you already have a new and empty Godot project created. So, to create a new hello world program from an empty project, you should right-click the *'Res://'* root inside the *FileSystem* dock, and then from the context menu choose *Create New > Script*. This will display the *New Script* dialog for creating a new Script file resource (see Figure 4.1).

The *Create a Script* dialog allows you to create a new script file, which is a plain text document containing coded instructions. From this dialog, ensure the chosen language is GDScript (it may be your only option), and

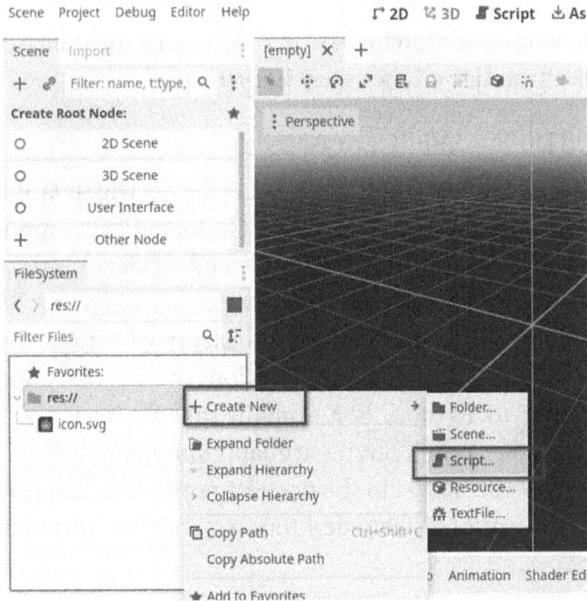

FIGURE 4.1 Create your first script file.

set the *Inherits* field to *Node*. The value of this field should vary, depending on your needs, as we'll see throughout the book. *Node* is used for the simplest of cases. Finally, name your file. I've set this to *hello_world.gd* (see Figure 4.2). When you're completed, click the *Create* button to confirm and apply the settings.

Once created, the GDScript script file lives as a file resource with the *FileSystem* Dock. For the program to run, the script must be instantiated by being attached to a Node (or object) inside the scene. That is, a script normally only runs when 'living on' a *Node* within the time and space of the scene. To instantiate the script, let's make a new 3D scene (although a 2D scene can also work). The newly created scene will feature a *Node3D* or *Node2D* object at the root. To attach the script, select the object from the *Scene* Dock, and then in the *Inspector*, click the empty drop-down box from the script field. Choose *Quick Load and* select the *hello_world* script (see Figure 4.3).

> NOTE. It doesn't matter whether you write your script first and then attach it to an object, or vice versa. You can attach the *same script to multiple objects*. A very important concept for efficient reuse of scripts. This causes the script to run separately for each object.

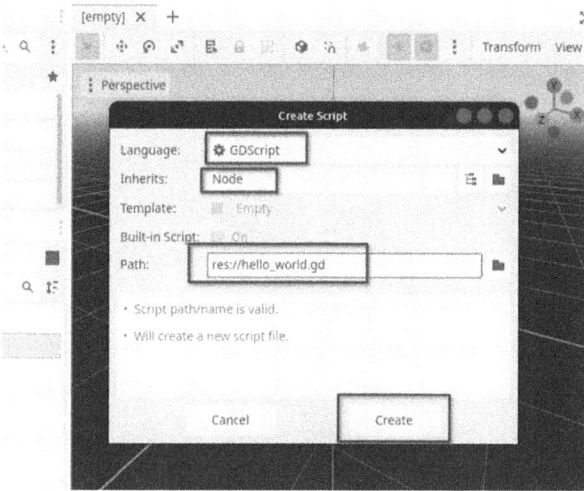

FIGURE 4.2   Configuring the created script file.

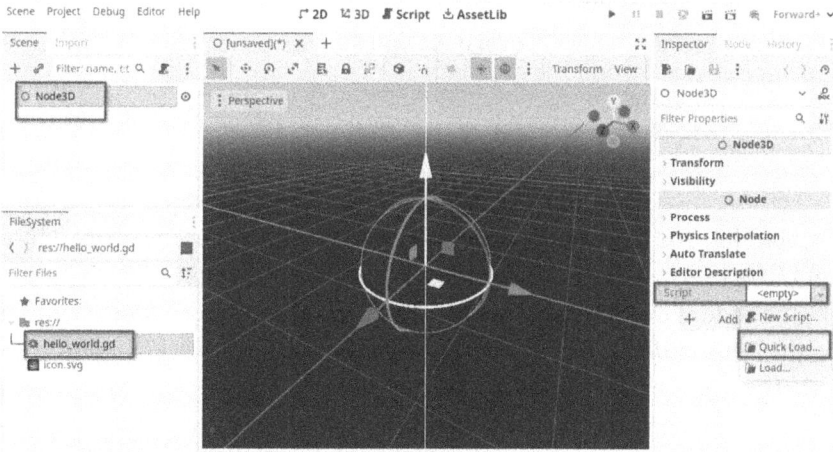

FIGURE 4.3   Attaching a Script file to an object.

Now let's write the script itself. For *GDScript*, Godot has a built-in Code Editor directly as part of the Editor interface. You can access it either by double-clicking the script file from the FileSystem Dock or by clicking the Script button from the top of the Editor. Then choose the Script file to view from the filter (see Figure 4.4).

The script file will already be populated with some Code, which can remain as is. See Code Sample 4.1. This code simply defines the type of object whose behavior we will be customizing; in this case, a *Node*.

FIGURE 4.4   Accessing the Godot Code Editor.

CODE SAMPLE 4.1

```
extends Node
```

Let's create a *Hello World* program. The full code is given below in Code Sample 4.2. You can simply copy and paste this code into the script editor and *Save* it. An explanation for the code is given below too.

The code above consists only of three lines. The keyword **func** is similar to the Python **def**. It marks the start of a *function definition*. That is, it's a function (hence the word *func*). A function names a block of code, which is clearly indented on the lines beneath, that can be referred to in shorthand form by the function name, and it can run as many times as needed simply by use of the name. The name of the function here is *_ready*. Function names are normally user-defined (by you) and can be whatever you want them to be, within naming rules. You should generally name

---

CODE SAMPLE 4.2

```
extends Node
func _ready():
        print("hello world")
```

functions that are meaningful to the context (close for exiting a program, fire for shooting a weapon, etc.). In Godot, however, there are some special names, which are reserved. This is because, when a function by any of those reserved names is included in a script, Godot will automatically run those functions at specific times, as an event. This is an application-specific convention rather than a language requirement. Godot uses the function name *_ready* as an event, which is run (executed) *only once when an object is added to the scene* for the first time during gameplay. 'The object' always refers to the node to which our script (hello_world) is attached. This means that any code inside the *_ready* function (code indented below its name) will be run at the level start in sequential order, line by line from top to bottom. In our case, we have only one line within the function, and so only one thing will happen. This line calls the *print* function (another function!) and includes the *argument* 'hello world'. An argument is an input parameter. In this case, it tells the print function which text should be output. An argument almost always adds additional details, controlling how a function should behave. A function can have multiple arguments.

So now let's run our code and see what happens. To do that, run the current scene by pressing F6 on the keyboard, or hit the Run Current Scene button from the toolbar (see Figure 4.5). If F6 doesn't work, or the button appears disabled, then make sure you have a 2D or 3D scene open in the viewport.

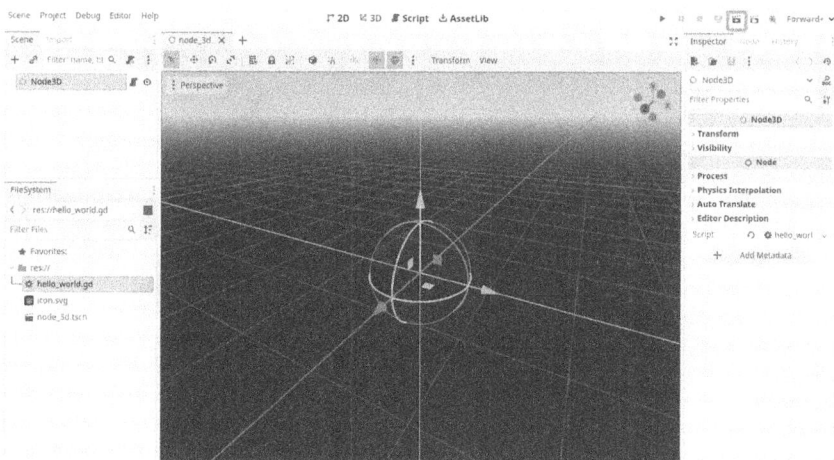

FIGURE 4.5   Running the active scene.

When you run your scene using the Play button, an empty window will pop up. This is your game in action, running a separate process. But you probably won't see anything inside the window because a default scene is created empty. It doesn't include any cameras, and it doesn't include any objects to see. If you've added these things yourself, then your scene may show some content. In any case, by attaching your *Hello World* script to a node in the scene, it will have run already, if attached and written correctly. If you close your game by closing the pop-up window, you can view the *Output* panel to see the results of your script file (see Figure 4.6).

The *Output* panel should display the message 'Hello World' because this is where all statements end up when run through the *print* function. This message is printed to the *Output* panel at the same moment the *print* command is executed, and the message remains in the *Output* panel for you to read later. If you don't see the message in the *Output* window, then ensure your script is attached to an object, and further that your call to *print* is included within the *_ready* function of that script. Printing messages this way is practically useful for debugging in game development because by seeing your messages appear in the *Output* panel, you can confirm that a specific line of code (the code featuring *print*) was reached and executed successfully. If your script were attached to multiple objects, then you would see the message printed once per object. Consider the revised code in Code Sample 4.3.

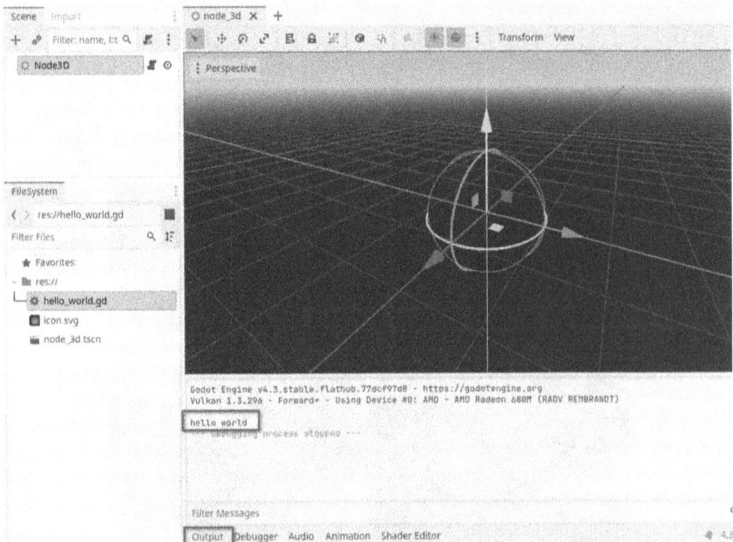

FIGURE 4.6   Viewing the Output panel.

CODE SAMPLE 4.3

```
extends Node

func _ready():
        print(name)
```

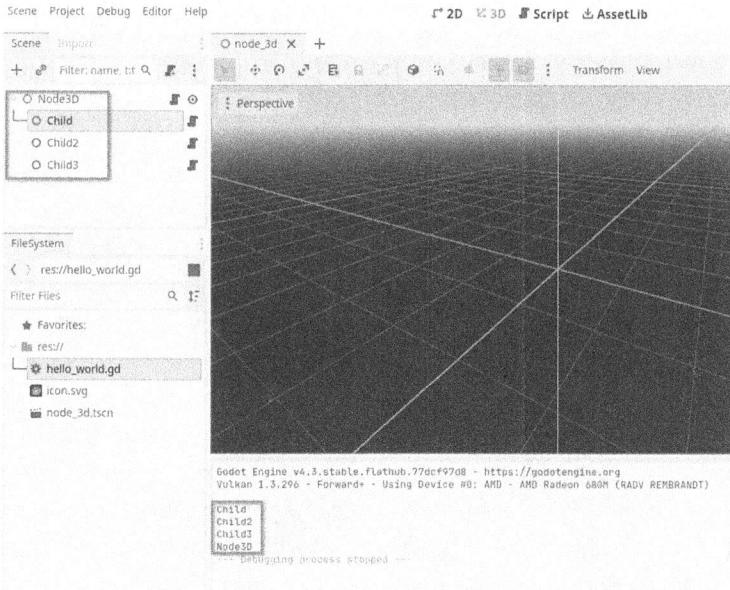

FIGURE 4.7   Printing to the Output panel from multiple objects.

This code replaces the literal message 'Hello World' with a variable *name*. This variable (called *name*) is included on all objects and refers to the user-defined name of the object (to which the script is attached) as it appears in the *Scene* tab. If you now add more nodes to the scene (such as empty nodes or meshes), rename each one, and then finally attach the script to each of those objects, you'll see the different names printed in the *Output* window when you hit *Play* again, as the script is run on each object (see Figure 4.7).

4.3 GAME CRITICAL EVENTS IN GDSCRIPT

The previous section explored the reserved, and Godot-specific, *_ready* function in the context of *Hello World*. The *_ready* function, as we saw, is a special *event*. It is called automatically by Godot for an object on the first occasion that it's added to a Scene. If the object is in the Scene from its beginning, then it will be called when the Scene begins too. But the function could be called later if the object (to which it is attached) is added to the scene later, such as when a bullet or ammo object is instantiated later when the trigger is pulled on a gun. In this sense, _ready is analogous to the *Start* function, featured in the Unity engine. The _ready event is critically important to gameplay programmers because it's often necessary to run initialization and configuration code when an object is first created. The _ready function is not the only important event that Godot offers us for running code. There are many others. This section explores the most common and widely used events in Godot.

4.3.1 The _process Event

Every object in the scene has its own heartbeat. This 'heartbeat' is referred to as *frames* or *processes*, and these processes typically occur *many times per second*. This ratio (*processes per second*) is literally the game's *frame rate*. Godot offers us the _process event to signify a single process (a single frame or heartbeat), which is run automatically for any script on an object. The _process event is therefore called many times per second – at least, when your game is working normally! Obviously, if the _process event were to happen less frequently than once per second (such as once for every two seconds), then it means the frame rate for your game has dropped so low that there is clearly a serious performance issue occurring. In fact, even once or twice per second is a terribly low frame rate. You don't want that. A more sensible range would be 50 or 60 frames per second. The _process event is the single most important opportunity to perform repeated or prolonged behaviors for an object. This includes making an object move, rotate, or change size; checking whether the object (if it's an NPC) has sustained damage; and checking whether the object (if it's the player character) should respond to input, such as a button press. Consider Code Sample 4.4.

CODE SAMPLE 4.4   ROTATE.GD – MAKING A 3D OBJECT SPIN AROUND ITS CENTRAL AXIS

```
extends Node3D
func _process(delta: float) -> void:
        var _rot_speed:float = 45
        rotate(Vector3.UP, deg_to_rad(_rot_speed *
delta))
```

NOTE. Go ahead and put this code (in Sample 4.4) onto a cube object in a 3D scene and then try it. Use a *MeshInstance3D* node to create a quick cube.

The above code, in Sample 4.4, should be attached to any 3D object, such as a Cube mesh (see Chapter 2). When attached to a 3D object in a 3D scene, combined with a camera and a light, the object will rotate continuously around its center at a user-defined rotational speed. This code uses the *_process* function to update an object's rotation forever. There are some important points to note about this code, as below.

1. This script file (rotate.gd) uses the extends command and extends from a *Node3D*, as opposed to a *Node*. A *Node* extension will cause your script to inherit all variables and functions that are essential to all nodes. A *Node3D* includes everything in a *Node*, plus additional functions and variables that are specific to 3D objects. This includes the *rotate* function, which is used later in the *_process* event.

2. The *_process* function accepts an input argument of *delta*, which is a floating-point value (a decimal number). This number is the amount of time in seconds since the previous *_process* was called for this object. A value of 1, for example, would mean that 1 second had elapsed since the previous *_process* occurred. It would also mean that the frame rate was 1 frame per second. A value of 0.5 seconds would mean 2 frames per second and half a second since *_process* was previously called. This value will therefore be of the form *1/frame_rate*. As a result, it will usually be a small, fractional value. The higher the frame rate, the smaller this number will be. This value is incredibly useful for ensuring that objects animate at predictable speeds over time, as we'll see.

3. This *_process* function uses a locally defined variable of *_rot_speed* (which is defined as float) for specifying the rotational speed of an object in degrees per second. The default value of 45 means the object will turn a total of 45 degrees in one second. This line does not actually rotate the object. Rather, it only defines the speed to rotate.

4. Next, the *rotate* function, which is inherited from *Node3D*, is used to rotate the object on each frame. It rotates the object relatively, in increments, turning the object by small fractions in each frame. The rotate function accepts two arguments. The first is the axis around

which rotation should occur, and the second is the amount of rotation to apply around that axis. The first argument is specified as a three-component number (a **Vector**). Specifically, the *Up Vector* is (0,1,0), creating a straight vertical pole along the Y axis through the center of the object, around which rotation will happen. The second argument converts the _rot_speed (in degrees per second) to radians per second. In Godot, angles are specified in the metric angular measure of *Radians*, as opposed to the commonly used and intuitive degrees.

5. Notice that the _rot_speed is multiplied with the *delta* variable. This is to keep the rotation speed constant over time since *speed * delta* will scale to the frame rate measure. If _rot_speed were not so multiplied, then the object would rotate at different rates on each frame, as the frame rate fluctuates.

NOTE. Find out more about *Node3D* from the Godot online documentation here: https://docs.godotengine.org/en/stable/classes/class_node 3d.html.

4.3.2 The _physics_process Event

The *_process* event has an important counterpart event, called *_physics_process*. It can be confusing to newcomers as to which one to use for prolonged multi-frame behaviors. *_process* is called once per frame and therefore reflects the game's true *frame rate*. The frame rate can vary, depending on what a computer is doing. Resource-intensive processes, for example, can cause frame rate drops. So, you can never be sure exactly how often *_process* will be called in any second. This isn't necessarily a problem because you can use variables, like *delta*, as a multiplier to speeds to ensure consistent behavior that is fixed to time. Nonetheless, Godot also features a dedicated physics system for handling object interactions (such as gravity and collision detection). This system typically updates at a lesser frequency than the frame rate. By default, the frequency of the physics system is 60 ticks per second. For this reason, if you're working with the physics system (such as checking for collisions), then you should use *_physics_process* to contain your code rather than *_process* when performing repeated and prolonged behaviors. For a broad discussion on _process vs. _physics_process, please see the online documentation here:

https://docs.godotengine.org/en/stable/tutorials/scripting/idle_and_physics_processing.html.

To change the physics frequency, you can use the Project Settings. Select *Project > Project Settings* from the application menu, and then choose *Physics > Common Category*. From here, you can specify the *Ticks per second* to control the frequency of the *_physics_process* function. You should try to keep this value as low as possible while still achieving the physical accuracy you need. I recommend leaving this setting at the default of 60 unless you have a compelling reason to change it (see Figure 4.8).

4.3.3 The _unhandled_input Event

If you need relatively low-level and direct access to input devices, such as the keyboard and mouse, then the *_unhandled_input* event is very useful. This event is run automatically by Godot whenever it detects that the mouse cursor moved, a mouse button was clicked, or a keyboard key was pressed or released, among other events. Using this function, in combination with checks and conditional statements, you can effectively determine

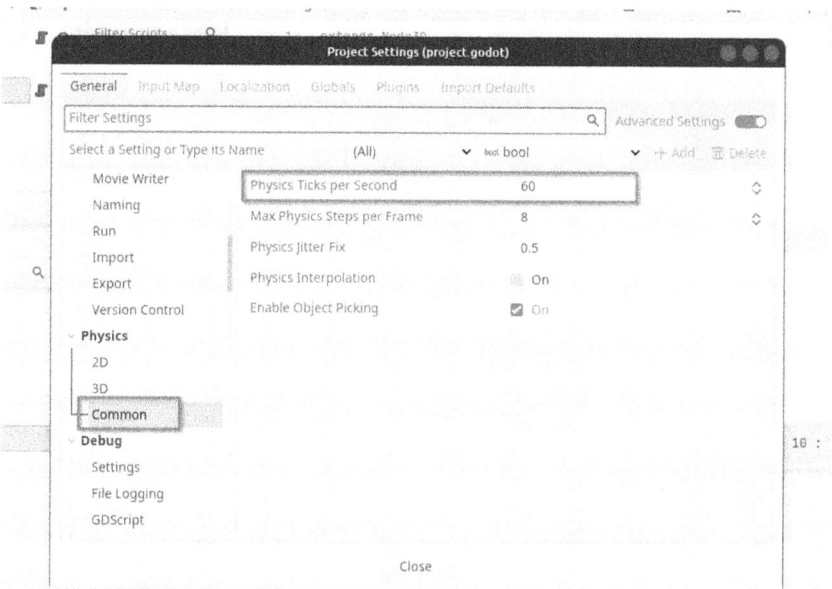

FIGURE 4.8   Controlling a project's ticks per second.

what input the player most recently provided. For example, the following code in Sample 4.5 determines whether the space bar was pressed on the keyboard and then prints a confirmation message to the *Output* panel in response.

CODE SAMPLE 4.5   CHECKING FOR SPACE BAR INPUT

```
func _ unhandled _ input(event):
        if event is InputEventKey:
                if event.pressed and event.keycode ==
KEY_SPACE:
 print("space bar pressed")
```

The main problem with this event, when used to read input data, is that it provides raw input data, unabstracted and totally dependent on the input device. For example, if the player changes from a keyboard to a gamepad, or the player changes keyboard mapping, or the player inverts the mouse controls, then your code remains fixed and inflexible to such player-defined customizations. This event may be useful at the prototyping or debugging stages of development, but you would not normally read player input this way in the final code. In this next section, we'll see a better approach to reading player input.

4.4 READING PLAYER INPUT

Input refers collectively to all the instructions that players provide a game-to-action command during gameplay: run, shoot, jump, turn, collect, stop, and others are examples of the commands. The list of commands in a game depends on the genre, style, gameplay, and design of the game. These instructions, nonetheless, are provided to a game through *Input Devices*, also known as *Input Peripherals*. This includes keyboards, mice, game-pads, joysticks, steering wheels, touch screens, hand controllers, and many more. The list of device types is almost endless. Ideally, we'd like to support all device types in all configurations to make our games as accessible as possible. That would be great, but this isn't normally practicable or economically possible for a developer, given the sheer variety and specificity of devices. So, the next best thing is to support the most common device types and their most common configurations. The way to approach this in a game engine, like Godot, is through abstraction; that is, by creating an *Input Map*. This map is a higher-order many-to-one database that sits above the physical hardware and connects our physical input devices, on the one hand, to in-game commands on the other. For example, it may connect both a *space-bar press* and a *left-mouse-click* to the in-game command *Jump*. Likewise, we may connect a *keyboard-left-arrow-press* and a *gamepad-left-arrow-press* to the in-game command *Turn Left*. The Input Map makes it possible to seamlessly reconnect the input hardware differently to the in-game commands, without the coder needing to rewrite any code. This allows the player easy customization of controls because our code won't directly read input from the devices. We won't assume that the controls themselves are predefined. Rather, our code will instead consult the intermediary Input Map to understand player input. Let's now see how this Input system is handled in Godot. To start, select *Project > Project Settings* from the application menu (see Figure 4.9).

4.4.1 Configuring an Input Map for Buttons

From the *Project Settings* menu, choose the *Input Map* tab. This displays an Input Map Editor. This is a complete database of *Inputs* connected to *Actions*. By default, the map is empty, and so it contains no entries (see Figure 4.10).

Let's configure an example *fire* or *shoot* button to get started using the Input Map. Crucially, this type of input (a button press) is a single one-shot button press that initiates an immediate in-game action when pressed, like shooting, jumping, or interacting. It doesn't have an analog component of

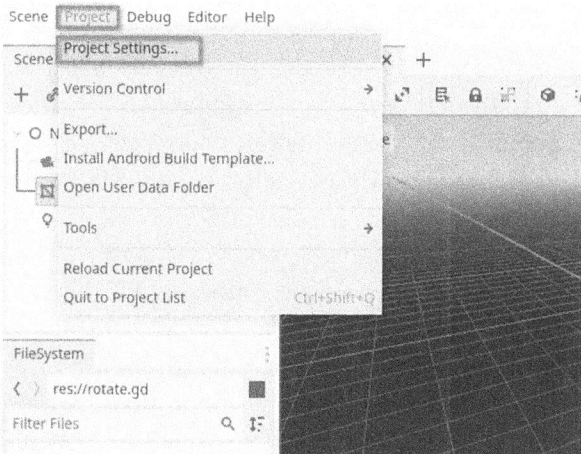

FIGURE 4.9   Accessing project settings from the application menu.

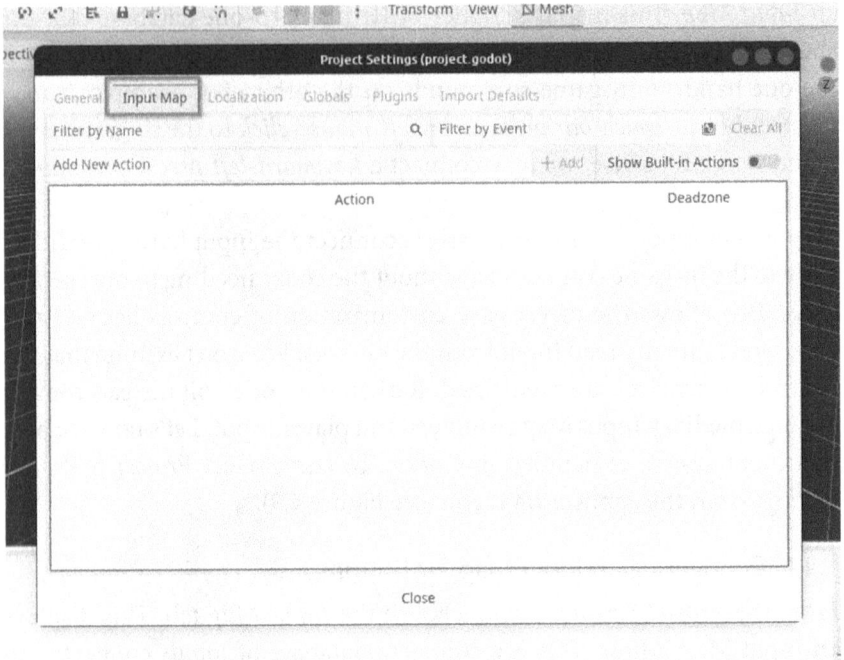

FIGURE 4.10   Getting started with Input Maps.

input, such as a joystick, which can be partially left or fully left. A button press is either on or off. To start, type in a new name of the Input Map connection to build. Typically, you'll name this connection after the in-game action the input will trigger. I will name this connection *Fire*. Once named, click *Add* to add a new entry to the Input Map (see Figure 4.11).

Next, let's connect physical inputs to this *Action*. Fire will be triggered by a *Ctrl* button press on the keyboard and by a *left-mouse-click*. To start, click the + icon in the new Fire entry (see Figure 4.12).

From the popup Event Configuration dialog, choose *Mouse Buttons*, then select *Left Mouse Button*, and finally click the *OK* button to confirm the change (see Figure 4.13).

Now let's add the keyboard button press. To do this, click the + icon again. From here, you could scan the entire list for the *Ctrl* button, but there are many keys to search through! Instead, click the Listen button, and then press Ctrl on the keyboard (see Figure 4.14).

You've now created two physical input connections to the Fire action in the Input Map. Check over your settings to ensure they're correct (see Figure 4.15).

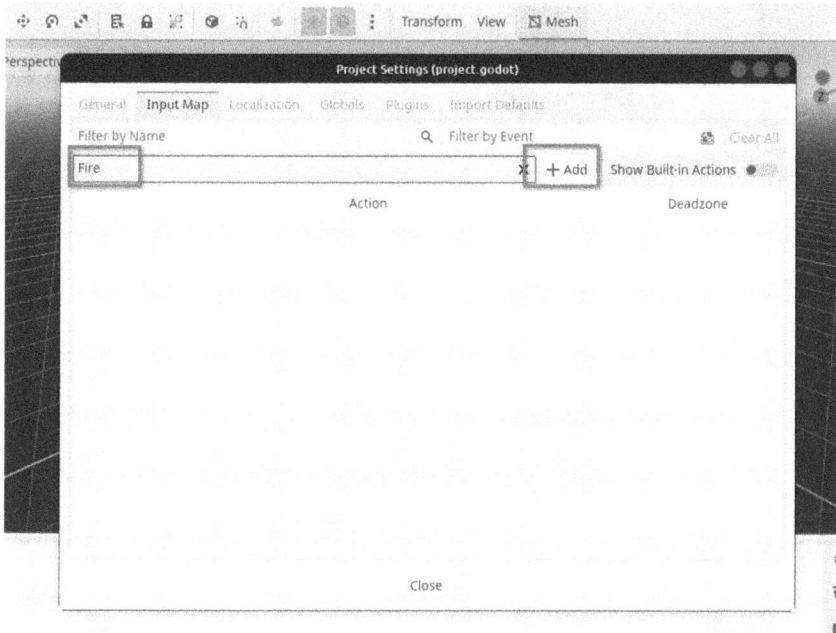

FIGURE 4.11   Creating a Fire Entry in the Input Map.

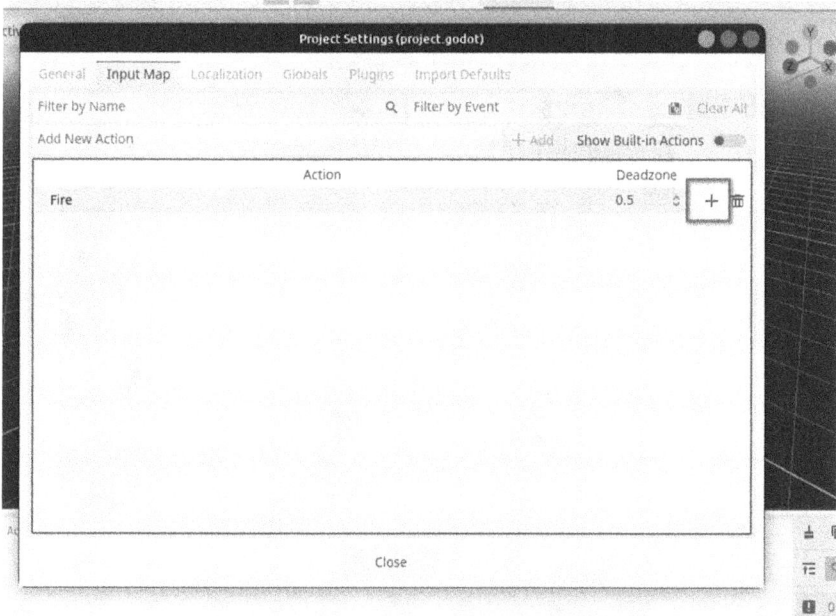

FIGURE 4.12   Building a physical button connection.

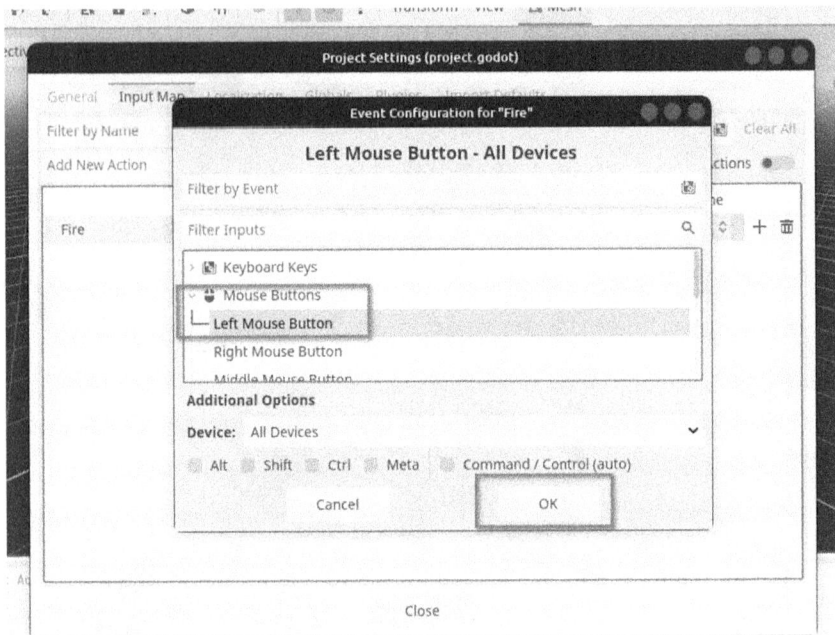

FIGURE 4.13   Confirming the Left Button Click.

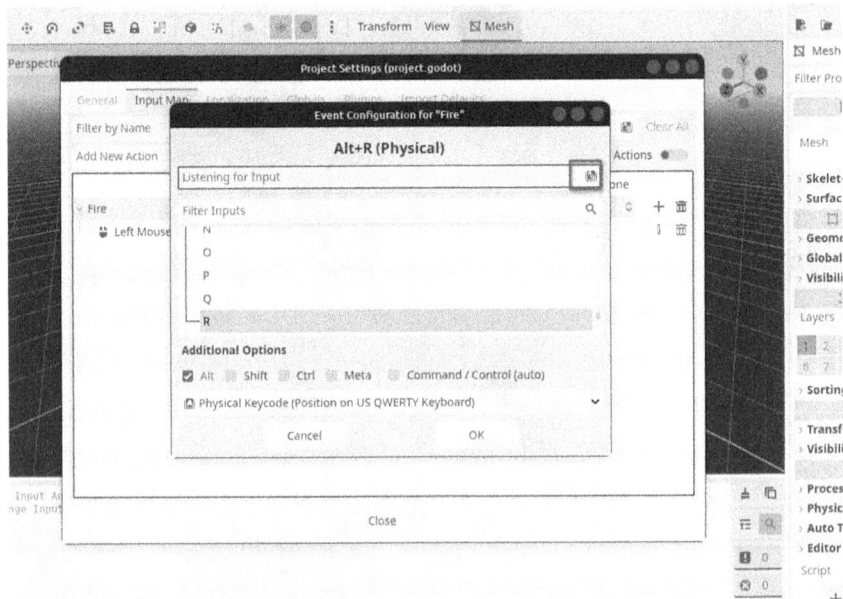

FIGURE 4.14   Listening for keyboard input.

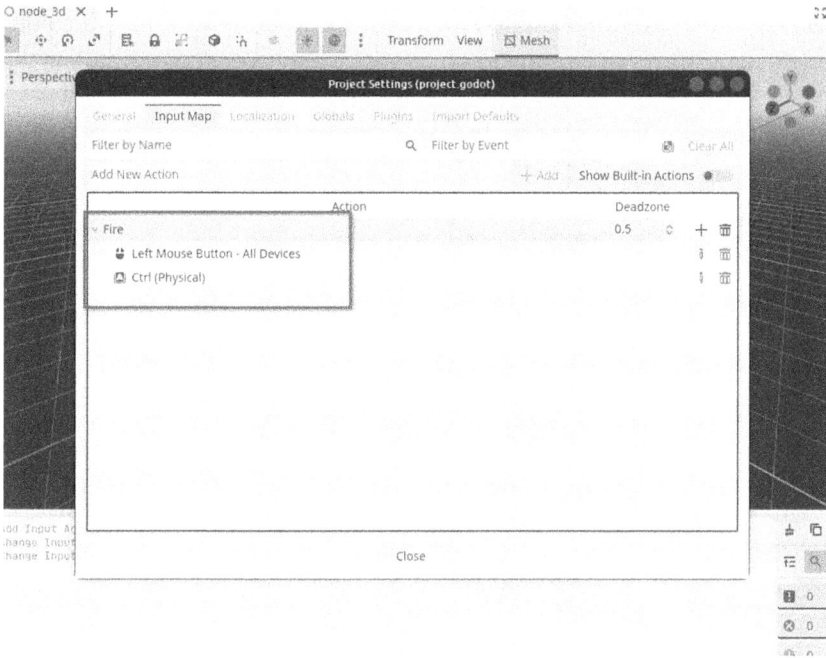

FIGURE 4.15   Reviewing the Fire button settings.

4.4.2 Reading Button Presses

Finally, let's see some code to read the Input Map and determine if Fire is being activated. To do this, consider the following Code Sample 4.6.

Here, in Code Sample 4.6 as above, the function *Input.is_action_pressed* is being used to determine if any input combination for *Fire* is currently being activated. This function will return true if either the left mouse button is being pressed or the Ctrl key is being pressed. It will repeatedly return true if these buttons are held down, and it will return true for as long as they are held down. Once released, or if never pressed at all, this function will return false. So, this method of reading the button press is

---

CODE SAMPLE 4.6   READ_INPUT.GD FOR READING USER INPUT

```
extends Node
func _process(delta: float) -> void:
     if Input.is_action_pressed("Fire"):
             print('Fire is being pressed now')
```

perhaps not useful for a single-*Fire* mechanic (such as a shot from a gun) in which only the first instance of a press is usually needed to simulate the trigger press. Instead, consider Code Sample 4.7.

CODE SAMPLE 4.7   READING INPUT FOR A ONE-SHOT MECHANIC

```
extends Node
func _process(delta: float) -> void:
        if Input.is_action_just_pressed("Fire"):
                print('Fire was pressed')
```

Code Sample 4.7 will return true on the first occasion that *Fire* is pressed, and then false thereafter. It will return true again only if *Fire* is pressed again. This function has a companion function of *Input.is_action_just_released*. This alternative returns true for releases rather than presses.

4.4.3 Creating Axis Controls with an Input Map

Determining whether a button is pressed or released, up or down, is ultimately a question about Booleans. The binary states of true and false are together sufficient for representing this kind of data meaningfully. But what about analog joystick motion for left and right or up and down? In this case, the joystick could be fully held left, partially held left, fully held right, partially held right, or not held at all. In essence, we have a number of lines of inputs. This has *0* at the center for 'not held', *-1* for fully held left, and 1 for fully held right. Fractional values are also possible in the *-1* to *1* range, such as *0.5* and *-0.3*, to express degrees of being held in either the left or right direction. The same applies up and down too. Let's configure the horizontal and vertical input axes for keyboard input using the Godot Input Map. To do this, open the Input Map window and create a new Action called *Left* (see Figure 4.16).

Next, click the + icon to add a new mapping, choose *Joypad Axis Left*, and assign the *keyboard left arrow* and the *keyboard A key* (for WASD controls) (see Figure 4.17).

Now let's do the same for the right axis and also for up and down, assigning the relevant keys and joystick states (see Figure 4.18).

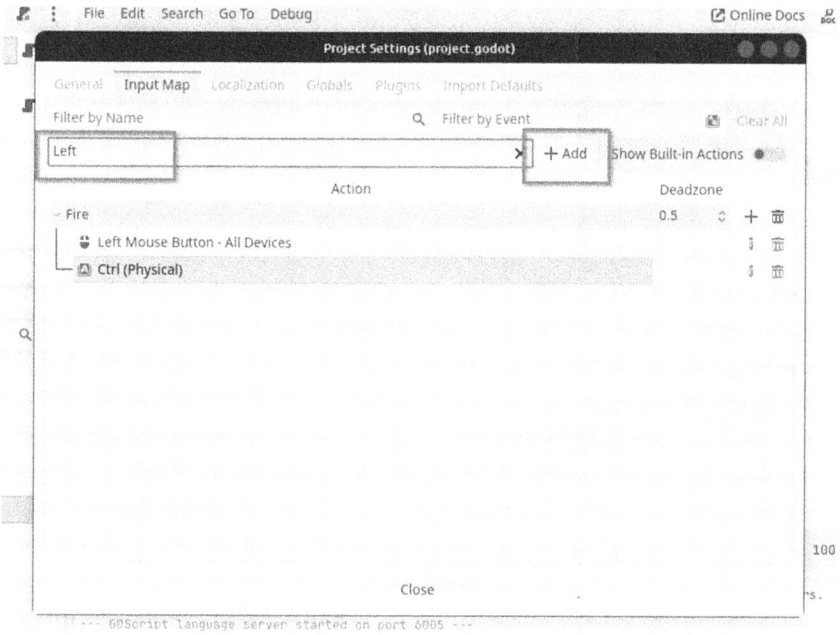

FIGURE 4.16   Creating a Left Axis.

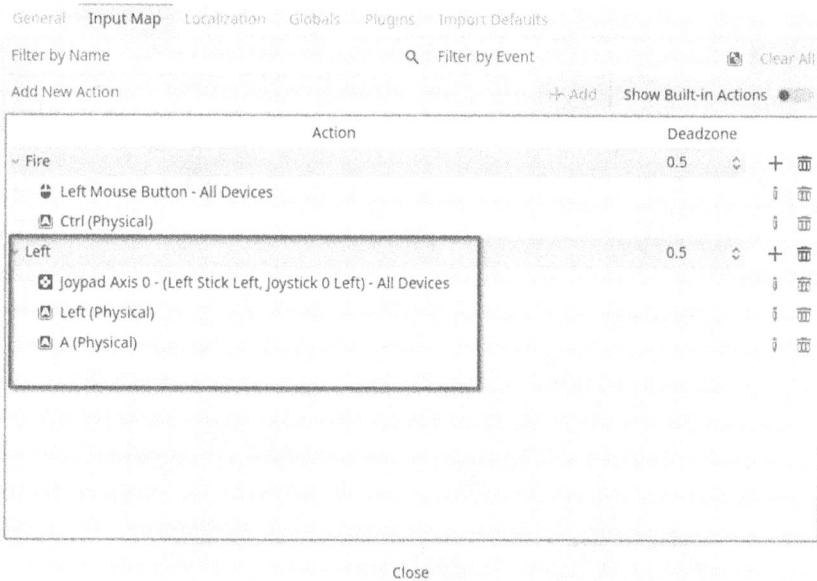

FIGURE 4.17   Completing the Left Axis.

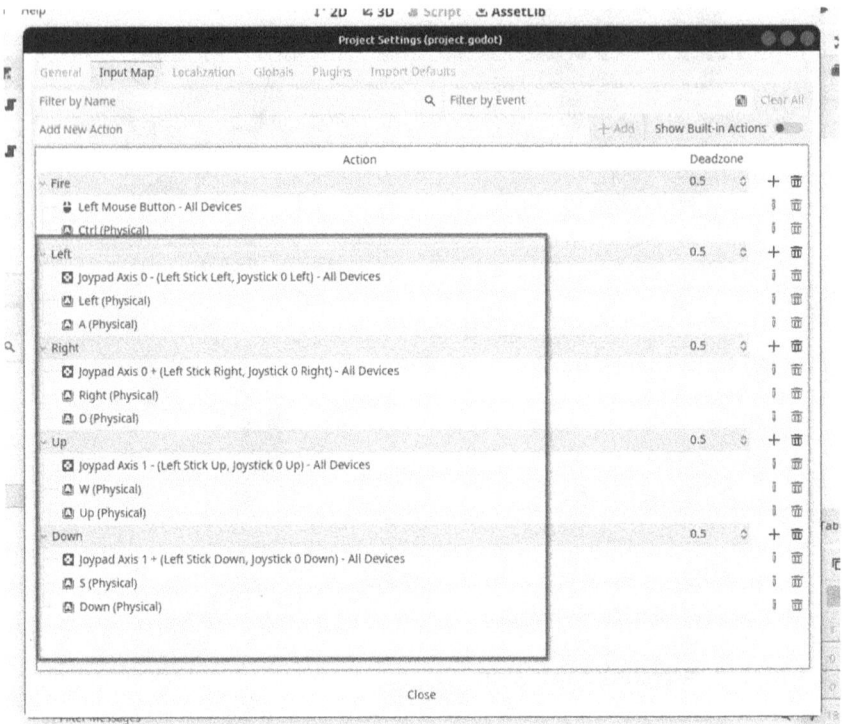

FIGURE 4.18   Completing all Input Axes.

4.4.4 Creating Axis Controls with an Input Map

In this section, we'll read input data from the directional axes, which include left and right and up and down. To do this, we'll add code to the _process event. See Code Sample 4.8.

CODE SAMPLE 4.8   READING DIRECTIONAL INPUT

```
func _ process(delta: float) -> void:
        var _left:float = Input.
get_action_strength("Left")
        var _right:float = Input.
get_action_strength("Right")
        var _up:float = Input.
get_action_strength("Up")
        var _down:float = Input.
get_action_strength("Down")
```

```
print("Left: " + var_to_str(_left))
print("Right: " + var_to_str(_right))
print("Up: " + var_to_str(_up))
print("Down: " + var_to_str(_down))
```

Each variable reads between 0 and 1, indicating whether the input is pressed and to what extent. Only the value of 0 signals that nothing is being pressed. We can go further with this idea and Vectorize the directional input for ease of reading and processing. Consider the following code in Sample 4.9.

CODE SAMPLE 4.9   VECTORIZING INPUT

```
func _process(delta: float) -> void:
        var _direction_input:Vector2 = Vector2.ZERO
        _direction_input.x = -Input.
get_action_strength("Left") + Input.
get_action_strength("Right")
        _direction_input.y = -Input.get_action_
strength("Down") + Input.get_action_strength("Up")
print(var_to_str(_direction_input))
```

The above code in Sample 4.9 converts the input data into Vector form such that left is (-1, 0), right is (1, 0), up is (0, 1), and down is (0, - 1). Combinations are possible too, such as (1,1) for up-and-right and (-1, 1) for down-and-left. If the player presses left and right simultaneously, or up and down, then *–1 + 1 = 0.*

4.5 EXPORTING VARIABLES

If a vehicle in a video game travels along a road, we need to specify *how fast*. If an NPC punches as a form of attack, we need to define *how hard*. If the player character jumps as a mechanic, then we need to express *how high*. In all these cases, and in many more, we use variables to define this kind of data. By default, variables are created and set in code, and they are hidden from the Inspector interface to avoid the Inspector becoming littered with unnecessary information. However, there are times – perhaps many times – when it is convenient and important to expose a variable to the Inspector interface, allowing its values to be read and set visually, saving us from editing the code directly. Godot supports this behavior using a special keyboard at the variable declaration. Consider Code Sample 4.10.

CODE SAMPLE 4.10   EXPORTING VARIABLES

```
extends Node3D
@export var __rot_speed:float = 180
func _process(delta: float) -> void:
        rotate(Vector3.UP, deg_to_rad(__rot_speed *
delta))
```

Code Sample 4.10, which rotates a mesh object, demonstrates the @ *export* keyword. This keyword exposes a variable to the Inspector. This allows the variable to be read and set directly via a type-in field in the Inspector, and the Inspector takes precedence. That is, if *__rot_speed* is initialized to *180* in code but this differs in the Inspector, where it is set to *90*, then the Inspector value is used (see Figure 4.19).

NOTE. There's a lot more to learn about Exported Properties in Godot. See the online documentation here: https://docs.godotengine.org/en/ stable/tutorials/scripting/gdscript/gdscript_exports.html.

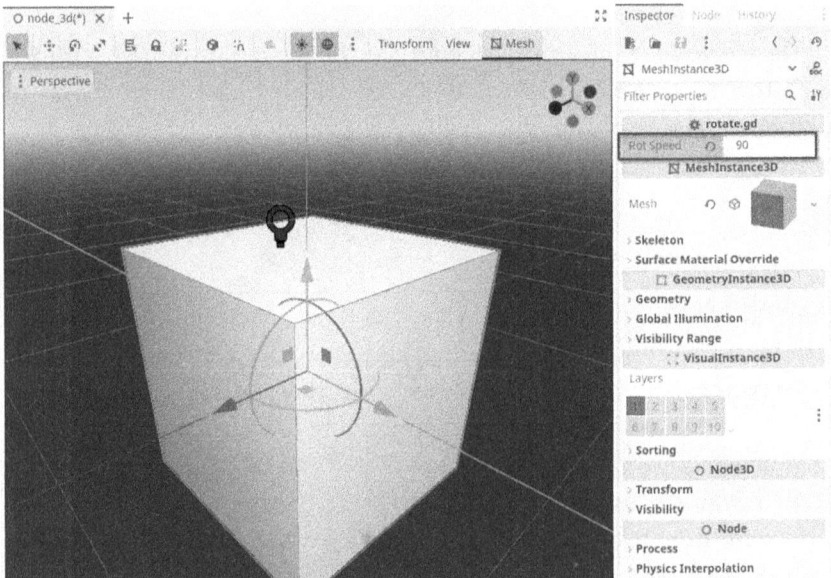

FIGURE 4.19   Exporting a variable.

4.6 SIGNALS AND THE OBSERVER PATTERN

Video games commonly feature many types of events that happen during gameplay; for example, the player jumps, an enemy shoots, the level begins, health is restored, a timer expires, a cutscene begins, an NPC starts patrolling, another NPC starts patrolling again, and the list goes on. The range of possible events, and their actual frequency in-game, is entirely determined by the game design. Each event itself can be the beginning of a knotty chain reaction of other events that flow as a consequence across the entire scene. For example, as the player collides with a dangerous enemy bullet, their health reduces in response, and if it reduces to below zero, the player then dies, and on their death, the level must reset, and so on. Now, this event complexity would get messy in code, especially for large games if the events are left unmanaged and unsystematized. We could end up with a nightmarish spaghetti code of ad hoc conditionals and fragile events that are wholly contingent and difficult to follow. Especially so for an outsider reading our code for the first time, and eventually for ourselves too after a short time has passed and the code is no longer fresh in our own minds. So, Godot offers a robust solution for working with events, specifically for connecting events to each other in predictable and clear ways. It's therefore important to know about this system before coding your first large game in Godot. This system is called *Signals*, and it implements the famous *Observer Design Pattern*, as we'll see. To start, we'll use the Signals system in code that is ready-made, and then we'll make our own Signals for our own objects.

4.6.1 Creating a Game Timer

Let's begin with a brand new and empty Godot project as a starting point for this section. From here, we'll build an empty *3D scene*, featuring a timer set to a specific period (measured in seconds), which counts down as soon as the level starts, until eventually it expires. On expiry, the game responds by printing the words 'Game Over' to the debug console. That is, we'll create some code in a script file that runs automatically when an event in another object (the timer) happens, namely, the timer expiry. Now, printing to the console is not an especially exciting response, but that's not important here. This section demonstrates the power of signals generally, allowing you to connect any number of events to a single in-game event. The key takeaway here is in understanding practically how any event can be wired to any number of responses purely by way of the signal system. To start, let's add a Timer object to a 3D scene. To do this, add a timer. Choose *Create Node and* then search for a *Timer* object. Click Create (see Figure 4.20).

Select the *Timer* object in the scene and use the *Wait Time* field to specify how long the timer should wait before 'expiring'. That is, how long (in seconds) before *sending a signal that other objects in the scene can listen for.* In this case, let's choose a *Wait Time* of 3 seconds (see Figure 4.21).

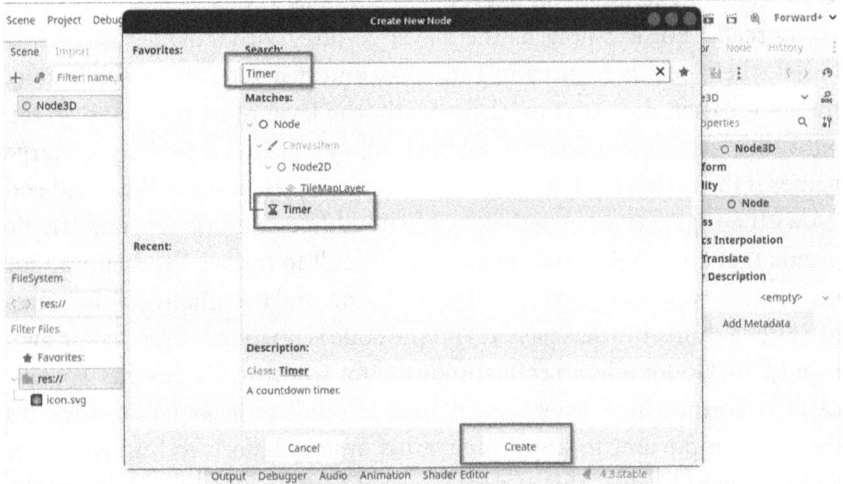

FIGURE 4.20   Creating a Timer node.

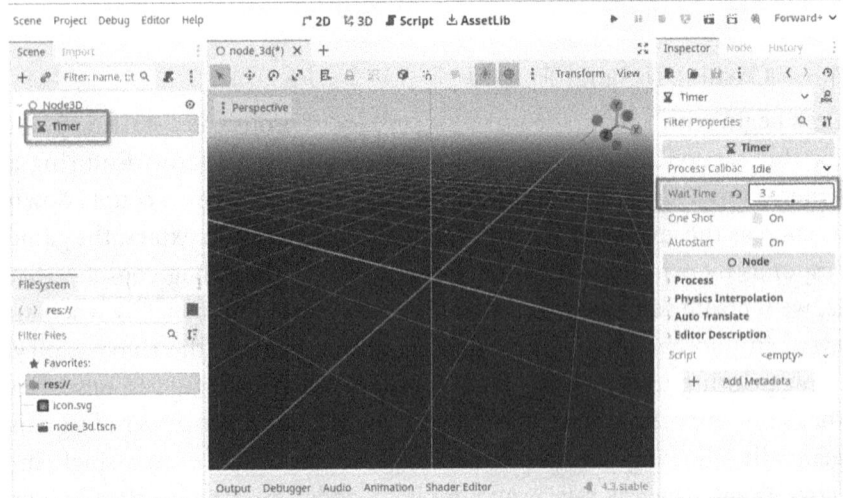

FIGURE 4.21   Setting the Wait Time for a Timer.

Now we'll create a new, empty object that will exist in the scene only to host a script file, which we will create shortly to respond to the timer expiry. Create a new Marker3D node (see Figure 4.22).

Next, let's create a new script named *TimedOut.gd*. This should be attached to the recently created Marker3D node and inherited from Marker3D (since it will be attached to a Marker3D node). See Figure 4.23, and then see Code Sample 4.11.

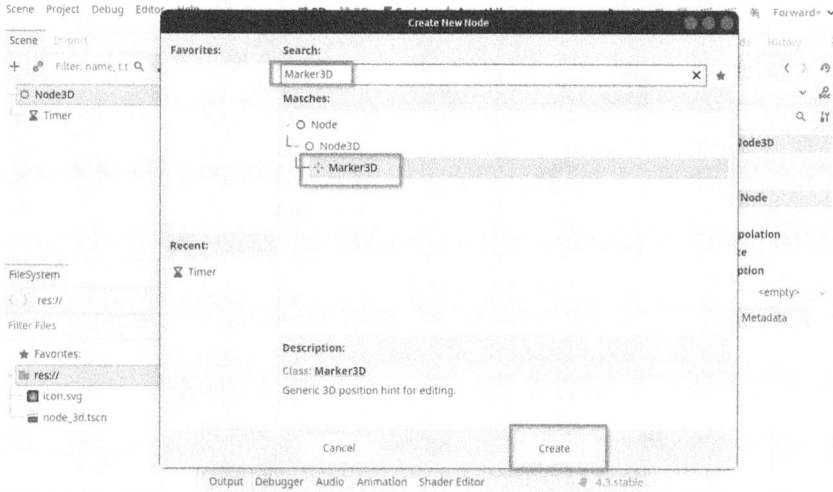

FIGURE 4.22   Create a Marker3D node for holding a Script File.

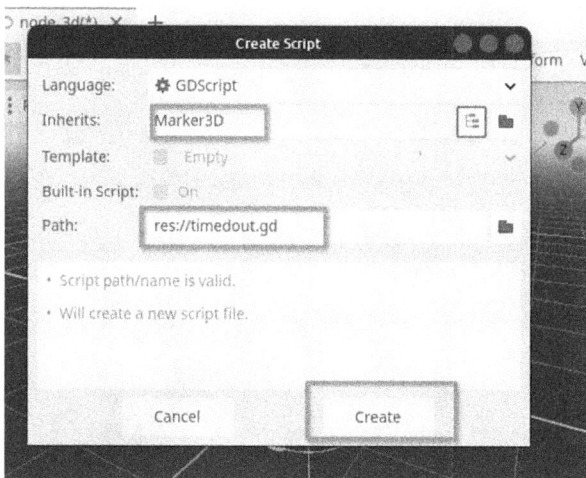

FIGURE 4.23   Creating a new script derived from the Marker3D class.

CODE SAMPLE 4.11   CREATING CODE
TO RUN ON A TIMER EXPIRY

```
extends Node3D
extends Marker3D
func on_timer_expiry():
        print("Timer has expired!")
```

The above code in Sample 4.11 contains only one function to print a message. As it stands, when this code is attached to a *Marker3D* node and when the scene is run, the code inside the function will not automatically execute because it is not yet attached to the *Timer* through Signals. To do this, select the *Timer* object, and from the Inspector, change to the *Node* tab. Within the *Node* tab, ensure the *Signals* tab is active to view all available Signals for the selected object (see Figure 4.24).

The *timeout* signal is invoked (executed) when the timer expires. That means *any and all* connected code to that signal will run on that event. You can connect multiple functions to a single Signal. It supports a *one-to-many* relationship. To connect code to this *Signal*, double-click the *Arrow* icon next to the **timeout** name, and this will display the *Signal Connection Window* (see Figure 4.25).

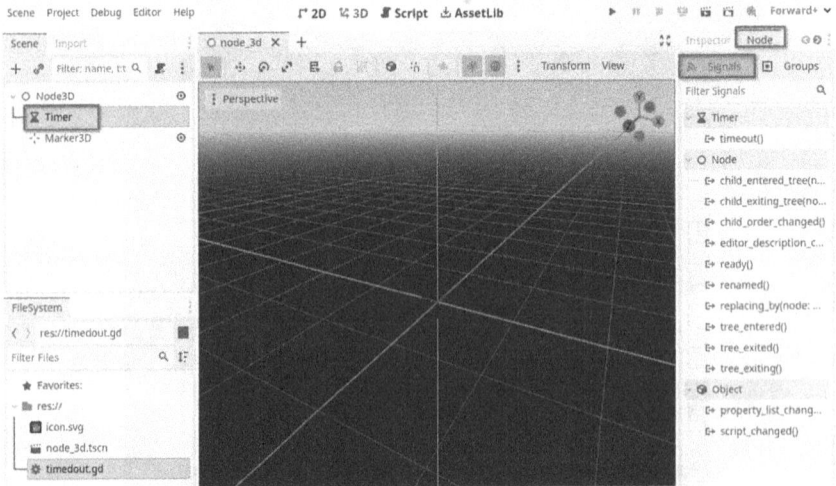

FIGURE 4.24   Finding relevant Signals for an Object.

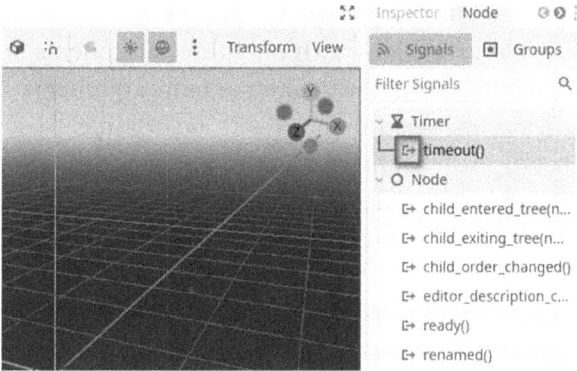

FIGURE 4.25   Opening the Signal Connection Window.

The Signal Connection Window lets you select objects and code to attach. In this case, we attached the *timeout* script (with a function inside) to a separate *Marker3D* object. From the Nodes list, select the *Marker3D* object. Then select the *Pick* button for the *Receiver* field (see Figure 4.26).

The *Pick* Dialog will show a list of all functions inside the script, which is attached to the object, that are compatible destinations for the Signal.

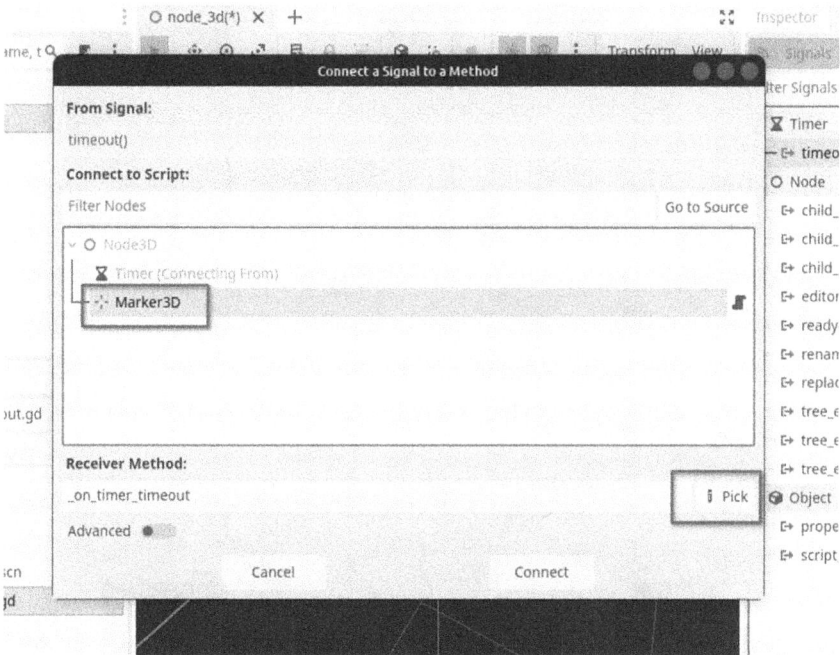

FIGURE 4.26   Find and select a Connecting Object.

That is all functions whose argument list matches the Signal expectations. If the Signal invokes functions with only three arguments, for example, then it will not show functions with fewer or more arguments. The *timeout* event for the *Timer* expects functions with no arguments, so all empty-argument functions will be shown for selection, including the one we created in Code Sample 4.11. Select our function *on_timer_expiry*, and then choose *OK*. Then choose *Connect* from the Signal Connection Window (see Figure 4.27).

You can confirm that a successful connection has been made, as a green entry now appears in the Signal list for the timer when viewed in the Inspector (see Figure 4.28).

Finally, return to the timer by selecting it and enabling the *Autostart* property from the Inspector. This ensures the timer starts as the scene begins (see Figure 4.29).

Now run the scene, and the timer expiry will cause our scripted function to run automatically every three seconds.

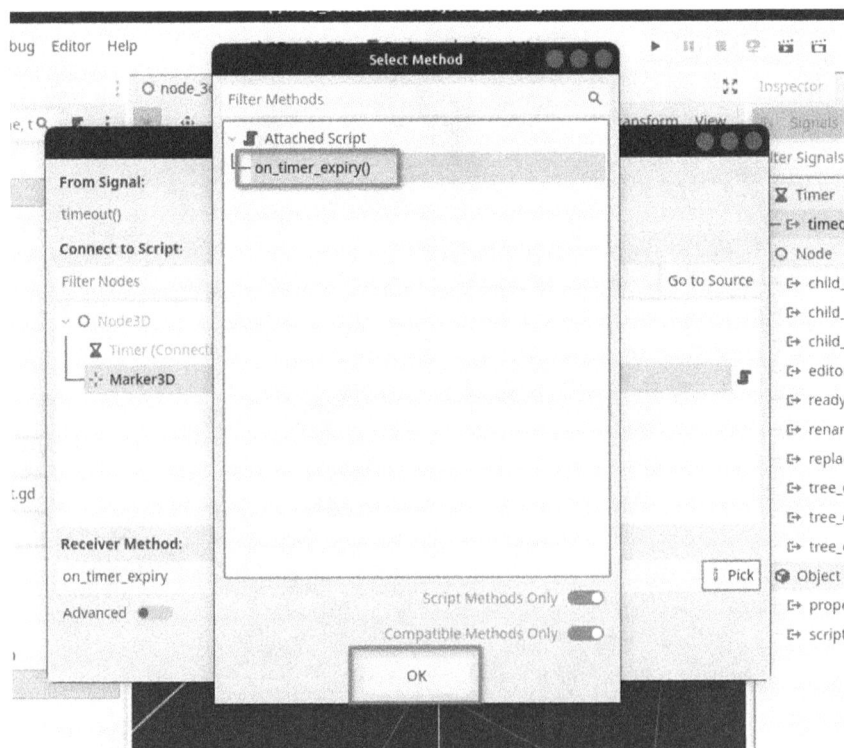

FIGURE 4.27   Connecting the signal to a named Function.

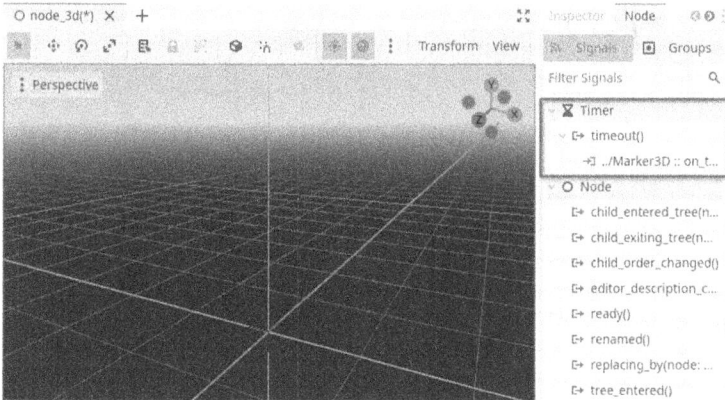

FIGURE 4.28   Confirming the Signal Connection.

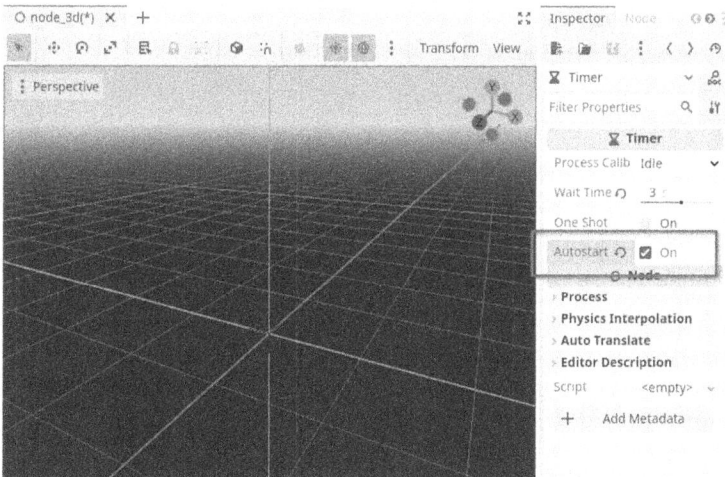

FIGURE 4.29   Enabling AutoStart

NOTE. To disconnect a Signal after it has been connected, right-click on the connection from the *Signals* tab in the *Inspector*, and then choose *Disconnect* from the context menu (see Figure 4.30).

4.6.2 Connecting a Signal in Code

The previous section demonstrated how to connect a signal from a timer to a function in a Script, manually and through the Godot UI via the Inspector. This is a convenient mouse-driven method for connecting one signal to one function with objects that already exist in the scene at design

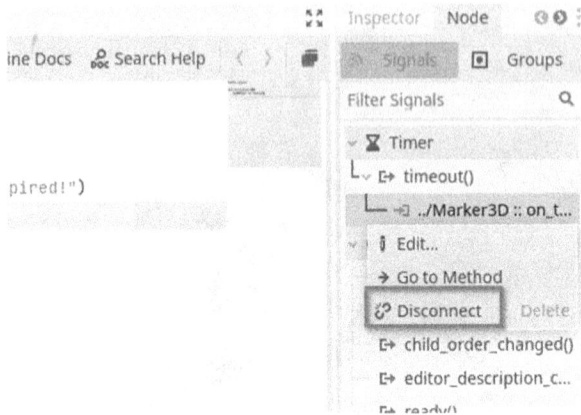

FIGURE 4.30   Disconnecting a Signal.

time, such as the *Marker3D* object and the *Timer* Object. But how would we connect a dynamically created object using Signals? That is, an object spawned at runtime. Or how would we connect thousands of objects via Signals and objects such as power-ups, collectibles, and NPCs? In these cases, it's much more convenient to connect them via code and automate the process, rather than connecting them one by one through the UI as we have done. So, let's disconnect the Signal from the *Timer*, which we config-ured previously, and see how to create the same connection through code rather than via the Inspector. To start, let's think more carefully about the relationship of our two objects. The *Marker3D* object, which contains our code for running, depends upon the *Timer* object. So, let's drag and drop the *Timer* object as a child of the *Marker3D*, using the Scene Hierarchy view. The *Timer* becomes indented (see Figure 4.31). This step is important later when writing the code, as we'll see.

Now let's redefine the code we created earlier in Code Sample 4.11. There, we defined only one function, which runs when invoked by a signal. Now, we'll write the code to include the same function as before but also include additional code to establish the signal connection beforehand. See Code Sample 4.12.

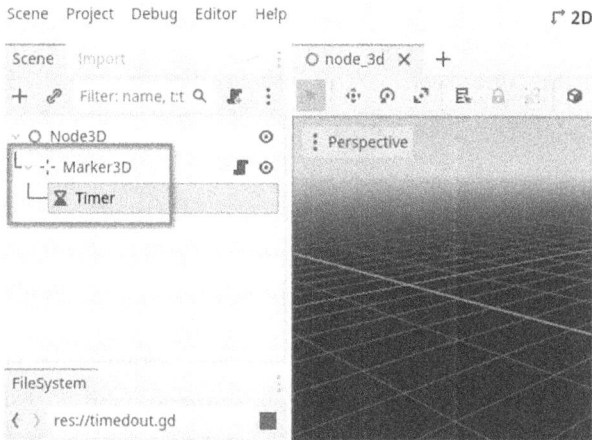

FIGURE 4.31　Moving the *Timer* to be a Child Object of the *Marker3D*.

CODE SAMPLE 4.12　CREATING CODE TO CREATE A SIGNAL CONNECTION

```
extends Marker3D
@onready var __Timer:Timer = $Timer
func _ready() -> void:
        __Timer.connect("timeout", on_timer_expiry)

func on_timer_expiry():
        print("Timer has expired!")
```

In Code Sample 4.12, there are two notable lines. First, the *@onready* command is used to auto-assign the variable *__Timer* a valid reference to the *Timer* object in the scene. This ensures that the *__Timer* object will be valid by the time the *_ready* event occurs, pointing to the timer object through which a Signal connection can be made. The constant *$Timer* value is a shorthand way to identify named objects in the scene if they are children of the current object (the object to which the script is attached). Thus, the *Timer* object is named *Timer* in the scene, and it is a child of the *Marker3D*. For this reason, *$Timer* refers to the *Timer* child. If the value were instead *$Node3D/Timer* then it would refer to a *Timer* object that was a grandchild of the current object.

The second line of interest uses the *__Timer.connect* function to build the connection. This function accepts two arguments at a minimum, namely the signal name (*timeout*) and the function to call when the signal occurs (*on_timer_expiry*). Now, when you run this code, it'll connect the signal from the timer, and our *on_time_expiry* function will run automatically for every timeout signal.

> NOTE. If this is the first time that you've seen the *Observer Pattern*, a common question is, why are we connecting two functions together (*timeout* and *on_timer_expiry*) in a complicated and indirect way through Signals, making our work harder? For our example, why don't we just amend the original *Timer* code internally to directly call *on_timer_expiry* when needed, without going through a Signals system at all? Surely, a direct function call between two objects is simpler than rerouting our entire function traffic through a separate events system? The reason is that the *Observer Pattern* tries to build *Object Decoupling*. Every direct function call between any two objects, X and Y creates a coupling, which is easy to break through code changes and needs continued maintenance to ensure the application runs smoothly. This is troublesome in the long term. We cannot be sure, for example, that in the future, new objects won't need to respond to our earlier events in new and different ways. So, by using a Signals system, we can easily connect multiple objects together in a managed way without having to revisit and recode any objects.

4.6.3 Creating Custom Signals

We saw previously that the *Timer* node supports a dedicated *timeout* signal, which runs any code attached to it whenever the timer expires. The *Timer* node is not alone in supporting Signals, however. The *VisibleOnScreenNotifier3D* node, for example, supports a signal that tells us when a specified 3D object becomes seen by a camera. Likewise, all Nodes support a *tree_entered* signal, which is invoked when the object enters the hierarchy of a scene, such as at the scene start or when an object is spawned dynamically into the scene. Almost every node type supports a range of public-facing signals like these, which we can connect code to as and when needed for our games. We also can define our own signals for our own scripts, making it easier to connect our code to other scripts and making it easier for third parties (including other team members and freelancers) to work with our code and connect it to their own. In this section, we'll create our own custom *Timer* object, which prints 'Hello World' at specified intervals and invokes a custom signal for each print. This allows other code to intercept those moments and add new behavior.

Consider the following Code Sample 4.14, which is a new script with signal functionality.

CODE SAMPLE 4.14   CODE FOR REPEATING A HELLO WORLD MESSAGE, WITH SIGNALS

```
extends Node
signal on_print_message(message_printed)
var __time_elapsed:float = 0
@export var __time_interval:float = 1
func _process(delta: float) -> void:
        __time_elapsed += delta
            if __time_elapsed >= __time_interval:
                __time_elapsed = 0
                var _message_to_print:String =
"hello world"
                print (_message_to_print)
        on_print_message.emit(_message_to_print)
```

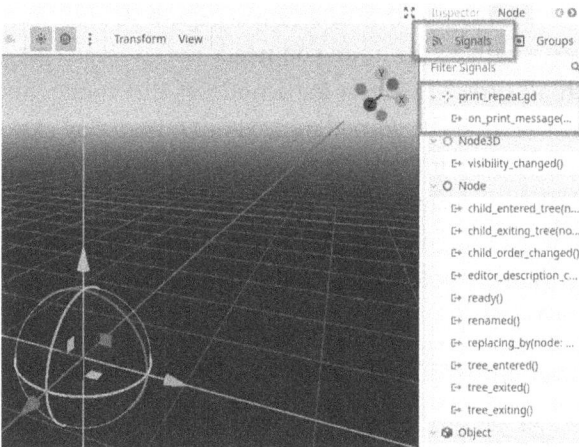

FIGURE 4.32   Adding custom signals to Objects.

When this code (in Sample 4.14) is attached to a node in the scene, you will see that the newly defined signal *on_print_message* is added to the Signals tab of the inspector. The **emit** function, which allows you to pass arguments, will call any functionality attached to the signal (see Figure 4.32).

4.7 NODES AND GROUPS

A Scene is a hierarchy of Nodes, and normally each node will be a derived class of the ancestor class *Node*, which contains all properties and behaviors common to all nodes. You can find more detailed information about this ancestor at the Godot online documentation here: https://docs.godotengine.org/en/stable/classes/class_node.html. An important skill in coding in GDScript is being able to reach outside of oneself and grab other surrounding nodes to interact with them. For example, NPC characters may need to connect with the Player object, wherever it is, to read the player's location in the scene. Likewise, if the player character is holding a weapon object in their hand, the player code will need to 'reach out' to the weapon code to check how much ammo is left. These examples, alongside many others, demonstrate that scripts and objects don't live in a vacuum but must reach out and connect with other scripts to fulfill their purpose effectively. This section explores some common ways to reference objects in the scene. Later chapters explore scenes in more depth.

4.7.1 Get Node

One of the most common ways to find a named object in the scene is to use the *get_node* function. This function accepts a string argument, which can be a relative path to the node you need. For example, *get_node('gun')* would search all direct children for a node of that name, and the function returns an error if the named node is not found. You can also specify paths to child nodes, for example, *get_node(hip/leg_01/foot)*, to access a foot object for a character that is nested further in the hierarchy. The following code accesses a child object and prints its name to the *Output Window*. See Code Sample 4.15.

CODE SAMPLE 4.15   PRINT CHILD NAME OBJECTS

```
print(get_node("child_gun").name)
```

4.7.2 Grouping Nodes

Godot scenes support Groups. A Group is a user-defined collection of related nodes, such as the NPCs or Collectibles in a scene. Any single node can be a member of more than one group, such as both the Collectibles and the NPCs groups. Groups have no limit to the number of nodes they can contain at any one time, and they are very useful for organizing objects in your scene. When managing large scenes, you'll make frequent use of Groups. They are also useful for searching a scene in code for multiple nodes of a common type. Let's explore Groups further. We'll start by assigning some objects to a group. Consider the following example scene in Figure 4.33, which features a collection of mesh objects that could represent Collectible coins in a side-scrolling platform game.

It's convenient to group together all similar objects into a single Group, or collection, to make it easier to refer to them in the scene and to process them in code if necessary. Let's add all these Collectibles together into a single group, called *Collectibles*. First, let's make a *Global Group*. That is a Group that has relevance and applicability throughout the project, as opposed to a single scene. To do that, select *Project > Project Settings* from the application menu, and then *Globals* and *Groups* (see Figure 4.34).

From the Group Creation Dialog, assign the Group a name (*Collectibles*) and then choose the *Add* button. This adds the new Group to the Groups list (Figure 4.35).

Close the Group Creation dialog, and then select each object in the scene. From the Inspector, switch to the *Nodes > Groups* tab, and enable the Collectibles check box. This ensures the selected node is assigned to the Group. Unfortunately, as of Godot 4.3, there is no way to assign multiple objects to the same group in a single operation using the Editor. You'd need to select each object separately and then assign it to the group (see Figure 4.36).

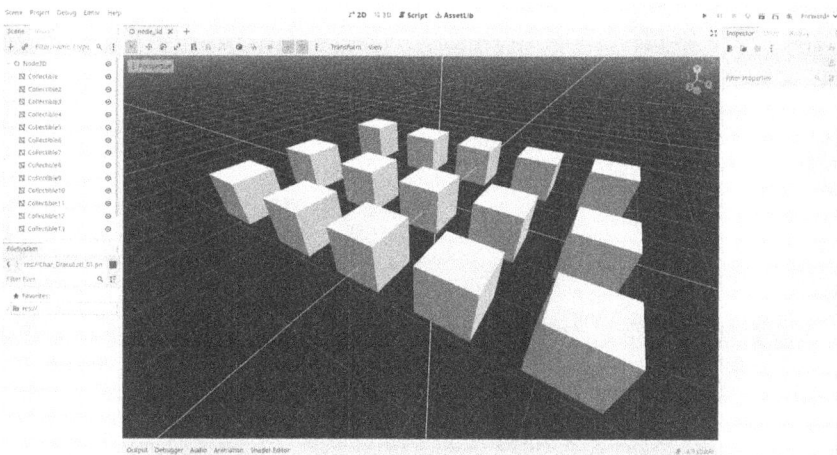

FIGURE 4.33 A collection of objects in a scene.

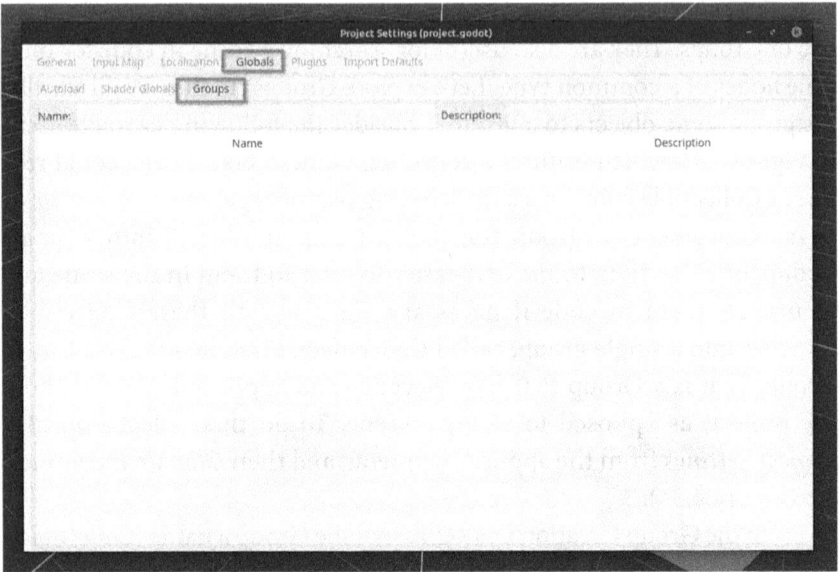

FIGURE 4.34   Accessing Global Groups.

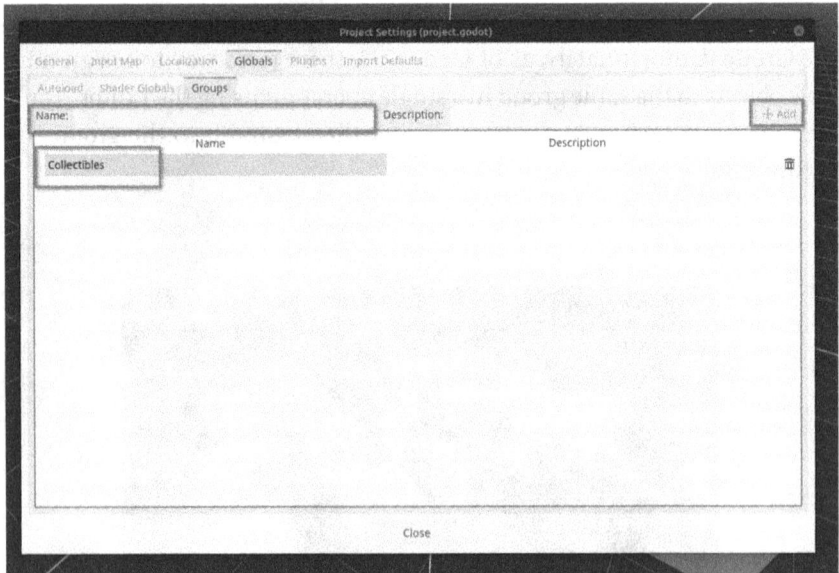

FIGURE 4.35   Creating a Global Group.

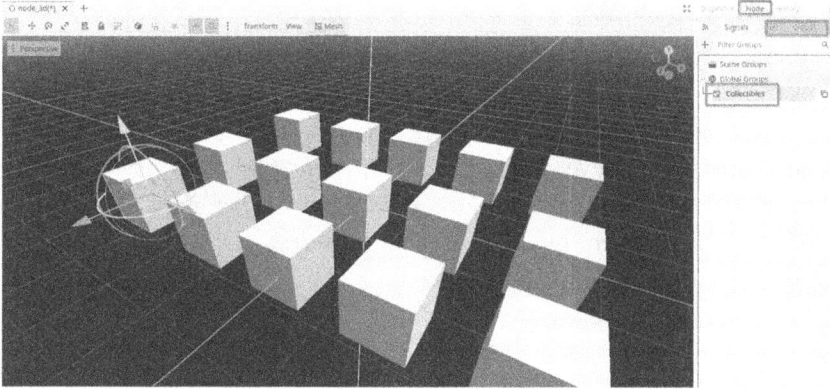

FIGURE 4.36   Assigning a Node to a Group using the Godot Editor.

You can also assign objects to groups using code too. See Code Sample 4.16 for an example script that could be attached to Collectibles.

CODE SAMPLE 4.16   AUTO ADD NODES TO GROUP

```
extends Node
func _ready() -> void:
        add_to_group("Collectibles")
```

4.7.3 Searching Groups

After you've assigned one or more nodes to a named Group, you can easily search a group in code for all members. This is useful if you need to know how many NPCs or Collectibles remain in the scene, or if you need to process all those objects (such as scaling or hiding them). Consider Code Sample 4.17, which iterates through all nodes in a Group.

CODE SAMPLE 4.17   ITERATE THROUGH GROUP MEMBERS

```
extends Node
func _ready() -> void:
        var _nodes = get_tree().get_nodes_in_group("Collectibles")
                for n in _nodes:
        print(n.name)
```

4.8 CONCLUSION

This chapter explored the foundations of coding inside *GDScript* for Godot. It explored everything a Godot developer should know to get started with gameplay scripting. This includes printing output to the debug console, understanding key events like *_ready* and *_process*, reading Input from different devices, and learning to use Signals to support communication between different nodes in a scene. The next chapters explore world-building in both 2D and 3D scenes.

CHAPTER 5

Building 2D Worlds

Sprites, Cameras, and Physics

G ODOT FEATURES THREE MAIN scene types, namely *UI*, *2D*, and *3D*. This
technical and nominal distinction, made by the Editor UI, may initially
make it seem that each scene type is mutually incompatible, as though every
scene type is separate and cannot work together with any other type. But
this really isn't true. As we'll see, scenes can be mixed in different and important ways, if needed. 2D scenes can be 'put into' 3D scenes, for example, and
vice versa. This chapter explores the fundamentals of 2D scenes: worlds that
exist within the flat Cartesian plane of X and Y. In this world, most objects
are flat and camera-facing, and the camera can slide left and right and up
and down, but it cannot rotate around its own axes to view other dimensions. Godot offers an incredibly powerful feature set for building 2D games,
and the comprehensive editor tools make 2D development an enjoyable
experience for developers. This chapter explores 2D scenes and many of
their related subjects in a specific order from the perspective of a developer
creating a movable player character in a scrolling 2D environment. We'll
begin with sprites and Animated Sprites, and then continue with cameras,
collisions, and more general world building. So, let's get started.

5.1 SPRITES AND ANIMATED SPRITES

Chapter 3 explored how to import many common asset types into Godot,
including textures, which are flat 2D images – such as TGAs and PNGs.
Consider the cartoon axolotl image (*Lottie the Lotl* by Evy Benita) in Figure 5.1.

DOI: 10.1201/9781003484523-5

This image, alongside others, is included in the book companion files, which allows you to follow along with the project work in this chapter. You can also use your own images or textures from Asset Libraries.

Textures are imported easily into Godot by dragging and dropping the texture files from the Operating System into the *FileSystem* Dock of the Godot Editor. You then add the imported textures to the 2D Scene as a *Sprite*, simply by dragging and dropping from the *FileSystem* Dock into a 2D scene. Try it now for yourself with the included image in Figure 5.1. Godot automatically instantiates images into a 2D scene as a *Sprite* Node. A *Sprite* is the *spatial instantiation* of a texture into the 2D space of a scene. Unlike a texture, a *Sprite* has an additional *position, rotation,* and *scale,* among other properties (see Figure 5.2).

Every Sprite has an *Offset* field, which is important. The *Offset* is ultimately a 2D Vector quantity of *(X, Y),* which defines the pixel position within the Sprite that represents its center of gravity – its pivot point. The location of a Sprite in the scene is measured from its *Offset.* By default, the offset is measured from the sprite center (*width/2, height/2*), but this can be disabled to change the offset to anywhere in the image. This is important because, typically, you'll want the offset to represent the center of motion for a movable character. For a humanoid player character, for example, the offset will usually be at the feet, where the feet contact the ground plane. For the character in Figure 5.1, the offset might be placed at the tip of the

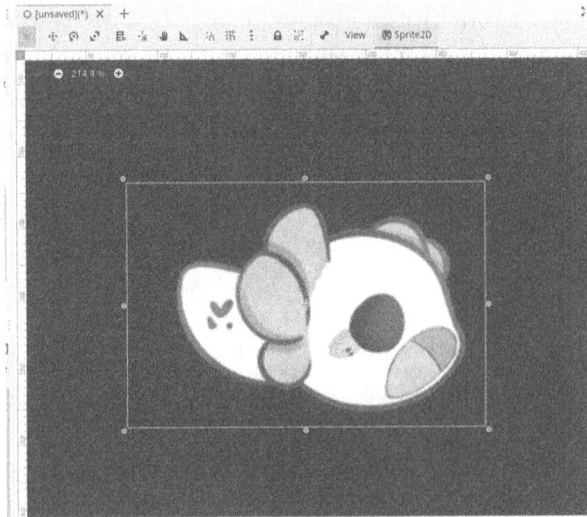

FIGURE 5.1   Cartoon Axolotl Texture image, imported into Godot.

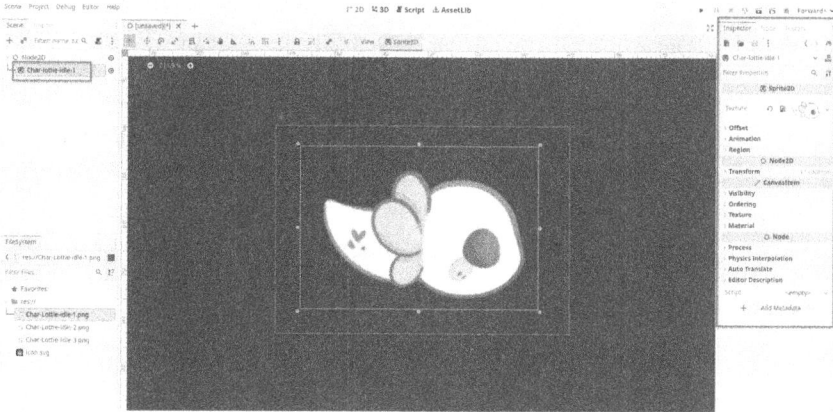

FIGURE 5.2   Adding a Sprite to a 2D scene.

nose, where the sprite first contacts a surrounding surface. To change the offset, disable the Centered Boolean field in the Inspector, and then enter pixel values for the X and Y Offsets (see Figure 5.3).

> NOTE. *Offsets* are measured absolutely *in pixels* and not in any normalized form (such as a fractional value between *0* and *1*). This means that if the texture for a sprite is changed to a texture of different dimensions, then any extant offset may be invalidated from the change.

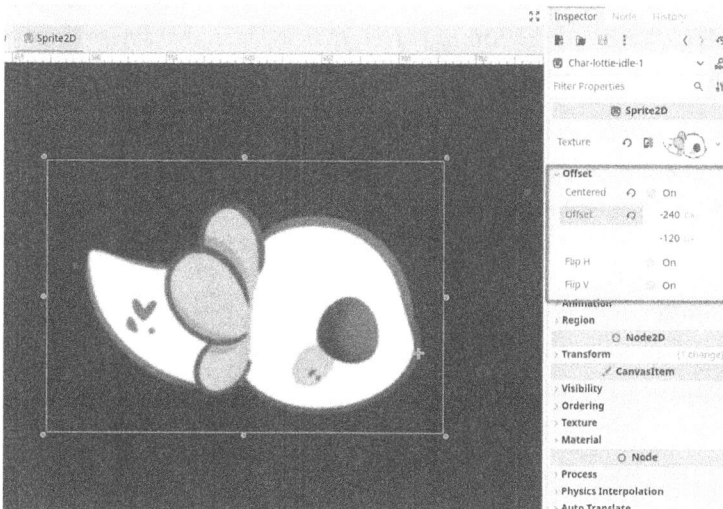

FIGURE 5.3   Setting the Sprite Offset.

5.1.1 Making Sprites Move

Typically, a 2D scene features many moving sprites, from scrolling back-grounds to walking characters. There are different ways to move a sprite, each method with unique advantages and disadvantages. Let's first consider the simplest method of motion, using a *Sprite2D* Node Script that adjusts the *X* and *Y* values of a position property over time. Consider the Code Sample 5.1 below, which can be attached to any Sprite2D node.

CODE SAMPLE 5.1   MAKING A SPRITE MOVE

```
extends Sprite2D
@export var __speed:float = 100
@export var __direction:Vector2 = Vector2.RIGHT
func _process(delta: float) -> void:
        position += __direction * delta * __speed
        if __direction.x != 0:
                scale.x = clampf(__direction.x, -1, 1)
```

The above Code Sample 5.1 moves a Sprite at a speed of __*speed* in the direction of __*direction*. __speed is expressed in pixels per second, and __*direction* is a 2D Vector expressing direction, where (1,0) is rightward and (-1,0) is leftward. (0,1) is up and (0, -1) is down. Combinations move in both directions simultaneously. This code also sets the X *scale* of the Sprite to conform to the direction of travel, making the characters look in the direction they are moving (see Figure 5.4).

> NOTE. The *Position*, *Rotation*, and *Scale* properties are part of *Node2D* and are inherited by *Sprite2D*. More information on *Node2D* can be found at the Godot online documentation here: https://docs.godo tengine.org/en/stable/classes/class_node2d.html.

5.1.2 Sprites and Pixel Art

Many 2D games made in Godot are rendered in the beautiful and classic pixel art style. This is a retro, old-style art form that is immensely popular and forms the basis for many excellent aesthetics. The examples in this book do not use the pixel art style, but if you're making a pixel art game, then you'll want to adjust some texture settings for your Sprites. If you're using pixel art for all textures, or most textures, then access your project

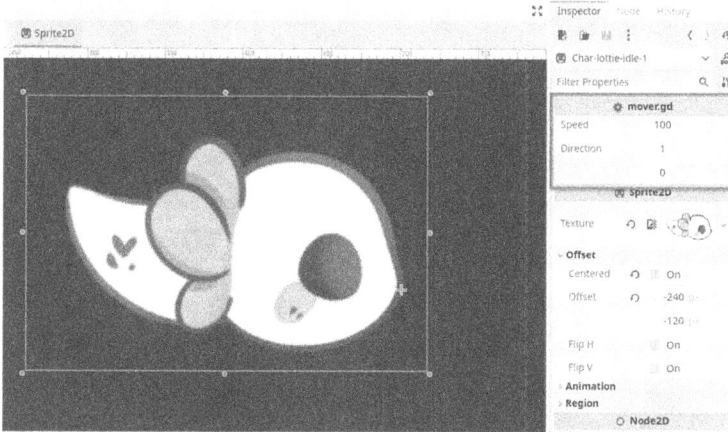

FIGURE 5.4   Moving a Sprite using *Node2D*.

settings by choosing *Project > Project Settings* from the application menu, and then choose *Rendering > Textures Group*, as shown in Figure 5.5.

You should choose *Nearest* for Pixel Art games and leave it as *Linear* for most other cases. This affects how pixels are rendered on screen. You should also select each Sprite and check its *Texture Filtering* mode. By default, it will use the default settings specified in the *Project Settings*, as we did above.

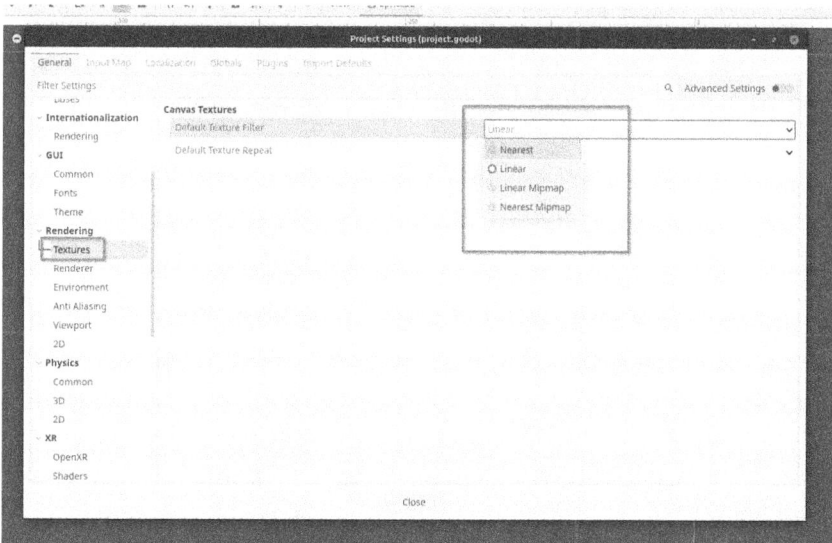

FIGURE 5.5   Setting Texture Filters for pixel art.

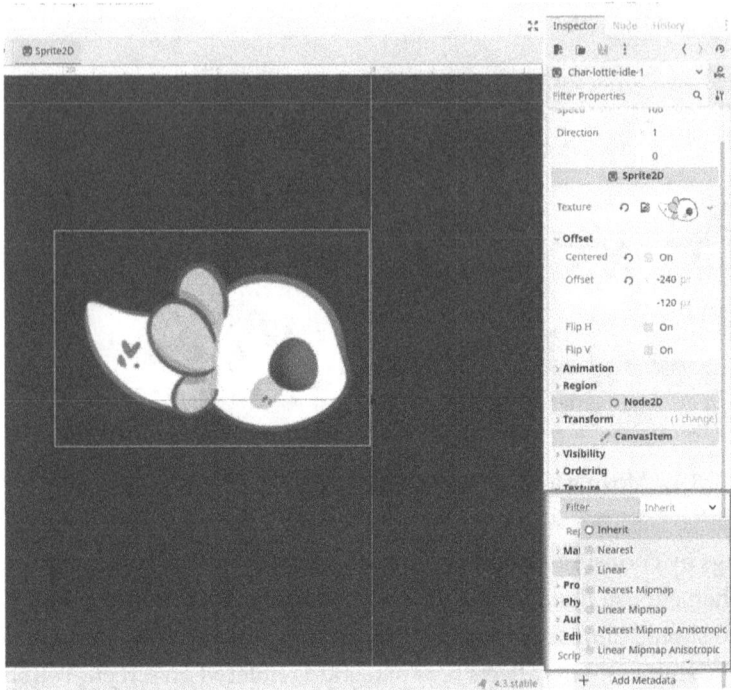

FIGURE 5.6 Setting Texture Filters for a Sprite.

Select the Sprite, and from the Inspector, expand the *Texture* rollout. The *Filter* field should be *Inherit* to match the *Project Settings*. But you can click the drop-down to override this setting for a specific Sprite if you need its filtering method to be different from the default (see Figure 5.6).

5.1.3 Making the Camera Follow a Sprite

2D Scenes are created without camera nodes. However, they do contain a static 'pseudo-camera' by default, making Sprites visible during gameplay even when no camera is technically in the scene. However, if any moving Sprites leave the default camera view by moving off the edge of the screen, the camera will not follow the sprite automatically. To follow the motion of an object, a *Camera2D* node needs to be added to the scene. *Camera2Ds* are essential whenever a 2D level is larger than the screen and you need to move the view. So, let's add a *Camera2D* node to the scene (see Figure 5.7).

To make a *Camera2D* follow an object in the scene, such as the player character, you'll need to attach a Script to the camera. Consider Code Sample 5.2.

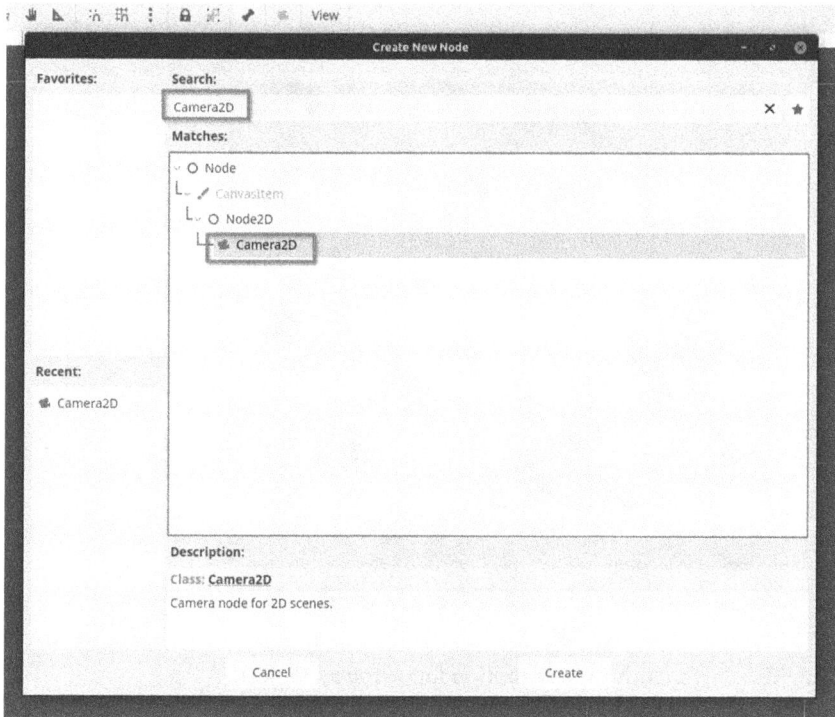

FIGURE 5.7 Adding a Camera2D Node to a 2D scene.

CODE SAMPLE 5.2   CAMERA SCRIPT TO FOLLOW A 2D OBJECT

```
extends Camera2D
@export var __target:Node2D = null
func _process(delta: float) -> void:
        global_position = __target.global_position
```

Once attached to a Camera 2D, you can then tweak the camera properties to create smoother motion, as it follows an object when it moves (see Figure 5.8).

5.1.4 Animated Sprites

The Animated Sprite is a specialization of the standard *Sprite* node. It offers additional features for 'flip book animation'; that is, animated frames, and this behavior is now quite comprehensive in the latest Godot. In this

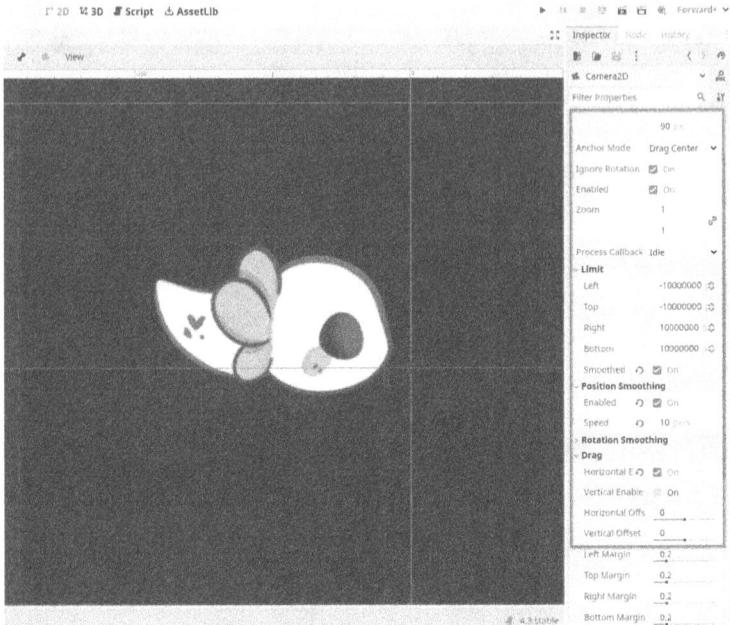

FIGURE 5.8 Smooth camera motion following an Object.

section, we'll explore how to configure two sets of animations for a single, for example, Animated Sprite (*Idle* and *Yawn*), which could be used for a player character in a 2D side-scroller game. The *Idle* plays by default, and the *Yawn* plays on demand, such as by a button press. An Animated Sprite can support many different animations (walk, run, jump, etc.), which can be dynamically switched during gameplay using code. Let's start by creating the *AnimatedSprite* node (see Figure 5.9).

The Animated Sprite node begins empty. It exists in the scene as a true object but has no renderability by default. To create the frames of animation, select the *AnimatedSprite* object, and then from the Inspector expand the animation rollout. For the *SpriteFrames* field, choose New *SpriteFrames* from the dropdown context menu. This option creates a new *Resource*. However, the resource is local to the scene by default and so does not appear in the *FileSystem* dock alongside project-wide resources, like meshes and textures. This isn't a problem but is worth noting (see Figure 5.10).

Next, after clicking the newly generated *SpriteFrames* menu entry from the Inspector, you'll be presented with the *AnimationFrames* Editor window, which is docked unmovably at the bottom of the editor interface, aligned horizontally. This window allows you to define all possible

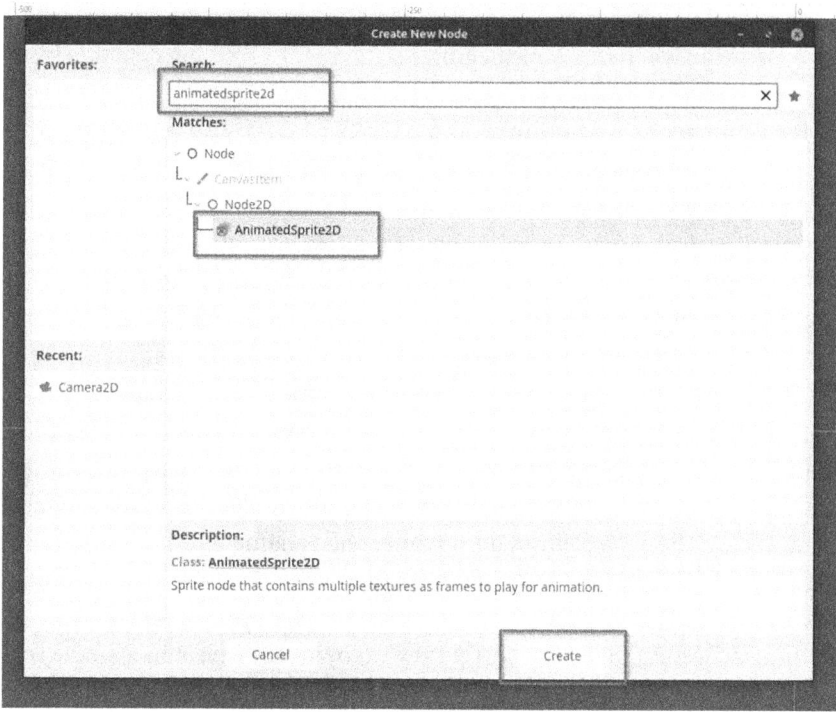

FIGURE 5.9   Creating an AnimatedSprite object.

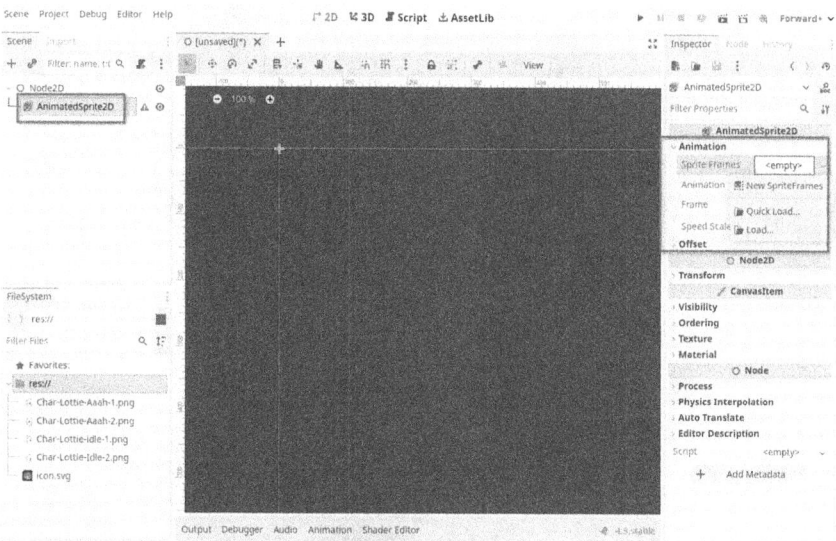

FIGURE 5.10   Creating an AnimatedSprite object.

animations for the sprite, including the default animation, which plays automatically when the scene begins. See Figure 5.11 for the default, empty *FramesEditor*.

Let's create our first animation for the sprite, the *Idle* animation. Idle animations for both player and NPC sprites are typically the default ones, and they play whenever no other activity is happening, such as shooting, running, or jumping. To create this animation, select all the *Idle* frames from the *FileSystem* Dock, and then drop them into the *Frames Editor*. For example, in Figure 5.12, there are only two frames, but *Idle* animations can contain many more. There is no official limit on the total number of frames in any animation besides what the computer can sustain.

Most *Idle* animations are intended to play on a loop and should play automatically when the level begins. To ensure this happens, enable the *Loop* and *AutoPlay* Commands from the *FrameEditor* Toolbar. Then additionally, double-click the *default* animation name, and rename it to *Idle*. Finally, hit the *Play* button from the *FrameEditor* window to preview the animation in the viewport. If the speed seems incorrect to the eye, you can adjust the *frames per second (FPS)* to control how many frames cycle in a single second. But a total of 5 frames works well for my example (see Figure 5.13).

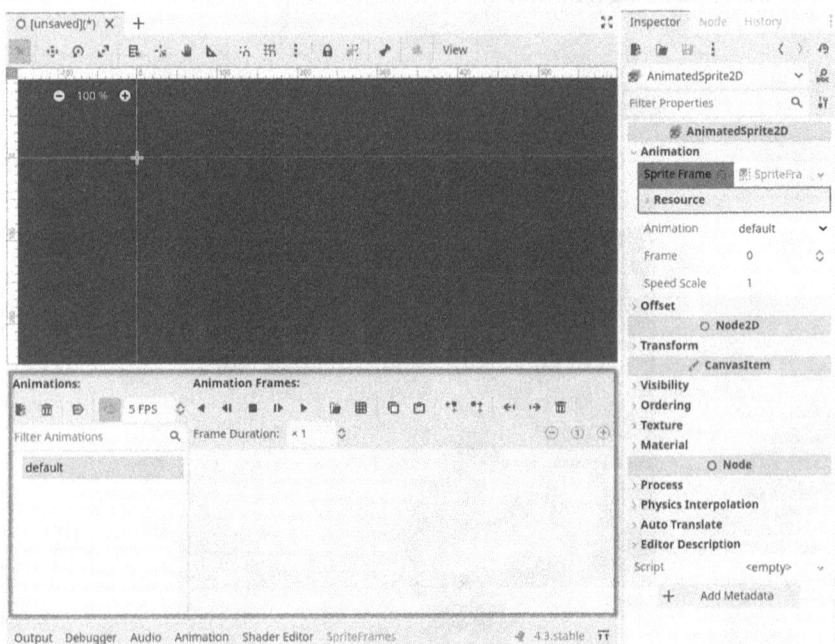

FIGURE 5.11 Preparing to use the FramesEditor.

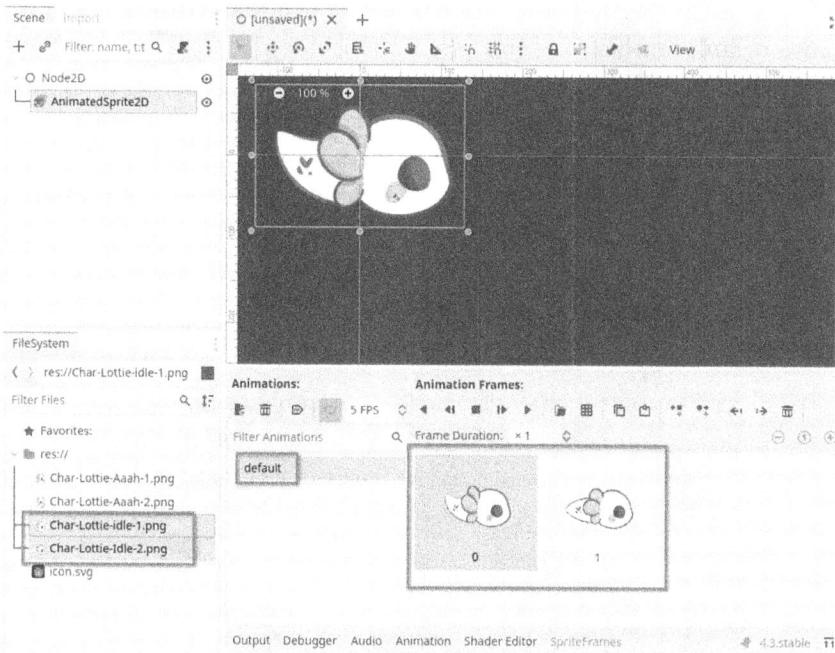

FIGURE 5.12   Adding our frames of animation.

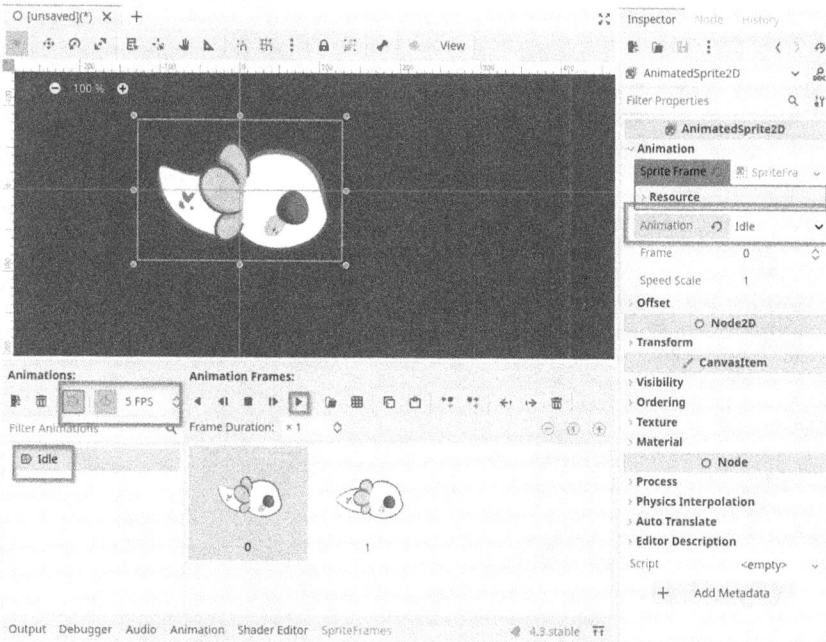

FIGURE 5.13   Completing a default, looping animation for Idle.

Let's make a second animation for our 'Yawn' state. Unlike the previous, default animation, this animation doesn't play automatically. It would typically be played during gameplay when an event happens. Thus, the animation is triggered by code. To build this animation, press the *New Button* from the *Frames Editor*, and then simply repeat the process above to name the animation and define the frames. Once created, make sure the Idle animation is set as the default for the *AnimatedSprite* by checking the *Animation* field from the Inspector (see Figure 5.14). If you now press *Play* on the Scene toolbar, the Sprite will animate as expected.

We can also control our Animated Sprite from code, which is critically important for creating believable 2D worlds. Consider Code Sample 5.3, which can be attached to any Sprite object that has an animation called 'Idle' and 'Yawn', as our sprite does.

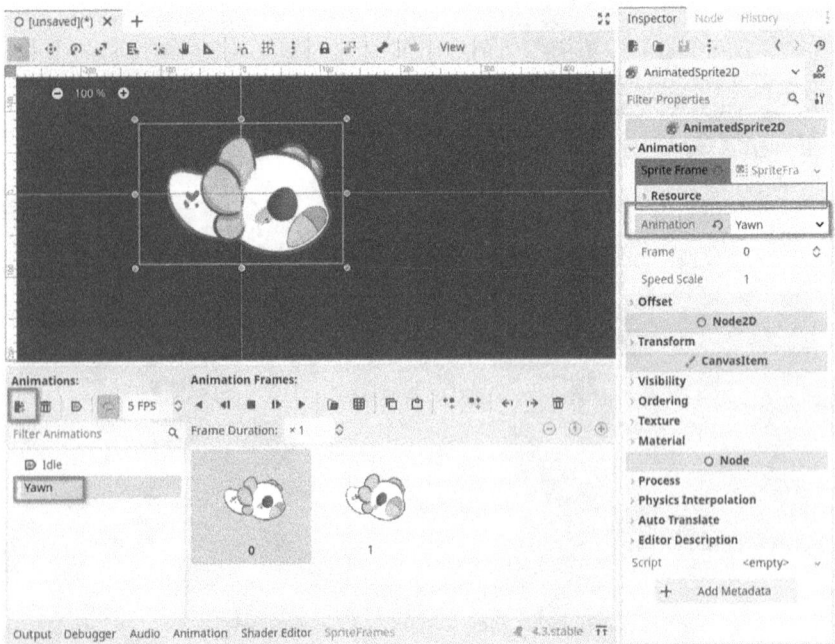

FIGURE 5.14   Completing a default, looping animation for Idle.

CODE SAMPLE 5.3   CONTROLLING SPRITE ANIMATION.

```
extends AnimatedSprite2D
func _ready() -> void:
#connect animation signals to sprite
connect("animation_looped", _on_animation_completed)
connect("animation_finished", _on_animation_completed)
#if a non-idle animation loops or ends, then return
to idle
func _on_animation_completed():
        if animation != "Idle":
        play("Idle")
#check input, and should we play a different
animation?
func _process(delta: float) -> void:
        if(!Input.is_action_pressed("Shoot")):
                return

        #Play yawn animation if Shoot is pressed
        play("Yawn")
```

NOTE. More information on coding with *AnimatedSprites* can be found online at the official Godot reference documentation here: https://docs.godotengine.org/en/stable/classes/class_animatedsprite2d.html.

5.2 PHYSICS AND COLLISIONS IN 2D

Previously, we saw how the *Sprite2D* and *AnimatedSprite2D* nodes are specialist node types, ultimately derived from *Node2D*. A *Node2D* is the main parent of all nodes existing inside a 2D scene. The *Node2D* object features a range of important properties, such as *Position*, for controlling the location and movement of objects within a unified Cartesian space. The problem with this setup for a developer seeking to create believable levels is that these positional properties of a *Node2D* are not fully validated at the time of being set. For example, Godot will happily allow you to set the position of a *Node2D* object to any specified (X, Y) location in the scene, regardless of whether another solid object, such as a wall, occupies that same location. As a result, you can easily make two or more objects overlap and intersect when they clearly shouldn't, assuming you want believable collisions and physics. This section explores how we can solve this problem by creating a moveable player character that won't pass through other solids. Godot makes it simple, but we need to configure our objects appropriately. Let's start doing that from an empty 2D scene.

5.2.1 Configuring a Movable Character with Physics

In this section, we'll build a movable player character. Now, we already did this already in Section 5.1.1. But in that case, we used a Sprite object, and our movement was neither constrained nor validated. Our movable Sprite could literally pass through solids. Here, however, we'll use a different object type that will respect other physical objects. To start, let's add a *CharacterBody2D* node to the scene. This node is used for any controlled object under the remit of physics. So, it should be used for player-controlled characters and NPCs. It should not be used for immovable physical objects, such as walls, trees, and buildings. And it should not be used for lifeless physical objects which can move, like falling branches, bales of hay, and marbles in a maze. A *CharacterBody2D* is an agent, and it *acts upon* things, as opposed to falling branches, which are *acted upon* by others (see Figure 5.15).

The *CharacterBody2D* is added to the scene, and a suspicious-looking exclamation triangle appears beside it in the *Scene* Dock of the Editor.

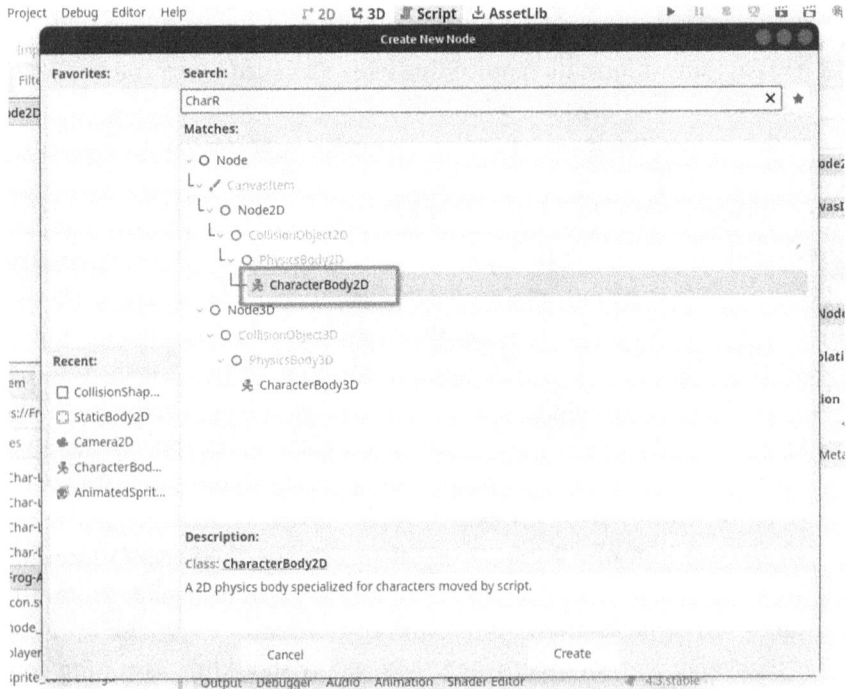

FIGURE 5.15   Creating a CharacterBody2D.

That means the *CharacterBody2D* node cannot operate properly until further steps are taken by us. In this case, the *CharacterBody2D* requires a *Collider* as a child node; that is, a special kind of node that defines the surface area and shape of the character. This data is *separate from* any pixels or from the sprites which define the character. This allows us to dress our characters in complex-looking sprites while maintaining a simpler underlying shape for faster collision calculations. So, let's add two child objects to the *CharacterBody2D*. First, an *AnimatedSprite* Object was created as above. And second, a *CollisionShape2D* node (see Figure 5.16).

As with *CharacterBody2D* objects, *CollisionShape2D* objects are created with a suspicious-looking exclamation next to them (see Figure 5.16). For the Collision Shape, we need to create the shape itself, as the object is created empty. To do this, click the *Shape* drop-down field in the *Inspector*, and select the most appropriate shape for your character. This choice can be more complex than it first appears. It's tempting to conclude that you should create a rectangle enclosing the entire sprite. And while this safely ensures that all sprite collisions are detected, it doesn't necessarily lead to the most believable or compelling gameplay. This is because technically correct collisions can include ones that don't look or feel right. For the character shown in Figure 5.16, I'll choose a *Circle*. Once selected, you can click and drag the red handle to scale the circle and enclose the character, and you can also click and drag from the circle center to reposition it to match the Sprite (see Figure 5.17).

NOTE. There are some really interesting additional properties for Collision Shapes. One is *Disabled*, which can be toggled on to deactivate the shape from the physics system (allowing objects to pass

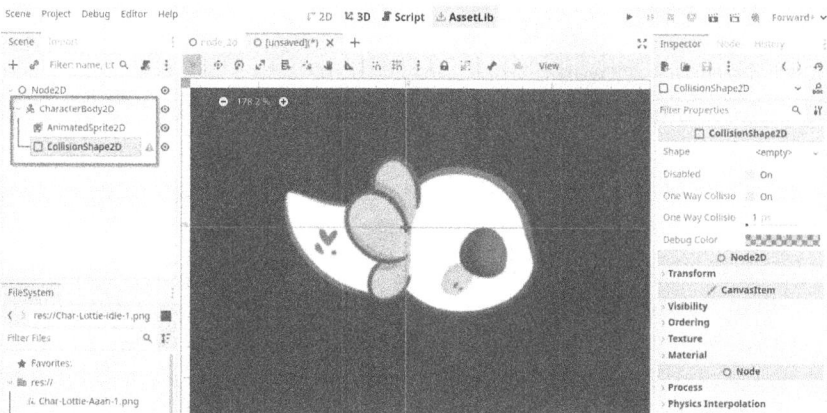

FIGURE 5.16   Creating a Sprite and CollisionShape Child Node.

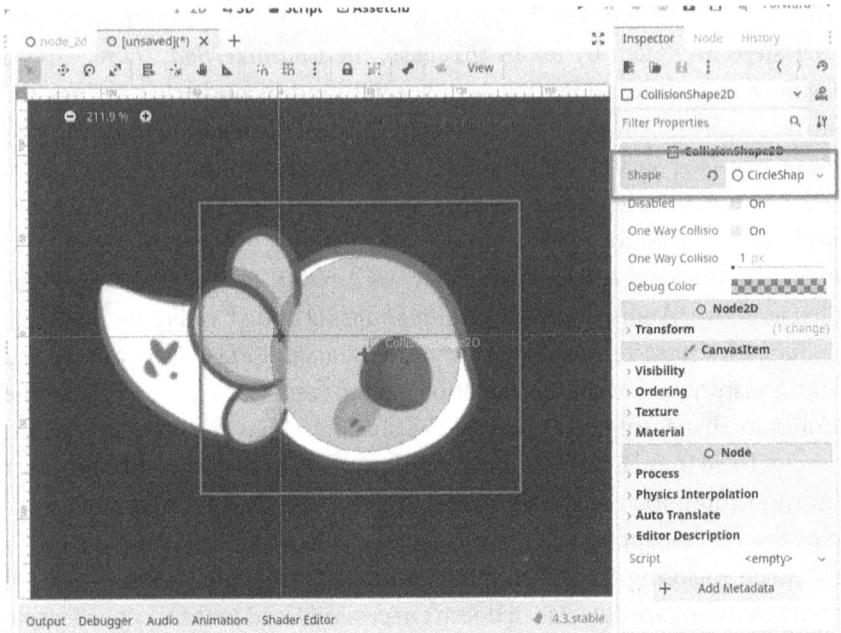

FIGURE 5.17   Create a Circle Shape around the Sprite.

through). The other is *One Way Collision*. This is useful for platform games, where characters that are standing on the ground can literally 'jump up' and through the bottom of the platform and then finally fall and land on the same platform as a solid object.

Finally, as our player character is a floating, or swimming, entity, we'll change the *Motion Mode* of *CharacterBody2D* from *Grounded* to *Floating* (see Figure 5.18).

5.2.2 Coding a Movable Character with Physics

We've now fully configured three related nodes that will work together as a single-player character, namely the *CharacterBody2D* node and its two children, *AnimatedSprite2D* and *CollisionShape2D*. At this stage, we can now attach a script to the *CharacterBody2D* and create a physics-compliant player-controlled character in *GDScript*. First, create a new script. As shown in Figure 5.19, called *player_controller.gd*.

Great. Now consider the following script in Code Sample 5.4. This code assumes Input Axes have been configured for up, down, left, and right on the keyboard or gamepad. Chapter 4 explores how to configure this in more detail.

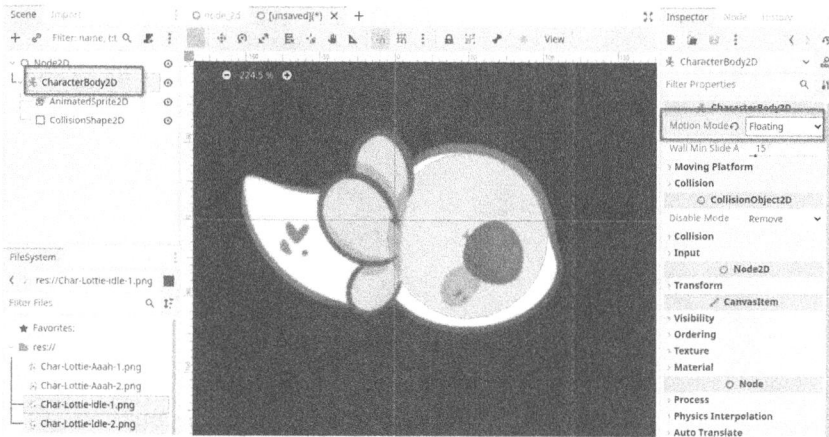

FIGURE 5.18   Configuring the CharacterBody2D.

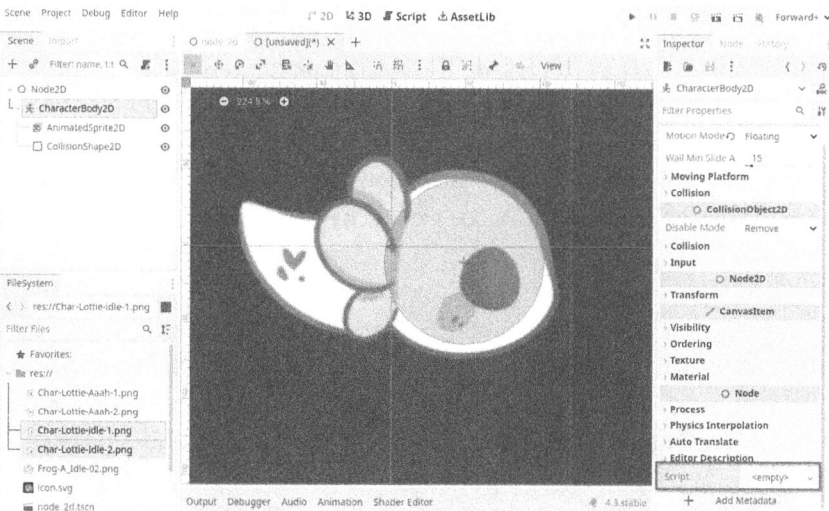

FIGURE 5.19   Creating a new Script.

CODE SAMPLE 5.4   CONTROLLING A CHARACTER WITH PHYSICS

```
extends CharacterBody2D
var __input_direction:Vector2 = Vector2.ZERO
@export var __speed:float = 200
func _process(_delta: float) -> void:
```

```
        __input_direction.x = -Input.get_action_
strength("Left") + Input.get_action_strength("Right")
        __input_direction.y = Input.get_action_
strength("Down") - Input.get_action_strength("Up")

func _physics_process(_delta: float) -> void:
        velocity = __input_direction * __speed
        move_and_slide()
```

Code Sample 5.4 features some key statements that make physics possible. First, the *__input_direction* variable vectorizes our input from the horizontal and vertical axes, as we saw previously in Chapter 4. This is later used in the *_physics_process* function, which is called once per physics step. That is, once per internal cycle of the physics system. This is likely to be multiple times per second, but less than the frame rate. The built-in variable *velocity* is a 2D Vector whose X and Y components describe the object's movement speed in pixels per second. The *move_and_slide* function is called to apply the velocity, and it will update the physics system with the object's motion. If you run this code now, along with a *Camera2D* in the scene, you'll be able to control the player character.

5.2.3 Creating a Static Obstacle

In this section, we'll create a static obstacle for the player to bump into. This object will prevent the player from passing through it. To build this, we don't even need any extra code. Let's get started. First, create a new *StaticBody2D* node. This should be a child of the root node and not a child of the player character (see Figure 5.20).

As with the *CharacterBody2D* node, the *StaticBody2D* node expects two children. A *Sprite2D* defines how the object looks, and a *ColllisionShape2D* defines how the object behaves physically. For the Sprite, I'll use a cute Frog Character (included in the book companion files), and for the collision, I'll use a *Circle* (see Figure 5.21).

And that's it! The player can now move around the level and will bump into static frogs! The physics system ensures that all collisions are respected.

5.2.4 Querying Collisions with GDScript

Our physics configuration so far has explored how to create a player-controlled character that can bump into static, solid objects elsewhere in the scene. Static obstacles could be used for walls, trees, streetlamps, statues,

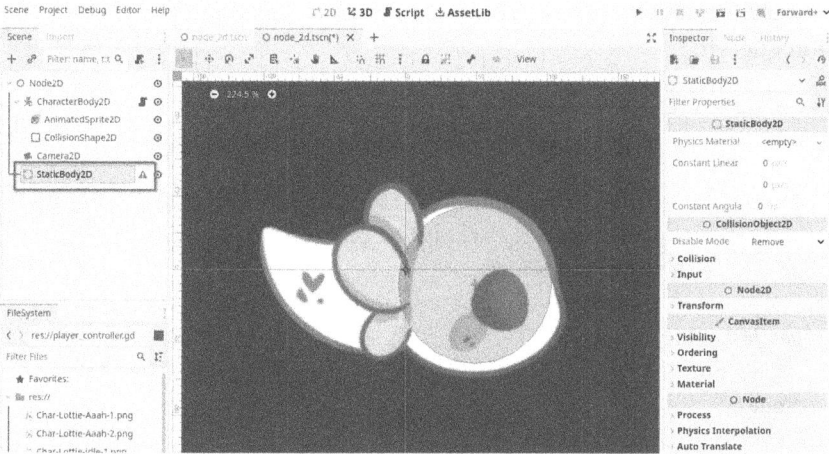

FIGURE 5.20   Creating a new StaticBody2D.

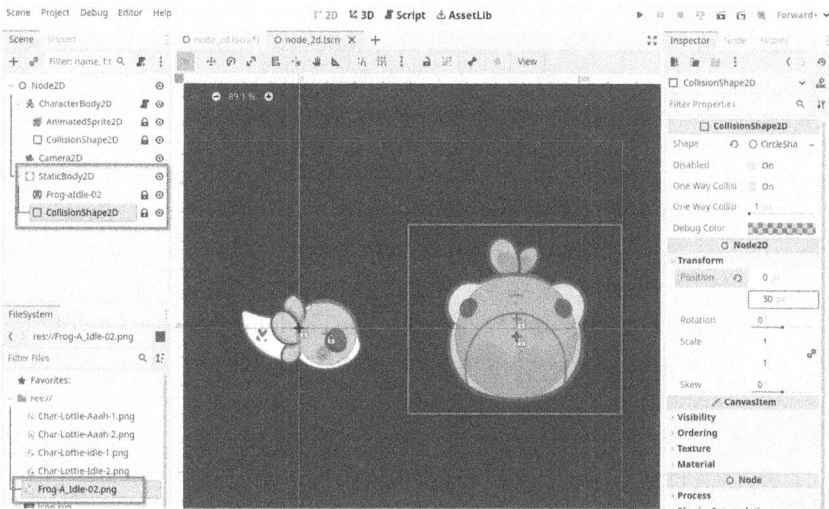

FIGURE 5.21   Configuring a Static Obstacle.

and more. The collisions and responses themselves are both detected and handled automatically by Godot through the *move_and_slide* function of *CharacterBody2D*. However, there will be occasions when you'll want to dig deeper into what is happening beneath the surface. Specifically, when a collision happens during gameplay, you may need to determine which objects collide. In the case of our player character, you may need to know which other object it contacted. This is important to know because not all objects are created equal. Bumping into a friendly cat is different from bumping into a wall of spinning saws. In the latter case, the player's health is likely to reduce from the collision. Consider Code Sample 5.5 for collision querying.

CODE SAMPLE 5.5   QUERYING COLLISIONS

```
func _physics_process(_delta: float) -> void:
        velocity = __input_direction * __speed
        if move_and_slide() :
                var _col_data:KinematicCollision2D =
get_last_slide_collision()
                var _col:Node2D = _col_data.get_collider() as
Node2D
                print(_col.name)
```

Code Sample 5.5 uses the *get_last_slide_collision* function to return information about the most recent single collision for the current *CharacterBody2D*. The *get_collider* function, cast as a *Node2D*, returns a reference to the colliding object during that collision.

NOTE. It's possible for a *CharacterBody2D* to collide with multiple objects in a single frame, such as hitting multiple enemies at once. In this case, you may need to query for all collisions, as opposed to the last collision. For this, you'd need the *get_slide_collision* function. More information can be found at the Godot online documentation here: https://docs.godotengine.org/en/stable/classes/class_character body2d.html.

5.3 REPEATING BACKGROUNDS WITH SPRITES

One important, creative decision when creating powerful 2D worlds is to choose a suitable background. Often, backgrounds are layered with multiple elements, one atop the other. One of the first decisions is to decide on a background color to fill the background as the furthest background layer, and then usually different elements will be layered on top, such as embellishments and details. To start, click on *Project > Project Settings*, and then choose *Rendering > Environment*. From there, select a background color that is consistent with your art style using the color picker dialog. Interestingly, this choice is project-wide, for every scene, as opposed to the active scene only (see Figure 5.22).

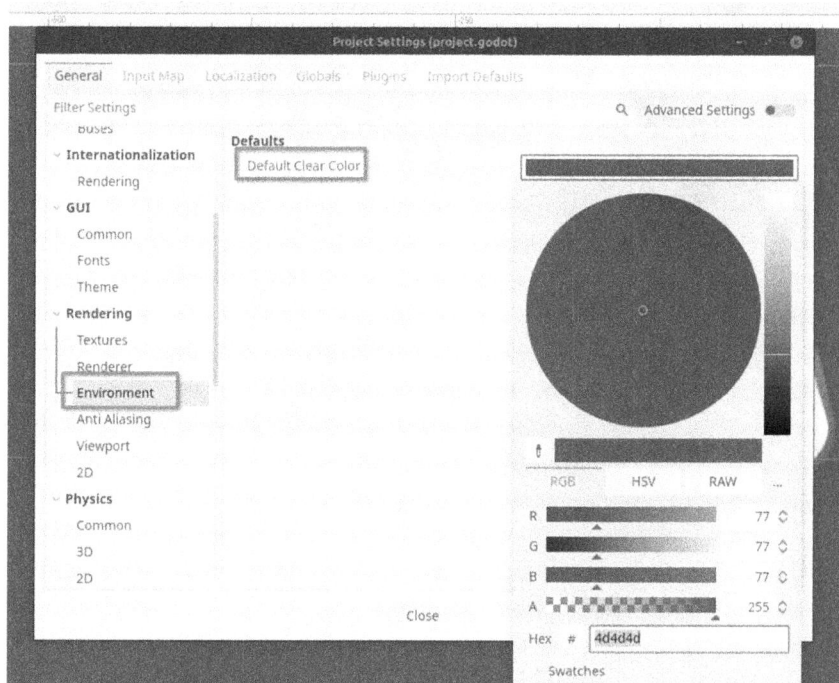

FIGURE 5.22   Choosing a Background Color.

NOTE. To set a different background color for each scene, you should use a *ColorRect* node, which is considered later with UIs.

Next, we'll create a repeating background using a *Sprite2D* node. To make this work for a left-to-right aligned world, you'll need a texture that repeats horizontally. I have included an example world background in the book companion files (*BG_05.png*), and I'll use that texture in this chapter, but you can use any repeating texture. Import the texture into the project and then drag and drop it into the scene as a standard *Sprite2D* (see Figure 5.23).

Next, select the background Sprite, expand the *Texture* rollout from the *Inspector*, and for the *Repeat* field, choose *Enabled* from the drop-down list (see Figure 5.24).

Now move to the *Region* rollout and choose *Enabled*. Region allows you to specify a smaller rectangle within the texture space to use for the *Sprite*. However, it also allows you to choose a *larger* Region into which the texture will be repeated when the *Repeat* field is enabled. As you enable the *Region* field, the Sprite vanishes. But it'll return when you enter the image

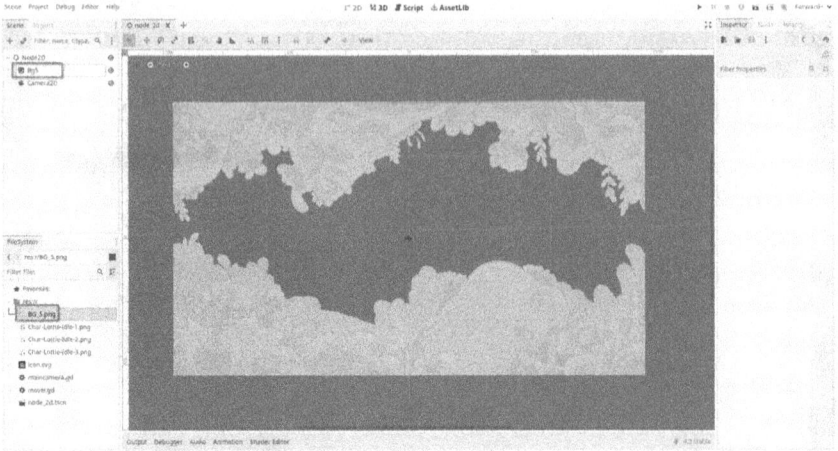

FIGURE 5.23   Using a Sprite for the background.

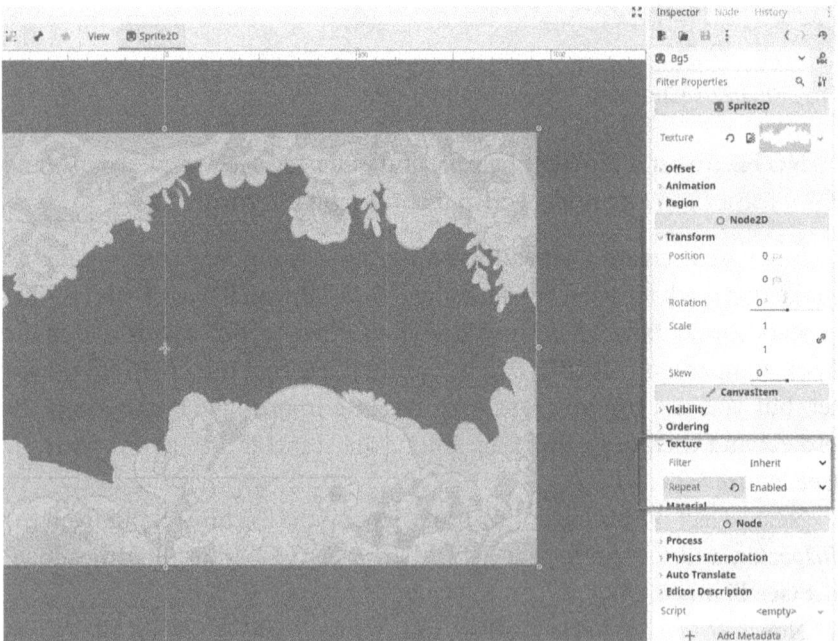

FIGURE 5.24   Enabling the *Repeat* Property for the Background Sprite.

dimensions into the *Rect* field. The default dimensions for my texture are *1920 x 1080* (HD resolution). If you're using a different texture, then be sure to check out its pixel dimensions (see Figure 5.25).

Finally, type the final pixel width *of the level* into the *W* field (Width). When you do this, the Sprite expands to meet that width, and the texture is repeated continually (rather than stretched) to fill that space (see Figure 5.26).

When you're happy with the scene width and appearance, click the padlock icon to lock the Sprite in place and prevent it from being selected

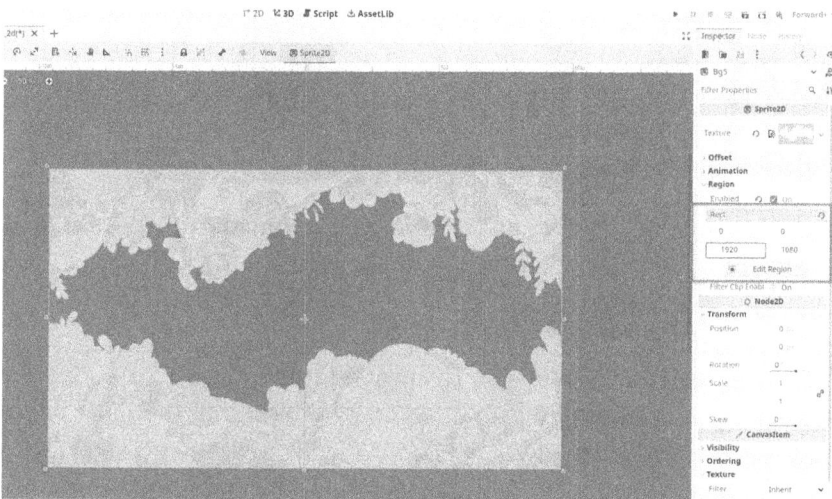

FIGURE 5.25   Setting the dimensions for a region-restricted Sprite.

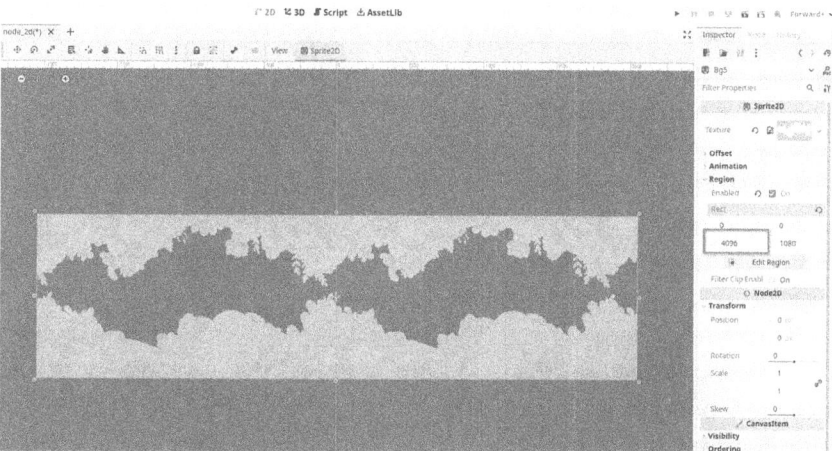

FIGURE 5.26   Repeating a Sprite to fill the width of a level.

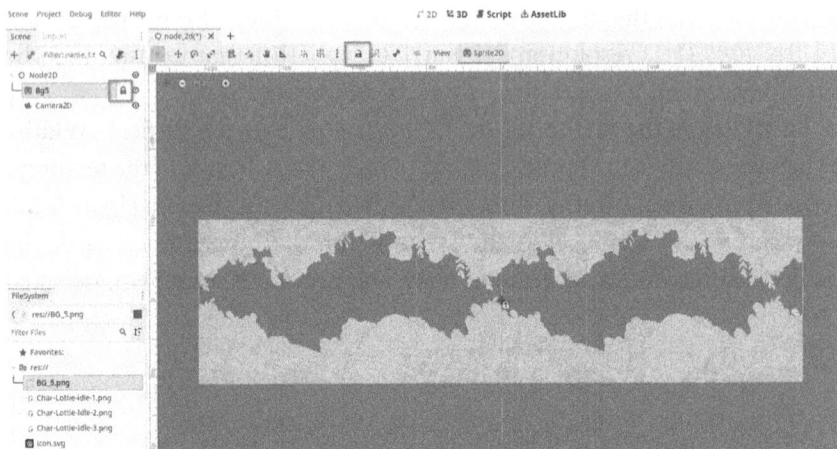

FIGURE 5.27   Securing the background in place.

accidentally. Given its size and location, a background sprite can easily be selected, so using the padlock is useful (see Figure 5.27).

5.4 TILEMAPS AND WORLD DESIGN

Large, expansive 2D worlds are frequently formed from *TileMaps*. Side-scrolling platformers, top-down RPGs and shooters, and even quirky little puzzle games feature worlds made from smaller, tileable images that are tightly packed together, like building blocks, into a large and meaningful grid. The grid forms the basis of all levels and scenes. Consider Figure 5.28 for a tileset, featuring tiles that can be rearranged to compose an underwater maze environment. Each tile in the map represents a unique building block, such as a straight section or a corner piece, which works in different orientations to build a larger world. In this section, we'll build an example level from a tileset (see Figure 5.28).

5.4.1 Creating a Texture Atlas for a TileMap

TileMaps typically begin from one of two places: either each and every tile is saved into a separate image file, one tile per file, or every tile is included together in a larger image, called an *Atlas*, where every tile is packed in grid formation. Godot expects the latter (one image), but it can work with the former case too. The former (individual tiles) require some additional steps in Godot, so we'll consider that case here to cover both scenarios. This book features a collection of tiles in separate images, which can be imported into Godot, but you can use any similar tileset to follow along (see Figure 5.29).

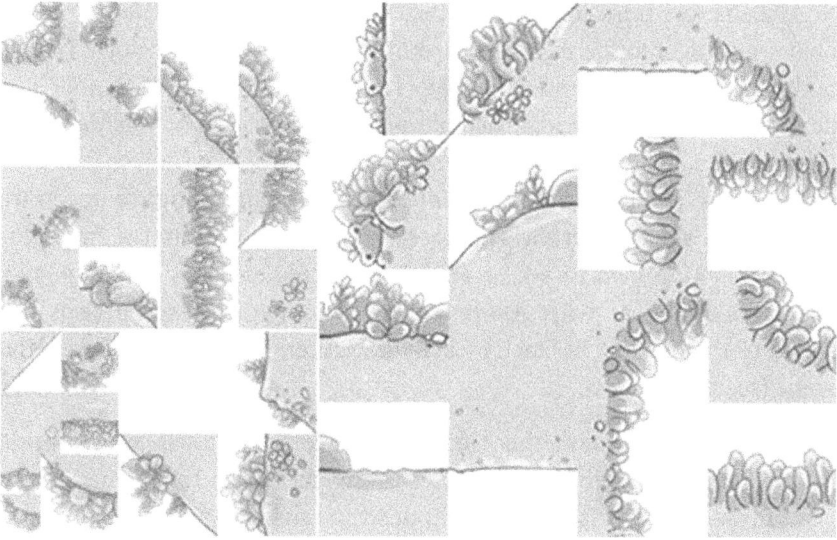

FIGURE 5.28   Exploring a Tileset.

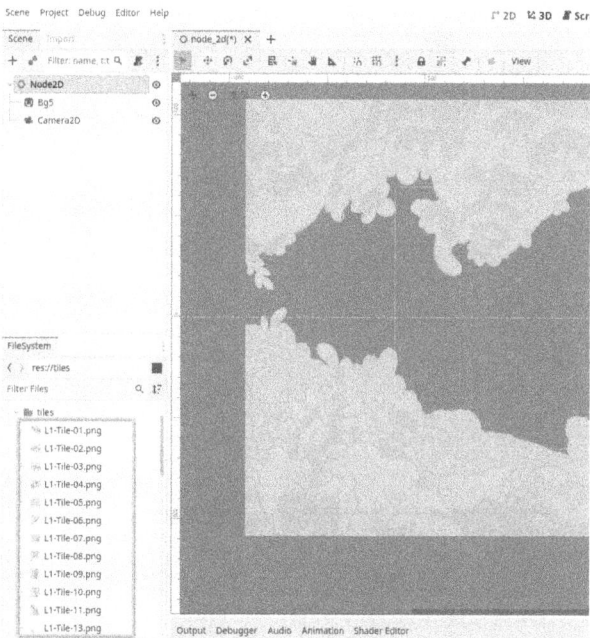

FIGURE 5.29   Importing multiple tiles.

After having imported tileset images, let's create a new *TileMap Layer* object, adding it to the scene. Be careful in choosing here; Godot 4.3 offers both a *TileMap* node and a *TileMap Layer* node. The *TileMap* node is a deprecated, legacy feature, which has now been replaced by *TileMapLayer* (see Figure 5.30).

From the newly created *TileMapLayer*, you can configure an entire *TileMap*. To start, select the *TileMapLayer* object, and from the Inspector set the *TileMap* field to a new *TileSet*. This creates a new *TileMapLayer* resource. Again, as with *AnimatedSprites*, the created resource is not added to the *FileSystem* Dock by default. Rather, it is stored locally in the scene (see Figure 5.31).

> NOTE. You can save the *TileSet* Resource as a global, project-wide resource by choosing *Save As* from the Resource Menu in the Inspector. This is useful if you need to reuse the same tileset across multiple scenes (see Figure 5.32).

Next, click on the *TileSet* resource from the *TileSet* Inspector field, and set the *TileSet* size in pixels. This defines the pixel *width* and *height* of each

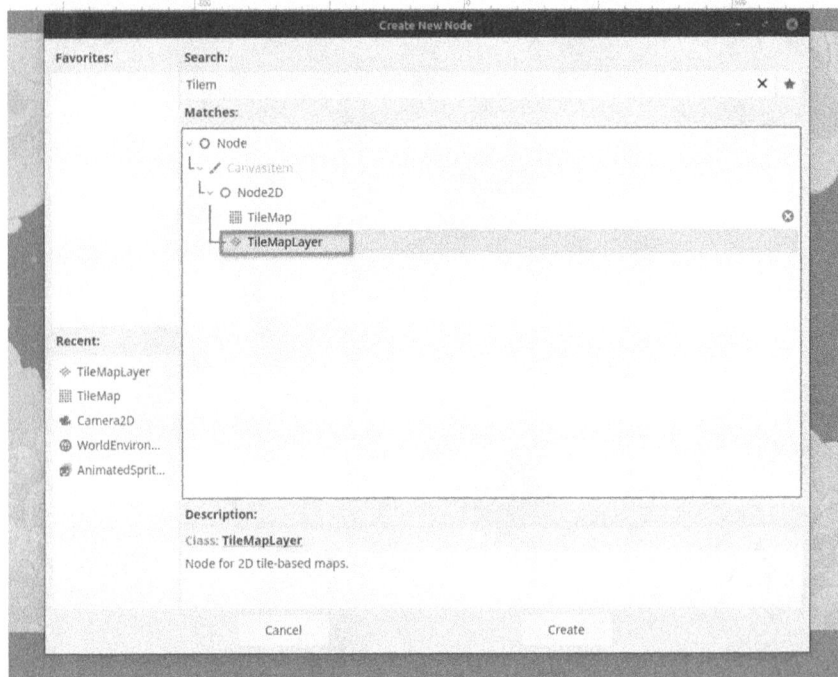

FIGURE 5.30 Creating a TileMapLayer Node.

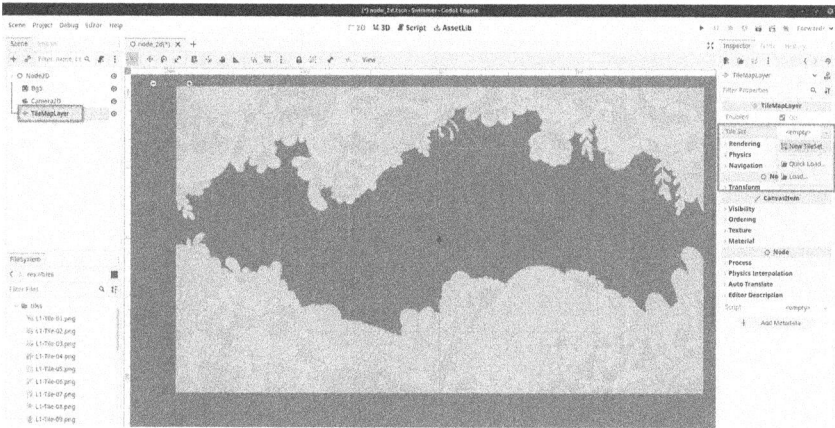

FIGURE 5.31   Creating a new TileSet Resource.

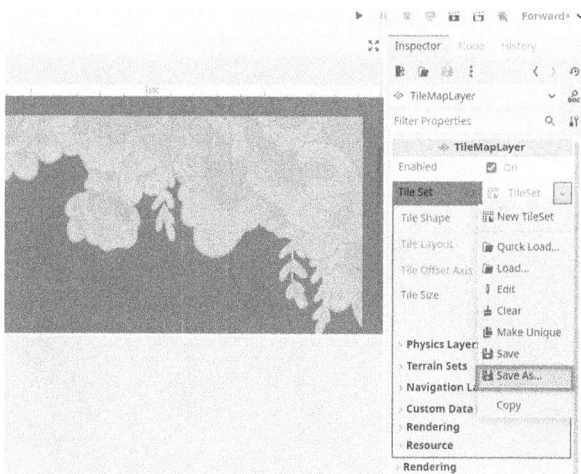

FIGURE 5.32   Saving a resource to the FileSystem Dock.

tile in the set, assuming all tiles are of equal size. Often, tiles will be square too, but Godot does not require this. For my example images, the dimensions are 64x64 pixels (see Figure 5.33).

After setting the tile unit size, jump over to the *TileSet* editor, which is docked at the bottom center of the Godot interface. Select all of the newly imported tiles and drop them into the Tiles list. This causes all imported tiles to be listed in a stack (see Figure 5.34). An obscure, and initially unhelpful, prompt may ask if you want to 'create all tiles in the atlas' and suggest the 'atlas has been modified'. You can answer 'No' to that question.

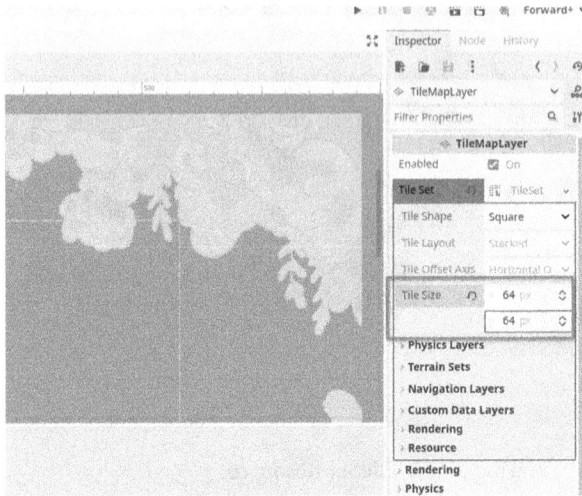

FIGURE 5.33   Setting the Tile dimensions.

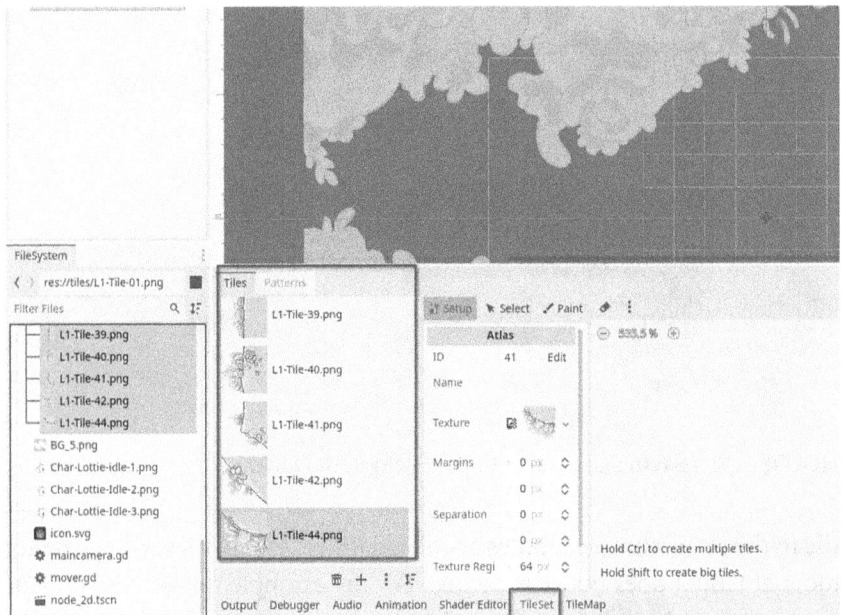

FIGURE 5.34   Adding tiles to the list.

Godot lets you generate a single, unified texture atlas from multiple textures. That is, a single texture that features all smaller tiles arranged in rows and columns. You'll need to generate this before creating a *TileSet*. To start, click the … icon and then choose *Open Atlas Merging Tool* from the context menu (see Figure 5.35).

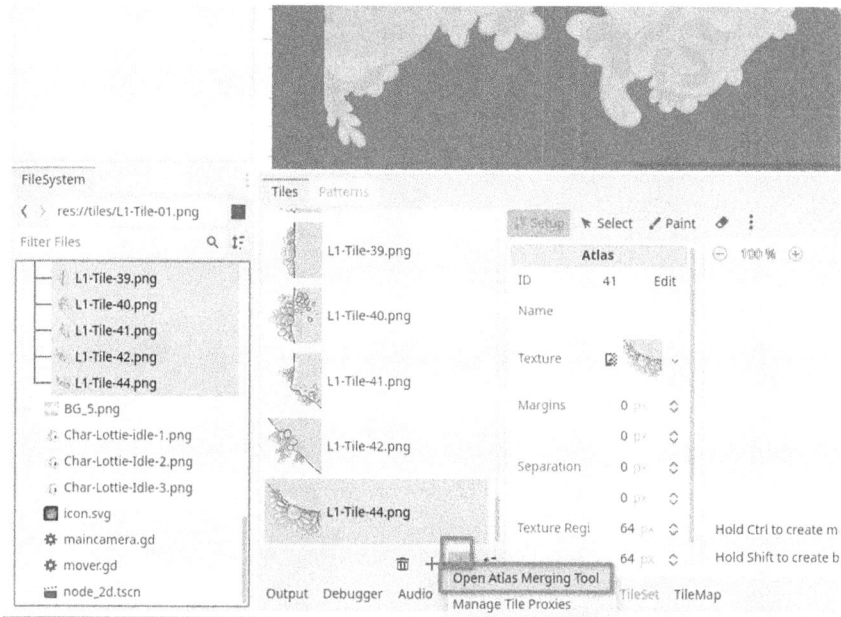

FIGURE 5.35   Generating an Atlas with the Atlas Merging Tool.

Select all textures in the list to include them in the Atlas and then choose the *Merge* button. From here, choose a Save Destination for the generated image file. This can be anywhere on the local file system. The file will be created as a single, collated *PNG* file. Once created, you can import the file back into Godot as a texture (see Figure 5.36).

The newly imported file is a texture atlas, and this can now be added to the *Tileset* list. This time, when the dialog prompts you to 'create tiles', choose *Yes*. In choosing this, all tiles in the atlas will be added from the *TileSet*, which is an image containing tiles, to the *TileMap*, which is a resource where all selected and extracted tiles appear in a palette, ready to use (see Figure 5.37).

5.4.2 Building Tile Collisions

Previously, we imported and configured a complete tileset for a 2D world from an atlas texture. At this point, we could use the *TileMapLayer* node in the scene to paint tiles and build an expansive world that characters can explore. However, beforehand, we should apply further configuration to our tiles, ensuring they behave as expected. Specifically, many tiles in the set may represent solid objects, such as rocks, corals, walls, doors, and other types of solids that should not allow physical objects, like the player and NPCs, to

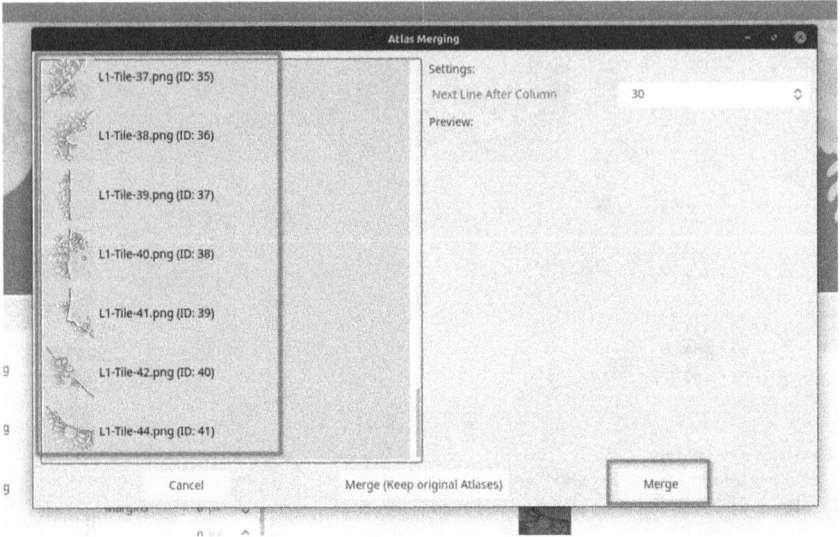

FIGURE 5.36   Creating an Atlas Texture.

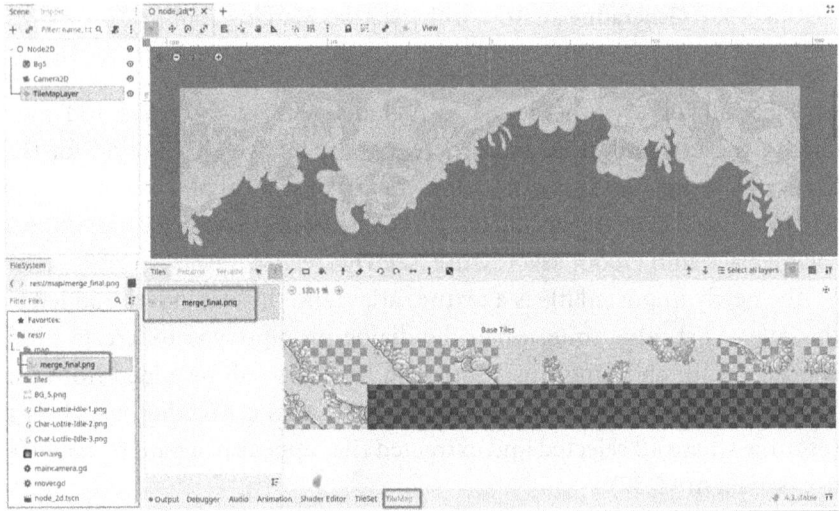

FIGURE 5.37   Creating a TileMap from a TileSet.

pass through. In these cases, we should attach collision data to our tiles. In this section, we'll create that. To start, enable *Physics* for the *TileMapLayer* node. Select the node in the scene, and from the inspector expand *Physics Layers*, and then click the *Add Element* button (see Figure 5.38).

Now that *Physics* is enabled, a new Physics Option will be made available in the *TileSet* Editor. Switch to the *TileSet* Editor, activate the *Select*

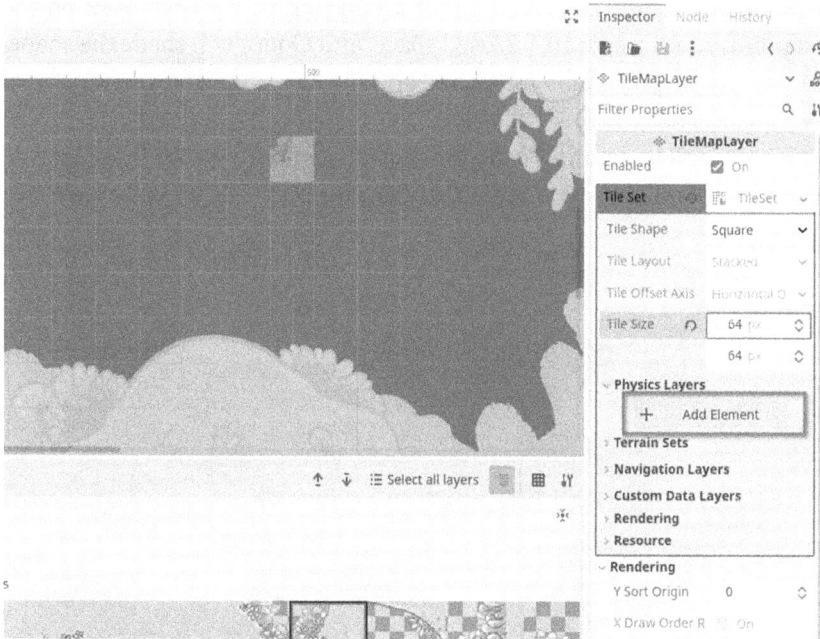

FIGURE 5.38   Add a physics layer to a Tileset.

tool, and pick a tile in the set. When you do this, expand the *Physics Layer* to see collision options (see Figure 5.39).

Next, let's create physics data for our selected tiles, one by one. Choose a tile from the set, and from the *Physics Editor*, you can activate the *Add Polygon* Tool to click and plot points to build a polygon. By clicking, point

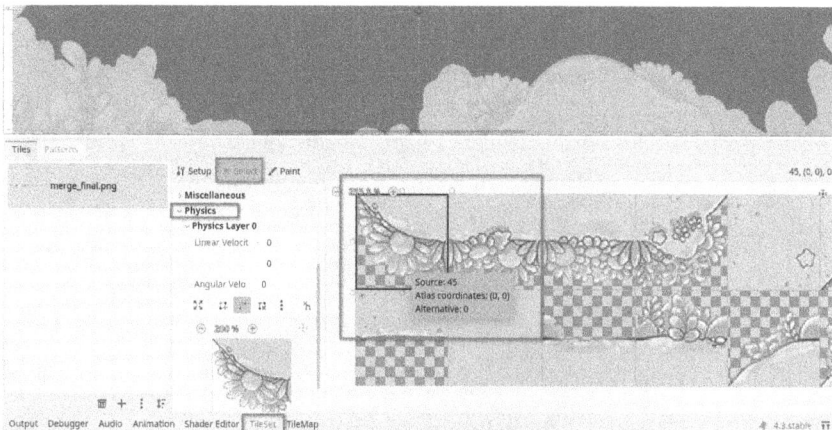

FIGURE 5.39   Accessing the physics for a Tile.

by point, you define new vertices for a polygon. If you click back on the first point, you'll create an enclosed space, and Godot will shade the shape. This means the polygon is completed and the collision data is now defined (see Figure 5.40).

Now complete defining collisions for all remaining tiles by repeating the process. You only need to do this once for each TileSet you create (see Figure 5.41).

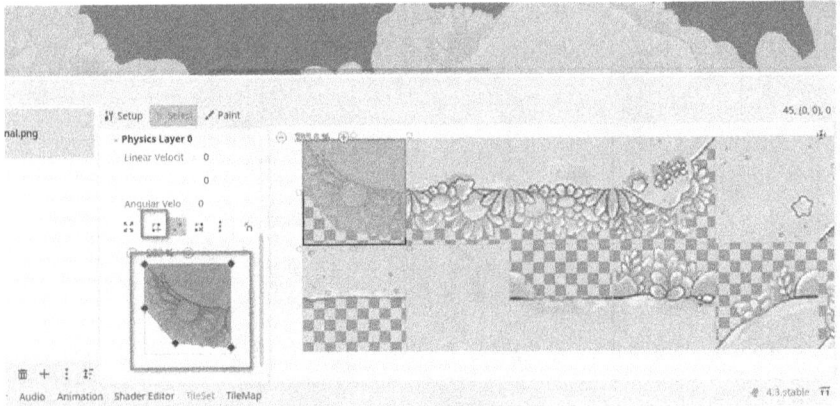

FIGURE 5.40   Building a collision polygon for a tile.

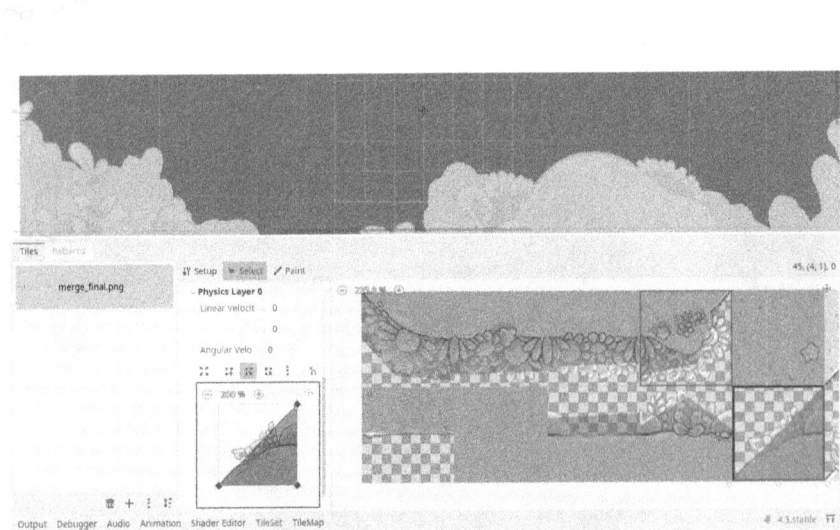

FIGURE 5.41   Completing the collisions for a tileset.

5.4.3 Painting TileSet Worlds

Now it's time for the fun of world-building using the *TileMap* painter. The *TileMapLayer* node allows you to paint selected tiles directly into the *Scene* viewport, building a world tile by tile according to your brush settings. To get started, activate *Paint Mode* from the *TileMap* tab. You can confirm that the *Paint* tool is active because a ghosted version of the selected tile will appear on your mouse cursor (see Figure 5.42).

You can now click and hold down the button to continually paint the selected tile into the viewport grid. You can then select a different tile from the palette and proceed to paint. Using this technique, you can build an expansive level (see Figure 5.43).

You can rotate and reflect tiles. To rotate a tile 90 degrees counterclockwise, press *Z*. To rotate 90 degrees clockwise, press *X*. To flip the tile horizontally, press *C*, and vertically press *V*. You can also use the tile toolbar from the TileMap Window (see Figure 5.44).

Finally, you can now move your player character around the level using the controller created earlier, and collisions will apply with the tiles.

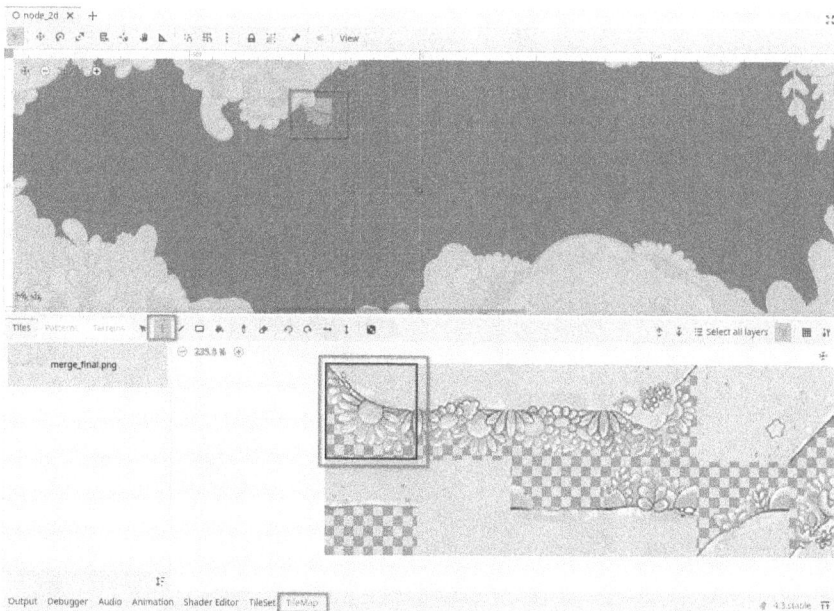

FIGURE 5.42   Painting tiles into the viewport

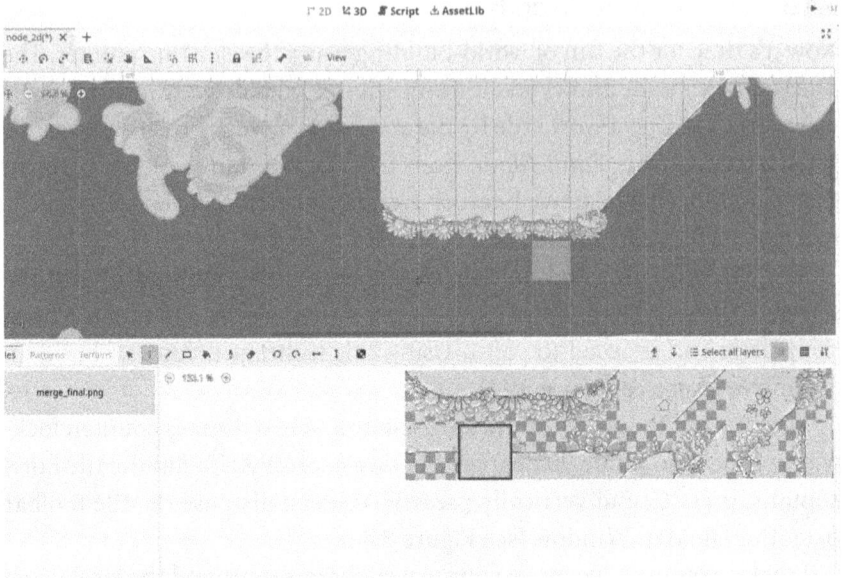

FIGURE 5.43   Painting a world from a TileMap.

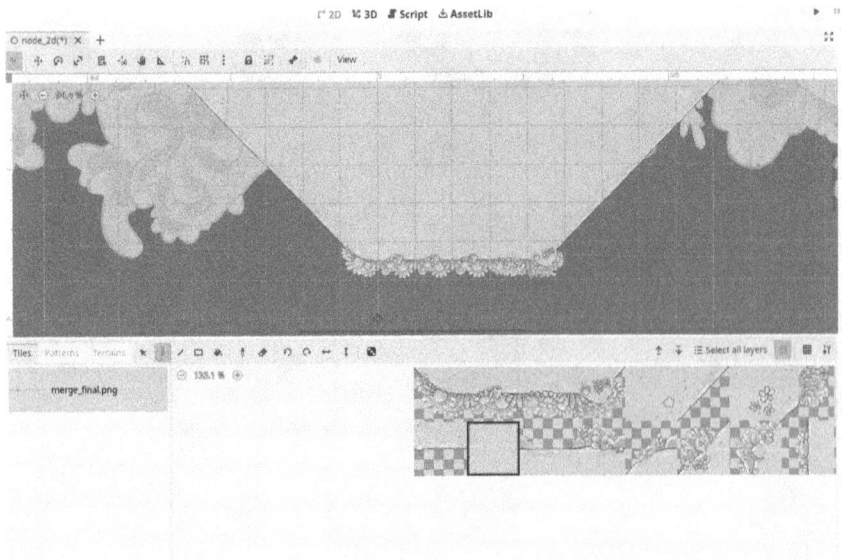

FIGURE 5.44   Transforming tiles.

5.5 2D PATHS AND PATH FOLLOWING

Many 2D space shooters and platformers feature NPCs and other objects that travel along predetermined and curved paths, such as flight paths. These kinds of paths can be hard coded and defined, but for long and complex paths, things can get complicated. So, Godot offers a handy tool for building and following paths. This section explores how to create and follow a predefined path. To start, add a new *Path2D* to an empty scene (see Figure 5.45).

Every newly created path is generated empty in the scene, and you need to add points manually to build a path. This is easy to do. First, select the *Path2D* in the scene and then click the *Add Points* button from the toolbar. By selecting this, you can click inside the viewport to add points. By default, the newly added points are connected by a straight edge (see Figure 5.46).

By default, the path is created by straight edges between points. You can add curvature to the path, however, which changes how the curve is

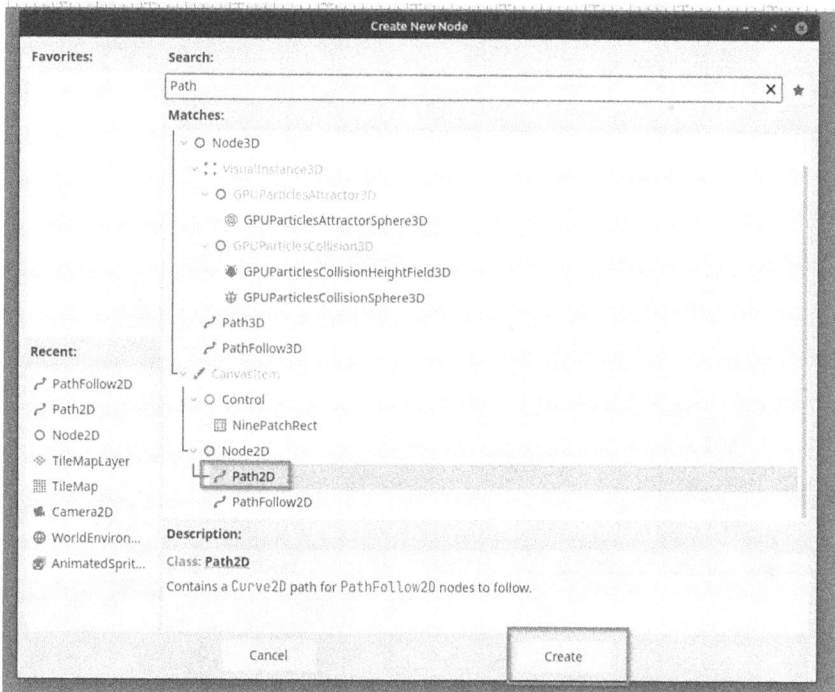

FIGURE 5.45   Transforming tiles.

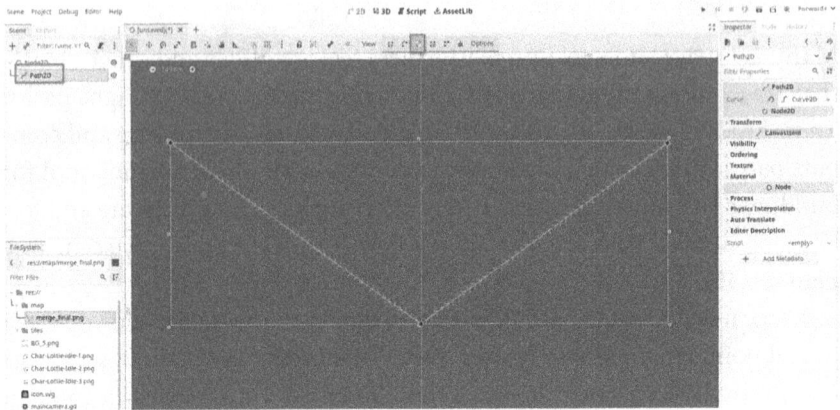

FIGURE 5.46   Creating a new Path by adding points.

generated between the same points. To do this, switch to the *Select Control Points* option by clicking its icon from the toolbar. When you click this, you can click on each control point and adjust its 'handle'. This is a straight, tangential reference line that extends on either side of the control points, and it can be clicked and dragged to adjust the curve of the path (see Figure 5.47).

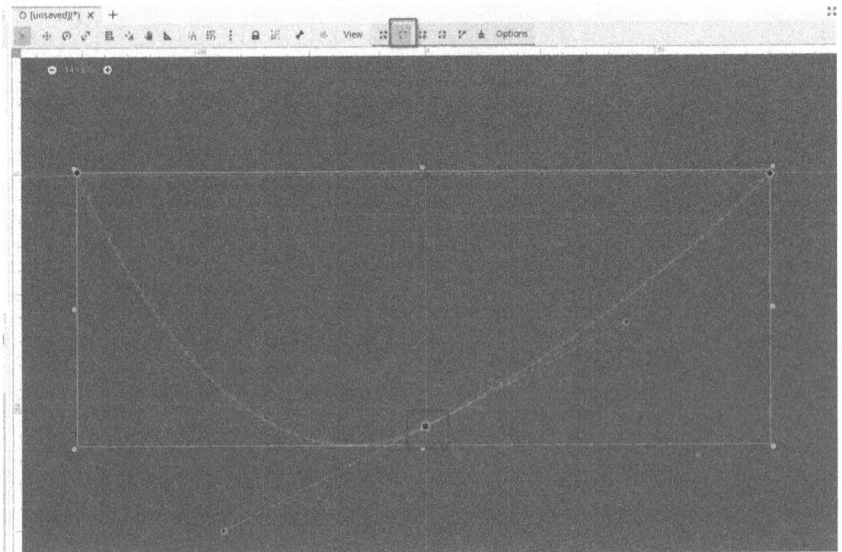

FIGURE 5.47   Adjusting point handles.

You can add as many points as needed to the curve. When you're happy with its structure, you can add a new *PathFollow2D* object to the scene. This should be added as a child of the *Path2D* that it should follow. Follow, in this case, doesn't mean that the object will move and rotate with the path, as its parent, as all children do. It means that the follower can procedurally travel along the curve, from start to end (see Figure 5.48).

The *PathFollow2D* node features two separate properties in the Inspector for measuring how the curve is navigated or followed. These are *Progress* and *Progress Ratio*. *Progress* controls the distance travelled along the curve in pixels, which can vary depending on the length of the curve. Progress Ratio normalizes the length of the curve, regardless of its actual length. The number 0 always means the start of the curve, and 1 always means the end. Fractional values between, such as 0.5, represent degrees between these two endpoints (see Figure 5.49).

As you traverse those numbers in the Inspector, scrolling the progress bar – either *Progress* or *Progress Ratio* – you'll notice that a red point scrolls along the curve, indicating the location of the follower object. The follower is not a visible object like a Sprite. Its purpose is to act as a parent and controller for one or more children who should follow the curve.

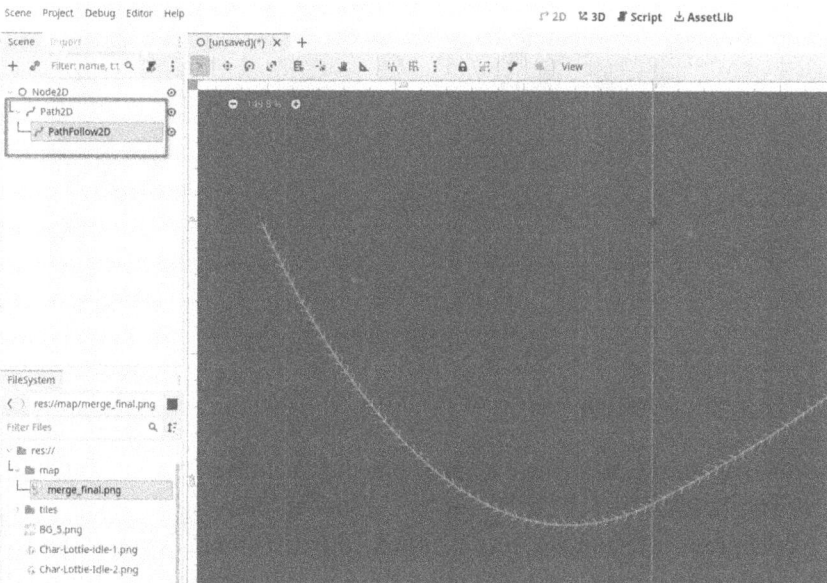

FIGURE 5.48   A follower should be the child of a curve.

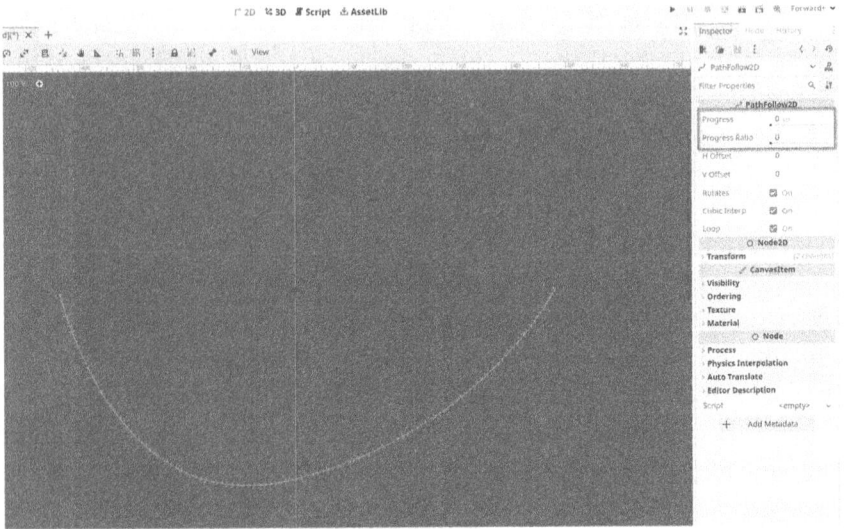

FIGURE 5.49   Two properties for controlling Curve Progress.

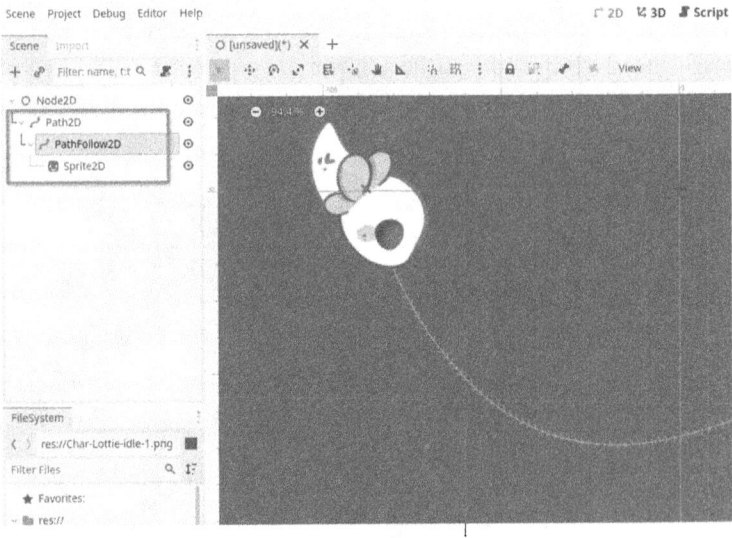

FIGURE 5.50   Attaching a Sprite as a child of PathFollow2D.

So, as an example, let's attach a Sprite object as a child of the *PathFollow2D* (see Figure 5.50).

With the Sprite attached as a child of the PathFollow2D, you can scroll through the Progress Ratio and move the Sprite along the path. The rotate property of PathFollow2D ensures the object rotates to conform to the curve (see Figure 5.51).

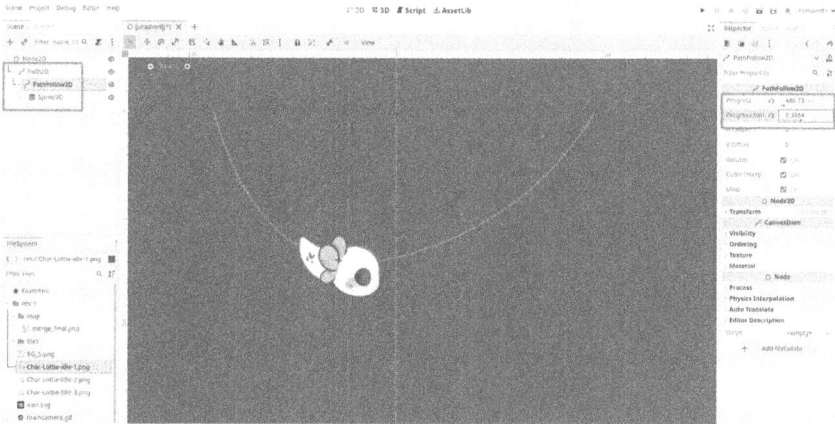

FIGURE 5.51   A Sprite Travels along a curve.

5.6 2D MODULATION

Let's now consider two useful features of renderable 2D objects generally in Godot, such as the *Sprite2D* and the *AnimatedSprite2D*. First are the *Modulate* and *Self-Modulate* fields, which are defined from the Inspector using Color Picker fields. Each defines a solid color that can be multiplied by the Sprite to 'tint' it a specific color. This is useful for flashing a sprite red whenever it takes damage or for turning the sprite blue when it gets frozen. Consider Figure 5.52.

The main difference between *Modulate* and *Self-Modulate* is how the color affects child objects. If Modulate is set, the color will affect both the

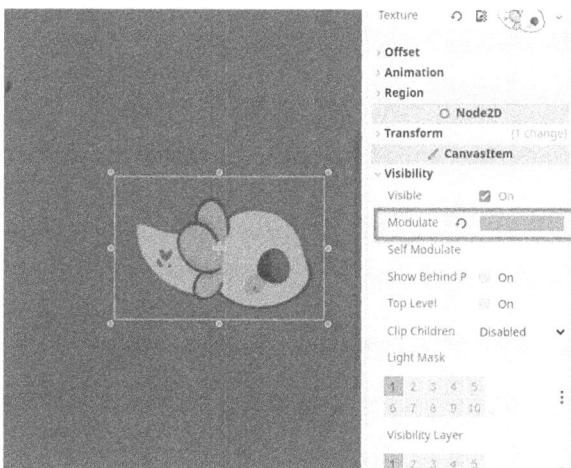

FIGURE 5.52   A Sprite's color controlled by modulation.

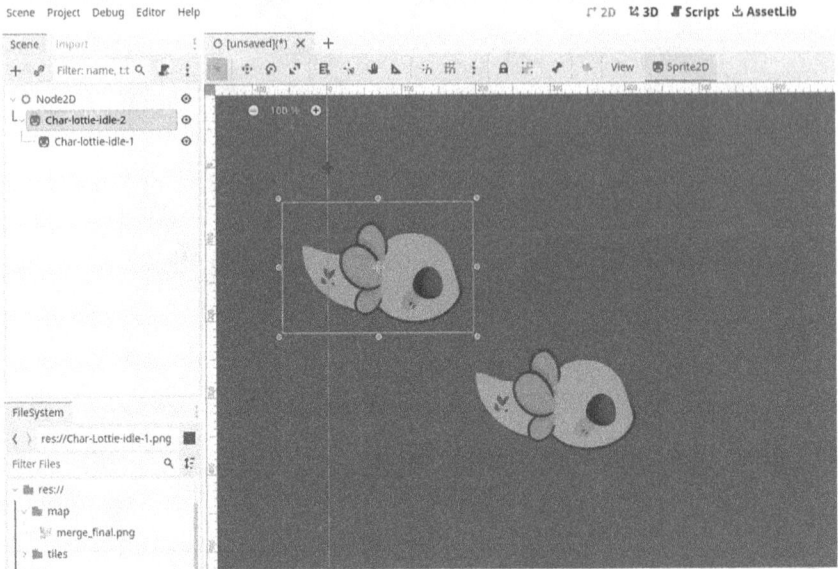

FIGURE 5.53 Modulate cascades down to child objects.

selected object and all the renderable children, making this a great choice for tinting multi-part objects, such as complex player characters holding weapons. By contrast, the Self-Modulate does not cascade down to child objects (see Figure 5.53).

5.7 CLIPPING

A truly excellent and convenient feature of 2D objects in Godot is the ability to use them as a clipping mask. That is, to use one object as a container for a child, preventing the child from being drawn outside the boundaries of its parent. In this case, each and every non-transparent pixel of the parent will reveal any overlapping child object and will otherwise hide it. Let's see how to configure that behavior. To start, add two Sprite objects to the scene, and make one the parent of the other. The parent acts as a mask, and the child will be hidden or revealed (see Figure 5.54).

Next, expand the *Visibility* section of the selected parent *Sprite2D*, and for the *Clip Children* field, choose *Clip Only*. When you do this, both the parent and child will seem to vanish, even though they are clearly present in the scene, via the Scene Dock (see Figure 5.55).

Finally, if you move the child object to any location that intersects the parent, you'll see the child to that extent and no further (see Figure 5.56).

FIGURE 5.54   Parents can act as masks for children.

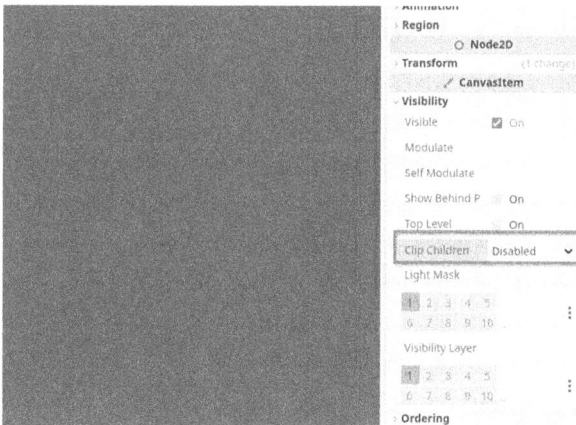

FIGURE 5.55   Choosing *Clip Only* for *Clip Children* will hide both parent and child…

This is a really powerful and easy-to-use feature that can create all kinds of interesting and fun transition effects between levels and scenes.

5.8 CONCLUSION

This chapter considered the most critical Godot features in 2D for building 2D games and 2D worlds. Of these, the *Sprite* and its associated objects are at the forefront. The *Sprite*, and the related *AnimatedSprite*, are the raw

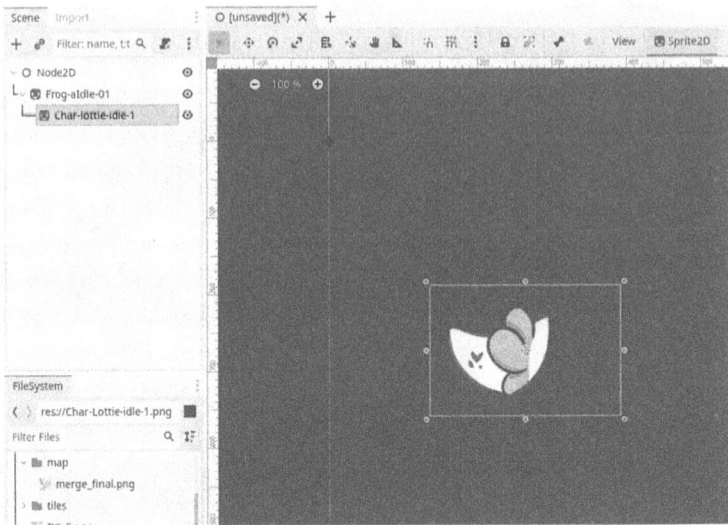

FIGURE 5.56   Parent objects can be used as a clipping mask for children.

materials for building 2D elements that move and are dynamic, such as the player character and NPCs. For static elements, however, such as environments and architecture, 2D TileMaps are usually the tool of choice. These objects are configured to draw lots of pixels to the screen in one operation. Together, Sprites and TileMaps are crucial. But these must usually be completed by physical objects, such as *CharacterBody2D* and *StaticBody2D*, as well as collision data embedded into tiles. In the next chapter, we'll move from the world of 2D into the world of 3D, which has very similar parallel concerns, as we'll see.

CHAPTER 6

3D Worlds

Meshes, Lights, and Cameras

THIS CHAPTER EXPLORES THE exciting world of three dimensions in Godot. 3D opens a new world of possibilities and creativity for game developers. In some ways, 3D scenes and worlds are simpler for newcomers to learn and build than 2D, because far more asset packs, tutorials, and examples are available for 3D than for 2D. For example, you can easily find 3D tutorials for most subjects in game development, from first-person shooters to third-person platformers. And yet, creating 3D worlds and making them truly believable poses a significant challenge both creatively and technically. Although there is so much about 3D that this chapter must necessarily leave unsaid due to space constraints, we'll nonetheless cover the foundations of working with 3D in Godot. This includes everything needed to start making 3D scenes and learn with confidence independently. This chapter assumes you've read the previous one on 2D scenes. You should complete that chapter before reading this one.

6.1 PROTOTYPING 3D SCENES WITH CSG

Nearly every 3D world in a production-ready game, from stylized dungeons to hyper-realistic towns, is formed from many custom-made 3D meshes arranged in a map, lovingly created over long periods of time by experienced artists and third parties. These meshes will normally be made in content creation software, such as Blender, and then finally imported into Godot for use inside scenes. Chapter 3 of this book explored common

DOI: 10.1201/9781003484523-6

resource types, including meshes, and their usual import process from third-party applications into Godot. In Chapter 3, we saw an especially excellent workflow between Blender and Godot, allowing you to edit and change meshes directly inside Blender with a live and updated connection in Godot. This intuitive pipeline creates an almost seamless bridge between the two applications. However, *before* such content is even made inside Blender, many game developers will initially be creating prototypes *in-engine*. Prototypes are early, experimental iterations of a game used to test ideas, try out experiments, see what works, and pre-visualize how a level looks and feels and works ahead of final assembly. Prototypes are a game developer's equivalent to an artist's sketch or to an architect's blueprints in progress. Almost everything about a prototype is subject to change, perhaps even massive change, and indeed, changes at the prototyping stage are considerably cheaper than those further along the line after much time and effort has been invested by the team. So, many 3D scenes begin not as part of a final project that must get everything right, but as part of a prototype where a developer is iteratively finalizing an idea before greenlighting the creation of final assets.

6.1.1 Creating a Room with a CSG Box

Godot features an excellent collection of prototyping tools to quickly build 3D levels from geometry directly inside the editor. These nodes are collectively referred to as *Constructive Solid Geometry* (CSG). They are not intended for use in final versions of a game but are great for 'blocking out' worlds to 'stand in' for elements that will, eventually, be replaced by final custom-made geometry. From the *Add New Dialog* of a 3D scene, you can view all related CSG nodes by typing CSG in the Search field (see Figure 6.1).

Now let's try working with some CSG to create a basic third-person 3D level. Let's start by making a room with a floor and four walls. To start, let's create a *CSGBox3D* node. As the name suggests, this action creates a cube mesh. However, unlike regular meshes, which are normally non-editable in the viewport, CSG can be changed, as we shall see (see Figure 6.2).

The newly generated room looks good initially: it's a box, and immediately, we have four walls, a floor, and a ceiling. But the box is facing outward and is always one-sided. If you move the viewport camera inside the box, its faces will turn transparent. This is due to a famous and pervasive technique known as *Backface Culling*. That is, the 'other side' of a polygon is never rendered by the engine. By default, all polygons are one-sided.

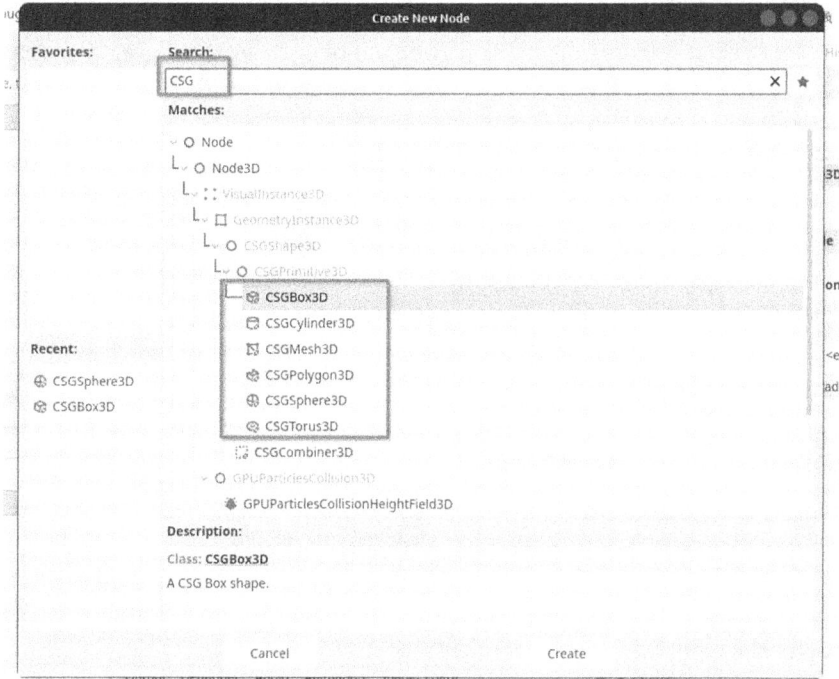

FIGURE 6.1   Searching for CSG nodes.

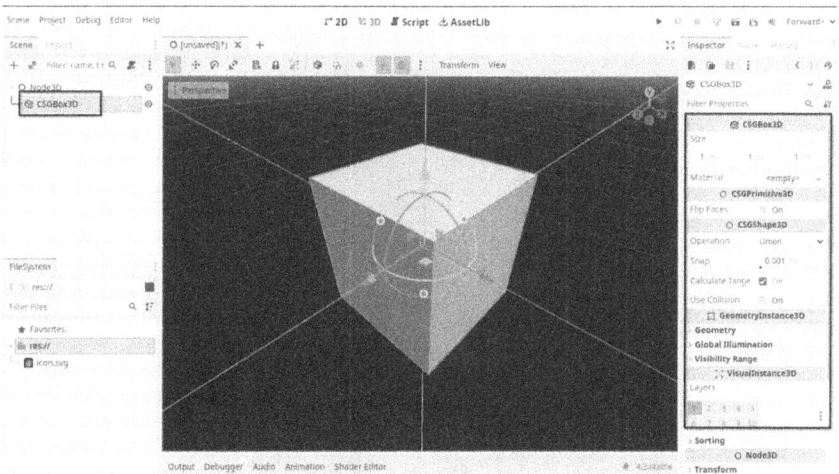

FIGURE 6.2   Creating a CSG box to build a room.

This is a render optimization to prevent the computer from having to calculate surfaces that probably won't or can't be seen by the player. So, what choices do we have here? One is to turn the cube 'inside out'. That is, to Flip all the faces so they face inside rather than outside. You can achieve this by enabling the option *Flip Faces* from the Inspector (see Figure 6.3).

Flipping Faces can be a good option for first-person games where all walls and surfaces are normally seen from ground level and through the eyes of the player character, who can never see the other side of any wall. However, for other camera view types, such as aerial, it can be problematic because it means your walls are paper-thin (without any thickness at all) and cannot be seen from the reverse side. So, for now, we'll disable *Flip Faces* in this case, and we'll build an actual room with thicker walls that are seen on both sides. After disabling *Flip Faces*, select the *CSGBox3D* in the Godot viewport and duplicate it (*Ctrl+D or* Cmd+D). You'll end up with two boxes overlapping each other exactly. Next, select the newly duplicated box, raise it from the ground slightly, and scale it smaller so that it's contained by the original on all walls and it peeks out above the top of the original box (see Figure 6.4).

Next, let's add a new *CSGCombiner* node. This node will soon control how other CSG meshes should interact and relate. Once created, make both of our CSG boxes a child of this node (see Figure 6.5). The order of

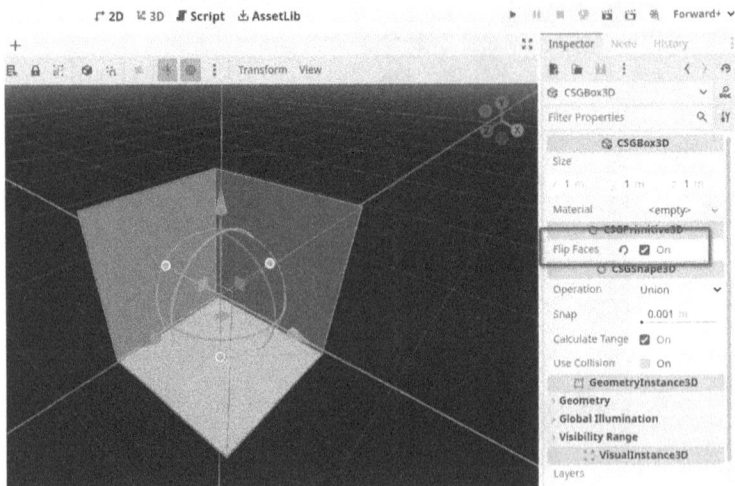

FIGURE 6.3   Flipping Faces to turn a Primitive inside out.

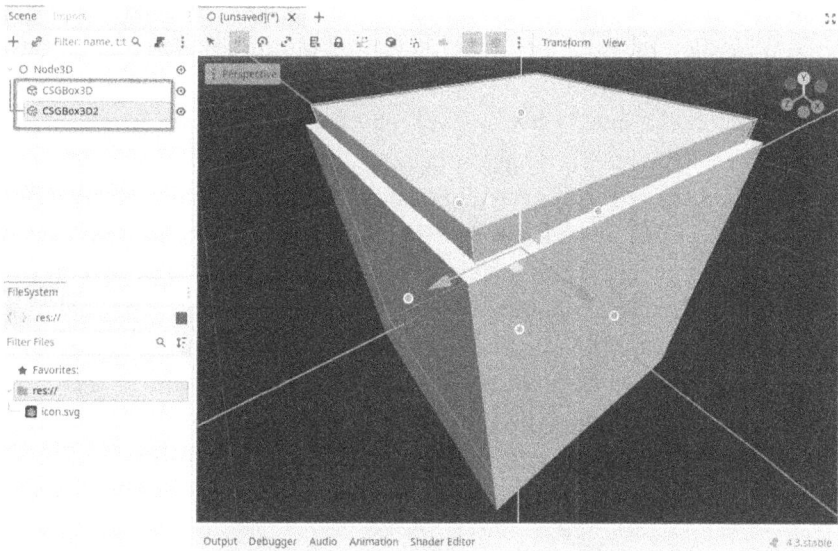

FIGURE 6.4   Positioning and scaling a second *CSGBox*, inside the original.

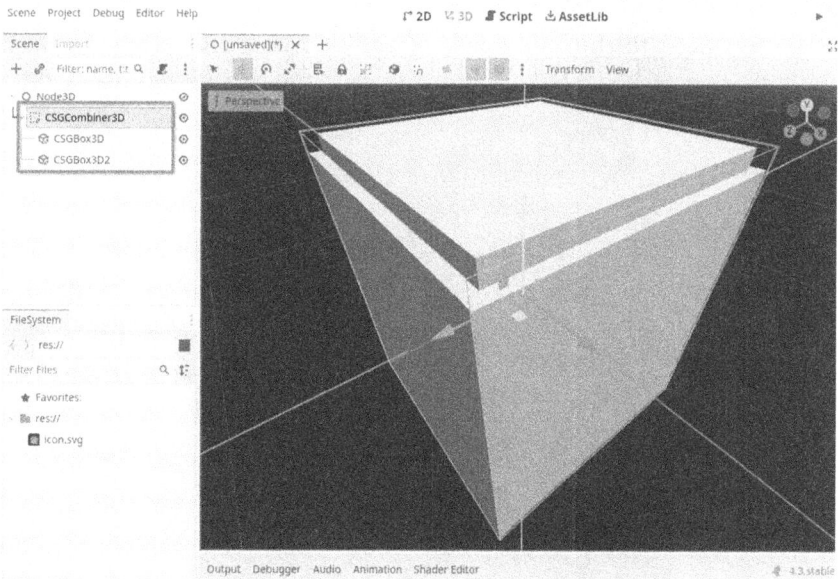

FIGURE 6.5   Creating a CSGCombiner node, and adding children to it.

nodes as children matters here, so be careful. The original CSG box should be the first (topmost) child, followed by the smaller box beneath (see Figure 6.5).

Now select the smaller box in the scene and choose *Subtraction* for the *Operation* field, using the Object Inspector. When you do this, the smaller box gets 'subtracted' from the bigger, overlapping box. Indeed, whenever two or more CSG objects are children of the *CSGCombiner* node, then they will each get combined with every overlapping mesh as defined by the *Operation* fields. The Combiner is therefore a form of Boolean modeling. It allows you to combine two or more meshes based on an *Operation*. The great feature of this technique is that you can still move the meshes around separately, and the Operations will still apply, allowing you to quickly make changes to any meshes. In reaching this far, then, we have now created our first room, with floors and walls (see Figure 6.6).

6.1.2 Creating a Connecting Hallway and Room

The previous section created a room with solid walls and floors using the *CSGCombiner* node. Here, we'll continue that work by expanding our environment further with CSG to include a hallway connecting to another room. If you were making this type of environment in Blender, Maya, or 3DS Max, you'd probably use extrusion and poly-modeling tools. But with CSG, you need to think in terms of addition and subtraction between multiple objects. To start, let's drag and drop the smaller room as a child

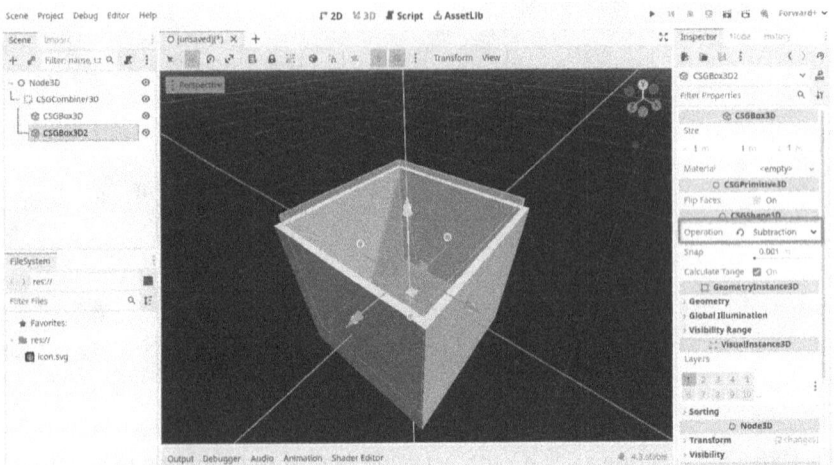

FIGURE 6.6   Combining meshes using a CSGCombiner node to create a room.

of the larger to treat them as one unit hierarchically. Select the larger room (as a parent) and duplicate it (along with the child) to make a second room further away (see Figure 6.7).

Next, let's make the hallway piece by duplicating one of the cube meshes, used for the rooms and deleting any interior space. And then use the scale tool, or the control handles, to resize the hallway as a connecting region. Ensure the two hallway ends pierce through each of the cube walls on either side. It's important for the hallway section to be a child of the same *CSGCombiner* node as the two rooms (see Figure 6.8).

Now duplicate the hallway section, and shrink the duplicate to create the interior space, but do not make it a child of the hallway because it must also affect the rooms as well as the hallway. Make sure the *Operation* is set to *Subtraction* (see Figure 6.9).

The final step in working with CSG is to make the meshes solid objects. By default, the CSG meshes are created without any collision data, which means any solid objects will pass through the CSG meshes as though they were substance-less apparitions. To enable collisions, you'll need to select the *CSGCombiner* node and then enable *Use Collision* from the Object Inspector (see Figure 6.10).

> NOTE. More information on CSG can be found here: https://docs. godotengine.org/en/stable/tutorials/3d/csg_tools.html.

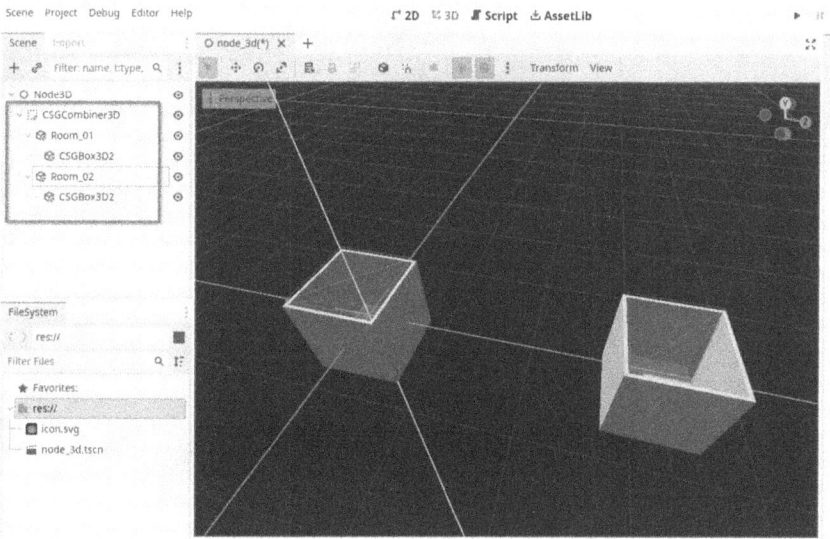

FIGURE 6.7   Creating a second room through duplication.

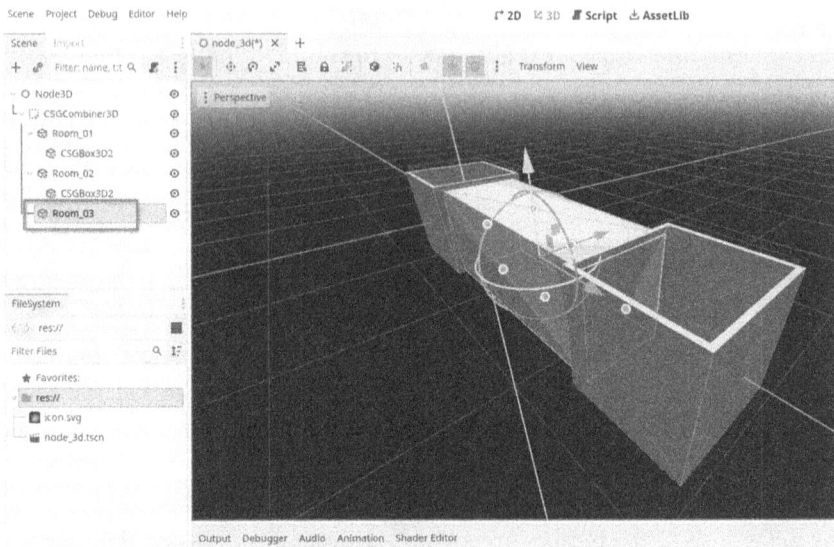

FIGURE 6.8   Creating the Hallway Outer Shell.

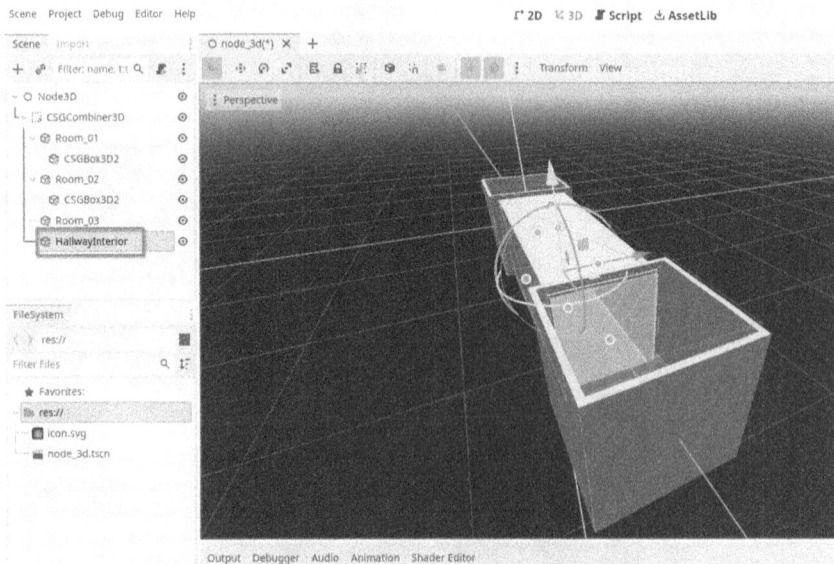

FIGURE 6.9   Creating a complete hallway section.

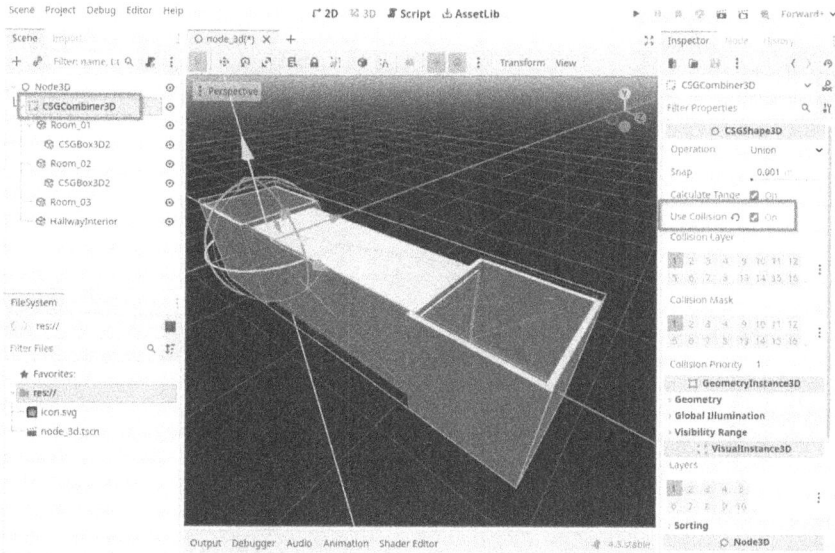

FIGURE 6.10   Adding Collision Data to CSG.

6.2 LIGHTING

The previous section explored how prototypical, and potentially complex, worlds may be constructed quickly from CSG. In this section, we'll move on to lighting in 3D, which is a huge subject that could occupy a book on its own. Here, we'll explore the basics. To start, let's create an empty 3D scene with a sphere and a plane. Chapters 2 and 3 explored how to create this kind of setup using *MeshInstance3D* nodes, along with materials (see Figure 6.11).

Now let's add a *Camera3D* to the scene, which will allow us to see the scene at runtime from a specified perspective. To do this, add a new *Camera3D* node, and then align the camera to the viewport by choosing *Align Transform with View* from the *Perspective* viewport menu. This action moves and rotates the selected object to match the viewport location and orientation. Note that it doesn't adjust the camera field of view or lens properties, so the camera view may still differ slightly from the viewport (see Figure 6.12).

If you now run the scene by pressing the *Play* button from the toolbar, you'll notice a striking difference between the scene view and the game view, even though both views present the scene from the same camera. The difference is in the lighting. This is because, by default, a different kind

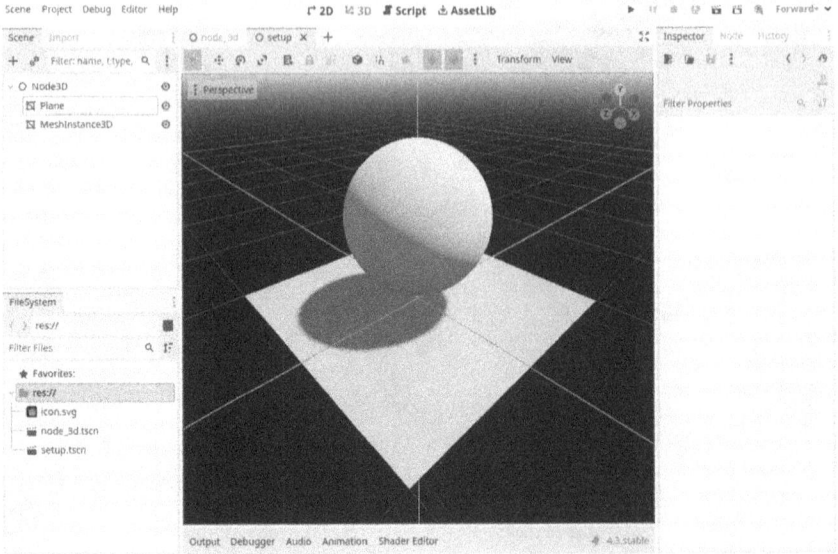

FIGURE 6.11   Creating a Scene with a Plane and Sphere.

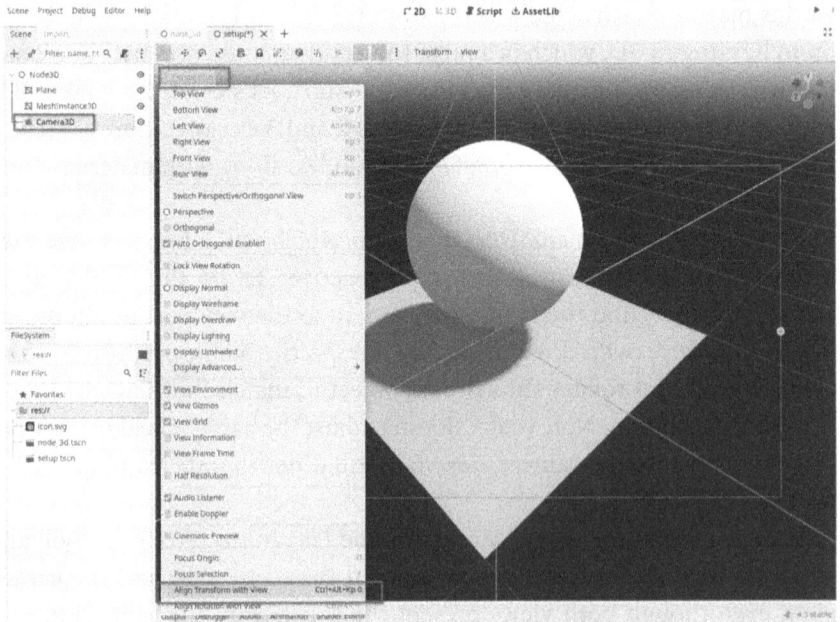

FIGURE 6.12   Aligning the camera to the viewport.

of lighting is applied to the scene in the editor to make editing and build-ing easier. However, it doesn't represent how the player will see the light-ing (Figure 6.13).

To make the editor viewport reflect the final lighting, be sure to disable the scene background and enable lighting using the Scene Toolbar (see Figure 6.14).

6.2.1 Ambient Lighting

To start lighting a scene, you'll first need to consider whether any extant lighting exists in the scene. After all, a world without *any* light sources *should* appear completely dark, and yet our scene is not as black as one might expect. Everything seems illuminated by a dull and pervasive light, casting illumination in all directions with an equal intensity for an infi-nite distance (see Figure 6.14). Indeed, this is known as the *Ambient Light*, or the *Default Clear.* It is, essentially, an artificial boost of illumination to render the contents of the scene visible. Although artificial, that doesn't mean it shouldn't be used and isn't useful. Indeed, the Ambient Light can help us in many ways. But it can prove a source of confusion if you're try-ing to create lighting from scratch and are wondering why your almost empty scene, without any lights, isn't rendering as black. The simplest way to control the ambient light is by using the *Project Settings.* From the

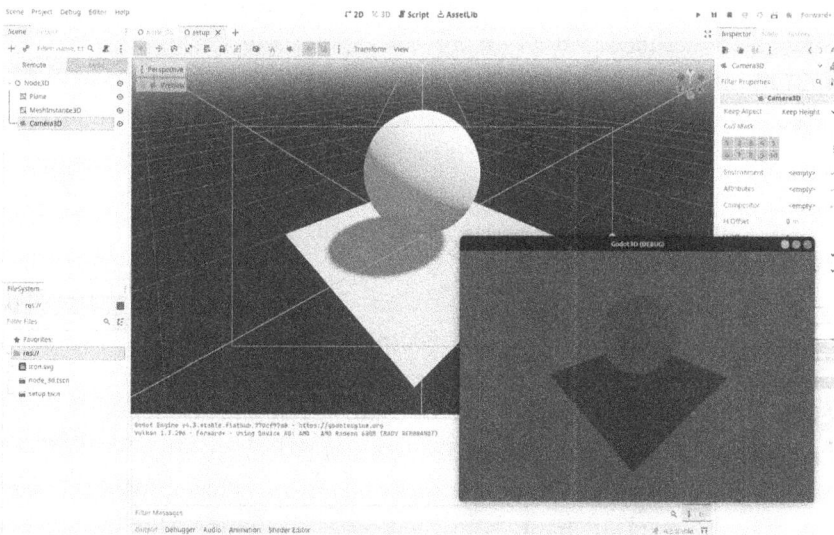

FIGURE 6.13   Comparing the game view with the scene view.

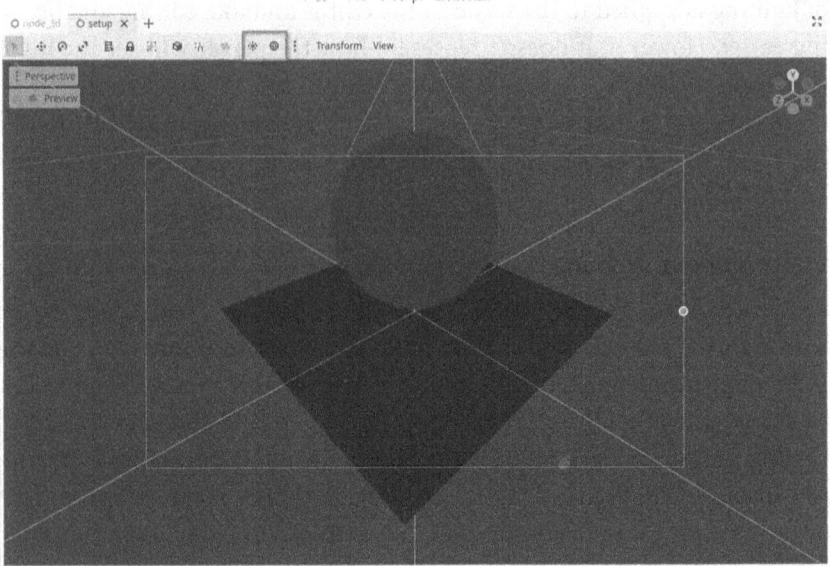

FIGURE 6.14   Creating parity between the scene and game views.

Rendering > Environment menu, you can set the *Default Clear Color*. This is set to a midtone by default. By setting this to black, you'll remove all lighting from the scene (see Figure 6.15).

The problem with the *Default Clear Color* setting is that it's global and not scene-specific. Changing this value affects the default starting color for all scenes. This may not be a problem if you set this value at the start of your project and always keep it in mind. But there are likely to be times when you don't want *all* scenes to behave in the *same* way. So, a more flexible way to control scene lighting is to use a *WorldEnviroment* Node, which can override the defaults. Let's create one of these now, as shown in Figure 6.16. Once created, create a new *Environment* asset via the *Environment* field in the Object Inspector.

Next, we'll override the *Default Clear Color* locally from the *Project Settings* by using the *Background* section and the *Mode* drop-down from the Inspector on the *WorldEnvironment* node. Specifically, set *Mode* to *Custom Color*, and choose *Black* as the color. This removes the ambient light from the scene, giving us a blank canvas to work from (see Figure 6.17).

Now, if you run the scene, it'll appear completely black. We have successfully removed all light from the scene. Of course, this is only an achievement if we want it, and we often will when designing our lighting.

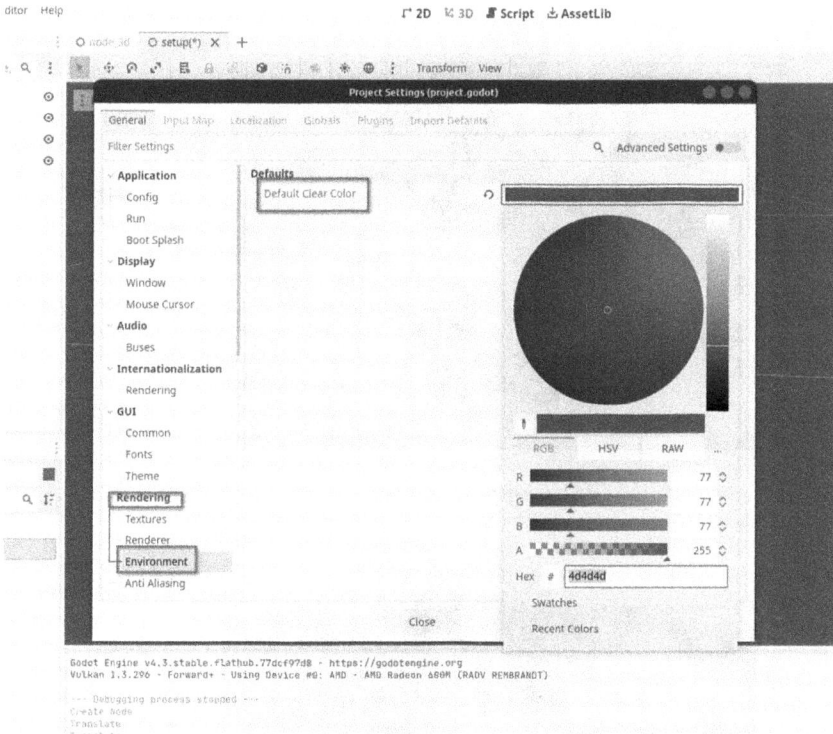

FIGURE 6.15   Setting the Ambient Light for 3D and 2D scenes.

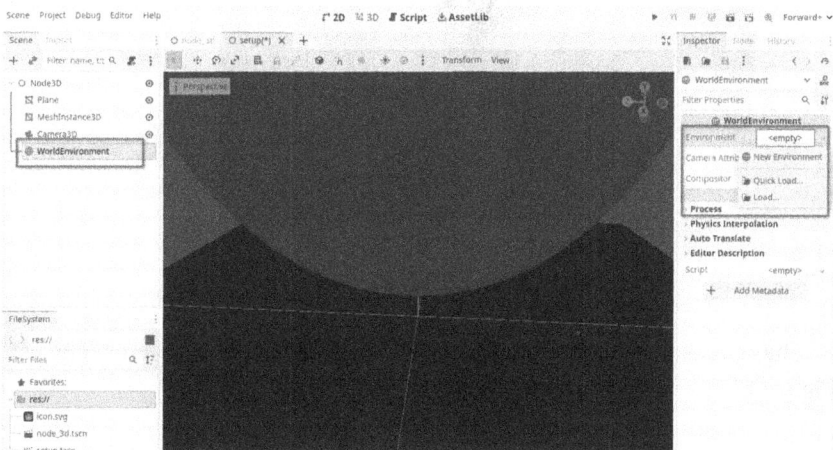

FIGURE 6.16   Creating a new Environment asset for an Environment node.

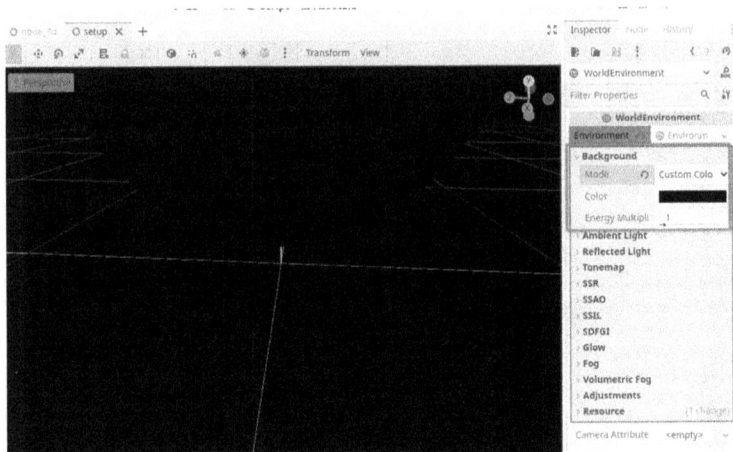

FIGURE 6.17 Setting the background for the Environment Node.

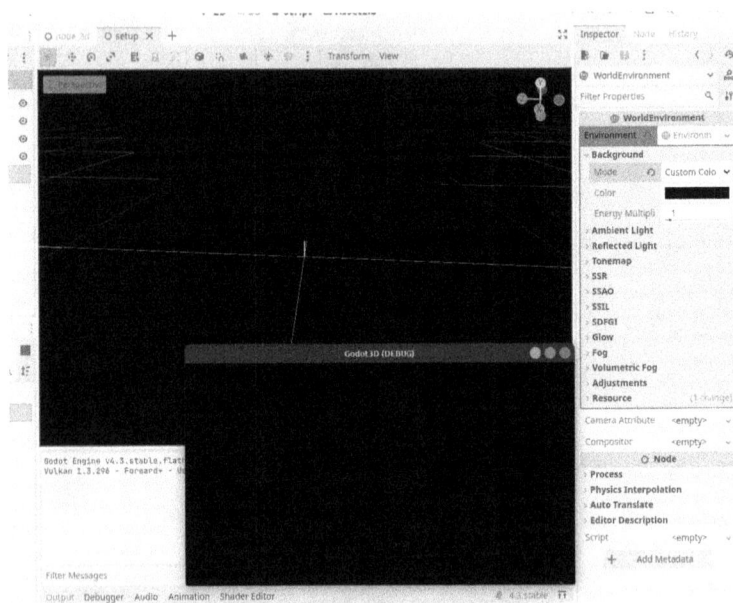

FIGURE 6.18 Light removed from a 3D scene.

We have reason to come back later and restore some ambient light (see Figure 6.18).

6.2.2 Directional Lights

Ambient Light is a pervasive light that isn't created by nodes or by objects but by global settings and controls from option menus. The Directional Light, however, is the first highly customizable and controllable light object that is a node type in scene space. You can add a Directional Light to the scene, as with any node. The node type is a *DirectionalLight3D*. This light type is the simplest kind of light and is also unusual in some notable ways. It's unusual because, even though you can position it at different locations in the scene, its position actually has no effect on its ability to cast light. Only its orientation matters. It will cast light for an equal intensity over an infinite distance in any single direction you specify by its orientation. This light type is useful for simulating large, astronomical, and natural light sources, such as sunlight and moonlight, as well as light from other large bodies, such as energy fields, a laser beam, and a spaceship explosion (see Figure 6.19).

The *Energy* field (which is a float) controls the light brightness from the Object Inspector, and the *Color* field lets you choose the light color. More complex, however, is the *Shadow* rollout, which enables shadow casting for the light. Shadows, when calculated in real-time in Godot, are both complex and computationally expensive. You'll want to have as few shadow-casting lights as possible. Or rather, the smallest number *needed* to achieve the look you *want*. I do not recommend enabling shadows for every single light you add, especially if you're creating a large scene with many lights (see Figure 6.20).

There are many settings to control shadows in Godot. The most important are *Bias*, *Opacity*, and *Blur*. Bias is ultimately an error adjustment field to correct rounding errors during shadow casting calculations. Practically, lower values slide the shadow closer to the casting object, and higher values slide the shadow away from it. If you go too low, the shadow creates a strange, self-repeating artifact appearance that looks erroneous. If you go

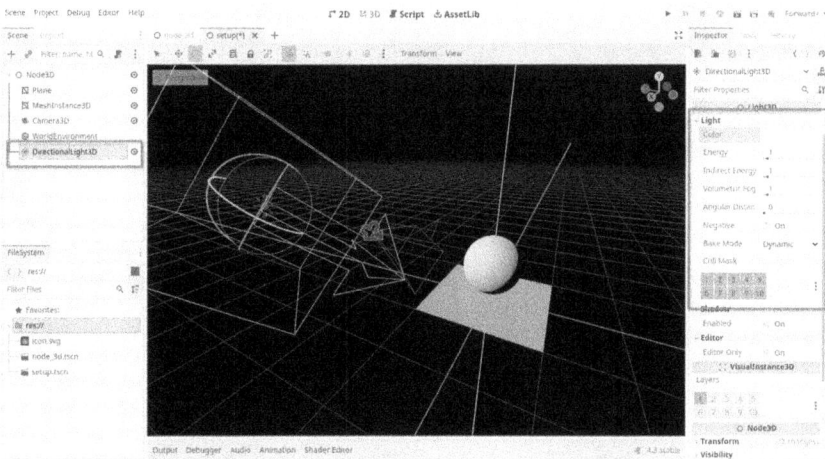

FIGURE 6.19   Creating a Directional Light.

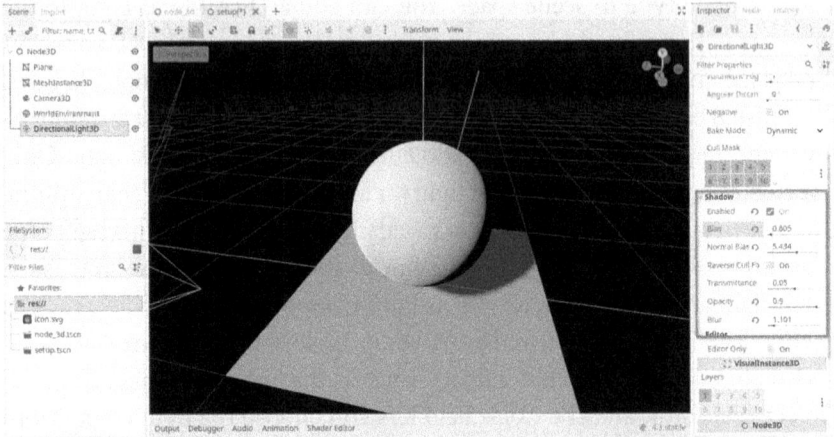

FIGURE 6.20   Enabling shadows for directional lights.

too high, however, the shadow slides too far from its casting object that it creates a sense of disconnectedness. Choosing the right value is an important balance that varies from object to object. Opacity ranges from 0 to 1 and controls shadow intensity. At 1, the shadow is a solid color (usually black), and at 0, the shadow is fully transparent. You would normally choose a value to achieve the most believable shadows. Finally, Blur softens the edges of shadows; again, values that are too low make shadows look hard and artificial, while values that are too high can erase or nullify the shadow altogether (see Figure 6.21).

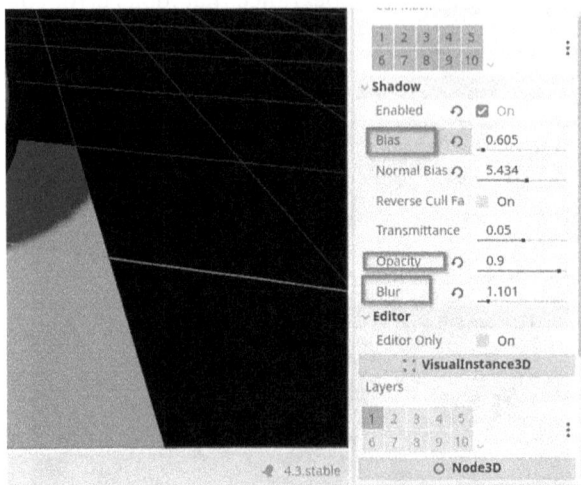

FIGURE 6.21   Adjusting shadow settings.

6.2.3 Omni Lights

The Omni Light is next on our list to consider. This is a moderately expensive light and is so named because it casts light in all directions from its location at a specified intensity and for a specified distance. Unlike the Directional Light, location matters here, and, as a result, the light diminishes in intensity the further it moves from its source location. The Omni Light (*OmniLight3D*) is the preferred method for simulating artificial light, such as light bulbs, fiery torches, and glowing portals or computers (see Figure 6.22).

Each Omni Light has a *Range* and *Attenuation*. The *Range* specifies the maximum radius, in meters, for the Omni Light's influence. Anything outside of the radius will be unaffected by light. Anything within the radius could be affected by the light, depending on its *Attenuation* settings. *Attenuation* controls how light dissipates within the Radius. That is, how the intensity of the light reduces from its center to its circumference. The best way to adjust these settings is normally by eye rather than by value. So, you would normally adjust these values while checking in the viewport to see the effects of your changes, settling on the values that look right aesthetically (see Figure 6.23).

6.2.4 Spot Lights

The final light primitive in Godot is the Spotlight (*SpotLight3D*) node, which is *directed* (like a Directional Light) but is also positional and

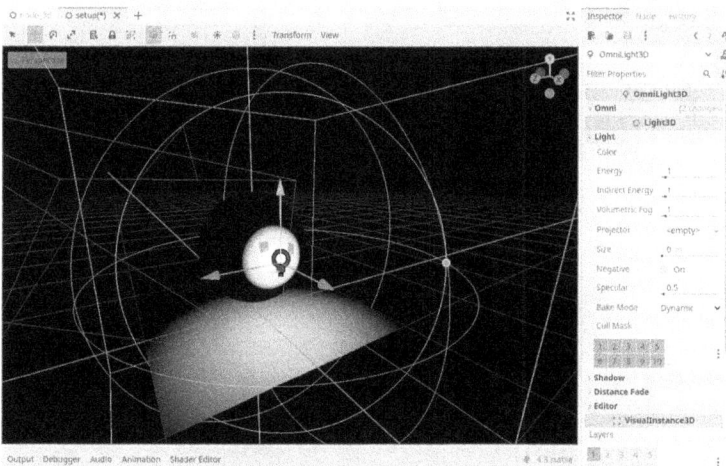

FIGURE 6.22   Adding an Omni Light to the Scene.

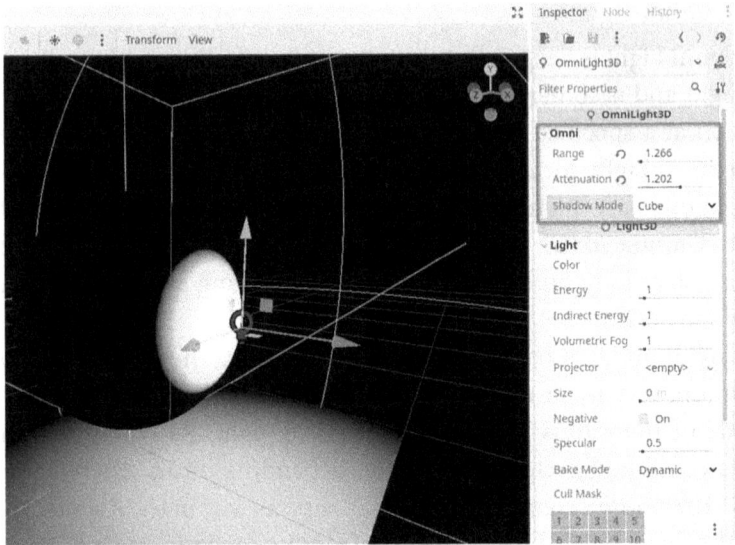

FIGURE 6.23   Controlling the Attenuation and Range for a Godot Omni Light.

limited like an Omni Light. The Spot Light is useful for creating artificial lights, such as ceiling lights, flashlights, and car headlights. The Spot Light has a range determined by two cones. The Outer Cone (controlled by *Angle* and *Range*) specifies the maximum range of the spotlight, both the circumference and the distance of the cone, respectively. The *Attenuation* and *Angle Attenuation* fields control the falloff of the light within the cone as it moves from the light source (see Figure 6.24).

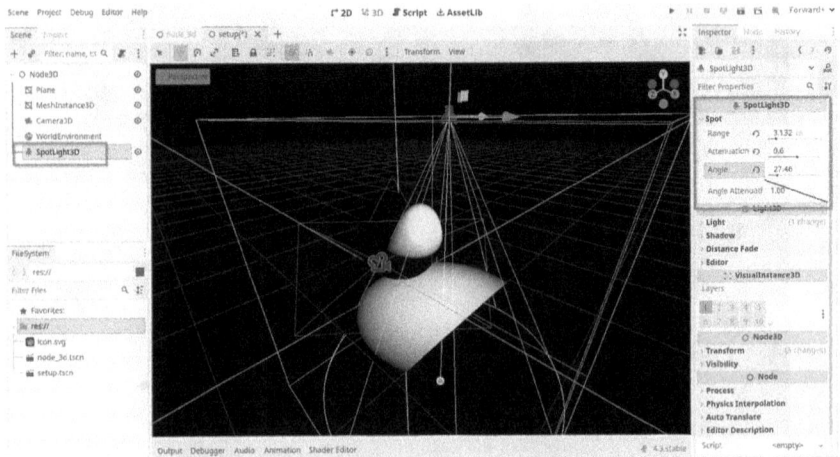

FIGURE 6.24   Creating a Spot Light Object.

6.3 TRANSFORM OBJECTS IN 3D

The previous two sections focus on prototyping and lighting 3D scenes, allowing you to create worlds to explore in 3D in a way where both *Edit* mode and *Play* mode can match each other faithfully in appearance. Now let's make 3D objects move dynamically through the scene from code, such as a camera fly-through or a sample player character. We'll start without any regard for physics and solidity. And then we'll explore how to achieve similar behavior but with physics included in the following section. Let's start with a new 3D scene and add an example character mesh. We'll create a Capsule Mesh for the player and a Plane Mesh for the floor. Both of these are created using a *MeshInstance3D*, as we have seen (see Figure 6.25).

Next, make sure you've setup the controls via the *Project Settings* Input Map. This is important for reading keyboard input to control object movement in the script (see Figure 6.26).

Next, let's add some code to create a player-controlled moving object. Be sure to attach the script to your object and then try it out on the capsule. Consider Code Sample 6.1 below.

CODE SAMPLE 6.1   PLAYER-CONTROLLED 3D OBJECT

```
extends Node3D
@export var __move_speed:float = 2
@export var __rot_speed:float = 90
func _process(_delta: float) -> void:
var _player_input:Vector2 = Vector2.ZERO
_player_input.x = Input.get_action_strength("Left")
- Input.get_action_strength("Right")
_player_input.y = -Input.get_action_strength("Down")
+ Input.get_action_strength("Up")

position += basis.z * _delta * _player_input.y * __move_speed;

rotate_y(deg_to_rad(__rot_speed * _delta * _player_input.x))
```

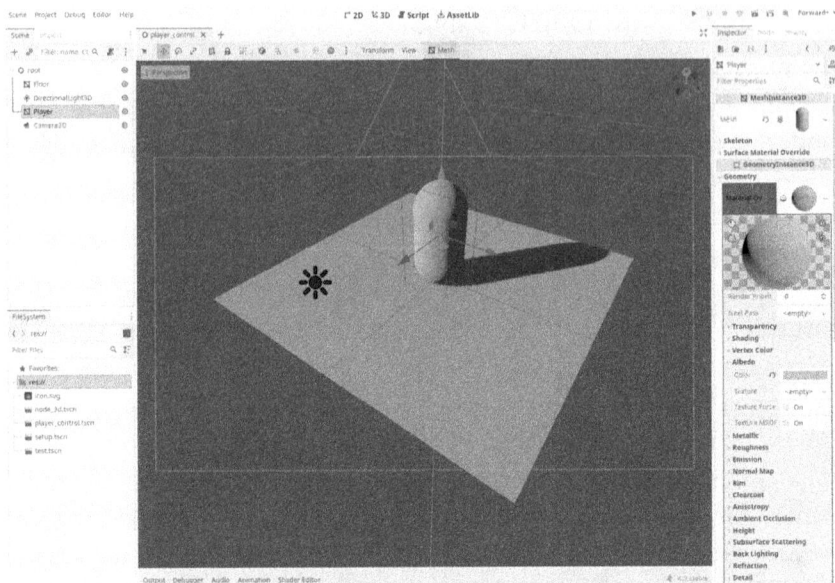

FIGURE 6.25   Creating a player from a capsule and a floor from a plane.

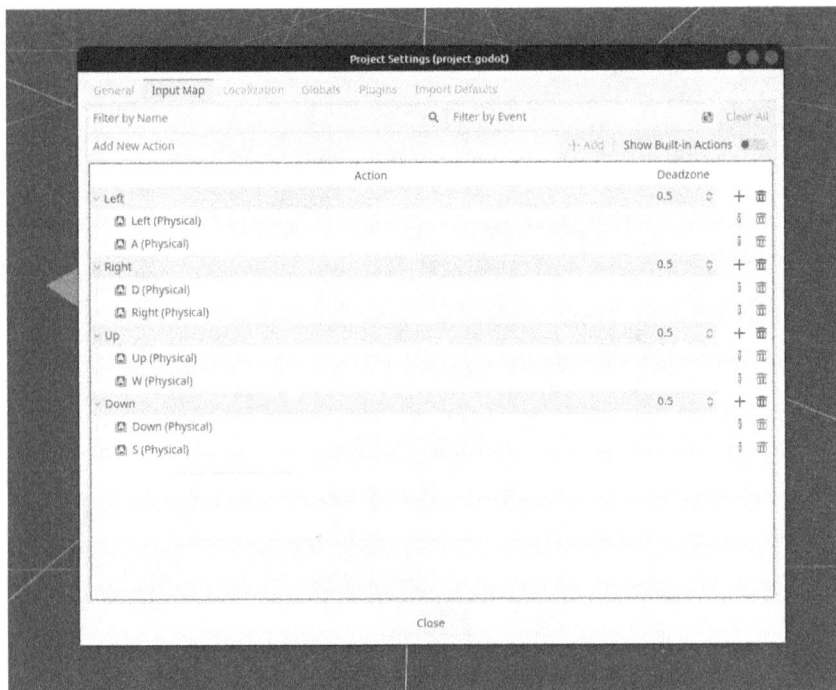

FIGURE 6.26   Configuring player controls.

Let's review some important details about this code:

- First, two variables are defined – *Speed* and *RotSpeed*. *Speed* defines the translation speed of the object (in meters per second) as we move through space by pressing the up or down arrow. *RotSpeed* is the angular speed at which the object will rotate as we press either left or right in degrees per second.

- The *_process* function is called automatically by Godot once per frame.

- The *get_action_strength* function returns input values between -1 and 1 to reflect keyboard input on either the left-right axis or the up-down axis.

- The *position* variable is part of *Node3D* and specifies the 3D location of the 3D object for this frame.

- The *basis.z* property is a 3D Vector. *Basis* contains three such vectors: X, Y, and Z. Each refers to *(X, Y, Z)* values. The Z property refers to the local Z axis in world space for that object. That is, it always points in the direction that the player is facing. It's the blue arrow (Z axis) in the viewport, which appears when the object is selected. For this reason, when *Z* is multiplied by other scalars, such as *speed, time,* and *input*, it offsets the player's position along the direction they are looking (creating forward or backward movement).

- The *rotate_y* function turns the player object *around* its local Y axis (that is, the axis pointing upward through its center). The angle in degrees is converted into the metric *Radian* angle measure as a function of the argument.

Great! In reaching this far, we have now created a player-controlled object using GDScript and the Node3D class. As shown in Chapter 2, this free-form movement can be useful, and it's good to know. But what about if we need collisions? Right now, our 3D object will move around and pass through solids and be unaffected by gravity. In the next section, we'll add physics to our workflow.

6.4 PHYSICS AND COLLISIONS IN 3D

This section continues from the previous in creating a movable, player-controlled object that respects physical interactions with other solids. Here, we'll expand on the previous scene, which features a capsule for the player and a plane for the floor. Additionally, we'll add some boxes which can be 'bumped into' as obstacles. Let's get started.

6.4.1 Configuring Solid Objects with Colliders

Let's first build a solid cube mesh. To do this, create a *StaticBody3D* node, which should feature two children, mirroring the 2D workflow. The children should be a *MeshInstance3D*, set to a *Box* mesh, and a *CollisionShape3D*, which is configured to a *Box* Shape. Together, these represent a solid obstacle (see Figure 6.27).

We should also apply the same thinking to the floor too because the floor is a solid object. So, let's make it a static body, coupled with a box collision shape (see Figure 6.28).

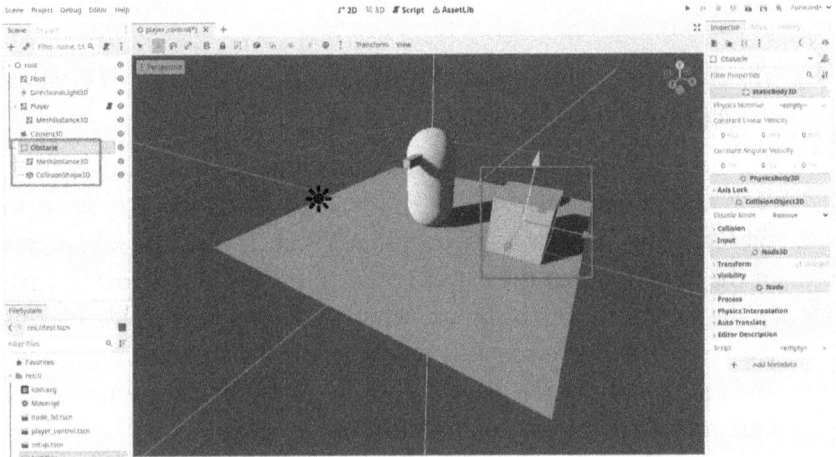

FIGURE 6.27   Cube mesh.

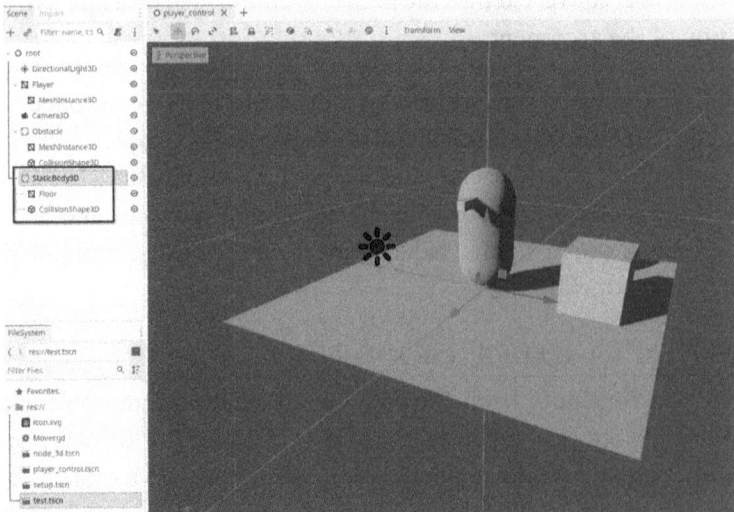

FIGURE 6.28   Creating a collider for the floor.

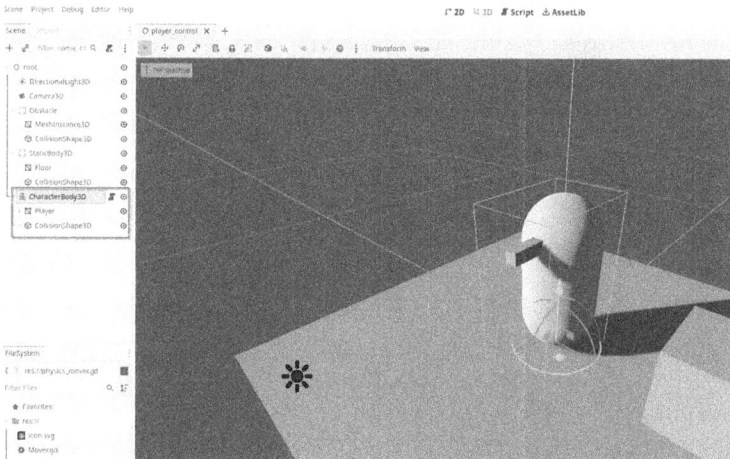

FIGURE 6.29   Creating a player object with collisions.

And now it's time to setup the player. The player should consist of three objects in a hierarchy. Namely, *CharacterBody3D*, with a mesh child and a representative collider (see Figure 6.29).

6.4.2 Creating a PlayerController with Physics

The *CharacterBody3D* is the critical movable physics object for in-game agents, like the player character or NPCs. This node contains the necessary functions and behaviors to easily build physically believable systems for games. Consider Code Sample 6.2, which should be attached to the *CharacterBody3D* for the player character.

CODE SAMPLE 6.2   PLAYER CONTROLLER

```
extends CharacterBody3D
@export var __move_speed:float = 2
@export var __rot_speed:float = 90
var _player_input:Vector2 = Vector2.ZERO
var _gravity:float = 0
func _ready() -> void:
        _gravity = ProjectSettings.
get_setting("physics/3d/default_gravity")
func _process(_delta: float) -> void:
        _player_input.x = Input.
get_action_strength("Left") - Input.
get_action_strength("Right")
```

```
        _player_input.y = -Input.get_action_
strength("Down") + Input.get_action_strength("Up")

func _physics_process(_delta: float) -> void:
        rotate_y(deg_to_rad(__rot_speed * _delta *
_player_input.x))
velocity = basis.z * _player_input.y * __move_speed

if(!is_on_floor()):
        velocity.y -= _gravity

move_and_slide()
```

Let's review some important details about this code:

- First, two *gravity* variables are defined in the *_ready* function as the scene starts. It reads the gravity setting from the *Project Settings*. This value is a float that defines the speed of gravity – the strength of its pull.

- The *_process* function is used here only to read input on the *horizontal* and *vertical* axes.

- The *_physics_process* function is called once per physics cycle.

- The function *move_and_slide* is used in conjunction with velocity to drive the player while taking into consideration physical collisions.

- The *is_on_floor* function returns true if the player is touching the ground. If this returns false, then gravity is subtracted from the velocity to pull the object down.

6.4.3 RigidBodies and Movables

So far, we've coded a player character that can move freely around the scene and collide with physical objects that are static bodies, such as boxes and floors. When the collision happens, further movement in that direction is prevented. In this section, we'll handle a physical interaction with a movable object, like a ball. Specifically, let's create a movable player character that can push a ball by colliding with it. To do this, let's create a movable ball object. We'll need three nodes for this: a *RigidBody3D* node as a parent and then two children: a sphere mesh and a sphere collider. See Figure 6.30 for the configuration.

Next, select the *RigidBody3D* object (the ball), and let's apply some important settings. Let's disable *Sleeping* and *Can Sleep*, as this object must continually monitor for collisions. Then set the *Solver* to *Continuous*. Again, to ensure the object will always respond to a collision (see Figure 6.31).

Finally, the Player Controller script, attached to the Player Agent, can be modified. It is given in full in Code Sample 6.3.

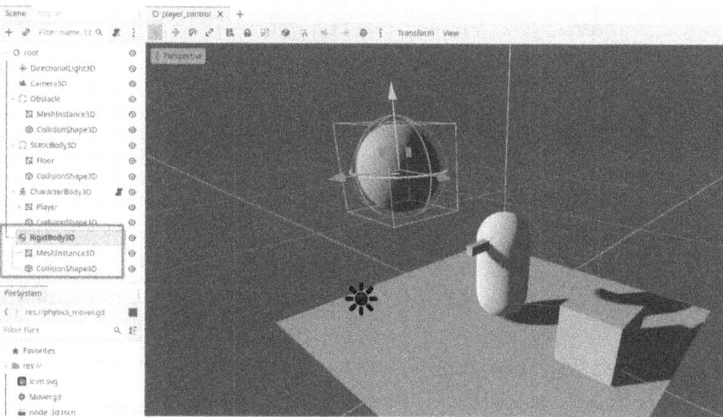

FIGURE 6.30   Creating a RigidBody object.

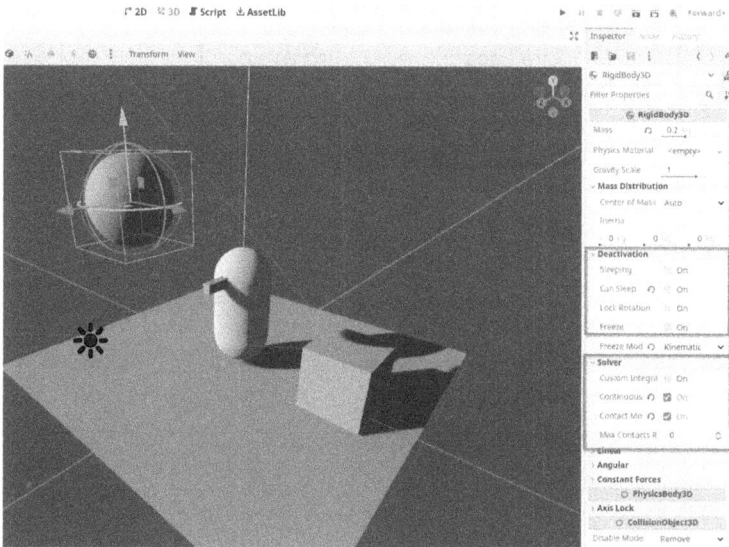

FIGURE 6.31   Configuring a RigidBody for collisions.

CODE SAMPLE 6.3   PLAYER CONTROLLER WITH COLLISION INTERACTION FOR RIGIDBODIES

```
extends CharacterBody3D
@export var __move_speed:float = 2
@export var __rot_speed:float = 90
var _player_input:Vector2 = Vector2.ZERO
var _gravity:float = 0
@export var _push_strength:float = 1
func _ready() -> void:
        _gravity = ProjectSettings.
get_setting("physics/3d/default_gravity")

func _process(_delta: float) -> void:
        _player_input.x = Input.
get_action_strength("Left") - Input.
get_action_strength("Right")
        _player_input.y = -Input.get_action_
strength("Down") + Input.get_action_strength("Up")

func _physics_process(_delta: float) -> void:
        rotate_y(deg_to_rad(__rot_speed * _delta *
_player_input.x))
velocity = basis.z * _player_input.y * __move_speed

        if(!is_on_floor()):
                velocity.y -= _gravity

        if move_and_slide():
                for i in get_slide_collision_count():
                        var collision =
get_slide_collision(i)

                        if collision.get_collider()
is RigidBody3D:
(collision.get_collider() as RigidBody3D).apply_central_
impulse(-collision.get_normal() * _push_strength)
```

Let's review some important details about this code:

- First, the *_push_strength* variable defines how strongly the player will push a rigidbody on a collision. This value is a multiplier, so a value of 2 means twice as strong as the default, 3 means three times, etc.

- The _physics_process function contains an additional statement to detect the collision. If a collision is detected with a Rigidbody, then an impulse is applied.

- The impulse is a vector, expressing the strength of a push. The *get_normal* function returns the 'direction of the collision' between the player and the ball. Thus, an inversion of this, multiplied by the push strength, will repel the ball away.

6.5 AREAS AND TRIGGERS

Sometimes, you don't want to block the player from entering an area of space, such as a box area or a sphere area. Colliders and physics have the effect of blocking. Instead, you'll often want to allow the player to enter an area but be notified when the entry happens so you can respond appropriately in code. An example would be when the player falls underwater, or when the player enters a dangerous region, or when the player enters an enemy's line of sight. In all these cases, notifications about the player's presence inside a specified area are helpful. In Godot, you use Area Nodes to identify these moments. Let's see how to use one. To start, let's create a new *Area3D* node, and it should have a child, which is also a collision shape, such as a box, sphere, or capsule. For this example, and for most instances, you'll probably use a box (see Figure 6.32).

Next, if you select *Area3D* and switch to the *Signals* tab in the Inspector, you'll notice many different types of events that you can listen for. Most of these events fall across two different types: body events and area events. Body events occur when a physical body, such as a *RigidBody* or *CharacterBody*, either enters or leaves the Area. Area events occur when two or more Area objects intersect (see Figure 6.33).

Let's listen for a *BodyEntered* event. This is called when a physics body first enters the Area. This event only happens once on the first occurrence. It will only happen again if the body first leaves and then re-enters the Area. To configure this, the following code can be added to our Player Controller, which we created in earlier sections (see Code Sample 6.4).

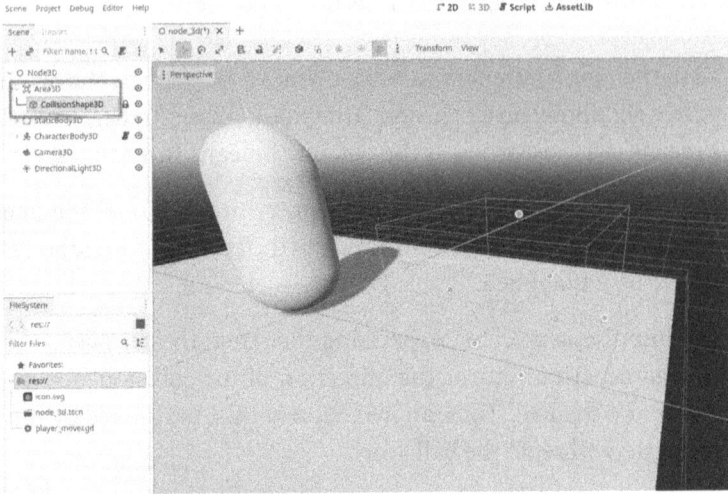

FIGURE 6.32   Creating an Area3D.

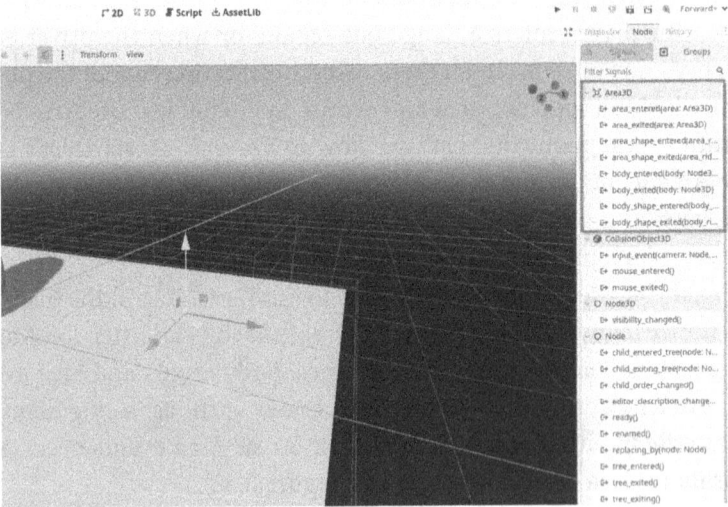

FIGURE 6.33   Areas support many event types.

CODE SAMPLE 6.4   CONFIGURING AN
AREA3D FOR ENTRY DETECTION.

```
func _ready() -> void:
        var _area:Area3D = get_node("/root/
MainScene/Area3D") as Area3D
        _area.connect("body_entered",
_on_body_entered)

func _on_body_entered(_body:Node3D):
        print("body entered")
```

Let's review some important details about this code:

- This script can be attached to the player's character. Although it interacts with the Area3D, it doesn't need to be attached to that object.

- Next, the *get_node* function is used inside *_ready* to find the Area3D node in the scene. This call uses the absolute path syntax. It begins with '/root/' and then is followed by the Node Name of the topmost node in the scene. This Path Syntaxis is useful in that you can absolutely identify any node by name, but it fails if this script is reused in a different scene with different names or if the current scene hierarchy changes. So, it's a very fragile way to refer to nodes. I include it here to show that it's possible to do if you want. But a better approach is to find nodes by groups, as you saw in earlier chapters.

- The *connect* function is used to link the *body_entered* event to a local function, which prints a message to the console.

6.6 PHYSICS QUERIES

Previous sections demonstrated both how to block object movement using *Bodies* and *Colliders* and how to be notified about object intersections with *Areas*. Together, these two nodes answer questions about events *as they happen now*, and so, they satisfy important needs for working effectively in 3D scenes. However, a third need arises, specifically queries. That is, you'll often need to ask questions about possibilities and counterfactuals, to take action, or to prevent action *in advance*. That is, you'll need to ask questions about what might happen if a certain event occurs. For example: *if* the player moves forward, will they collide with any dangerous traps? *If* an NPC runs forward, will they fall off the edge of a platform? *If* the player is teleported to the other side of the world, will they land on the floor? Answering these questions is important, especially for creating NPC AI, to make good decisions and to avoid dangers that could radically affect gameplay. To run these kinds of queries, we can use *Raycasts* and *Shapecasts*.

6.6.1 Ray Casts

A ray in Godot is a finite line segment that is non-rendered and is used only to test for intersections with surrounding objects. It detects whether the line intersects either a body, an area, or both. Rays are often attached as children to movable objects, such as NPCs and the player character, to detect nearby objects. For example, a ray may be attached to the front of a walking NPC object to determine when a wall is approached. Let's attach a *RayCast3D* to the player character to express their line of sight (see Figure 6.34).

Now let's explore some of the most important settings, which are available from the Object Inspector. *Exclude Parent* and *Hit From Inside* are two useful settings! Often, the RayCast object will be positioned *inside* a mesh looking outward, such as from the eye socket of the character looking outward to the world. The Raycast will usually be added as a child of the moving object too (such as the player), to ensure the Raycast moves

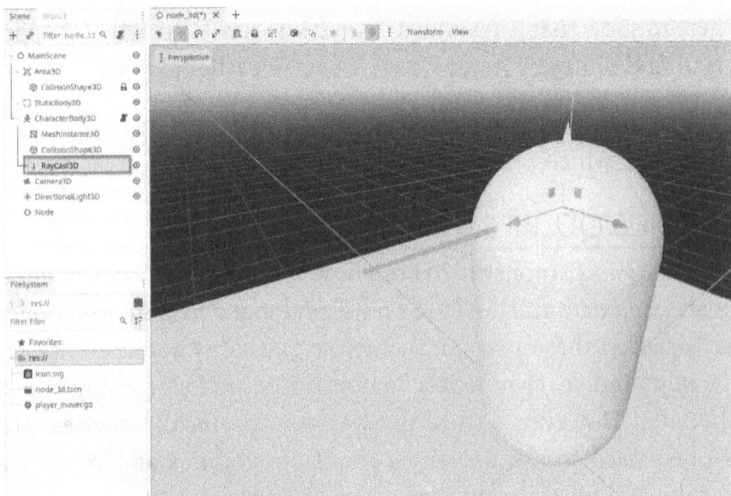

FIGURE 6.34 Attaching a Raycast to a Player Object.

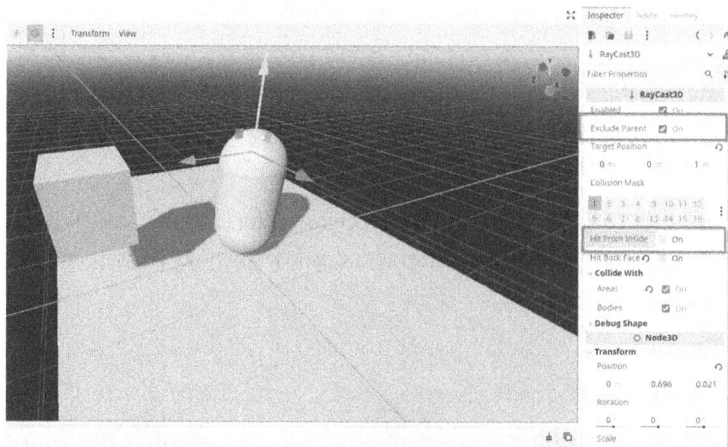

FIGURE 6.35   Configuring a Raycast.

with the object. Now, if you disable *Exclude Parent* and enable *Hit From Inside*, then the Raycast will hit the inside faces of the mesh that it's contained within. That's not normally what you want; it's a self-collision. Self-collision is usually bad. So be sure to enable *Exclude Parent* (to exempt the parent object from collisions) and disable *Hit From Inside* (to prevent hitting any interior faces), unless you have a compelling reason not to do so (see Figure 6.35).

Finally, be sure to specify the *Target Position* Vector, which is relative to the position of the Raycast. A value of *(0,0,1)* for example, means that the Raycast will point forward. A value of *(0,-1,0)* means the Raycast will point downward. Now let's create some code to work with the *RayCast3D*. This can be added to any existing code, such as the Player Controller. Consider Code Sample 6.5.

CODE SAMPLE 6.5   WORKING WITH RAYCASTS.

```
@onready var —raycast:RayCast3D = $RayCast3D

func _physics_process(delta: float) -> void:
        if __raycast.is_colliding():
                if __raycast.get_collider() is StaticBody3D:
                        var _staticbody:StaticBody3D = __
raycast.get_collider() as StaticBody3D
                        print(_staticbody.name)
```

Let's review some important details about this code:

- The *is_colliding* function can be called on each physics frame, and it returns a boolean expressing whether the RayCast object intersects anybody or any area.

- The *get_collider* function retrieves a reference to the first eligible object that the Raycast intersects, allowing you to determine what was hit.

6.6.2 Shape Casts

There are some problems inherent with Raycasts, which limit how and where they can be used. They are generally performant and simple to use, but they can pose problems for specific cases. For example, consider the line-of-sight case in the previous section where the Raycast is used as a handy line of sight, projected from the character's eyes, looking for solid walls ahead. This Raycast setup may initially seem to make sense, but what happens if the wall ahead is shorter than the Raycast level? Consider another example for a ground check: If the Raycast points downward from a character and hits the ground below, we can classify the character as having finally landed on the ground after falling from a jump. But what happens if there is a small hole in the floor through which the Raycast is unlucky enough to travel even though the character's legs have touched the ground on either side? In both cases, the Raycast will return false, and the resultant behavior will be undesired: the player will continue through the wall in the first case and will fall through the floor in the second one. This is because there are times when the Raycast, by its very nature, isn't enough. So, instead, we can use a *Shape Cast*. This method basically creates a non-renderable collider, like a box or a sphere, and throws it ahead of the character along a line to test for intersections. Because the shape has a width, height, and depth, it's likely to produce a more accurate result for collision testing, at the expense of being more expensive than a Raycast. Let's start. Create a new *ShapeCast3D* node and attach that as a child of a movable character, like an NPC (see Figure 6.36).

Next, let's create some code that detects collisions with a ShapeCast. Consider the following Code Sample 6.6.

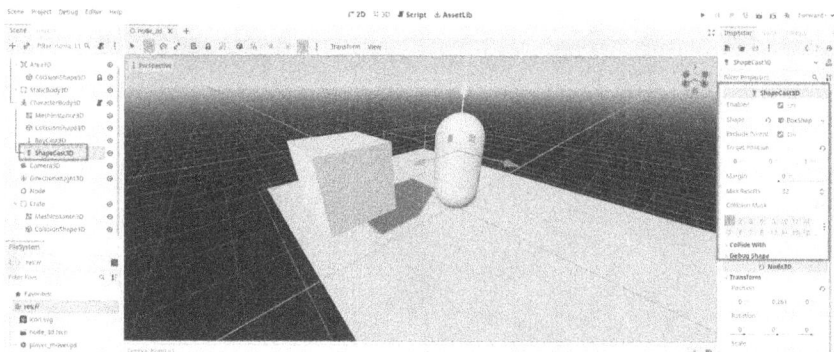

FIGURE 6.36   Setting up a Shape Cast Node.

CODE SAMPLE 6.6   WORKING WITH SHAPECASTS

```
@onready var _shapecast:ShapeCast3D = $ShapeCast3D

func _physics_process(delta: float) -> void:
     if _shapecast.is_colliding():
          for i in _shapecast.
get_collision_count():
                    if _shapecast.get_
collider(i) is StaticBody3D:
                         var _
staticbody:StaticBody3D = _shapecast.get_
collider(i) as StaticBody3D
                         print(_staticbody.
name)
```

6.7 TEXT IN 3D

When creating rapid prototypes of games in 3D, it's often useful to display text data besides 3D objects. This is especially useful for live debugging inside the editor, allowing you to quickly see important data. The text may be used to display properties of objects in the viewport, such as the name of an object, the health of a player, the time remaining for a level, or the location of an object. In these cases, the often-overlooked *Label3D* object can be your friend, as it saves you from printing lots of messages to the debug console. *Label3D* is a standard Node3D-derived object and can be attached as a child to an object (see Figure 6.37).

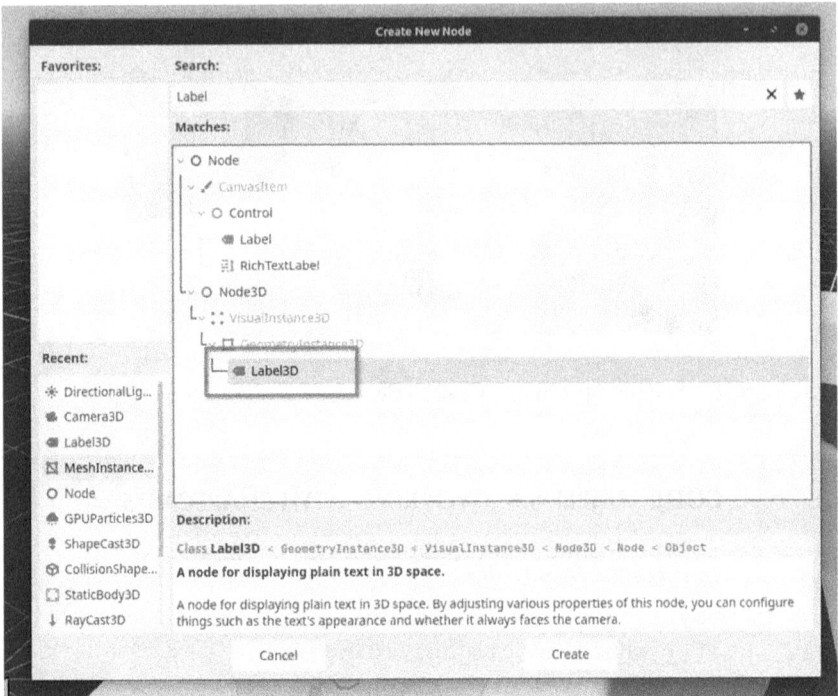

FIGURE 6.37   Adding a Label to an Object.

FIGURE 6.38   Setting Text through the Inspector.

Next, you can enter your text directly through the *Inspector*, using the *Text* rollout and the *Text* field. The *Font Size* controls text size (see Figure 6.38).

You can also set text through code. Consider Code Sample 6.7, which sets the Text of a *Label3D* child object.

CODE SAMPLE 6.7   SETTING THE TEXT OF A LABEL OBJECT.

```
extends Node3D
@onready var __text_object:Label3D = $Label3D
func _process(delta: float) -> void:
        __text_object.text = name
```

Each Label features a *Billboard* property, which can be enabled. When enabled, the text will always rotate to face the active camera directly, so it can be read without any rotation.

6.8 CONCLUSION

This chapter introduced the exciting world of 3D scenes in Godot, and there are many powerful nodes to use here, from CSGs and Meshes to Physics and Areas. There is, certainly, a lot more to be said about every one of these objects. And, indeed, more of them will be explored further in the coming chapters. Next, we enter the world of user interfaces.

CHAPTER 7

User Interfaces

T HIS CHAPTER IS A project-based chapter. Here, we'll work together, step by step, to create a working user interface for a main menu screen, used for a potential 2D space-shooter game called *Space Ranger*. We'll create this project from scratch, from importing assets to hitting play on the final version. By completing a working project like this, we'll learn many core features of user interfaces in Godot and game development more generally. By 'user interface' (UI) I am referring to menu screens, option menus, HUDs, popups, message boxes, information screens, and many other relevant elements. UIs are typically 2D but can exist in 3D spaces too, such as health bars that appear above a 3D character's head, and Godot offers features for both 2D and 3D. This chapter is concerned with 2D, but we'll explore implications for 3D too (see Figure 7.1). This shows an example of the interface we'll create, considering a range of problematic and interesting issues along the way.

> NOTE. *Space Ranger* is actually a real game made by me and Evy
> Benita using the Godot engine! You can access the full game here:
> https://thelotls.itch.io/lotl-space-ranger. You can also check a video
> play session of the game here: https://www.youtube.com/watch?v=
> yO2N2J8nsZM.

DOI: 10.1201/9781003484523-7

FIGURE 7.1   The Interface to create in this chapter.

7.1 IMPORTING ASSETS

The first step in creating a main menu interface for a game is to import all our needed texture assets into the project. These will feature as different elements on the screen. We may not end up using all of them, and that's fine. You can easily remove unneeded assets later by simply deleting them from the project. Remember, if you delete something from the Godot project, the file is removed from your computer too. So be sure to have a backup somewhere safe in case you need to restore the file or files at any time later. To import our textures, as always, drag and drop the contents of the included *UI* folder directly into the Godot project, into the *FileSystem* panel, and all assets will be imported (see Figure 7.2).

7.2 STARTING THE USER INTERFACE

Now let's configure our scene and the foundations of our UI. To start, create a new *UI Scene* by choosing 'User Interface' from the *Scene* dock, as opposed to a *2D* or a *3D* scene. Although a UI is, strictly speaking, a 2D scene, the UI nodes nonetheless operate differently from standard 2D nodes (see Figure 7.3).

The scene is created with only one node present, that is, a *Control* node. Rename this topmost node to *Root* for clarity, and then from the *Inspector* be sure to choose *Full Rect* for the *Anchor Preset* from the *Layout* section of the node. Choosing this option forces the control to continually stretch

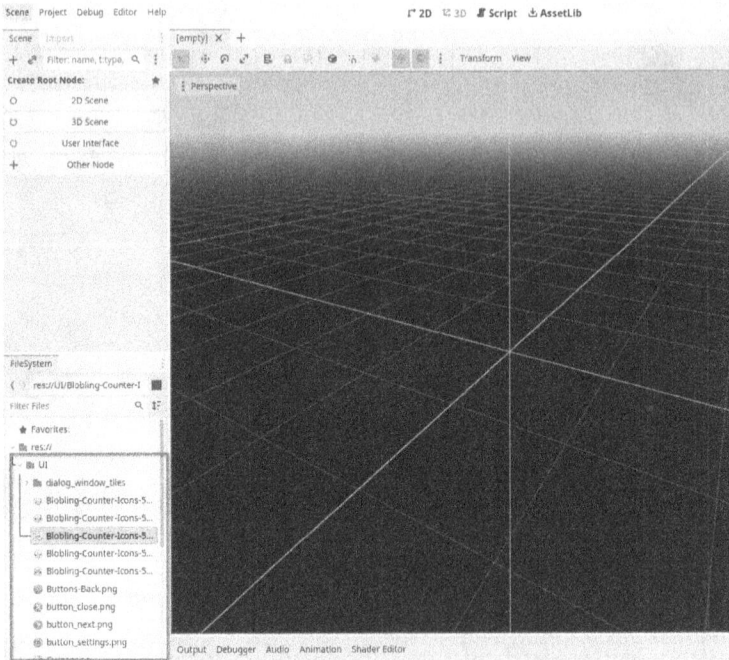

FIGURE 7.2   The Interface to create in this chapter.

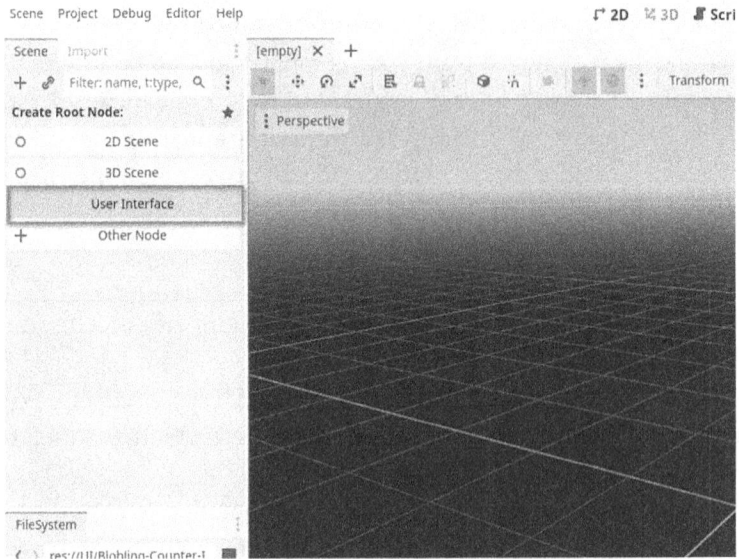

FIGURE 7.3   Creating a new UI Scene.

its width and height to fill the screen, whatever its size, and allow for any changes at run time, such as window resizing. By default, the node is transparent and doesn't have any appearance at all. Rather, it simply marks out a region of the screen (namely, *the entire screen*), and this will be relevant for child nodes, which we will add soon. Specifically, the size of the parent determines the space 'available' to children within the interface. You might be wondering why this process is necessary. Surely, we can just define the position and sizes of objects in pixels and not need to worry about any other way of measuring screen size and position? The answer is 'yes', technically we can. But this route of specifying position and size in absolute pixels is far from ideal, because the UI may appear wrongly at different sizes on different screens and devices where the number of pixels in height and width may differ from the dimensions you used when making the interface. Therefore, we usually want the UI to look the same, or at least equivalent, in all cases, and we only want to make one adaptive UI in the engine, rather than one static version for every size and screen. The latter approach would be tedious for one person (see Figure 7.4).

We've created our root control for the UI, but we still need to define how Godot should behave for scenes generally, both 2D and 3D, if the window were resized by the player during gameplay, or if the game were presented on a screen that is smaller or larger than the intended size. One option, in the case of larger screens with more pixels, is simply to expand the range of a level that the camera can see, allowing more things to be

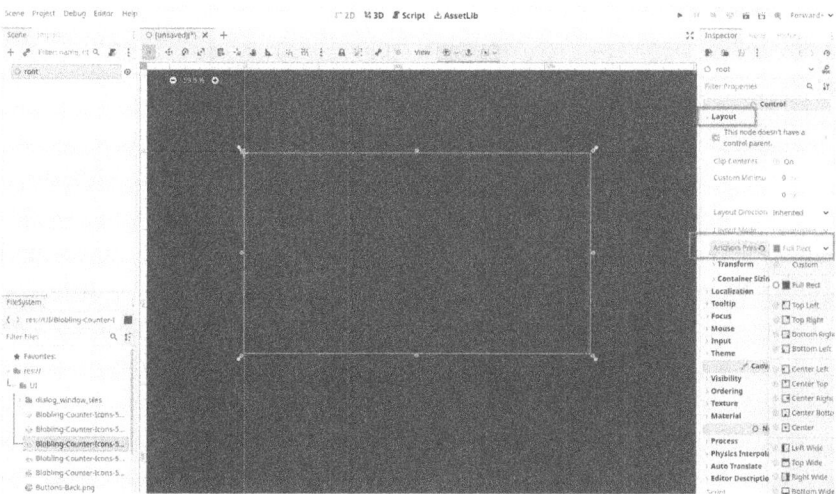

FIGURE 7.4   Setting the Root Control to Fill Rect.

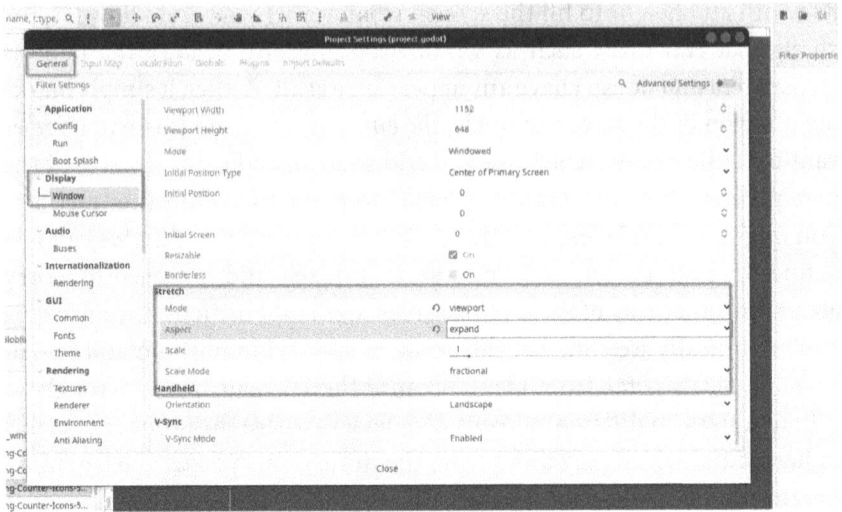

FIGURE 7.5   Setting the Window for the Display.

seen than could be seen on a smaller screen, such as off-screen enemies and objects. The alternative, which we will use here, is to keep all graphical elements the same scale but enlarge or shrink them to fit the new window size, ensuring the game looks the same on all screens. To do this, access *Project Settings* from the application menu. From the *Display* > *Window* section, choose *Viewport* for the *Mode* and *Expand* for the *Aspect*. This setting ensures the contents of the viewport (all the in-game graphics) are expanded to fit the aspect of the window (see Figure 7.5).

7.3 CREATING THE BACKGROUND

Let's create the background layer of the UI – the furthermost layer to the back. This should be a bold color, and I'll choose a dark purple/pink style. To create this, we could set the Default Clear Color of Godot, as we did in previous chapters. But here, we only need to set the background for this scene specifically. I'll use a *ColorRect* node to do this. As the name suggests, this node fills a specified rectangle with a selected color. Create the *ColorRect* node and, like the root node, set the *Layout Mode* to *Anchors* and set the *Anchors Preset* to *Full Rect*. This resizes the rectangle to fill the screen automatically (see Figure 7.6).

Finally, choose the background color via the Color Picker, and then click the Padlock icon from the toolbar to lock the object in place. As a background item, it'll be easy to accidentally select and move in the viewport, creating unwanted changes, and so, by locking the *ColorRect* in place, we keep its settings intact (see Figure 7.7).

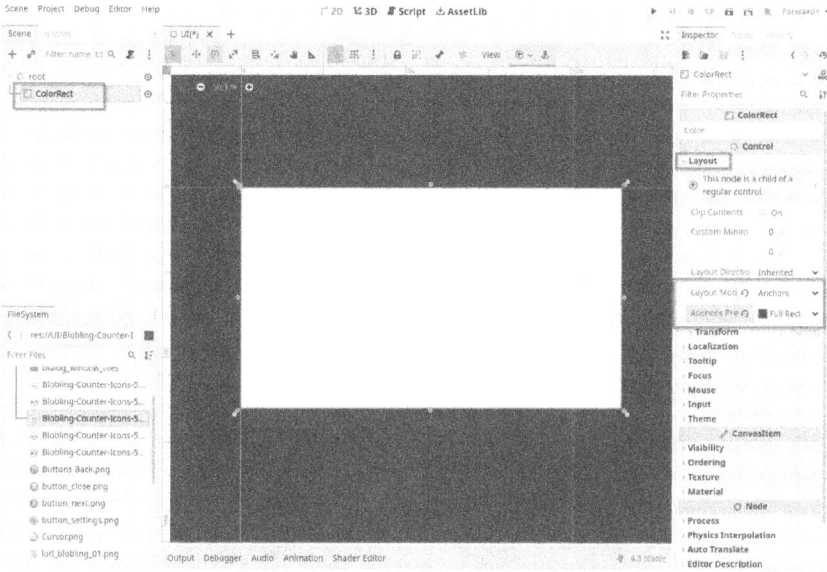

FIGURE 7.6   Resizing the ColorRect to fill the screen.

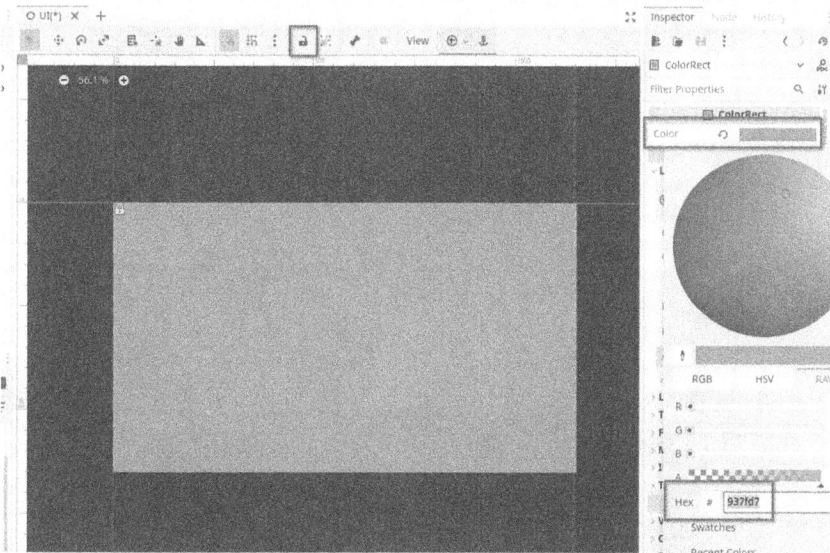

FIGURE 7.7   Setting the background color and locking the position.

7.4 ADD A UI TITLE

The title of our example game is 'Space Ranger', and we've already imported a texture for this in Section 7.1. The title should appear on the menu, *fixed* close to the top of the screen. The word 'fixed' is used here, and the word 'anchored' is also appropriate. It means that the title should always appear at the top-center of the screen *regardless* of how the window may be resized by the user or regardless of the screen size on which the UI is being viewed. To start, select the root node, and then create a new *TextureRect* node. The *TextureRect* fills a rectangle with a texture. Once created, choose the *Texture* slot from the inspector, and select

Quick Load from the context menu. Pick the 'Space Ranger' title, and this will be displayed in the viewport (see Figure 7.8).

Now let's size and position the title in place, with precision and exactitude. First, you'll notice a small red crosshair at the top-left corner of the title, which marks the pivot point and default center of the texture, that is, the location within the texture from which its position is measured. Since we're aligning the title to the top-center of the screen, and not the top-left, let's move this point as close to that top-center as we can. From the Inspector, expand the *Layout* Section and the *Transform* Section. From there, set the *Pivot Offset* on X to 400 pixels; 400 is half the width of my texture. Then let's set its scale to 0.6 (see Figure 7.9).

You'll also notice a green crosshair that appears by default at the top-left center of the screen. These are the *Anchors*. They control which locations of the screen that the control should absolutely be attached to. This means

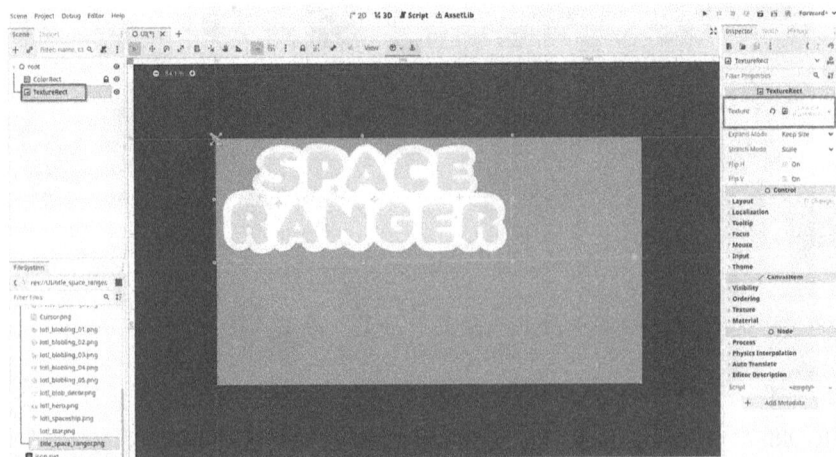

FIGURE 7.8   Adding a UI title to the UI.

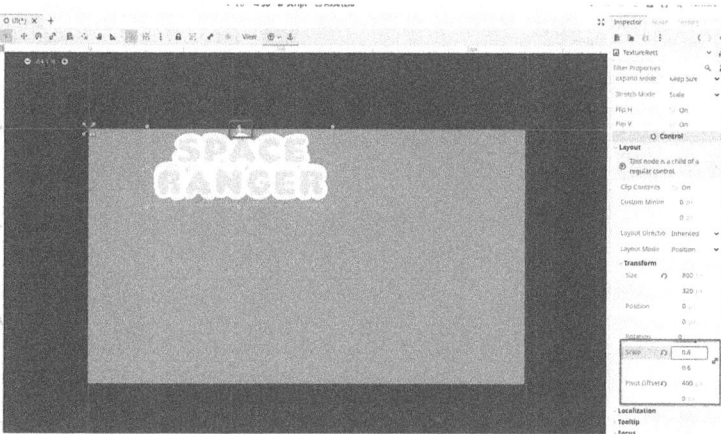

FIGURE 7.9   Setting the Pivot for the TextureRect.

the control will always conform, by moving or resizing, to respect those screen locations, even if the screen or window is resized. When all four Anchors appear together, it means they all specify the same location. In this case, let's attach the title to the top-center of the screen. To do this, select the title object and, from the toolbar, select the Anchor drop-down. From the drop-down, choose the Center-Top preset (see Figure 7.10).

The game title is now fixed to the screen top-center, which is excellent. However, the top edge of the texture touches the edge of the screen, and I'd like to leave some margin or padding to avoid the UI looking overcrowded. We can do this by using the *Position Y* field and adding a pixel offset from the Anchor location. I'll enter a value of 30 pixels to push the title down from the Anchor by 30 pixels (see Figure 7.11).

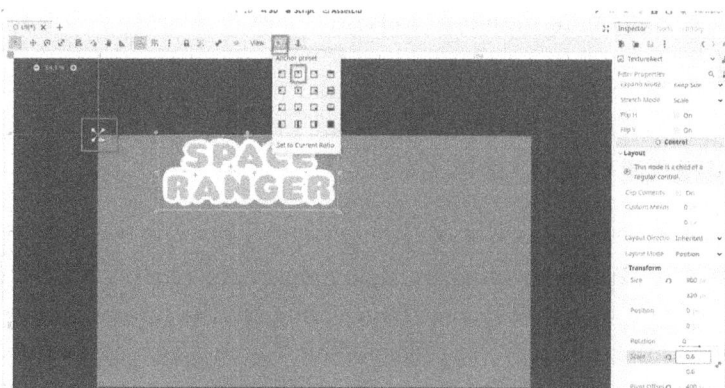

FIGURE 7.10   Setting the Title to the top-center of the screen.

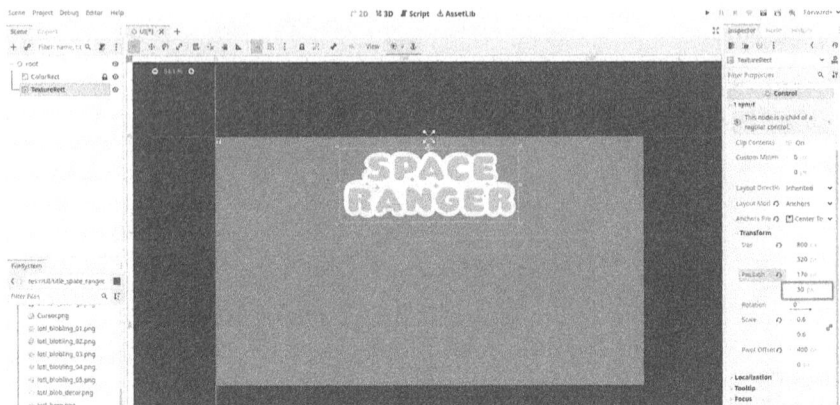

FIGURE 7.11   Pushing the title away from the top edge of the screen.

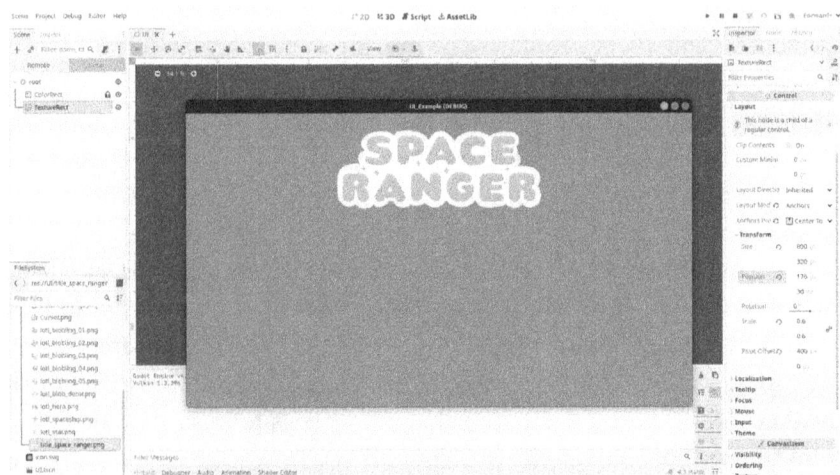

FIGURE 7.12   Running the project and testing the UI.

Finally, lock the title in place. And now take the project for a test run where you can resize the window, and you'll see the title fixed in its proper place. Good work! (see Figure 7.12).

7.5 CREATING A CURSOR

This section explores creating a custom mouse cursor for our UI. For desktop platforms, such as *Windows*, *Linux*, and *Mac*, the cursor expresses the mouse location on the screen. For mobile devices, such as *Android* and *iOS*, we'll typically hide the course, as these will be touchscreen devices. The cursor allows us to click elements on the screen, such as buttons.

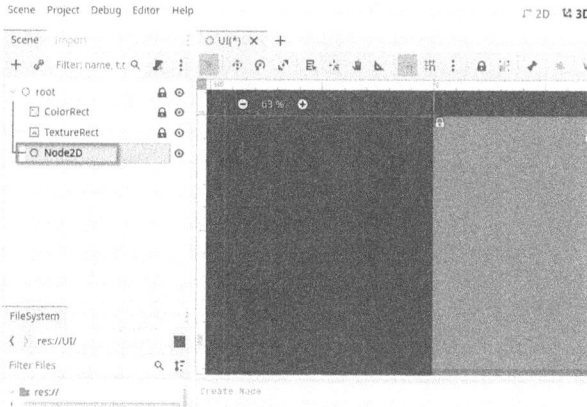

FIGURE 7.13   Creating a Node2D as the start of a mouse cursor.

To get started, let's create a new *Node2D* (see Figure 7.13). Interesting to note here that this object normally belongs in a 2D scene (it has blue color coding, rather than green). However, 2D and UI objects (and even 3D) can co-exist in the same scene!

Next, let's name the node *Cursor*, and we'll create a new script and attach it to the node. This script contains all the needed functionality for the cursor (see Code Sample 7.1).

CODE SAMPLE 7.1

```
extends Node2D
#------------------------------------------------------
---------
@export var _arrow_texture : Texture2D
@export var __cursor_timeout:float = 3
var __OS_name:String = ""
var __is_visible:bool = false
var __is_enabled:bool = false
var __time_elapsed:float = 0
var __manual_override:bool = false
#------------------------------------------------------
---------
func _enter_tree():
        __OS_name = OS.get_name()
```

```
        if __OS_name != "Android" and __OS_name !=
"iOS":
                __is_enabled = true
 show_cursor()

#---------------------------------------------------
---------
func show_cursor():
        if __is_enabled:
                Input.set_mouse_mode(Input.
MOUSE_MODE_VISIBLE)
                Input.set_custom_mouse_cursor
(_arrow_texture)
                __is_visible = true
                __manual_override = false

#---------------------------------------------------
---------
func hide_cursor(override=false):
        Input.set_mouse_mode(Input.MOUSE_MODE_HIDDEN)
        __is_visible = false
        __manual_override = override

#---------------------------------------------------
---------
func _input(_event): if !__is_enabled: return
if __manual_override:
  return

if _event is InputEventMouseMotion:
    __time_elapsed = 0
if !__is_visible:
    show_cursor()

#---------------------------------------------------
---------
func _process(delta):
        if !__is_enabled or !__is_visible:
                return
        __time_elapsed += delta
        if __time_elapsed > __cursor_timeout:
                hide_cursor()
#---------------------------------------------------
---------
```

Let's explore this code in more depth, as follows:

1. The *enter_tree* function is called as the Node2D enters the scene. Unlike _ready, which is called at object creation only once in the lifetime of the node, the enter_tree can be called more than once. It's called once each time the node enters the scene hierarchy. Normally this will be once. But if the object were ever removed from the scene and then later returned, *enter_tree* would happen a second time.

2. Inside the *enter_tree* function, we determine which OS is being used. If the OS is *Android* or *iOS*, the cursor is hidden entirely.

3. If the cursor is to be shown, two native Godot functions are called. Namely, *Input.set_mouse_mode*, and *Input.set_custom_mouse_cursor*. The first enables the mouse cursor inside a Godot Window, allowing the cursor to move freely and generate events. The latter allows us to use a texture for the cursor image inside the window.

4. I've also added a timer feature, which causes the cursor to disappear when unmoved for a specified period.

After the script has been attached to the cursor node, let's configure it inside the Inspector. For the *Arrow Texture* field, choose the mouse cursor texture, which we imported earlier alongside many other textures (see Figure 7.14).

Excellent. Now, the cursor should appear during gameplay.

FIGURE 7.14 Configuring the cursor texture.

7.6 CREATING A HERO IMAGE AND SUPPORTING IMAGES

The 'hero image', or the 'hero asset', is the primary feature and most striking highlight of a composition. Our menu includes a collection of Axolotl characters lined up and supporting NPC characters floating around them. Let's start with the Axolotl characters. Create a new *TextureRect* node and load the characters into it as the texture (see Figure 7.15).

The newly created image should be fixed to the screen center. Again, we can use Anchors and Offsets to achieve this. Set the offset to roughly the center of the image (see Figure 7.16).

This time use the Anchor Presets from the toolbar to center align the hero asset and adjust the scale by eye to create a pleasing composition (see Figure 7.17).

Now run the game and compare different screen configurations to the original in the editor, checking different width and height sizes for the window to see how the hero asset behaves and aligns with the title aligned at the top-center (Figure 7.18).

Next, we'll add random NPC creatures scattered around the central hero asset on the main menu. Since the NPCs must complement the hero asset, orbiting it radially in design, it's therefore important for them to anchor to the same location as the hero at the screen center; otherwise, the NPCs can drift away from the center under different window sizes.

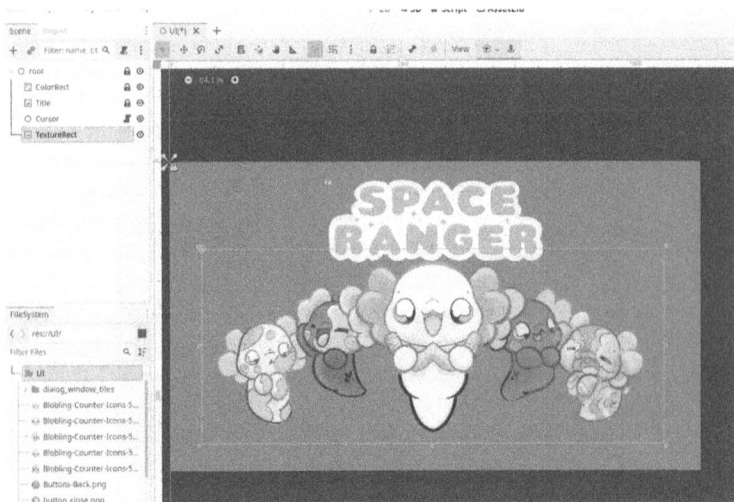

FIGURE 7.15   Adding a Hero image to the menu.

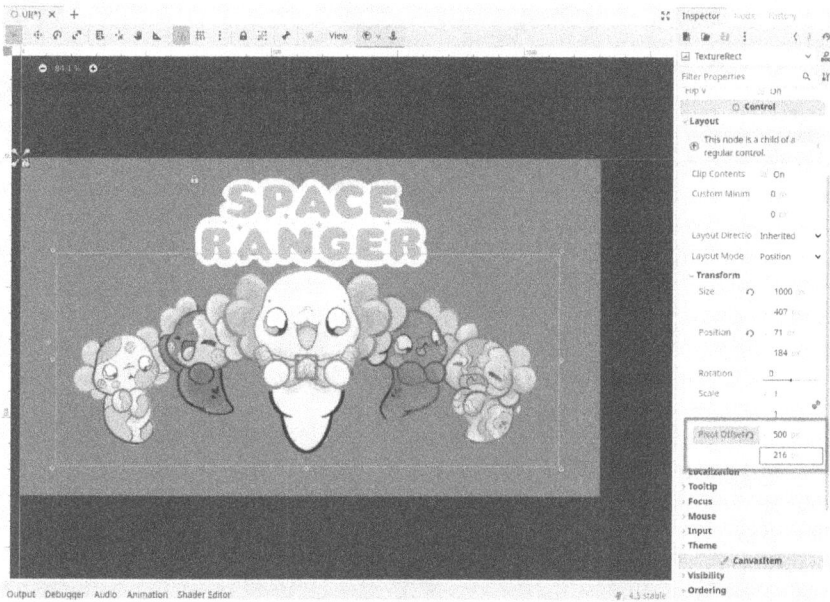

FIGURE 7.16   Using offset to set the image center.

FIGURE 7.17   Center the Hero Asset.

Our method will be to create the first NPC, configure it correctly, and then duplicate it for other variations. To start, create a *TextureRect* node. Load any NPC texture and adjust the offset to the image center (see Figure 7.19).

The newly added NPC looks quite intense compared to the hero asset. It'll probably direct attention away from the center, which is shortly where

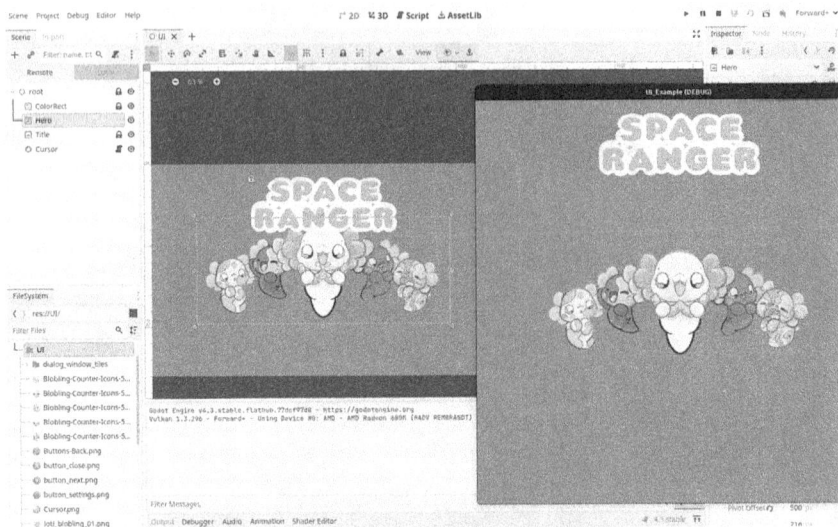

FIGURE 7.18   Testing different UI dimensions.

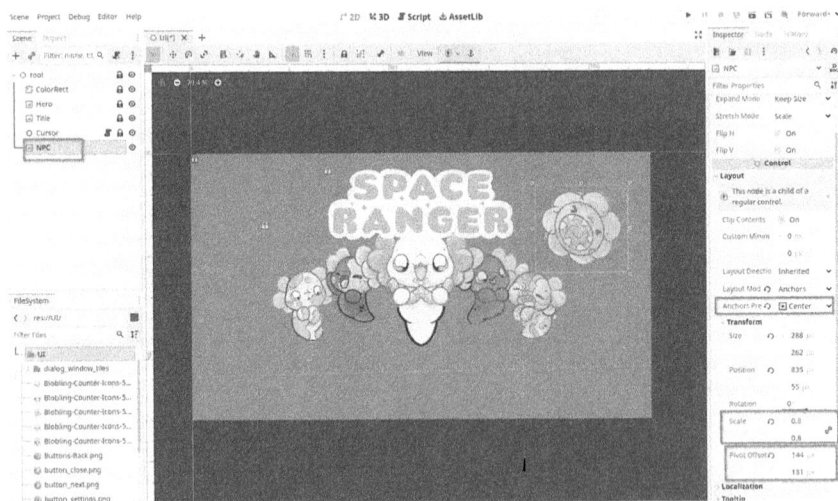

FIGURE 7.19   Adding an NPC character.

we'll be positioning some buttons. These NPCs are designed flourishes to complement the central elements. So, let's reduce its opacity. To do that, select the NPC and expand the *Visibility* rollout. From there, click the *Self Modulate* field, and reduce the *Alpha* to control its transparency (see Figure 7.20).

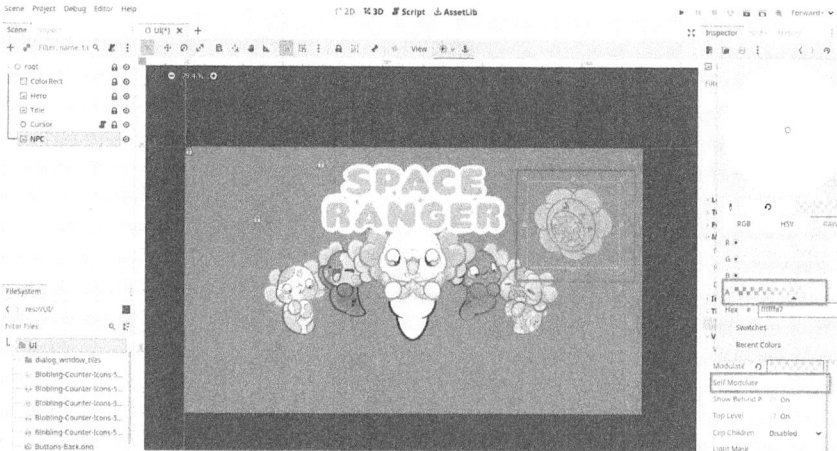

FIGURE 7.20   Controlling NPC opacity.

Now duplicate a few times, assigning a different image to each duplicate, and then reposition each around the scene, ensuring the anchor is
still at the screen center (see Figure 7.21).

Excellent. We're getting there. Next, we'll start to add buttons and functional controls to the UI that links to code.

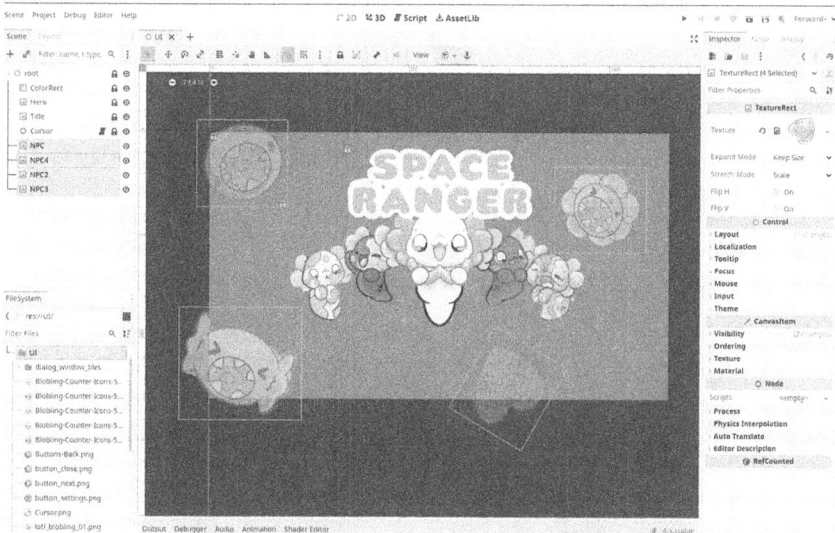

FIGURE 7.21   Adding other NPCs to the scene.

7.7 CREATING UI BUTTONS

Our interface will feature three buttons arranged in a single line or horizontal row. This will be *Play*, *Settings*, and *Exit*. Now, we could simply add the buttons to the scene and use all of the positioning techniques covered already, such as anchoring, to find appropriate locations. This will work, but there's a better way. In cases where you're working with many elements that appear equally in a regimented, grid-like formation, Godot offers some powerful tools for auto-arrangement. We'll explore those here. To start, let's create a *CenterContainer* node. This node represents a rectangular region of space, which can be anchored, and inside which all children will automatically be aligned to the center. Once created, draw out a rectangular strip, by clicking and dragging, spanning the width of the window and anchoring to the center (see Figure 7.22).

> NOTE. When you click and drag the *CenterContainer* to align with the edges of the screen, you can enable *Snapping* for exact alignment. To enable Snapping, click the Snapping button from the Editor toolbar (see Figure 7.23).

You can easily test the *CenterContainer* by adding any visible node, such as a *TextureRect*, as a child. On making an object a child of the *CenterContainer*, it will auto-align to the vertical and horizontal center – *not to* the center of

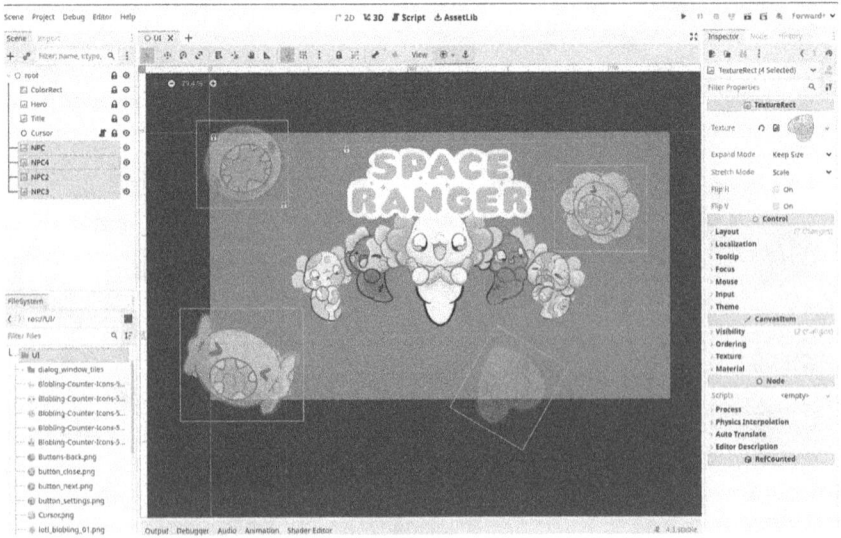

FIGURE 7.22   Adding a CenterContainer Object.

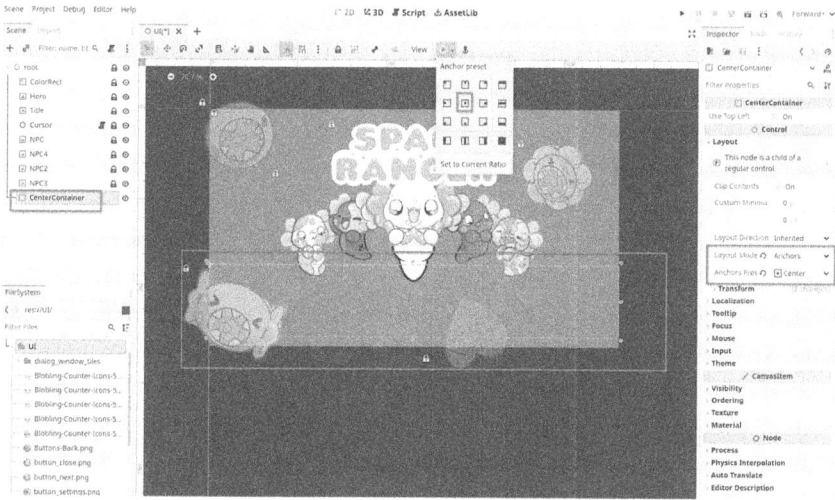

FIGURE 7.23   Activate snapping to perfectly align a container to the screen edges.

the screen, *but* to the center of the container. Next, we'll create a new object, called a *GridContainer*. The *GridContainer* aligns its children neatly in rows and columns, and we'll use this to make a list of button nodes. Create a *GridContainer* now (see Figure 7.24).

The *GridContainer* doesn't have many options. So, let's explore how it works. Start by creating a *TextureButton* object as a child of the

FIGURE 7.24   Creating a GridContainer to house all button objects…

GridContainer. This node works much like a *TextureRect* in that it displays a texture over a rectangular region, but it also acts as a button that is interactive. Specifically, it can be clicked or tapped (see Figure 7.25).

With the new TextureButton Object created in the scene, let's assign it a texture appearance. Previously, in Section 7.1, we imported a range of texture assets to use here. Select the *TextureButton*, and then *Quick Load* a texture into the *Textures > Normal* rollout from the Inspector (see Figure 7.26).

The *TextureButton* features several options under the textures rollout, such as *Normal, Pressed, Hover, Disabled,* and *Focused.* Let's explore the

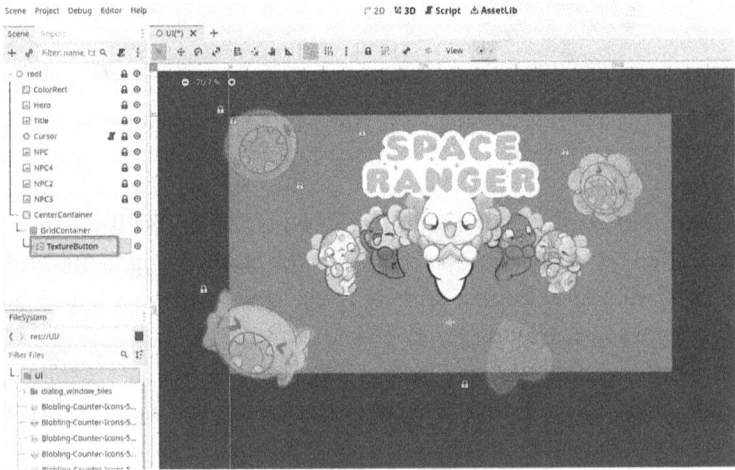

FIGURE 7.25   Adding a Button as a child of the GridContainer.

FIGURE 7.26   Quick loading a texture into a TextureButton.

definitions of each, as they are important concepts for any interactive UI element.

1. **Normal**. This refers to the default appearance of the button. When the scene begins, or when no interaction is occurring, the Normal texture will be used and shown.

2. **Pressed**. This texture will be shown if it exists when the button is being pressed and held down. This is typically when the user clicks or taps the button but hasn't yet released the click or tap to confirm the interaction.

3. **Hover**. This normally applies only to mouse-driven interfaces. This texture will be shown, if it exists, when the cursor moves over the button, but the button hasn't been pressed yet.

4. **Disabled**. This texture will be shown if it exists and if the button is temporarily deactivated and cannot be used at all. This texture will often be a faded or grayed-out version of Normal.

5. **Focused**. This texture will be shown if it exists when the control receives 'focus'. This relates to keyboards, gamepads, and other devices that do not express 'position'. The focused control is the one that will respond to the keyboard or gamepad input. Normally, the leftmost button in a series will receive Focus automatically, allowing the player to move between the buttons with left and right arrow presses.

Now let's duplicate the newly created *TextureButton* twice, creating two more buttons. When you do this, you'll end up with Figure 7.27, and there are some interesting points to note.

The buttons are auto-aligned into a column by the grid container, stacking one on top of the other, making sure there is no overlap. This is a powerful feature, supporting the fast and versatile creation of aligned elements in a UI. Select the *GridContainer*, and from the Inspector, change the *Column* count to 3. This allows a row to form, which is capped at three elements, before a new row is created (see Figure 7.28).

Next, change the texture for each button, allowing one for closing the application, one for starting gameplay, and one for accessing a settings menu (see Figure 7.29).

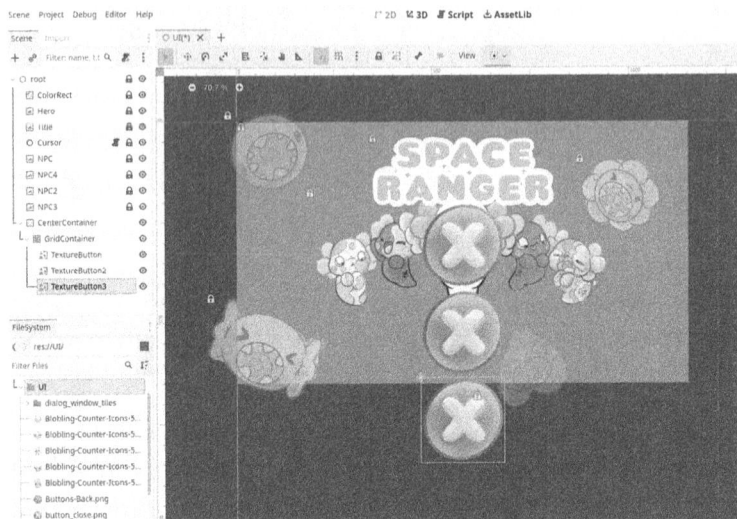

FIGURE 7.27   Adding more buttons to the *GridContainer*.

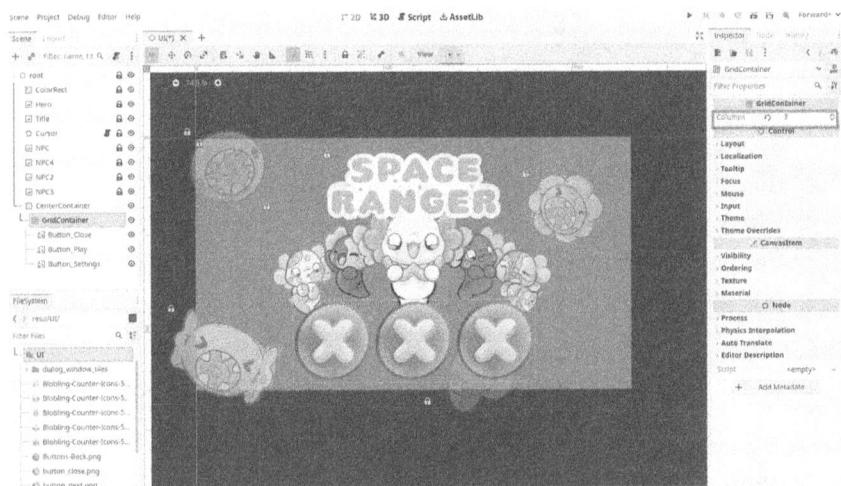

FIGURE 7.28   Aligning buttons into a single row.

Finally, we'll probably want to add some padding, or spacing, between the buttons to ensure they don't simply align together at the edges, pixel by pixel. In my example, the spacing looks acceptable, but this is only because some transparency is already added to the button edges. To add spacing, select the *GridContainer* node, and from the Inspector, open the *ThemeOverrides* rollout. From here, enable *H Separation (Horizontal)*

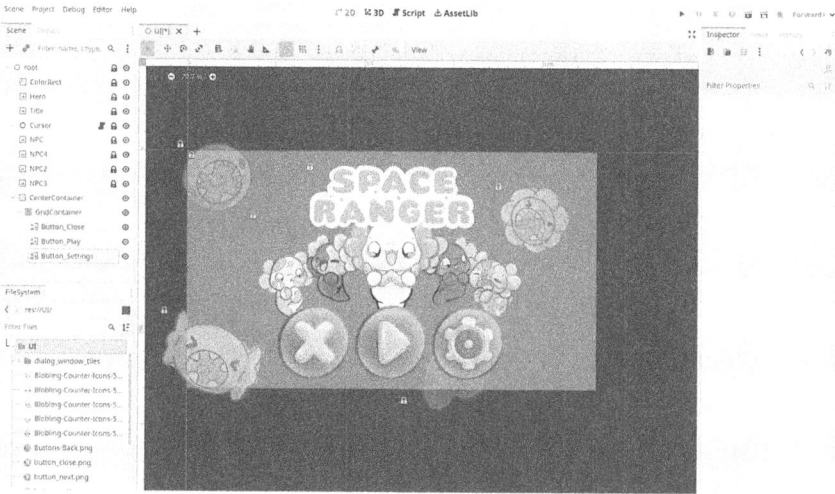

FIGURE 7.29   Assigning textures to our button panel

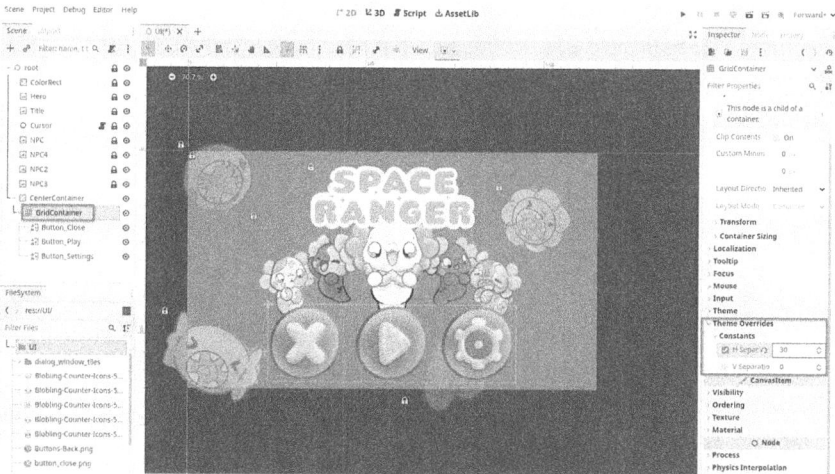

FIGURE 7.30   Adding horizontal separation between the buttons.

and enter a value of 30 (30 pixels of separation). The buttons will then be spaced further apart (see Figure 7.30).

7.8 CREATING BUTTON FUNCTIONALITY

The interface created here features three unique buttons, each with a specific purpose commonly found in games. On selecting each button and moving to the Node tab of the Inspector, you'll see that each button supports four signal types, which we can connect to for responding to different types of events. These are as follows:

1. **Button Down**. This signal is fired when the button is first pressed. At this point, it's likely that the mouse button is still being held down.

2. **Button Up**. This signal fires when the button is first released from a click. It may also be called if the button is pressed down elsewhere and then released separately while the cursor is hovering over the button.

3. **Pressed** is when a success button press occurs, that is, when the button is pressed down and then released.

4. **Toggled** applies to a different kind of button, like a checkbox, which can be switched on or off.

In this section we'll handle the different button clicks through a single overarching class, which will be attached to the root node. Consider the following Code Sample 7.2, which is attached to the scene root node as a starting point for connecting the button pushes to functions inside a script file.

CODE SAMPLE 7.2

```
extends Node
@onready var __button_close:TextureButton =
$CenterContainer/GridContainer/Button_Close

@onready var __button_play:TextureButton =
$CenterContainer/GridContainer/Button_Play
@onready var __button_settings:TextureButton =
$CenterContainer/GridContainer/Button_Settings

func _ready() -> void:
        __button_close.connect("pressed",
_on_close_press)
        __button_play.connect("pressed",
_on_play_press)
        __button_settings.connect("pressed",
_on_settings_press)

func _on_close_press():
        print("close pressed")
```

```
func _on_play_press():
      print("play pressed")

func _on_settings_press():
  print("settings pressed")
```

7.8.1 Coding the Close Button – Quitting the Game

The close button should terminate the application and return the gamer back to the OS. Closing an application in Godot is straightforward. Consider Code Sample 7.3 for the _on_close_press function.

CODE SAMPLE 7.3

```
func _ on _ close _ press():
      get_tree().quit()
```

NOTE. Usually, before running *Quit*, games will call other functions and behaviors, such as sound effects and animations, to create a smooth exit. The *Quit* function is the final command that is executed by a game prior to its termination entirely.

7.8.2 Coding the Play and Settings Buttons – Changing Scenes

The play and setting buttons assume your project consists of more than one scene; that is, more scenes besides the UI. Normally, a different scene will be the destination where the player should arrive when *Play or Settings are clicked from the menu.* So, essentially, either of these buttons will invoke a Scene change, moving you from the menu scene to another. Consider the completed code in Code Sample 7.4.

CODE SAMPLE 7.4

```
extends Node
@onready var __button_close:TextureButton =
$CenterContainer/GridContainer/Button_Close
```

```
@onready var __button_play:TextureButton =
$CenterContainer/GridContainer/Button_Play
@onready var __button_settings:TextureButton =
$CenterContainer/GridContainer/Button_Settings

@export var __game_scene : PackedScene
@export var __settings_scene : PackedScene
func _ready() -> void:
        __button_close.connect("pressed",
_on_close_press)
        __button_play.connect("pressed",
_on_play_press)
        __button_settings.connect("pressed",
_on_settings_press)

func _on_close_press():
        get_tree().quit()



func _on_play_press():
     get_tree().
change_scene_to_packed(__game_scene)

func _on_settings_press():
     get_tree().
change_scene_to_packed(__settings_scene)
```

After completing the code, select the root object and set its key properties (see Figure 7.31).

7.9 ANIMATING UI ELEMENTS – THE ANIMATIONPLAYER

In this section, we'll use the *Godot* animation system to create a predefined, multi-object animation across the entire UI scene. Specifically, we'll make the background NPCs vary their opacity at different rates to create a tranquil sense of dynamism from the menu. Godot has a powerful and easy-to-use animation system that is capable of creating complete cutscenes and cinematics. To create a new Animation object, add a new *AnimationPlayer* node to the scene. Despite the name of AnimationPlayer, this node is also used to create animations. This node should be a child of

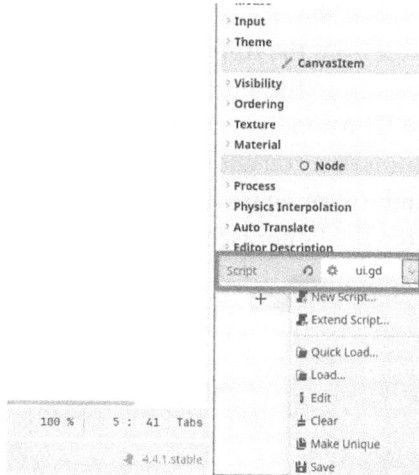

FIGURE 7.31   Configuring the Main Menu object.

the root object. It doesn't matter where in the hierarchy this node is created, but it can be problematic and involve lots more work if you relocate the *AnimationPlayer* node *after* creating your animations. So, I recommend you locate the object in a good, well-reasoned place in the hierarchy before building animations (see Figure 7.32).

> NOTE. The Animation System can be used to animate any object in any scene type. It's not limited to UIs.

To start creating animations for the UI, select the *AnimationPlayer* node in the scene hierarchy. With the *AnimationPlayer* node selected, make sure the *Animation* tab is visible in the *Output* Window area of the Editor (see Figure 7.33).

FIGURE 7.32   Creating an AnimationPlayer node

Create a new Animation called *UI Animation*, by choosing the *Animation* drop-down from the *Animation Editor*. Then select *New* from the context menu and assign the animation a name (see Figure 7.34).

The newly created UI Animation should run as soon as the scene starts and should play continuously on a loop, over and over again, to create an animated background. To configure this, enable the *Repeat* button and the *Auto-play* button from the Editor (see Figure 7.35).

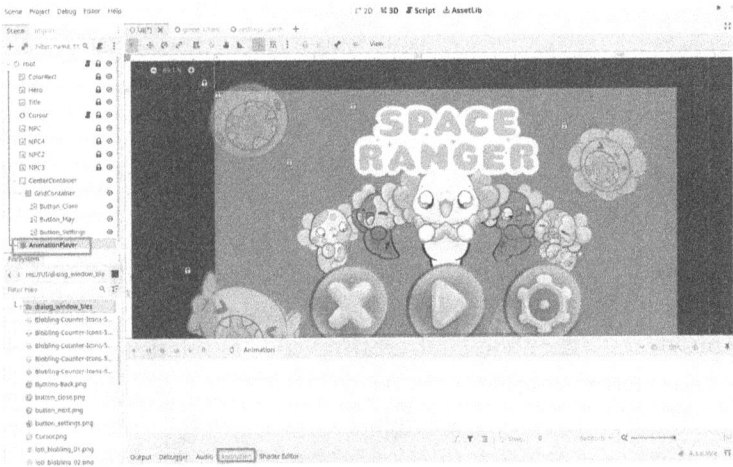

FIGURE 7.33   Accessing the Animation Editor.

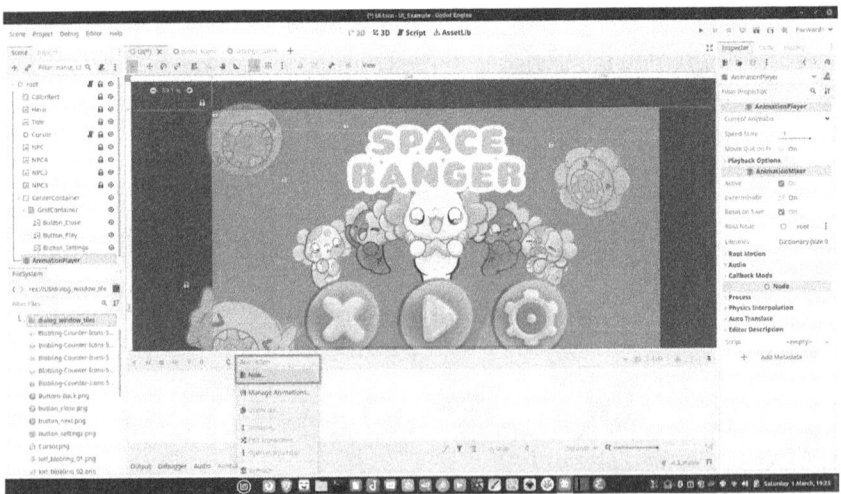

FIGURE 7.34   Creating a new animation from the Animation Editor.

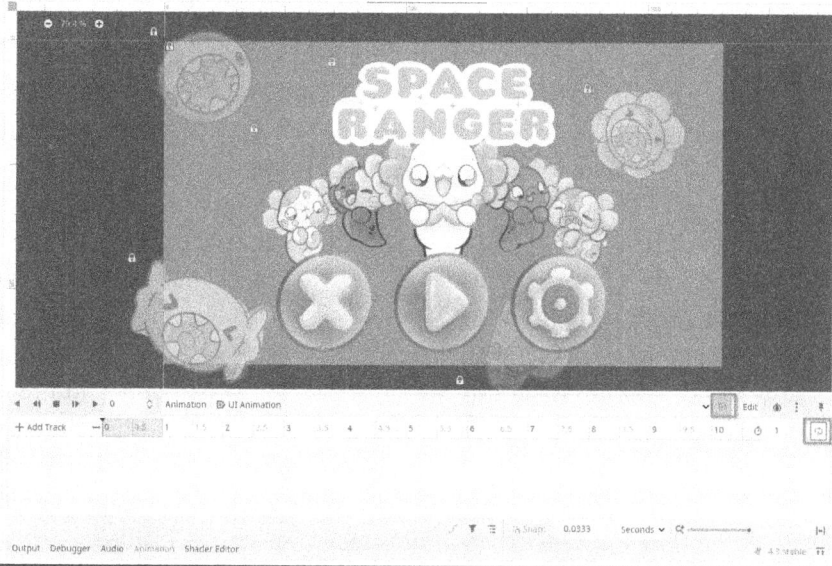

FIGURE 7.35   Enabling repeat and auto-play.

Next, we'll start building the animation itself. In Godot, each animated element is defined in the *Animation Editor* by an *Animation Track*. A track defines how a property of a specified object, such as its position or scale, changes over time. Using this system, an animation is therefore a collection of relationships of a *property* to *time*. In our animation, we'll be relating NPC opacity to time. Click the button *Add Track* and choose *Property Track* from the context menu (see Figure 7.36).

FIGURE 7.36   Creating an animation Property Track.

After choosing the *Property Track*, it'll ask you to select an object for animation. Here, since we're animating the NPCs, choose one of them and click *OK* (see Figure 7.37).

Now choose the property to animate from the property list. Here, it should be *self_modulate*. This is a *color* field in the form of RGBA (*Red, Green, Blue, and Alpha*). The alpha component specifies opacity and ranges from 0 to 255. This color is multiplied with the material to change its tint and shade overall. Once selected, choose the strangely named *Open* button to confirm your selection (see Figure 7.38).

The animation track is now presented in a horizontal timeline measured in seconds. The default total time for the animation is 1 second, and I recommend leaving this setting as-is. An animation can always be accelerated or slowed down through a global *Speed Scale setting* on the *AnimationPlayer* object, as we'll see. Click and drag the time slider to the first frame, at *position 0* in the timeline. Once there, right-click your mouse inside the timeline, along the *self_modulate* track, and choose *Insert Key* from the context

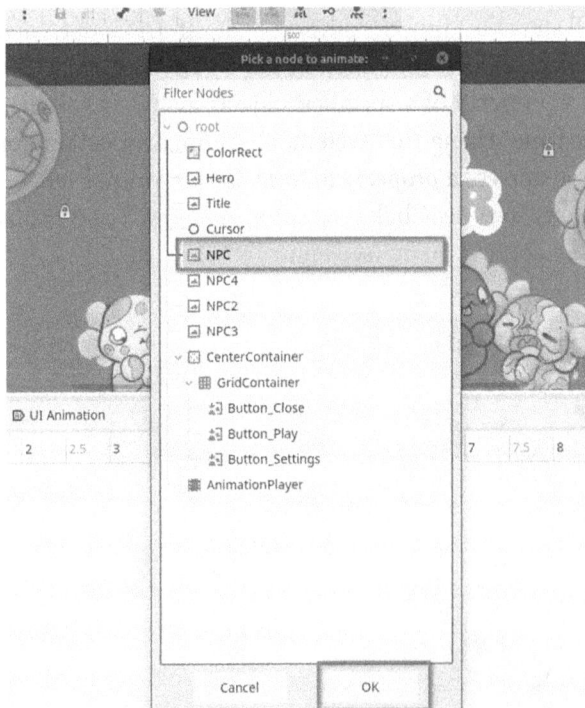

FIGURE 7.37 Next, choose an object to animate

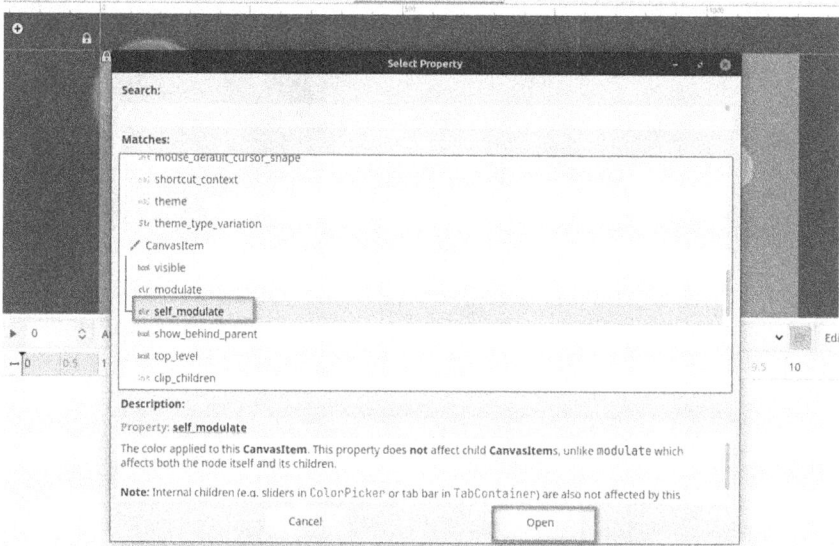

FIGURE 7.38   Finalizing a property track.

menu. A key (*Keyframe*) locks in the value of a setting at that time, and the *AnimationPlayer* calculates (*Interpolate*) the value for the property between the known keyframes (see Figure 7.39).

Now insert a keyframe at the end of the animation, at *time 1*. This locks the timeline value at the end of the animation and further creates an interpolated space between (see Figure 7.40).

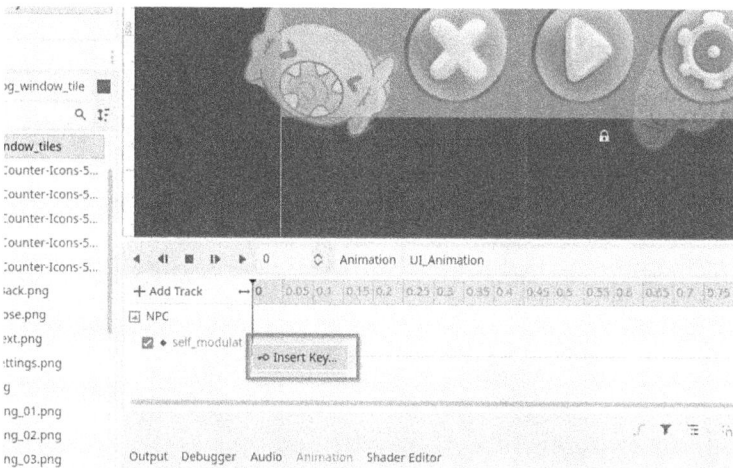

FIGURE 7.39   Inserting a keyframe into the Property Track.

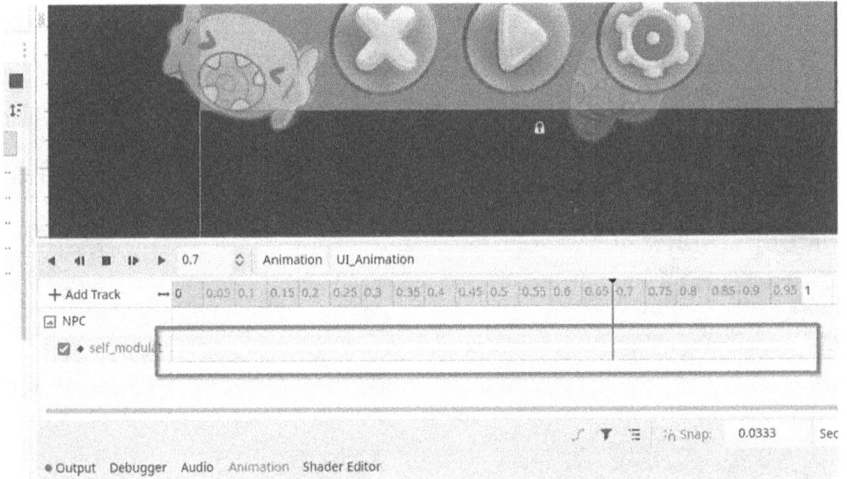

FIGURE 7.40   Inserting a keyframe at the end of the Property Track.

Now that we've created keyframes at the start and end of the track, we should create some at random points between, at times when the opacity should change, either up or down. The two keyframes at the start and end lock the opacity at its default value. So, insert new keyframes between, and then click each keyframe to set its color in the inspector (see Figure 7.41).

For each selected keyframe, click the *Value* field and set its color with a different opacity value. Be sure to keep the opacity value for the first and last keyframes (see Figure 7.42).

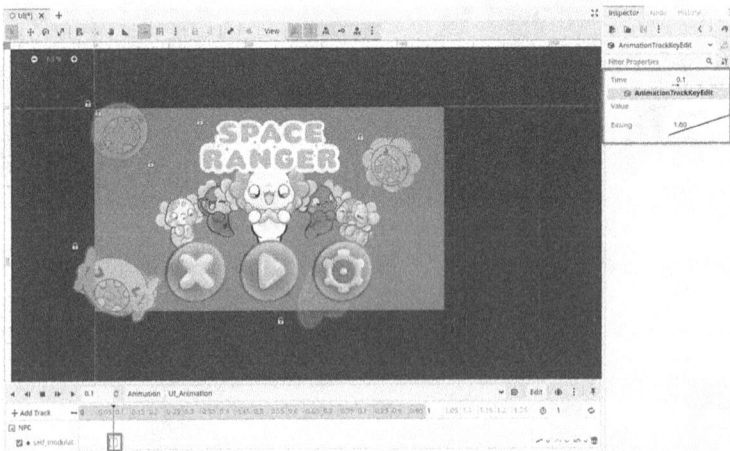

FIGURE 7.41   Select a keyframe to view its properties in the Inspector.

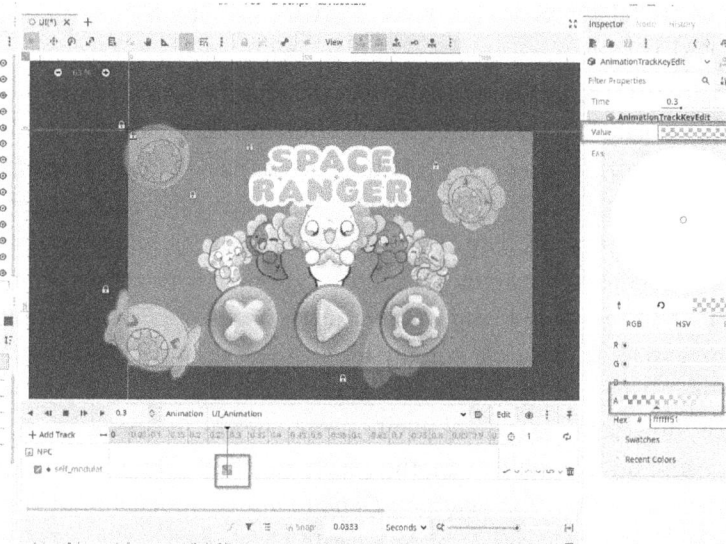

FIGURE 7.42 Animating NPC opacity values.

If you now play the scene, you'll see the animation take effect immediately. It'll probably appear way too fast; that is, the speed will be inappropriate for the context. We can easily change this. Select the *AnimationPlayer* object and then change the *Speed Scale* from 1 to 0.4 to reduce the playback speed (see Figure 7.43).

Now repeat this process for the other NPCs in the scene to create an organic and dynamic background.

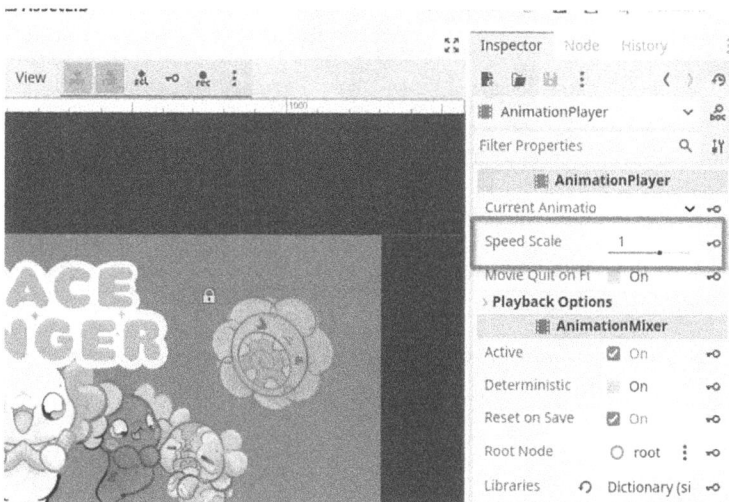

FIGURE 7.43 Changing playback speed.

7.10 AUTOLOADS – THE SINGLETON DESIGN PATTERN

The main menu screen is rarely, if ever, a destination for the player. Nobody launches a game to spend all playtime only on its menu screen. Rather, the menu screen is a location that the player visits on their way to *somewhere else*, such as the first level, or to resume gameplay from a later level. Nonetheless, the player may make important, and even gameplay-defining, decisions on the menu. Settings or choices applied there, at the menu, must often be referred to and read in other levels and scenes during gameplay. This may include checking volume levels, reading the player's name, and checking on game difficulty. However, this raises a problem of persistence. Namely, how can data created in one scene, such as the menu, continue to survive and be accessible in another, such as a level? This section explores one method, namely the *Singelton Design Pattern*, which Godot supports through *Autoload Objects*. First, let's create a basic data object in GDScript. Right-click the *FileSystem* menu and choose Create *New > Script* from the context menu (see Figure 7.44).

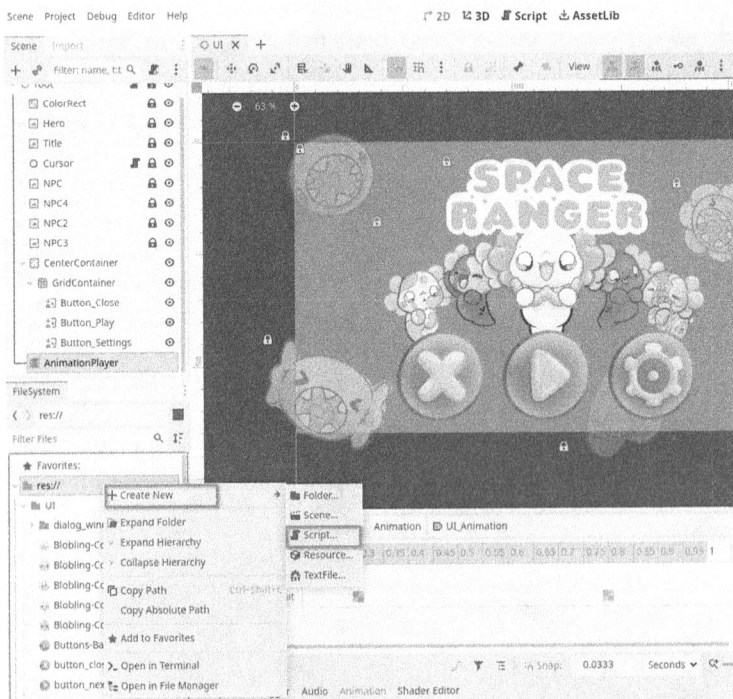

FIGURE 7.44   Creating a New Script from the FileSystem Dock.

As this script encodes only data and has no position within a scene, the script should derive from *Node*, as opposed to *Node2D* or *Node3D* or *Control* (see Figure 7.45).

Consider Code Sample 7.5, which contains an example game data class. This class could contain many different properties for a game.

CODE SAMPLE 7.5

```
extends Node
@export var game_difficulty:int = 0
@export var player_name:String = ""
@export var volume:float = 15
@export var run_full_screen:bool = true
```

Now we need to make this class a Singleton. A Singleton is a class that always has one and only one instance available at any one time during gameplay. The Singleton does not permit duplicate instances, and the single, available instance contains important data that is accessible to every class everywhere, always. This makes it a useful structure to keep track of single, global properties, such as Score, Player Name, Volume Levels, and more. It would not be suitable for keeping track of instance-specific properties, such as NPC health, as this varies from instance to instance across

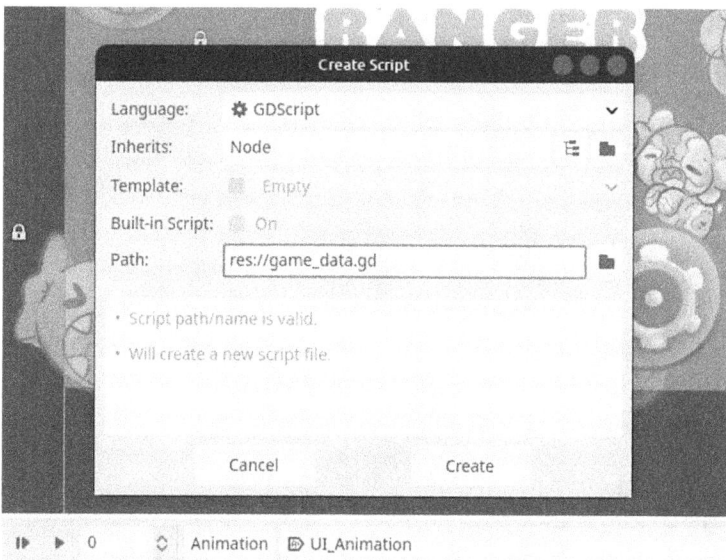

FIGURE 7.45 Creating a new Singleton from Node.

potentially many instances. To make our newly created class a Singleton, select its GD file in the FileSystem and then right-click, choosing *Copy Path* from the context menu (see Figure 7.46).

Next, select *Project > Project Settings* from the application menu, and switch to the *Globals* tab. From there, select the *AutoLoad* tab (see Figure 7.47).

Now paste your copied path into the *Path* field, and enter a *Global Name* into the *Node Name* field. This is the name by which your script should be

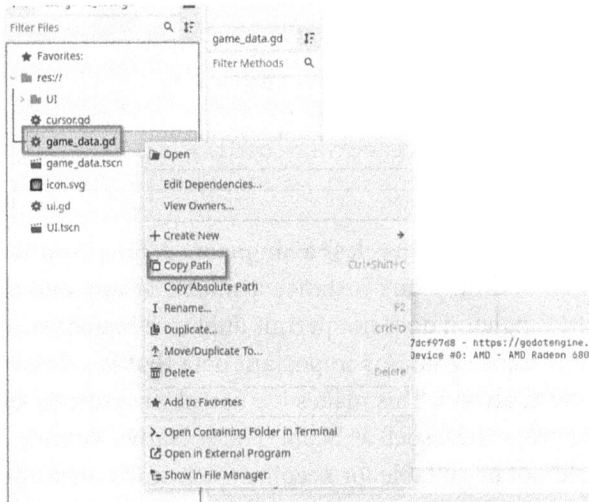

FIGURE 7.46   Copying the path for a selected Script File.

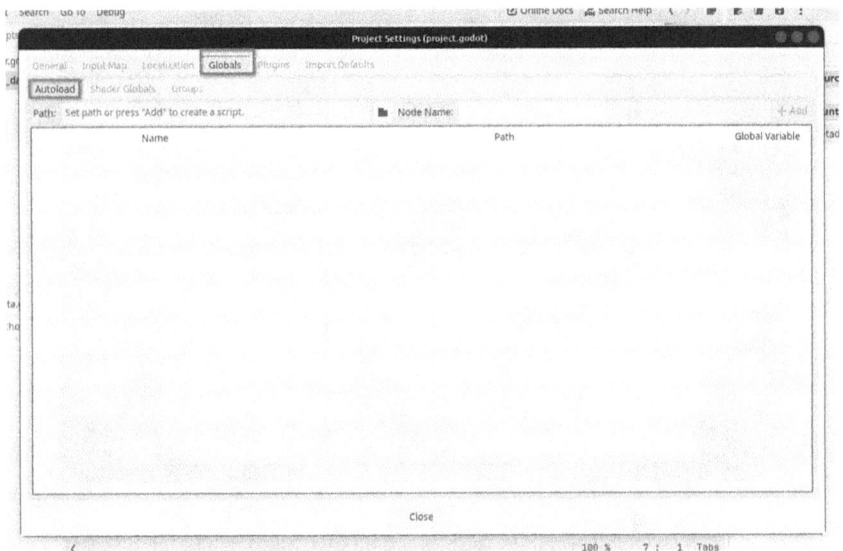

FIGURE 7.47   Accessing the AutoLoad Tab.

known – it is Singleton Name. In this case, I have used the name *GameData* (see Figure 7.48).

Once added, make sure that *Enable* is checked for the *Global Variable* field. This ensures that your Singleton class is available to access everywhere, to every node in every scene (see Figure 7.49).

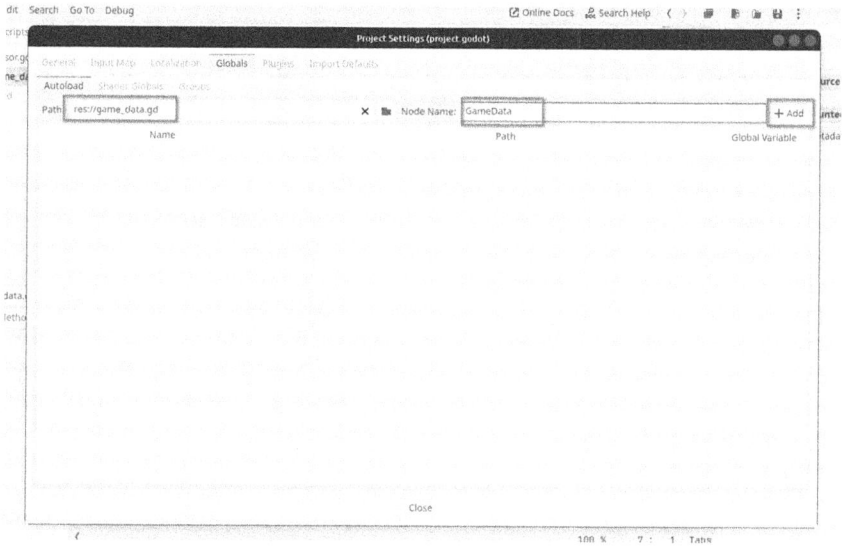

FIGURE 7.48   Adding a GameData Singleton.

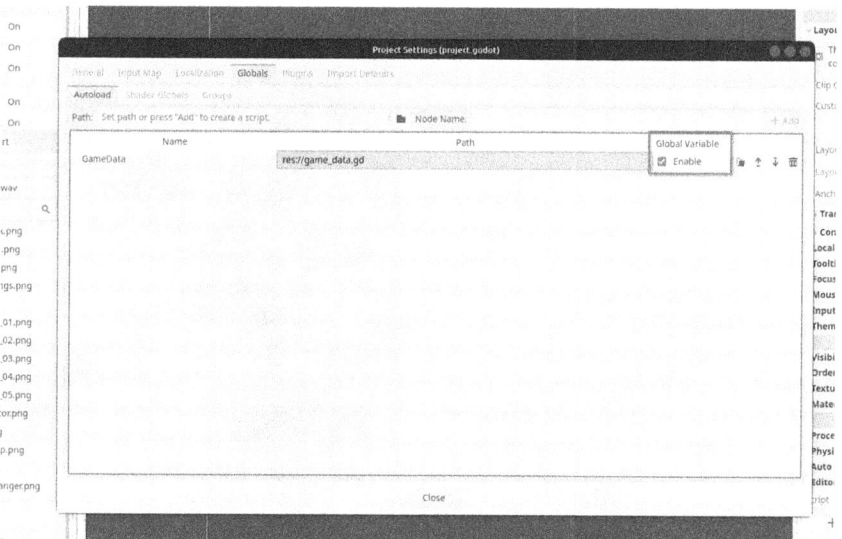

FIGURE 7.49   Enabling Singleton Behavior.

You can now access your Singleton Object everywhere in the code, as shown in Code Sample 7.6. You can include this code in any script file. The Singleton is accessible to every object and is never destroyed. If a scene changes, the Singleton remains with all its values.

CODE SAMPLE 7.6

GameData. `run_full_screen = true`

7.11 ADDING BACKGROUND MUSIC FOR THE MENU

Let's add some audio and music to our menu. This book does not include any music tracks, but there are many resources online where music can be downloaded both for free and cheaply. In our menu, there should be a continually playing music track that plays immediately and loops endlessly to set the mood and context for the menu. To start, import our music into the project. Music can be either in *WAV* or *OGG* format (see Figure 7.50).

Select the music in the FileSystem and switch to the Import tab to view the default properties for audio import. For a menu screen music track, we want the track to auto-repeat each time playback ends. To do this, enable the *Forward* setting for the *Loop Mode*. This means the music track should continue playing the music as normal on each repeat (see Figure 7.51).

NOTE. Make sure to click the *ReImport* button after making changes to confirm your settings.

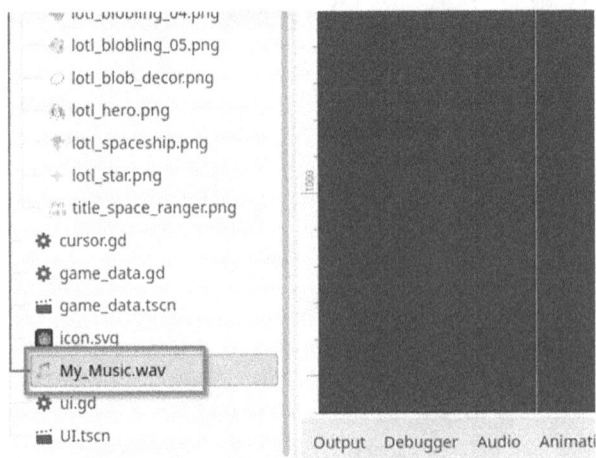

FIGURE 7.50   Importing a Music Track.

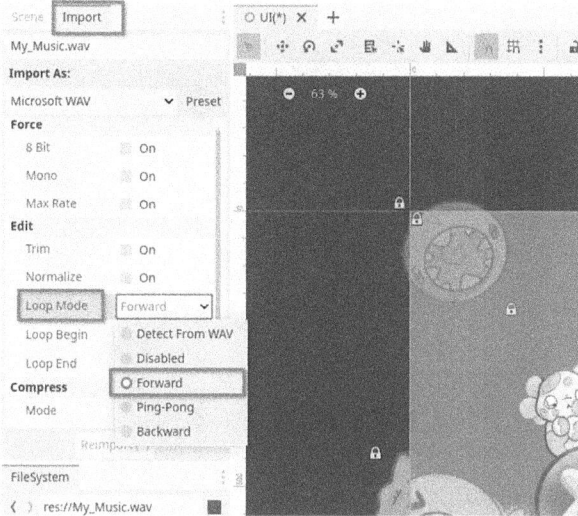

FIGURE 7.51   Enabling Looping Playback.

Next, create a new *AudioStreamPlayer2D* to the scene. From the Stream setting in the *Object Inspector*, choose *Quick Load* and select your music track (see Figure 7.52).

Now enable the *Autoplay* field from the Inspector, and also set the *Playback Type* to *Stream* to prevent Godot from loading the entire sample into memory, thereby increasing level loading times (see Figure 7.53).

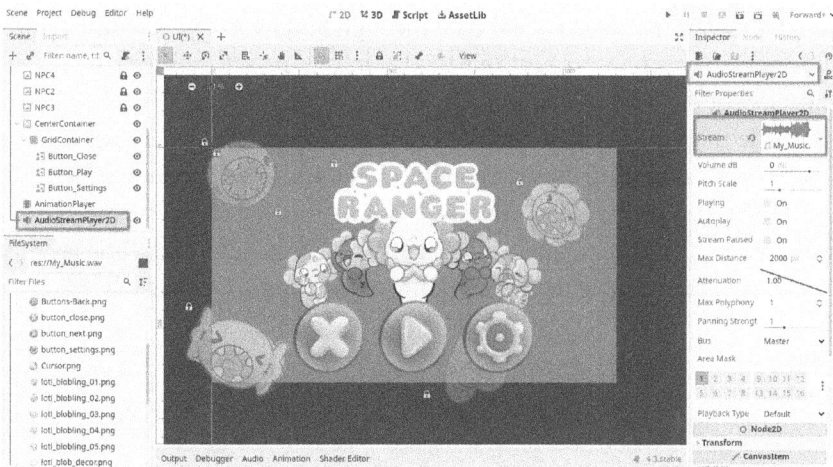

FIGURE 7.52   Using Quick Load.

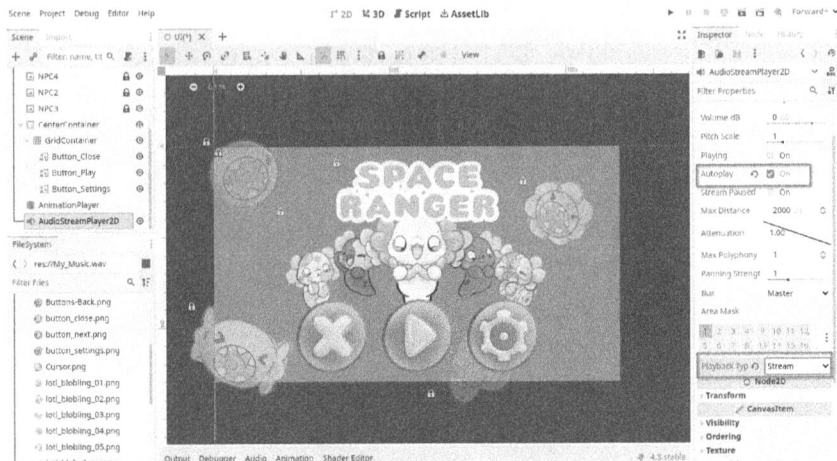

FIGURE 7.53   Configuring streaming audio.

And that's it! Your scene is now configured to play a looping audio track on the menu. Press run from the toolbar and enjoy a completed menu with music.

7.12 CONCLUSION

This chapter explored a step-by-step workflow for creating a UI menu screen for an example game named *Space Ranger*. In creating this menu, we saw a range of useful and important features, many of which have an application beyond UIs specifically. We saw how to create a mouse cursor, how to connect buttons to interactions, and how to use the *AnimationPlayer*, as well as how to create persistent data through Singleton Objects. Singletons especially have an important role to play in storing settings for games that must live beyond any single scene and must move through all scenes, being available to all objects. In completing this chapter, you have seen how to work with scenes of all kinds, namely 2D, 3D, and UI. As we move forward, we'll focus less on the scenes themselves and more on the game mechanics we can create for them, and we'll see different functions and libraries that Godot makes available to us for coding many kinds of behaviors.

CHAPTER 8

Game Mechanics

Creating a First-Person Controller

THIS CHAPTER IS A project-based chapter, just like the previous one. Here, however, we'll explore many Godot features and tools and *GDScript* functions to support the creation of important gameplay elements. Namely, we're going to build a functionally complete first-person controller from scratch, complete with collisions, mouse and keyboard controls, jumping and gravity, and more. The first-person controller is a commonplace and historically important mechanic in 3D games, being the cornerstone of many 3D shooters and narrative-driven walking simulators. By constructing a first-person shooter from the ground upward, we'll learn a lot of transferable knowledge about Godot, which has applications in many areas across 2D, 3D, and user interfaces. For this reason, please don't skip this chapter by thinking that 3D is not relevant for you if you're planning to make 2D games. This is because so much content here – such as methodology, approach, and problem-solving – all have their relevant 2D parallels. By the end of this chapter, we'll have a feature-filled first-person controller that can easily navigate around a 3D level using traditional *WASD* first-person controls, alongside mouse movement for head rotation. So, let's get started.

8.1 STARTING A NEW GODOT PROJECT AND ASSET IMPORTING

Our development journey begins by creating a new Godot project. We've seen this process before in earlier chapters, but let's recap. From the *Godot*

Project Creation Window, choose the *Create* button, and then complete important project details. I've named the project *FPS Sandbox,* and I've selected a *Forward+* Renderer. After this, press *Create and Edit* to confirm the details and enter the Editor. See Figure 8.1.

For this project, there's only one very simple mesh asset to import. It's a prototype mesh environment with a ground plane and some basic cube obstacles as walls for testing our first-person controller with collisions as we build it in-engine. This mesh was created in the 3D modeling software Blender, which we saw earlier in Chapter 2. The mesh was exported from Blender as a GLTF file with the naming suffix of *–col* for all objects inside the file, meaning that colliders will automatically be generated by Godot for the mesh at import time. This saves us from having to generate colliders manually inside Godot using nodes and other objects. We can import the mesh, and it's ready to use, and that's all. The mesh is included in the book companion files, in the Chapter 8 folder. Drag and drop the file into Godot in the *FileSystem* Dock. See Figure 8.2.

For a sanity check, let's confirm that the colliders were generated for the imported mesh, as we expect them to be. To do this, double-click the imported mesh from the *FileSystem* Dock to open its contents in the

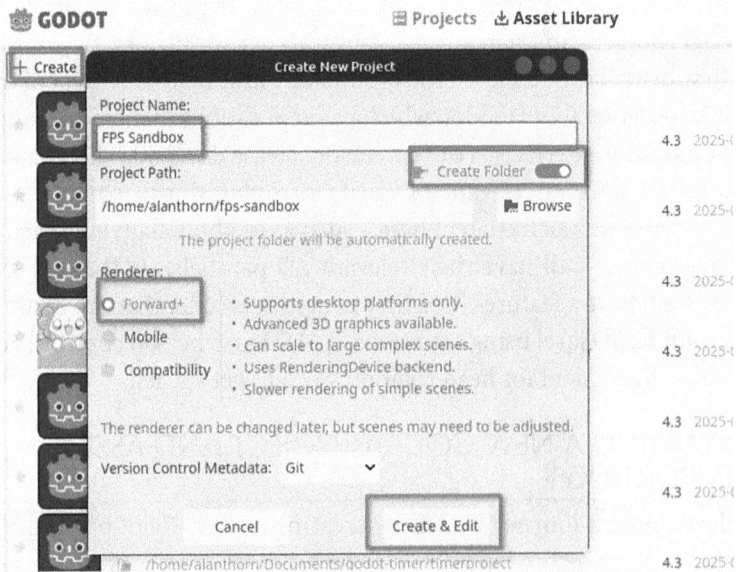

FIGURE 8.1   Creating a new project for a first-person controller.

Advanced Import Settings Dialog. In the *Scene* tab, inside the hierarchy, you'll notice that some additional physics objects have been appended to the hierarchy automatically; namely, a *StaticBody3D* and a *Collision-Shape3D*. The *CollisionShape3D* uses the mesh itself as the colliding volume. See Figure 8.3.

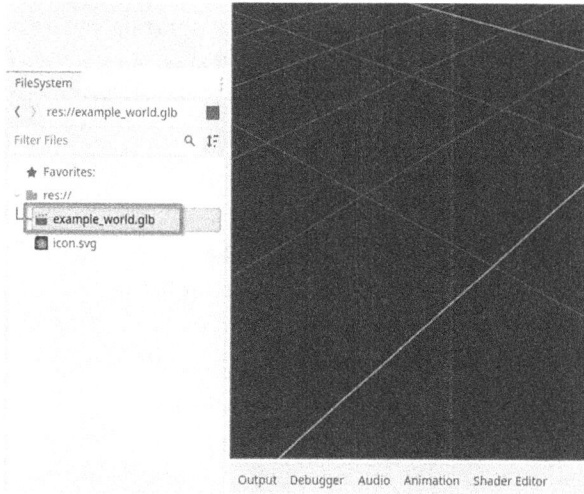

FIGURE 8.2   Import a mesh environment asset into Godot.

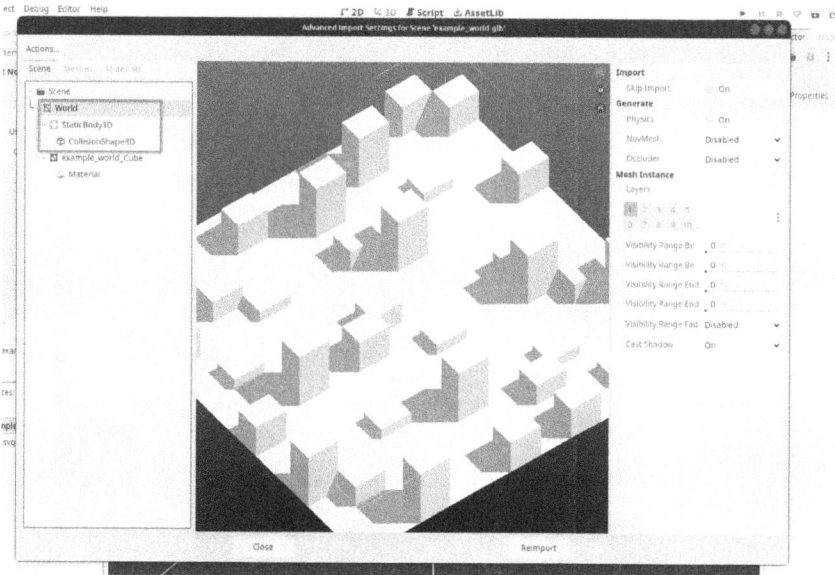

FIGURE 8.3   Checking a mesh's collision data.

8.2 BUILDING THE ENVIRONMENT SCENE

Although the first-person controller will be *part* of our game world, it will also be *separate* from it. We will be building the first-person controller in such a way that it can be easily reused across many different 3D scenes and projects, and it's not attached to any specific scene or level. To achieve this, it's important to see both the environment, inside which the controller will live, and the controller itself as separate but related entities, just as the fish is separate from water. We'll start here by creating the 3D environment first, ensuring the world is ready to accept a character. To do this, create a new, empty 3D scene and rename the root node (the topmost node) to the *environment*. See Figure 8.4.

Drag and drop the newly imported mesh environment from the *FileSystem* panel into the scene, locating it at the world origin and using the padlock feature to prevent the mesh from being selected and moved accidentally. See Figure 8.5.

The scene looks well illuminated in the editor's viewport. However, as we've seen before in earlier chapters, this is only a sample lighting setup in editor mode. So, we'll need to add some in-scene lighting for a game-ready setup. Let's add two nodes for this: first, a *WorldEnvironmentNode*, and second, a *DirectionalLight*. See Figure 8.6.

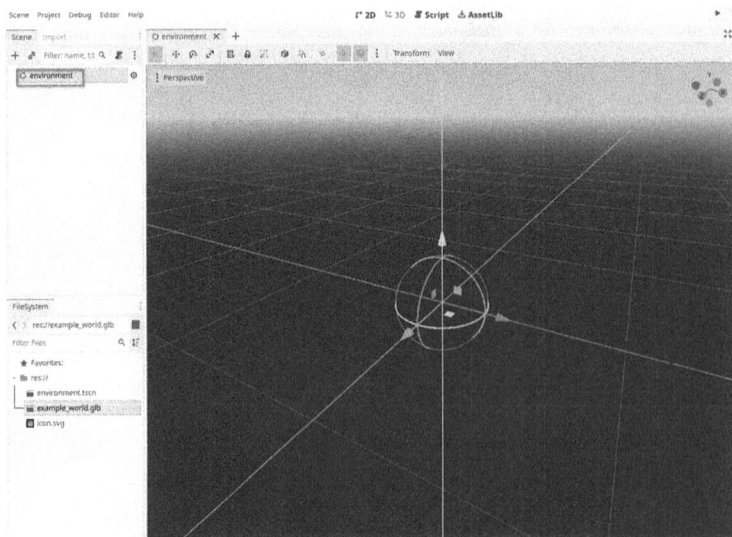

FIGURE 8.4   Creating an empty 3D scene.

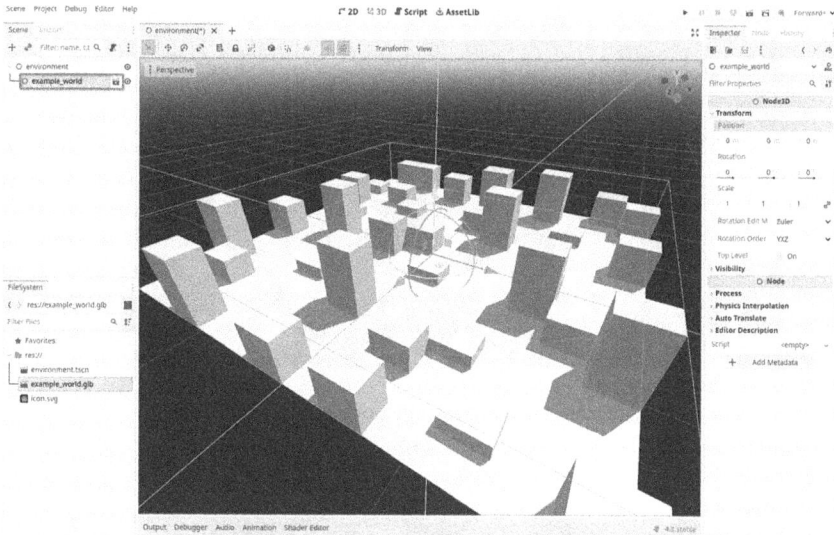

FIGURE 8.5   Importing the mesh environment.

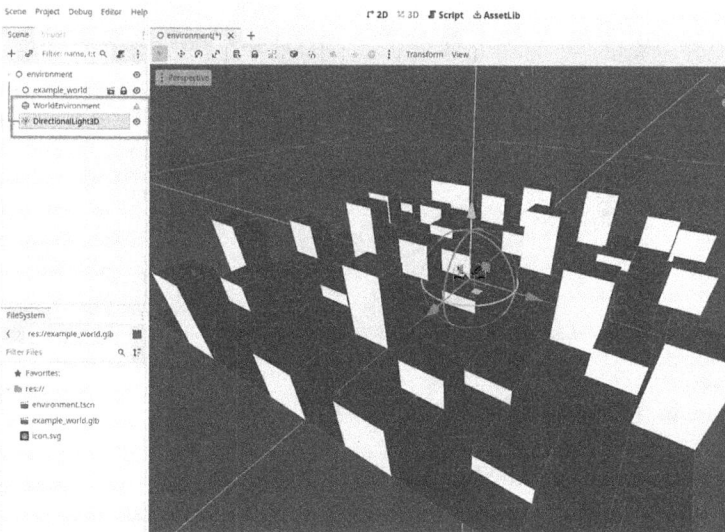

FIGURE 8.6   Creating a lighting setup.

The newly created *WorldEnvironment* node requires some attention, as indicated by the exclamation mark icon beside its name in the hierarchy. Select this node and choose *New Environment* under the *Environment* field in the Inspector. See Figure 8.7.

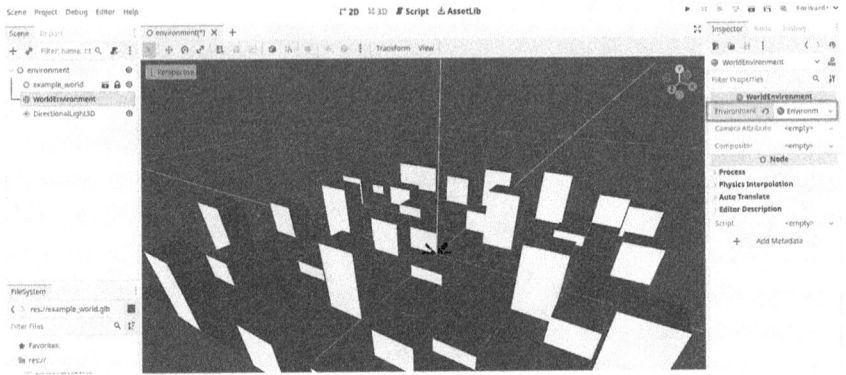

FIGURE 8.7   Creating a new Environment node.

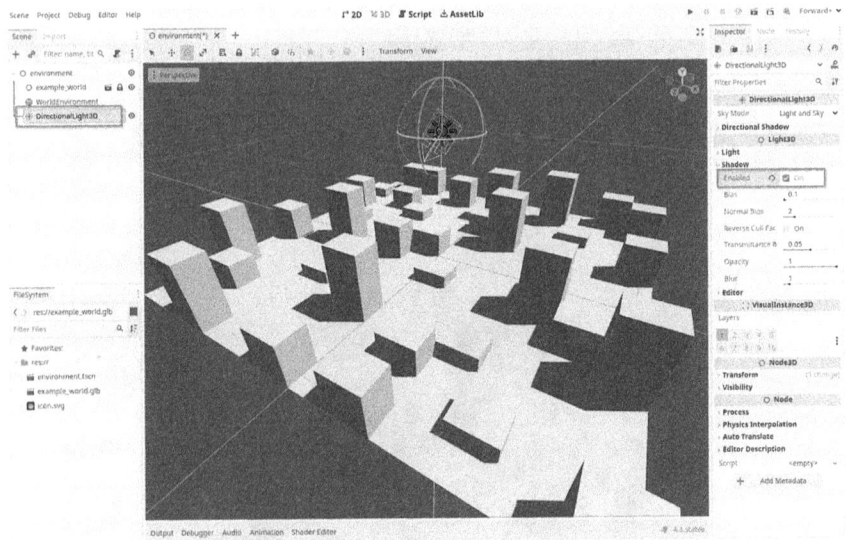

FIGURE 8.8   Orienting a directional light in the scene.

Let's now configure the lighting itself. Select the *Directional Light* node, pull it up into the sky for our convenience, and then rotate it to cast light downward onto the scene. Find an orientation that works well for your level, then enable shadow casting. See Figure 8.8.

8.3 BUILDING THE PLAYER CHARACTER AS A SCENE

This section explores a truly powerful methodology for working with nodes in Godot scenes. Here, we'll create the player's first-person controller in its *own* 3D scene, separate from the 3D world we just made, where the player will eventually be added as a linked instance. In addition to defining worlds, scenes in Godot are used as *containers* for objects, like NPCs and player characters, and props. Each scene can be reused many times in many places. The first-person controller will be its own miniature world, inside its own scene, and this scene will eventually be embedded in our larger scene of 'the world'. But, in being added to another scene like this, the player will still retain its *connections* to the original scene from where it was made. Consequently, any changes made to the original scene are updated and reflected automatically in any other scenes or worlds where it is embedded as an instance. This is because the embedded scene is not a copy or a duplication but is an instance that is still connected to the original scene. In this way, scenes may exist inside other scenes, and there is no limit to the extent of scene embedding – scenes within scenes and so on, each instance maintaining its connection to the original scene. Let's start. To do so, create a new 3D scene. Add a *CharacterBody3D* object and right-click on it in the Hierarchy. Choose *Make Scene Root* from the context menu to position the new node at the top of the hierarchy. See Figure 8.9. Afterward, you can delete the child node, *Node3D*. We won't need it.

Next, we'll give the player a mesh, which will be a capsule. This will probably be hidden at run time, but it's useful to have a mesh representation of the player for debugging purposes, helping us to see where the player is

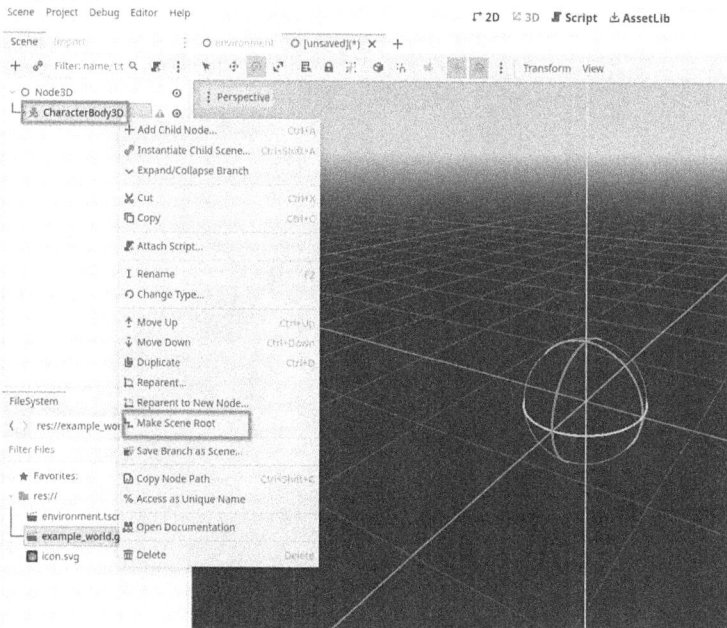

FIGURE 8.9   Making a CharacterBody3D the root node.

inside the scene. Otherwise, the player is simply a disembodied camera floating around. To do this, create a *MeshInstance3D* node as a child of the *CharacterBody3D*, and assign it a *Capsule* Mesh. See Figure 8.10.

Whenever you work with movable objects, like NPCs and player characters, you need to be especially careful about pivot points. These mark the location in the scene from which the position of the object is measured; it's the object's center or origin. By default, the capsule mesh has its origin at the world origin, and so, the capsule appears centered, half above and half below the ground level. We want the capsule to stand on the floor, with the pivot touching the ground for the character's feet. Select the capsule and set its Y value to 1. See Figure 8.11. This moves the capsule to ground level.

Now we'll add two Colliders for this character. First, let's add the regular collider. This is a *CollisionShape3D* set to a capsule, and again it should be lifted on the Y axis to 1. This object will be a child of the *CharacterBody3D*. See Figure 8.12.

We'll be working with two colliders because the player character can walk and crouch. In the crouch position, the character technically becomes shorter as their posture changes, and so their collision data also changes. In crouch mode, the player can fit into smaller spaces. So, let's create our second collider, which is also a capsule, but we'll reduce its height by half. See Figure 8.13.

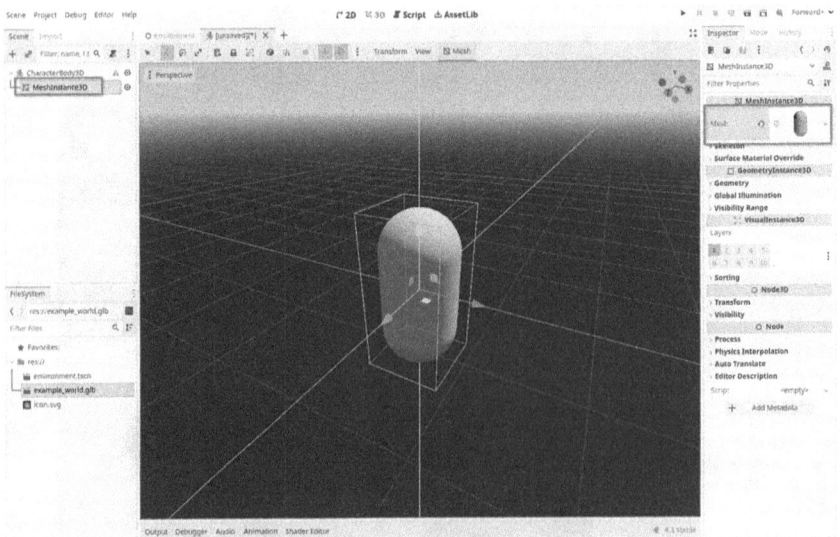

FIGURE 8.10 Creating a Capsule mesh for the character.

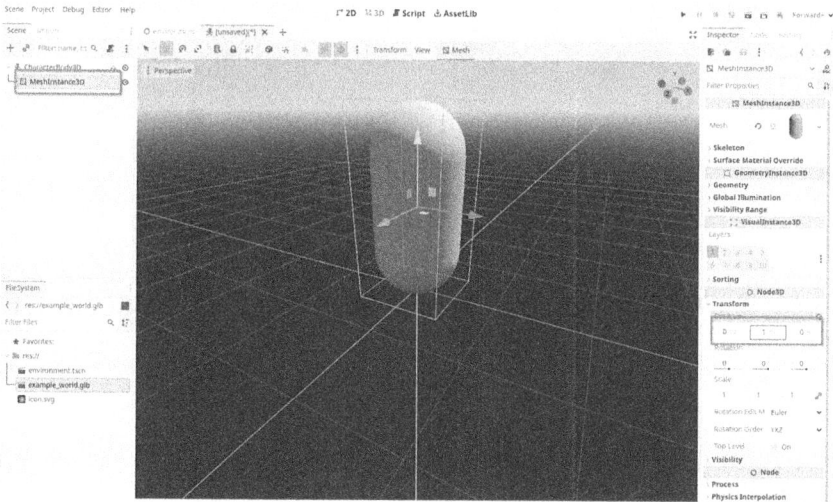

FIGURE 8.11   Positioning the capsule to the ground.

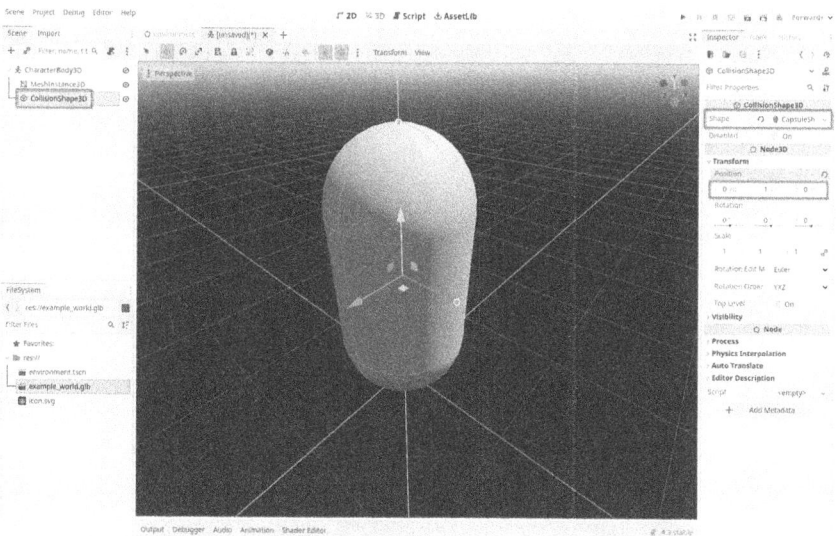

FIGURE 8.12   Adding a collider for the player.

Let's rename both objects for clarity. One is *CollisionShape3D_Standing*, and the other is *CollisionShape3D_Crouching*. See Figure 8.14. The names will be important later in the code.

NOTE. Only one of the two colliders will be active at any one time, depending on whether the player is walking or crouching.

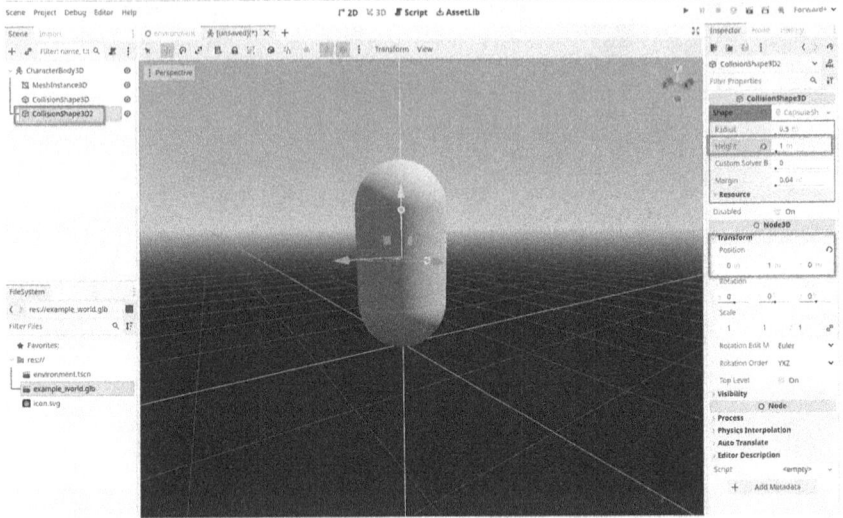

FIGURE 8.13   Halving the height of the crouch collider.

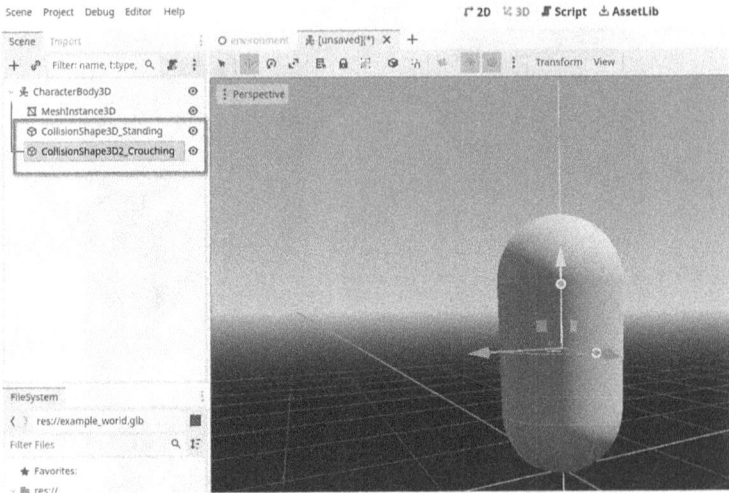

FIGURE 8.14   Naming the colliders.

Now let's add a *Camera3D* node, which will become the player's eyes, as a child of *CharacterBody3D*. Position the camera upward inside the scene, inside the mesh, at eye level. We can easily adjust later. Also, be sure that the forward vector of the camera (blue arrow, or Z Axis) matches the blue arrow of the *CharacterBody3D*. Rotate the camera if needed to ensure both objects are facing in the same direction. See Figure 8.15.

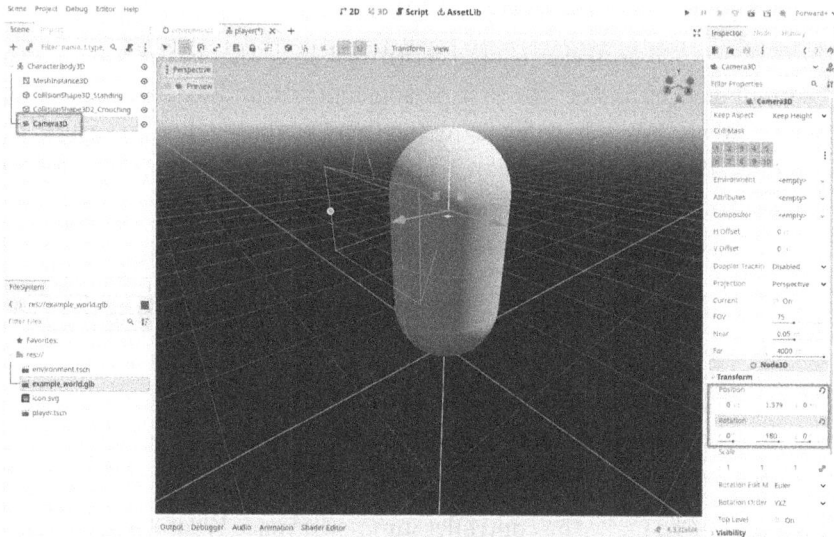

FIGURE 8.15   Aligning the camera to the eyes

Finally, save the player scene, and then drag and drop the saved scene file from the *FileSystem* dock into the other environment level, positioning the player at the suitable location. In the future, if you need to make changes to the player, you should do so in the original Player scene. Any changes will be automatically updated at the environment level. See Figure 8.16.

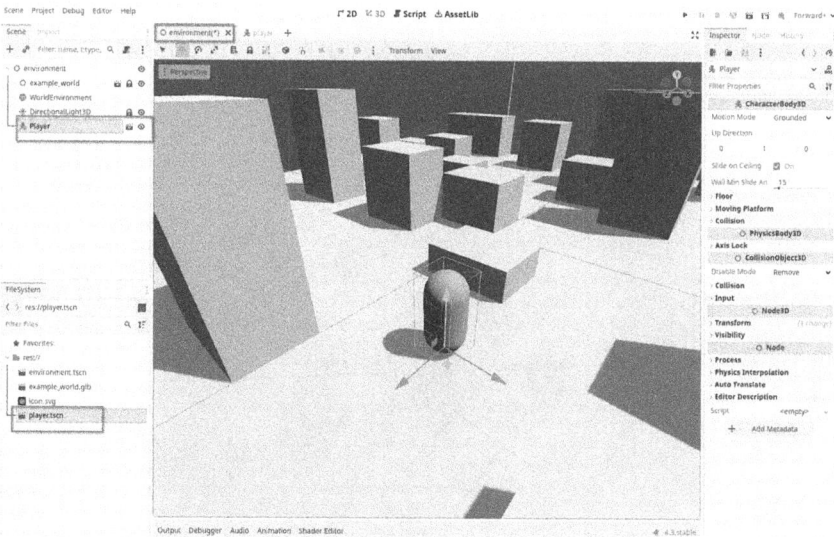

FIGURE 8.16   Adding the Player to the level.

8.4 CONFIGURING PLAYER CONTROLS

The first-person controller needs a control scheme. That is, the player must use input devices to steer the first-person controls, and we'll need to setup those controls. We'll do so by using the Input Manager that we've already seen in earlier chapters. You can access this by choosing *Project > Project Settings* from the application menu. See Figure 8.17.

Let's review the needed controls, as follows:

- *Left, Right, Up, and Down* (the WASD controls for moving the first-person controller).

- *Look_Left, Look_Right, Look_Up, and Look_Down* (these are IJKL keyboard controls for moving the head of the first-person controller, like mouse movement).

- Jump – To make the controller jump on a space bar press.

- Crouch – To make the controller crouch, reducing its height.

- Run – Finally, when the run is held down, the controller will move faster.

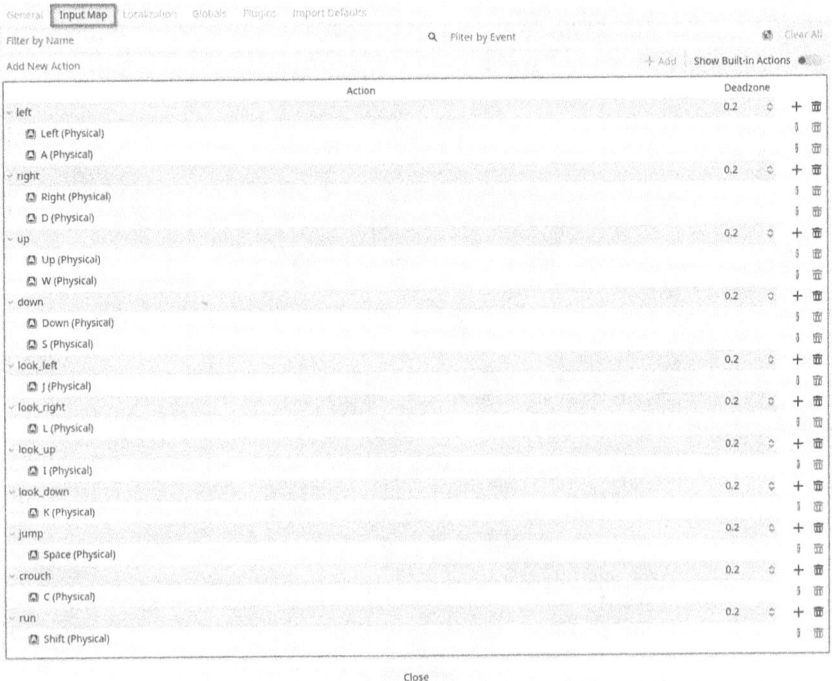

FIGURE 8.17 Defining controls from the Input Manager.

8.5 CREATING THE PLAYER CONTROLLER SCRIPT

Now we'll create our *Player Controller* script, which will be attached to *the root object of the player scene*. It's very important that our script is attached here, to the root object *inside* the player scene. Do not attach it to a child object anywhere, and do not attach it to the root object as it appears in the environment scene. Be sure to use the player scene so that the changes will be reflected wherever else the player is embedded. Select the root object, and from the *Inspector* expand the *Script* field and create a new script file named *PlayerController.gd*. See Figure 8.18. This script will be derived from *CharacterBody3D*.

To start, let's define a set of exported variables, which will control important properties for the first-person controller. Consider Code Sample 8.1.

CODE SAMPLE 8.1

```
#Controls walking speeding of player (meters per
second)
@export var _walk_speed:float = 2
#Determines how fast player runs when run is held
down (meters per second)
@export var _run_speed:float = 4
#Controls how much head movement responds to mouse
movement
@export var _mouse_sensitivity:float = 2
#Controls how fast head movement moves based on
keyboard input
@export var _controller_head_rot_speed:float = 90
#Should the cursor be hidden when first person
controller is active?
@export var _capture_mouse:bool = true
#How far in any direction can the head turn when
player is standing still (degrees)
@export var _head_rot_limits:Vector2 = Vector2(-80,
80)
#How much should speed reduce when player stops
@export var _movement_damping:float = 4
#How quickly should head turning reduce when stopped
@export var _rotation_Damping:float = 10
#How high or low should the head move when walking
@export var _headbob_amplitude:float = 0.03
```

```
#How often should head move when walking
@export var _headbob_frequency:float = 0.002
#What should the height of the player be when
crouching
@export var _crouch_amout:Vector3 = Vector3(0, 0.5,
0)
#How fast can we move when crouching (meters per
second)
@export var _crouching_speed:float=1000
#Can player controller be controlled by input?
@export var _input_enabled:bool = true
#Should the grey mesh capsule be hidden to avoid
shadow casting during gameplay?
@export var _hide_player_mesh_on_start:bool = true
```

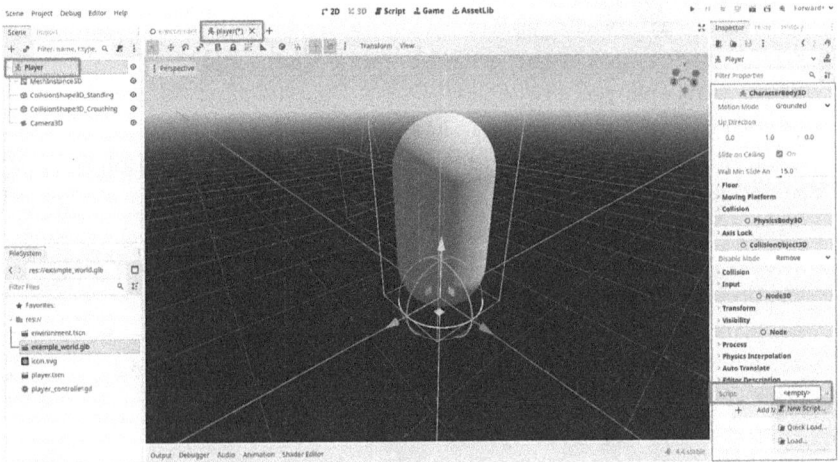

FIGURE 8.18   Creating a new script on the Player Controller root object.

If you now save this code, when attached to the root object, you'll see all the defined properties appear in the Object Inspector. See Figure 8.19.

NOTE. You will also be able to see and change variables on the script when the object is selected in a different scene.

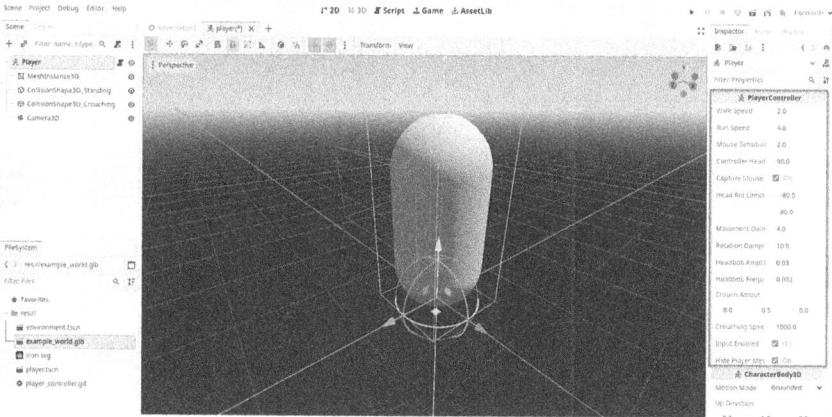

FIGURE 8.19   Creating player controller variables.

8.6 CODING HEAD ROTATION

With a first-person controller, the world is seen through the eyes of the player. This typically means that the camera represents our head. We see the world through the camera lens from its position, orientation, and perspective. For this purpose, we can also divide camera behavior into two types: walking motion, which determines camera *position* in the world, and head rotation, which determines camera *orientation*. We'll focus on the latter here. Orientation is controlled by both mouse movement and by the keyboard keys *IJKL*. Using this input, we must be able to rotate the head left, right, up, and down. And indeed, within this rotational space, there are limits too. We should not normally rotate the head 360 degrees in any direction, for example. Let's start. So, first, we'll need a reference to the camera object itself to rotate it as needed. See Code Sample 8.2.

CODE SAMPLE 8.2

```
@onready var _camera_3d = $Camera3D
```

Next, we want to keep track of relative mouse movement since the previous frame. Greater mouse displacement leads to faster header turning, within preset limits. We can keep track of this with a Vector2 variable. See Code Sample 8.3.

CODE SAMPLE 8.3

```
var _relative_mouse:Vector2 = Vector2(0,0)
```

Now, before we measure mouse motion itself, we need to understand more clearly what we're measuring. Mouse motion will be defined in terms of pixel displacement. That is, how *much the cursor has changed in pixel position* since the previous frame. This sounds straightforward. However, what happens if the user resizes the window and the game re-scales to a new size? Or what happens if the first-person controller view is only shown on part of the screen (such as a pop-up), rather than for the whole of the screen? In these cases, the ratio between pixel displacement of the cursor and the viewport scale is not always 1:1. So, we'll need to define this ratio first to ensure there is a consistent displacement applied to our rotation calculations later. If we don't do this, then the rotational head speed will vary depending on the viewport scale. Consider Code Sample 8.4.

CODE SAMPLE 8.4

```
func _input(event):
        if !(event is InputEventMouseMotion):
                return
_default_viewport_size = get_viewport().size
scaled_view.x = get_window().size.x /
_default_viewport_size.x
scaled_view.y = get_window().size.y /
_default_viewport_size.y

#measure how much mouse cursor has moved, for
controlling head motion
#godot doesn't scale mouse motion if the window
is shrunk or enlarged
#this ensures the mouse movement behaves at the
same speed for every resolution
_relative_mouse.x = event.relative.x *
scaled_view.x
_relative_mouse.y = event.relative.y *
scaled_view.y
```

Great! The above code in Sample 8.4 will scale the vector _relative_mouse by the viewport scale to ensure that there is a 1:1 relationship between pixel displacement (*delta*) of the cursor and viewport scale. Now, in addition, we also need to keep track of the mouse delta from the previous frame, whatever it was. This value will be needed for a calculation later so that we can add a 'smoothing' effect to our head rotation. If head rotation were allowed to be driven directly by mouse movement alone, then any ugly jittering or shaking of the physical mouse by the user's hand would be reflected immediately in messy head turning for the first-person controller in-game. This kind of immediate sensitivity between mouse and head can enhance a sea-sickness feel from first-person controls, as well as make the game feel unnatural. To fix this, then, we create one degree of separation between physical mouse movement, on the one hand, and the head-turning in the first-person controller on the other. We do this by having head-turning always play a game of 'catch-up' by rotating smoothly in numbers from where it was previously to a rotational destination ahead, as determined by the latest mouse displacement. Let's examine the _process function, which happens automatically on each frame, as shown in Code Sample 8.5.

CODE SAMPLE 8.5

```
func _ process(delta):
        #update head rotation
        if(_input_enabled):
                _last_look_input = Vector2(((-
Input.get_action_strength("look_left") + Input.
get_action_strength("look_right")) * _controller_
head_rot_speed) + _relative_mouse.x, ((-Input.
get_action_strength("look_up") + Input.get_action_
strength("look_down")) * _controller_head_rot_speed)
+ _relative_mouse.y)
 else:
        _last_look_input = Vector2.ZERO
 _target_rotation.y = -_last_look_input.x * _mouse_
sensitivity * delta

 _yaw = lerp(_yaw, _target_rotation.y, delta *
_rotation_Damping)
```

```
    rotate_y(deg_to_rad(_yaw))


_target_rotation.x +=  _last_look_input.y * _mouse_
sensitivity * delta

        _target_rotation.x = clamp(_target_
rotation.x,  _head_rot_limits.x, _head_rot_limits.y)

        _pitch = lerp(_pitch, _target_rotation.x, delta*
_rotation_Damping)

        _camera_3d.rotation.x = -deg_to_rad(_pitch)

        if(_relative_mouse.x != 0 or _relative_
mouse.y !=0):
            _relative_mouse = Vector2.ZERO
```

Let's consider some of the key points here in the code:

1. The _process function happens once per frame.

2. If input is allowed, we record the latest head movement as a vector _last_look_input, combining mouse displacement with keyboard input, if any.

3. _target_rotation is a vector detailing where the rotation *should aim* toward. This is what our head rotation would be if it were linked directly to mouse movement.

4. The target rotation is clamped by rotational limits. This prevents the head from rotating 360 degrees, or from turning upside down.

5. The rotate_y function turns the camera around the Y axis by a 'lerped' quantity, moving smoothly from a previous value to a new destination.

6. The *rotation.x* property controls up and down camera rotation; again, it controlled by a lerped value and within rotation limits.

Before moving forward, let's take our code for a test run. Click *Play*, and your head rotation should now be working. See Figure 8.20.

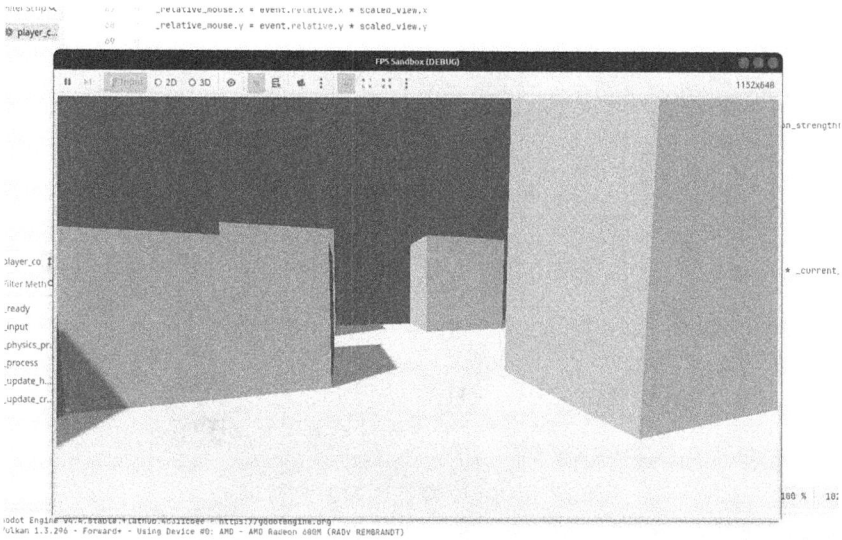

FIGURE 8.20   Testing head rotation.

8.7 CODING CAMERA MOVEMENT

In this section, we'll focus on player controller *movement*, complete with physical collisions to ensure the player cannot and does not pass through solid objects, like the floor and walls. This process involves the *move_ and_slide* function of *CharacterBody3D*, which we've seen before in earlier chapters. Movement occurs during the _physics_process event, called once per physics cycle. Consider Code Sample 8.6.

CODE SAMPLE 8.6

```
func _ physics _ process(delta):
        #update movement
        #check if movement is allowed. Useful to
disable motion on game pauses etc
        if(_input_enabled): _last_move_input =
Vector2(-Input.get_action_strength("left") + Input.
get_action_strength("right"), -Input.get_action_
strength("down") + Input.get_action_strength("up"))
        _current_speed = _walk_speed
```

```
        if(Input.is_action_pressed("run") and is_on_
floor() and !_is_crouching):
                _current_speed = _run_speed
        else:
                _last_move_input = Vector2.ZERO

        _target_velocity = (transform.basis.z * _
last_move_input.y * _current_speed) + (transform.
basis.x * -_last_move_input.x * _current_speed)

        if(!is_on_floor()):
                _target_velocity.y -= _gravity
        else:
                if(Input.is_action_just_
pressed("jump") and _input_enabled and ! _
is_crouching):
                _target_velocity.y += 80

        velocity = velocity.lerp(_target_velocity,
clamp(delta * _movement_damping, 0, 1))

        move_and_slide()
```

Let's discuss this code in more depth, as below.

1. First, we check if input is allowed. This might be disabled during a cutscene or when the game is paused.

2. Second, we must determine the moving speed of the player to use for the current frame. This is normally a choice between walking or running speed, depending on whether the *run* is being held down by the player.

3. Third, the Vector *_target_velocity* is calculated based on the local X and local Z axis. Local X is projected from the right side of the CharacterBody3D and it defines movement left and right (side steps). The local Z axis is projected from the character's nose and defines forward and backward movement. This is calculated based on combining player input with speed.

4. Fourth, we check if either *jump* or *crouch* is pressed.

5. Finally, we *Lerp* the velocity to add inertia and smooth motion, which we pass on to the *move_and_slide* function.

You now have motion and rotation coded. Test this out again by pressing play on the toolbar.

8.8 CODING CROUCHING BEHAVIOR

Crouching is a functional mode of the first-person controller. In this specific mode, the player moves slower and is shorter in height, able to crawl through more narrow spaces, like air ducts and ventilation shafts. Engaging in this mode is caused by pressing and holding the C key. Consider the following function to enable crouch behavior, which can be called from the *_process* function. See Code Sample 8.7.

CODE SAMPLE 8.7

```
func _ update _ crouch(delta):
        if _input_enabled: _is_crouching = false
        _is_crouching = is_on_floor() and Input.
is_action_pressed("crouch")

        _walk_collision.disabled = _is_crouching
        _crouch_collision.disabled = !_is_crouching

        _camera_3d.position = _camera_3d.position.
lerp(_camera_starting_pos - (_crouch_amout * int(_
is_crouching)), clamp(delta * _crouching_speed, 0
,1))
        _camera_resting_pos = _camera_3d.position
```

8.9 CODING HEAD BOB

Head bob is the sinusoidal tendency of the head to naturally move up and then down repeatedly because the body is simply going through the kinematic motions of walking. The movement of the head up and then down creates a natural feel to the first-person controller, and it should be enabled whenever you need to stress the humanity and dynamism of the character. You may choose to accentuate the effect whenever you need to focus on vulnerability or stressful situations. You may choose to reduce the effect or remove it entirely when you need an ethereal, powerful, and surreal character. Head Bob is, essentially, a minor modification to the Y position of the camera, making sure the camera does not elevate so far as to move above its own surrounding collider. Consider Code Sample 8.8, which is another function to be called once per frame from the _process function.

CODE SAMPLE 8.8

```
func _ update _ head _ bob(delta):
        #if we are falling, there should be no head
bob var bob_multiplier = 0
        #update head bob if we are grounded
              if is_on_floor():
                  if _last_move_input.length_squared() !=
0:
                        bob_multiplier = _current_speed
+ 8
                  else:
                        bob_multiplier = 1

                  _bob_target = _camera_resting_pos +
(_camera_3d.basis.y * (sin(Time.get_ticks_msec()
* _headbob_frequency * bob_multiplier) * _headbob_
amplitude * bob_multiplier))
                        _camera_3d.position = _camera_3d.
position.lerp(_bob_target, delta)
```

8.10 COMPLETING THE FIRST-PERSON CONTROLLER

We've now arrived at our destination, which is the completion of the first-person controller. By reaching this point, your controller can move forward, backward, left, and right. It also has a freely rotating head to look in different directions. It will collide with physical obstacles, and it can jump and fall to the ground under gravity. Furthermore, we can run and crouch, and we can also enable a head-bob for natural motion. See Code Sample 8.9 for the full source code for the first-person controller, and this is also included in the course companion files.

CODE SAMPLE 8.9

```
extends CharacterBody3D
class_name PlayerController
@export var _walk_speed:float = 2
@export var _run_speed:float = 4
@export var _mouse_sensitivity:float = 2
@export var _controller_head_rot_speed:float = 90
@export var _capture_mouse:bool = true
@export var _head_rot_limits:Vector2 = Vector2(-80,
80)
@export var _movement_damping:float = 4
@export var _rotation_Damping:float = 10
@export var _headbob_amplitude:float = 0.03
@export var _headbob_frequency:float = 0.002
@export var _crouch_amout:Vector3 = Vector3(0, 0.5, 0)
@export var _crouching_speed:float=1000
@export var _input_enabled:bool = true
@export var _hide_player_mesh_on_start:bool = true
@onready var _mesh = $MeshInstance3D
@onready var _camera_3d = $Camera3D
@onready var _walk_collision =
$CollisionShape3D_Standing
@onready var _crouch_collision =
$CollisionShape3D_Crouching
var _relative_mouse:Vector2 = Vector2(0,0)
var _pitch:float = 0
var _yaw:float = 0
var _gravity:float = 0
var _last_move_input:Vector2 = Vector2.ZERO
var _last_look_input:Vector2 = Vector2.ZERO
var _target_velocity:Vector3 = Vector3.ZERO
var _target_rotation:Vector3 = Vector3.ZERO
var _camera_starting_pos:Vector3 = Vector3.ZERO
var _camera_resting_pos:Vector3 = Vector3.ZERO
var _bob_target:Vector3 = Vector3.ZERO
var _default_viewport_size:Vector2 = Vector2.ONE
var _is_crouching:bool = false
var _current_speed:float=0
func _ready():
```

```
        #hides mesh representation of player at scene
start
        _mesh.visible = !_hide_player_mesh_on_start
        _gravity = ProjectSettings.
get_setting("physics/3d/default_gravity")
        #get gravity strength from project settings
        #gets the active viewport for this scene.
This could be the game window, or an embedded view
            _default_viewport_size = get_
viewport().size


            #hide system mouse cursor?
            if _capture_mouse:
                    Input.set_mouse_mode(Input.
MOUSE_MODE_CAPTURED)


            _camera_starting_pos = _camera_3d.
position
            _camera_resting_pos =
_camera_starting_pos
            _current_speed = _walk_speed


func _input(event):
        if !(event is InputEventMouseMotion): return
        #compare window to viewport size
            #this can be different. For example, if
a small game world is stretched to fill the window
            var scaled_view:Vector2 = Vector2.ZERO
            scaled_view.x = get_window().size.x /
_default_viewport_size.x
            scaled_view.y = get_window().size.y /
_default_viewport_size.y


            #measure how much mouse cursor has
moved, for controlling head motion
            #godot does not scale the mouse motion
if the window is shrunk or enlarged, so let's scale
it here
            #this ensures the mouse movement
behaves at the same speed for every resolution
```

```
                _relative_mouse.x = event.relative.x *
scaled_view.x
                _relative_mouse.y = event.relative.y *
scaled_view.y

func _physics_process(delta):
        #update movement #check if movement is
allowed. Useful to disable motion on game pauses etc
        if(_input_enabled):
                _last_move_input = Vector2(-
Input.get_action_strength("left") + Input.
get_action_strength("right"), -Input.get_action_
strength("down") + Input.get_action_strength("up"))
        _current_speed = _walk_speed

                if(Input.is_action_pressed("run") and
is_on_floor() and !_is_crouching):
                        _current_speed = _run_speed
                else:
                        _last_move_input = Vector2.
ZERO

        _target_velocity = (transform.basis.z * _
last_move_input.y * _current_speed) + (transform.
basis.x * -_last_move_input.x * _current_speed)

        if(!is_on_floor()):
                _target_velocity.y -= _gravity
        else:
        if(Input.is_action_just_pressed("jump") and
_input_enabled and !_is_crouching):
                _target_velocity.y += 80
        velocity = velocity.lerp(_target_velocity,
clamp(delta * _movement_damping, 0, 1))

        move_and_slide()

func _process(delta):
        #update head rotation
        if(_input_enabled):
```

```
                _last_look_input = Vector2(((-
Input.get_action_strength("look_left") + Input.
get_action_strength("look_right")) * _controller_
head_rot_speed) + _relative_mouse.x, ((-Input.
get_action_strength("look_up") + Input.get_action_
strength("look_down")) * _controller_head_rot_speed)
+ _relative_mouse.y)
        else:
                _last_look_input = Vector2.ZERO
_target_rotation.y = -_last_look_input.x * _mouse_
sensitivity * delta
_yaw = lerp(_yaw, _target_rotation.y, delta *
_rotation_Damping)
rotate_y(deg_to_rad(_yaw))

_target_rotation.x += _last_look_input.y * _mouse_
sensitivity * delta;
_target_rotation.x = clamp(_target_rotation.x, _
head_rot_limits.x, _head_rot_limits.y)
_pitch = lerp(_pitch, _target_rotation.x, delta*
_rotation_Damping)

_camera_3d.rotation.x = -deg_to_rad(_pitch)

if(_relative_mouse.x != 0 or _relative_mouse.y !=0):
    _relative_mouse = Vector2.ZERO

_update_head_bob(delta)
_update_crouch(delta)

func _update_head_bob(delta):
        #if we are falling, there should be no head
bob
        var bob_multiplier = 0
        #update head bob if we are grounded
                if is_on_floor():
                        if _last_move_input.length_
squared() != 0:
```

```
                                bob_multiplier = _
current_speed + 8
                      else:
                      bob_multiplier = 1

            _bob_target = _camera_resting_pos +
(_camera_3d.basis.y * (sin(Time.get_ticks_msec()
* _headbob_frequency * bob_multiplier) * _headbob_
amplitude * bob_multiplier))
                _camera_3d.position = _camera_3d.
position.lerp(_bob_target, delta)

func _update_crouch(delta):
      if _input_enabled: _
              is_crouching = false
          _is_crouching = is_on_floor() and Input.
is_action_pressed("crouch")

              _walk_collision.disabled =
_is_crouching
              _crouch_collision.disabled =
!_is_crouching

              _camera_3d.position = _camera_3d.
position.lerp(_camera_starting_pos - (_crouch_amout
* int(_is_crouching)), clamp(delta * _crouching_
speed, 0 ,1))
              _camera_resting_pos = _camera_3d.
position
```

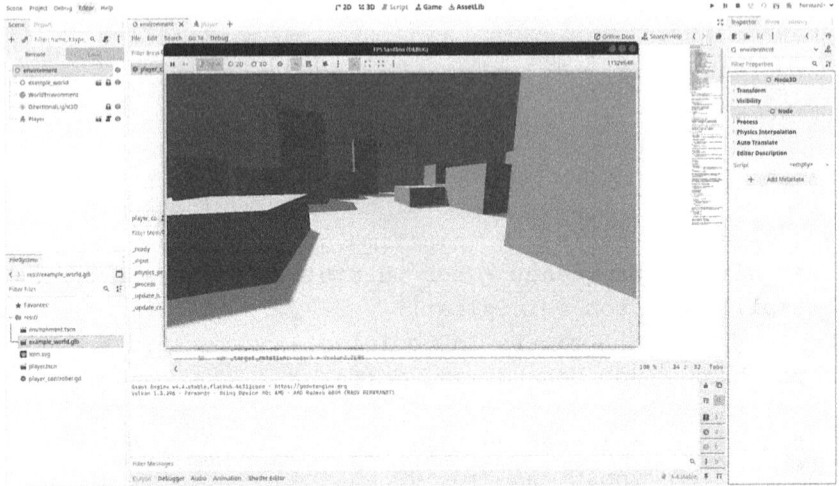

FIGURE 8.21 The completed first person controller.

Now press play and enjoy your completed first-person controller. See Figure 8.21.

8.11 FEATURES TO ADD A CHALLENGE

This section focuses on some potential improvements that you could make independently to the first-person controller to expand its functionality for a variety of game genres, and even for purposes beyond games. Let's consider some of the most important improvements.

- Interaction

   Interaction is the ability of the player to approach objects in the world and 'interact' with them. This may be as straightforward as approaching a closed door and then pressing a button on the keyboard to open it, but it may include more complex interactions too, such as lassoing a rope around a distant tree branch and swinging to a moving platform. Interaction involves adding detection points around objects and the controller, such as through Area Nodes, to determine when the controller enters the proximity of an interactable. Once detected, you'll need to establish the kind of interaction needed. Decisions as to which objects or nodes are responsible for the interaction behaviors are engineering decisions. One approach is to use the Command Design Pattern, which is an approach to coding games.

- Inventory

  An additional feature of the first-person controller, commonly found in puzzle and adventure games, is the inventory. It essentially represents the very deep pockets of the player. If the player collects a key, it goes into the inventory; if they collect a medi-kit, it goes into the inventory. For this reason, the inventory is a memory for keeping track of everything the player has ever collected and which is immediately accessible to them right now. At first sight, the inventory seems easy to implement: it's surely an array of objects. But a closer inspection reveals that things are not so straightforward. For example, if the player moves from one level to another, the inventory usually goes with them. If the player restores the game from an earlier session via a saved state, the inventory is also restored. Thus, the inventory is normally a persistent system. That is, inventory data survives the temporariness of any single play session, and it lives across multiple. To create this, a developer would normally save data to a file. Godot offers multiple ways to do this, including JSON.

- Embodiment

  The first-person controller that we've created is ultimately a floating camera nested inside a collider. There's nothing wrong with that, per se. Many games work successfully like that. Historically, the majority of first-person controllers have worked that way. But it's not the only way. You can also create a character mesh to accompany the controller, allowing the player to see the character's hands, legs, body, and feet. Doing this gives the first-person controller a deeper sense of embodiment, but it comes at the price of both technical complexity and psychology. If the player can see themselves in first person, it changes how the player relates to the character. Without a body, the player could imagine themselves as a protagonist. But with a body, the player may need to make an additional jump into the shoes of another, seen through their eyes.

- Weapons

  Many first-person games involve a hand at the bottom center of the screen, clutching onto a weapon. This is usually a pistol, rifle, rocket launcher, or chainsaw. The creation of weapons entails a weapon system, which is an inventory of weapons, allowing the player to change from one to another and reload them.

- Reactions

  The world is full of dangers, hazards, healing potions, and blatant near-misses. All of these things have an important effect on the player, and the player must respond appropriately. The response here refers not to the player's actions or mechanics, but to the way that a first-person controller automatically behaves to signal these events to the player. The screen might shake and flash red when hit, the field of view might distort and then heal, and the vision might become scrambled when influenced by a tractor beam from a nearby spaceship. As a result, many first-person controllers are usually accompanied by post-processing systems.

8.12 CONCLUSION

In this chapter, we created a first-person controller that could be used for a walking simulator-type game. There are many further directions this controller could be taken, but even by creating the controller that we have already, there are many interesting explorative experiences that we could make. The next chapter moves forward and considers a range of tips and tricks for working in Godot.

CHAPTER 9

Godot Tips and Tricks

THIS CHAPTER IS A helpful selection box of tutorials for common and important tasks when making games and applithe name of the active camera to the consolelocations using Godot. These tips and the name of the active camera to the consoletechniques do not properly belong in any chapter alone, but they are nonetheless useful applications of many ideas and concepts that we've seen already simply by exploring scene creation across 2D, 3D, and UI. The techniques in this chapter are presented in no special order, and it's likely that you'll need to make use of them all at some point during your career. What is, perhaps, both surprising and impressive is how easy and straightforward Godot, as an engine, makes some of these techniques compared to some other engines. So, let's get started.

9.1 MOUSE PICKING

Mouse picking simply refers to being able to select objects in the scene during gameplay, especially in 3D scenes, by using the mouse cursor and clicking. This may seem simple at first sight, but on closer inspection, there are quite a few complexities to contend with. For example, how should one *detect* when the cursor clicks on a 3D mesh? What if another 3D object is *in front of* the object you want to select? What happens if you click when a scene has multiple cameras, which view the same object from different angles? All of these considerations, and more, make object selection by the mouse (or even by tapping) more complex than one might first think. Here, we'll consider the following example scene, as shown in Figure 9.1. This scene features a green cube on a blue floor, seen by a 3D camera. The cube is configured with an *Area3D* node and a *Box* collider shape.

DOI: 10.1201/9781003484523-9

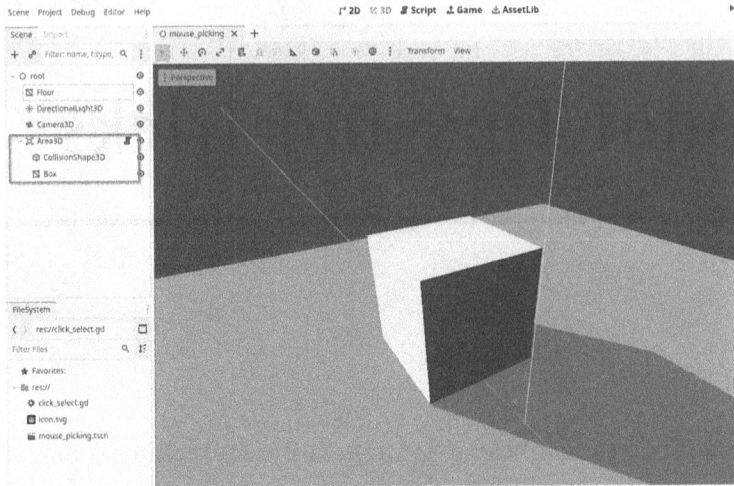

FIGURE 9.1   A basic scene with a selectable cube object.

The *Area3D* node features an important signal for detecting clicks and other types of input. Select the *Area3D* node in the scene, and from the *Signals* tab of the Inspector, you'll see the *Input_Event* signal. This signal executes for any *relevant* input event. That is, if the cursor hovers over the object, the object will be notified of any mouse events, so long as the cursor remains hovered. See Figure 9.2.

Now, attach the following script in Code Sample 9.1 onto your object; that is, onto the *Area3D* object. By doing this, your object will detect mouse clicks. In our example here, we'll print the name of the active camera to the console.

CODE SAMPLE 9.1

```
extends Area3D
func _ready() -> void:
 connect("input_event", _on_click)

func _on_click(_cam:Node, _input_event:InputEvent,
_event_pos:Vector3, _norm:Vector3, _shape_idx:int):
        if _input_event is InputEventMouseButton:
                if _input_event.pressed:
                    print(_cam.name)
```

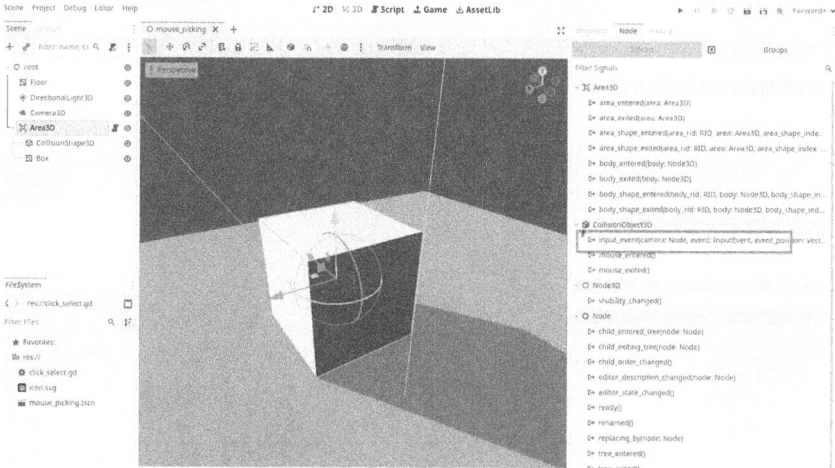

FIGURE 9.2   The InputEvent signal will execute for any input relevant events on an object.

NOTE. In a scene where multiple cameras are active at once, such as split-screen games, you'll probably need to check the camera name or group during the event to ensure the click or interaction happened from the relevant camera.

9.2 CUSTOM RESOURCES

With some game types and genres, you'll work with lots of data. An example is a competitive trading card game, or a battle card game, where different cards in a deck represent different collections of statistics, such as strength, mana, and speed. Likewise, an RPG game may feature many character types, from warriors to mages, and each instance of a type may share many different and complex properties. In these cases, you could select each instance in the scene and use the Inspector to set the object's properties variable by variable, as needed. Setting health, mana, speed, and so on. However, Godot allows you to create your own custom resource to hold many properties as a preset, which can be assigned to an object instance, and more as needed. Thereby, the data can be shared and referenced by many. Let's see an example of this. First, create a new script file derived from the resource class, as shown in Code Sample 9.2.

CODE SAMPLE 9.2

```
##Data for a custom character type in an example
game
extends Resource
class_name CustomCharData
@export var CharacterType:String
@export_range (0,100) var Strength:int
@export_range (0,100) var Speed:int
@export_range (0,100) var Mana:int
@export_range (0,100) var Health:int
@export var BlendColor:Color
```

Next, create a new resource based on this script. If the script were defining data for a character type, such as a mage or a warrior, then each resource would represent a unique type – one resource for each. See Figure 9.3.

Now, by selecting the newly created *Resource* in the *FileSystem* dock, you can set its properties in the Inspector. Remember, any objects that

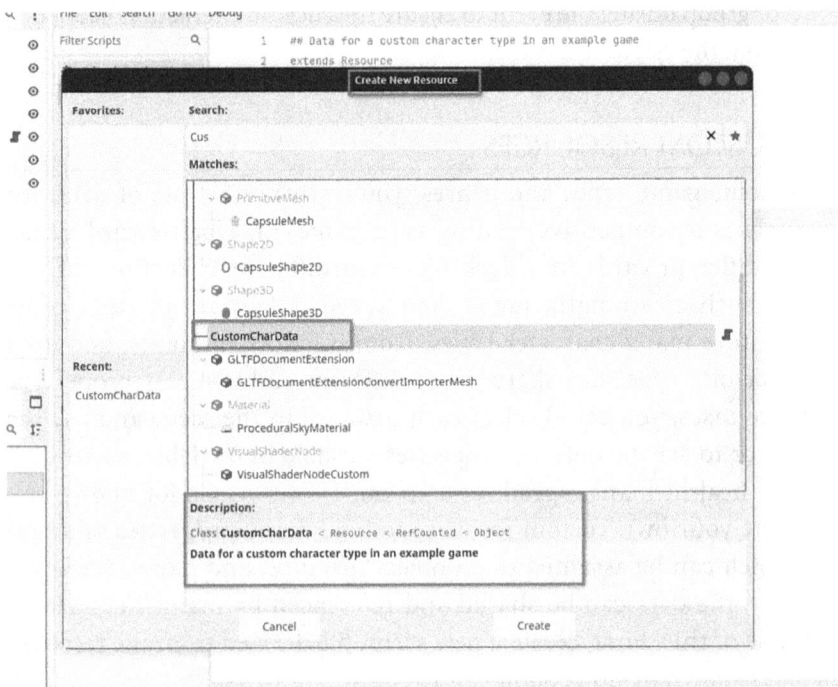

FIGURE 9.3   Creating a new Resource based on a custom type.

reference this resource will be updated in all scenes everywhere, making this a great option for sharing data. See Figure 9.4.

The remaining question now *is* how does a single object in a scene, such as a character mesh, access and reference a custom resource asset, such as character data, reading values from it, such as health? See Code Sample 9.3 below.

CODE SAMPLE 9.3

```
extends Node3D
@export var Starting_Data:CustomCharData
func _ready() -> void:
        print("My starting health is " + var_to_
str(Starting_Data.Health))
```

Code Sample 9.3 above allows you to attach character data, as a project-wide resource, to a specific character instance in a scene. This means that if, later, you decide to change the core properties of a character type, you can edit the original resource and thereby have the changes propagate everywhere to all instances. See Figure 9.5.

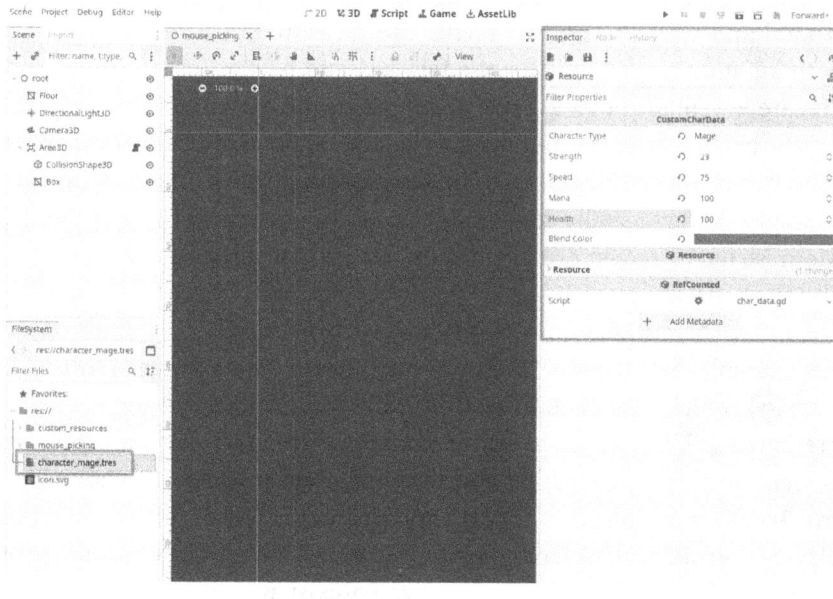

FIGURE 9.4   Setting properties for the new resource.

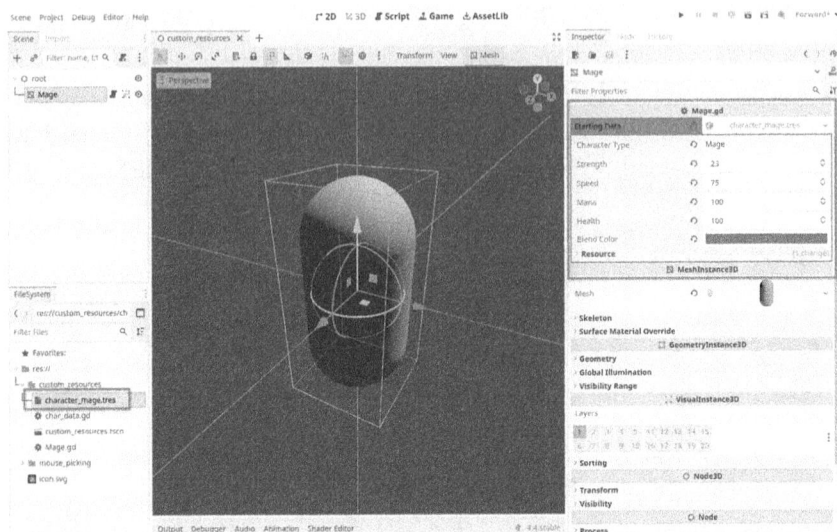

FIGURE 9.5   Attaching resource data to an instance.

9.3 MIXING 2D AND 3D SCENES

We've seen already that Godot supports three major scene types, namely *2D*, *3D*, and *UI*. 2D scenes have a *Node2D* as their root by default, 3D have a *Node3D*, and *UI* has a *Control* node. In 2D scenes, nodes live in a Cartesian space of two dimensions: X and Y, corresponding to the horizontal and vertical axes. 3D scenes are measured in three dimensions, with an additional Z axis for the forward and backward direction. And UIs are, essentially, in a 2D space, but with additional, precision controls to attach scene nodes to the edges of the screen. In many cases, these scene types never meet: a 2D side-scrolling platformer game with 2D sprites, for example, doesn't usually contain 3D elements, as character meshes, and a Main Menu UI screen doesn't usually feature gameplay, such as shooting and jumping, in either 2D or 3D. However, there are important gameplay scenarios where scenes do seem to blend with one another and must do so. For example, first-person 3D games often feature a HUD (i.e., *Heads Up Display*), which may contain an overhead map, health bars, and elements presented as UI or 2D elements fixed to the screen. Similarly, a 2D Menu Screen for character creation and customization might feature an adaptive 3D character, one that changes and updates based on settings that the player controls, such as hair color, physical size, and costume. In all these cases, and more, different scene types co-exist with each other in real time. Let's see how to set up these kinds of scene connections. Specifically, we'll consider two main cases.

9.3.1 Inserting UI Scenes into 3D Scenes

Let's start with the most common case, displaying a *UI* scene inside a *3D* scene. Some common examples of this would be to show a health bar over a 3D character, or to show a high score or an on-screen speedometer for a 3D racing game, or even a mini-map view for a first-person shooter. There are many commonplace situations in games where this would be useful. So, let's get started and see the methodology, which scales from simple to complex scenes. To start, create a simple UI scene and a simple 3D scene. Consider Figures 9.6 and 9.7, which are our starting points. You can use different scenes if preferred.

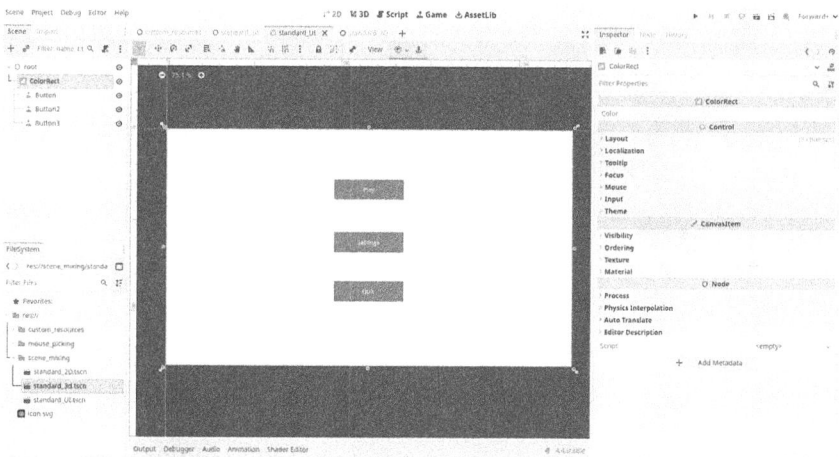

FIGURE 9.6   A UI scene.

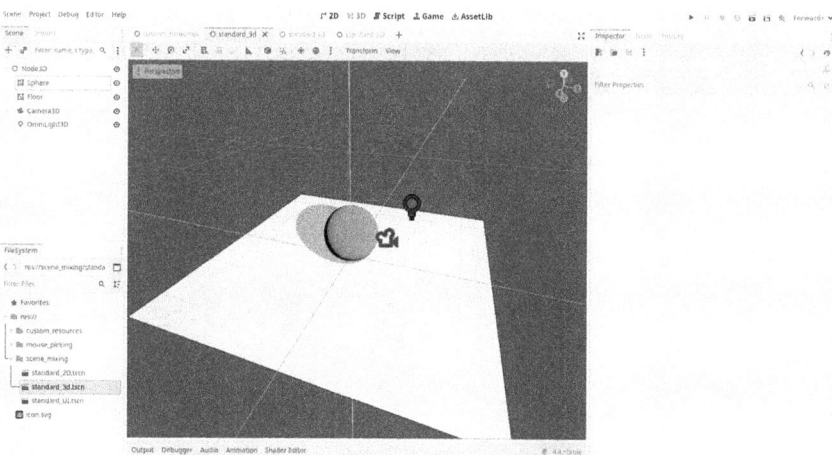

FIGURE 9.7   A 3D scene.

Next, open the 3D scene in the editor. We should always start with the destination scene. Let's create a surface inside which the UI scene will be shown as a texture. To do this, create a new *MeshInstance3D* and generate a *Plane*. See Figure 9.8.

Now we'll create a *SubViewport* Node. This renders the contents of its child nodes to an internal texture, as opposed to the screen directly. By itself, the node doesn't show anything. Rather, it renders its children into pixels inside a texture, which is hidden. You can use the *SubViewport* roll-out in the *Inspector* to choose the *Size* of the texture. Here, I'll set the size to 512 by 512 pixels. The size should be no larger than you need. See Figure 9.9.

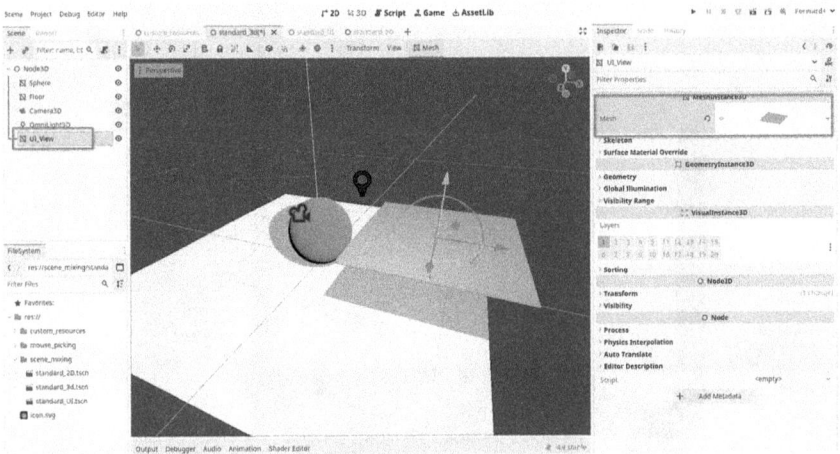

FIGURE 9.8   Creating a plane mesh for a UI view.

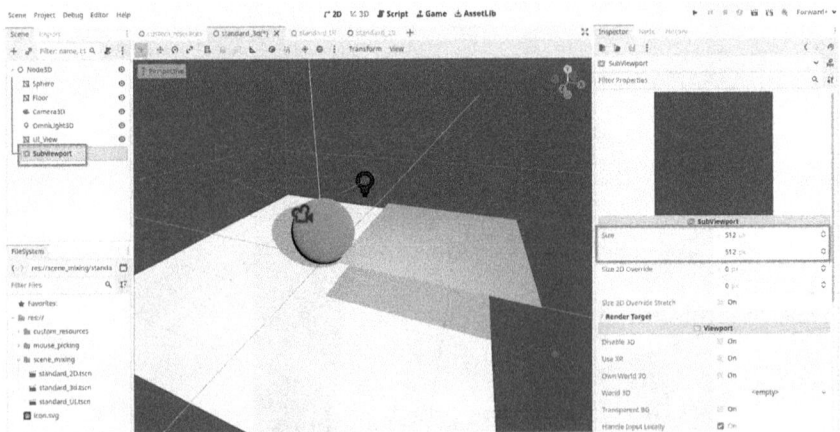

FIGURE 9.9   Setting the render texture size.

Next, drag and drop the UI scene from the *FileSystem* into the Scene as a child node of the *SubViewport*. Make sure it's a child of the SubViewport. At this point, the display of the 3D view in the editor may change as it tries to show you the contents of the UI scene. You can easily return to the normal 3D view by selecting one of the 3D nodes from the *Scene* panel. See Figure 9.10.

In this configuration, the *SubViewport* node is now rendering its children to a texture. Let's now configure the newly created *Plane* object to display the *SubViewport* texture on its surface to show the UI in the scene. To do this, select the plane mesh and, from the Inspector, open the *Surface Material Override* field. From the drop-down of slot 0, choose *New StandardMaterial3D*, to create a new material.

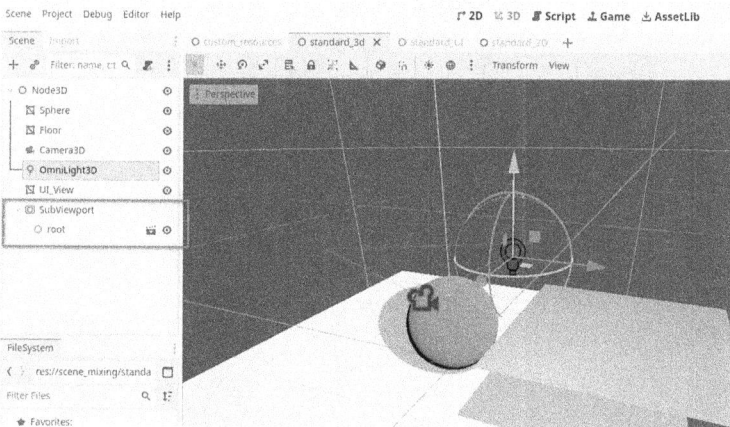

FIGURE 9.10   Adding a UI scene to the 3D scene.

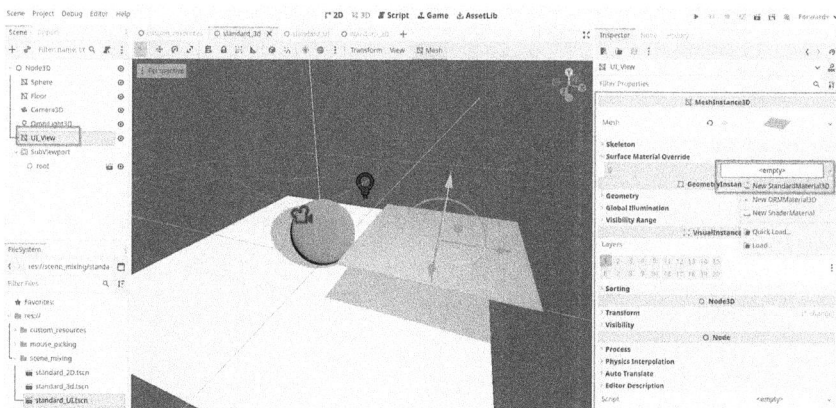

FIGURE 9.11   Creating a new standard material.

For the *ViewportTexture* to work correctly and show the UI scene, you'll first need to scroll to the bottom of the material and enable the *Local to Scene* checkbox. This ensures the material is not a project-wide resource but a scene-specific resource. This will be needed to reference the scene-specific viewport texture in the next step. See Figure 9.12.

Next, expand the material's *Albedo* slot, and from the texture field drop-down, choose *New Viewport Texture*. See Figure 9.13.

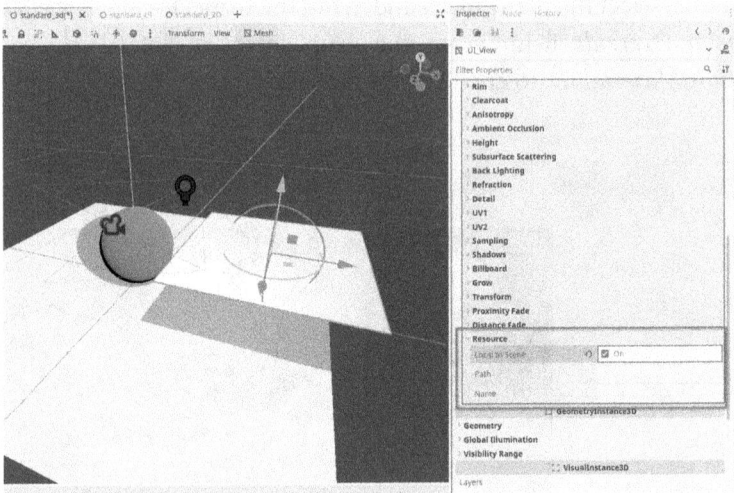

FIGURE 9.12   Creating a *Local to Scene* material.

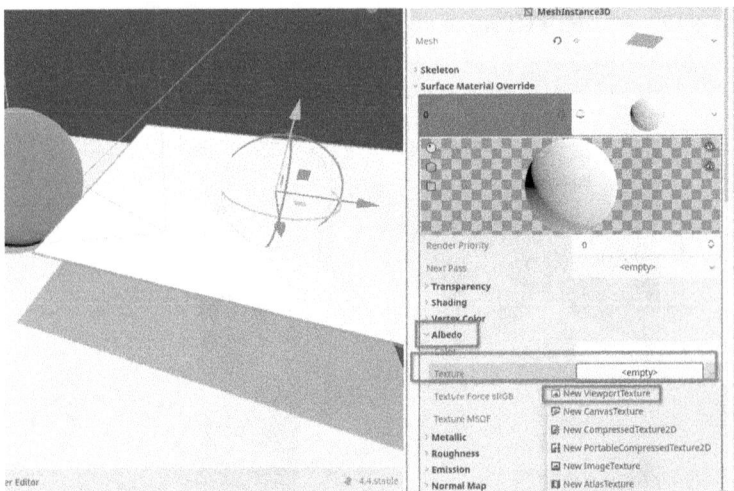

FIGURE 9.13   Creating a new Viewport texture.

After choosing *New ViewportTexture* from the drop-down, expand the *ViewportPath* field and click the *Assign...* button. Then choose the *SubViewport* object. When you do this, a connection is made between the *Albedo* Texture and the internal *ViewportTexture* that is generated by the *SubViewport*.

And that's it! You did it. Your textured quad is now displaying the contents of the selected UI scene, using the Viewport. See Figure 9.15.

9.3.2 Inserting 3D Scenes into 2D Scenes

Now we'll try another use case. Specifically, showing a 3D scene inside a 2D scene. The process is very similar to showing a UI scene in a 3D scene, as we did above. To start, let's create a new 2D scene and add a *Camera2D* object. Then we'll add a *MeshInstance2D*. This is a 2D mesh object. See Figure 9.16.

Next, move to the Inspect and click on the *Mesh* drop-down. From the drop-down, choose *PlaneMesh*. See Figure 9.17.

Now set the *width* and *height* of the mesh to *100x100*. This is set in pixels. And then set the *Orientation* to *Face Z* to align the mesh to the camera in the 2D plane. See Figure 9.18.

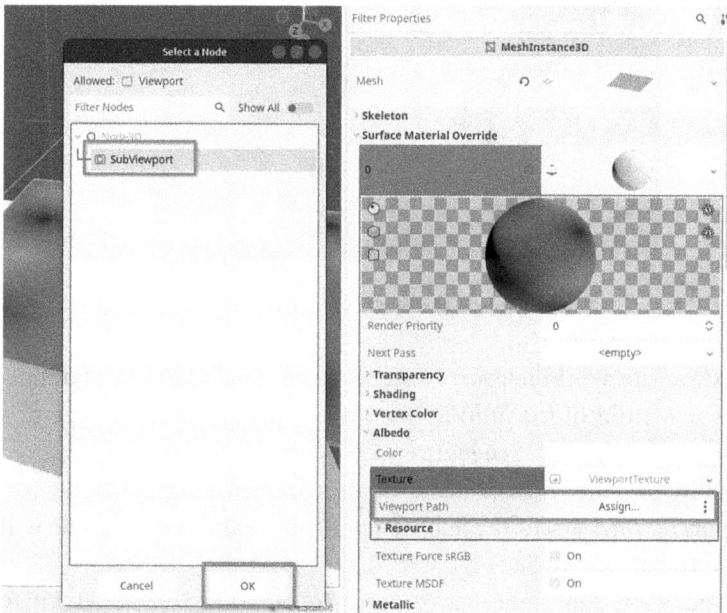

FIGURE 9.14   Connecting Albedo to the Viewport Texture.

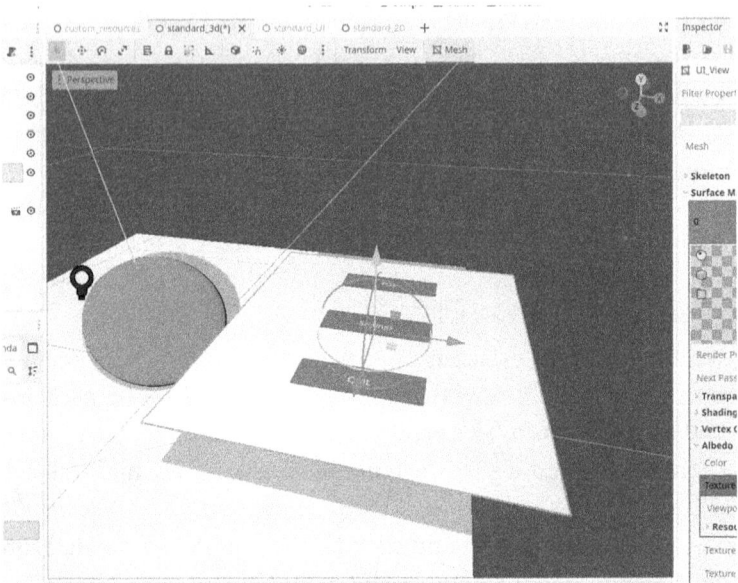

FIGURE 9.15 Rendering the UI on a 3D surface in a 3D scene.

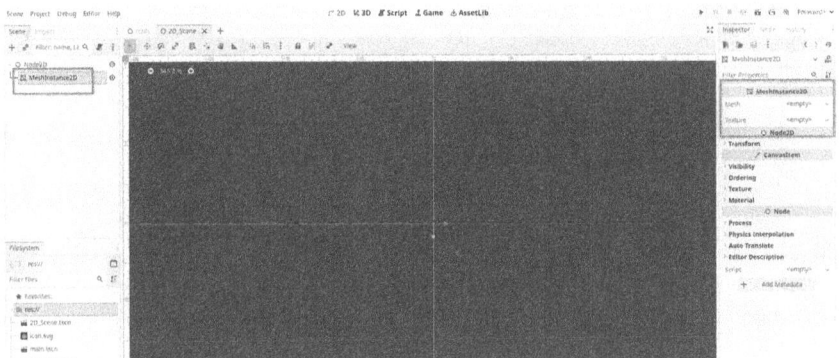

FIGURE 9.16 Creating a Mesh2D object.

Next, create a *SubViewport* Node set to a size of 512x512, and make the 3D scene a child of the *SubViewport* node, using the same type of setup that we created earlier. See Figure 9.19.

Finally, set the *Texture* field of the *MeshInstance2D* node to be a *ViewportTexture*. Select the SubViewport node, and the 3D scene will display on the 2D mesh. See Figure 9.20.

If you want the scene background to be transparent, return to the *SubViewport* node, and enable *TransparentBG* from the Inspector. See Figure 9.21.

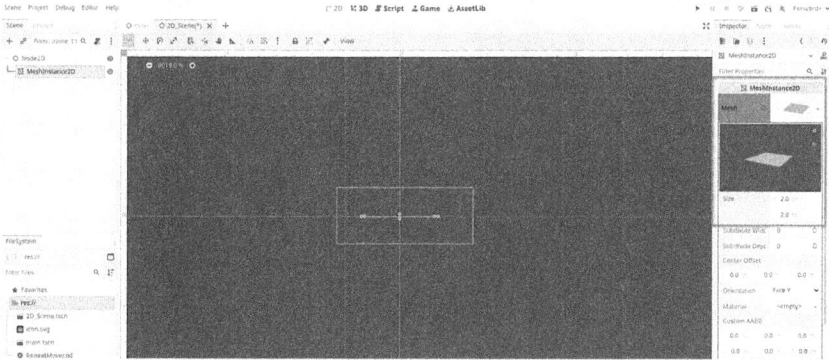

FIGURE 9.17   Create a new Plane Mesh.

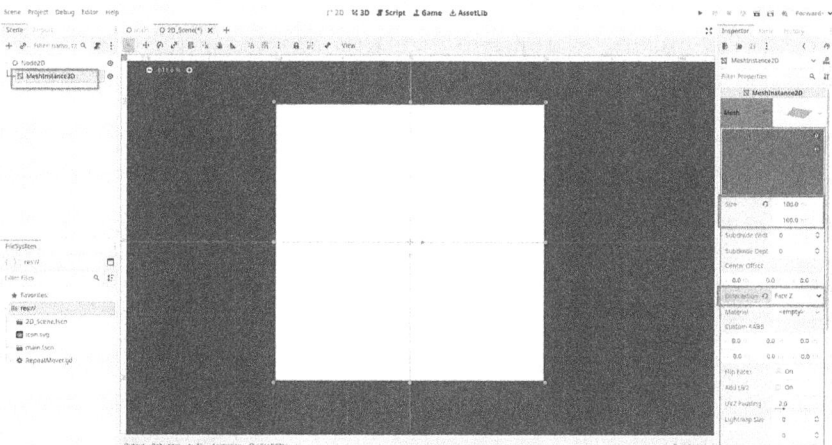

FIGURE 9.18   Creating a new Plane Mesh aligned to the camera.

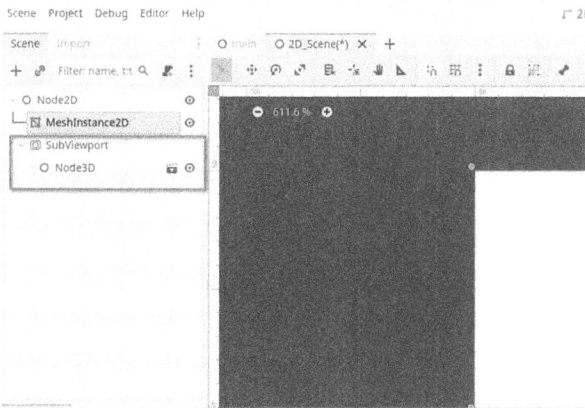

FIGURE 9.19   Creating a SubViewport node.

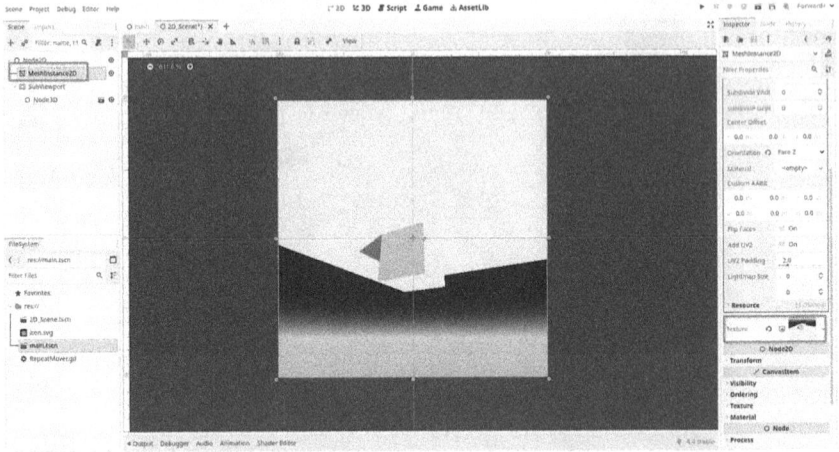

FIGURE 9.20   Adding a Viewport Texture to the MeshInstance2D node.

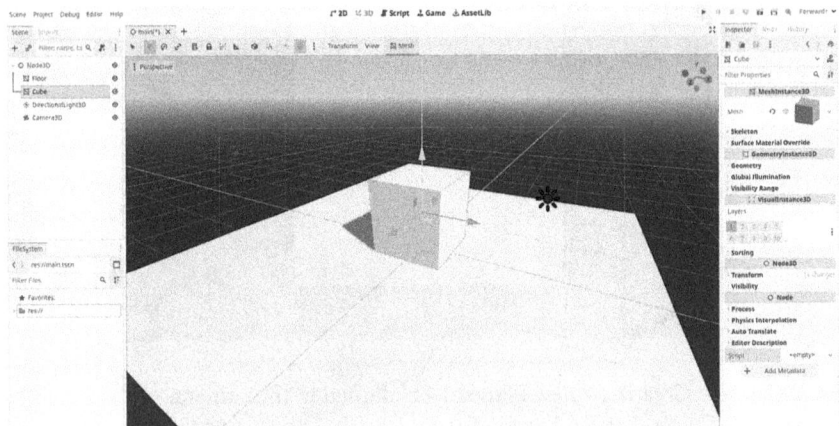

FIGURE 9.21   Enabling a transparent background.

9.4 USING CURVES

This section explores curves in Godot. The curve is not a node like a *MeshInstance*, but a special type of object available in *GDScript*. The curve object allows you to plot points on a graph by using the Inspector, and then a smooth curve is generated between the points, which can be sampled in code along the horizontal axis to read the corresponding Y value. Curves are especially useful for creating dynamic animations, smooth motion, and for reading statistical data, such as character stats and vehicle metrics. In this example here, we'll use it to repeatedly move a 3D object up and down smoothly, such as a moving platform in a platformer game.

Let's get started. To begin and explore the workflow, we'll use a basic 3D scene, which features a ground plane and a cube mesh on top. We'll be moving the cube up and down on the Y axis, based on a curve. Consider the following 3D scene in Figure 9.22.

Now consider the following code in Sample 9.4, which should be attached to the cube mesh in the scene.

CODE SAMPLE 9.4

```
extends MeshInstance3D
@export var main_curve:Curve
@export var sample_speed:float = 1
var _sample_point:float = 0
func _process(delta: float) -> void:
        _sample_point += delta * sample_speed
        position.y = main_curve.sample(wrapf(_sample_
point, 0, 1))
```

The above code features a *Curve* object, which is used later by the *Sample* function. The Sample function will return the Y value of the graph by accepting the X value as input. See Figure 9.23 to create a curve in the Inspector.

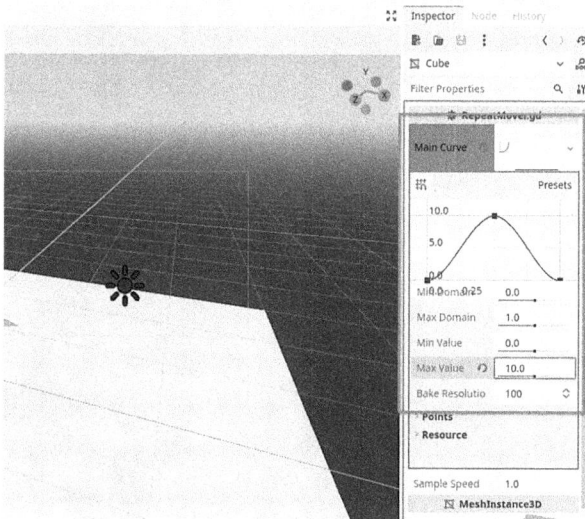

FIGURE 9.22   Starting with a 3D scene; a cube on a floor mesh.

Click on the graph to add points, and then click and drag the points to move them. Be sure to set the *Max Value* to control the upper limit of the graph.

Click Play on the toolbar and watch the cube move up and down in the scene. Remember to add a 3D camera in the scene to display its contents in the viewport. See Figure 9.24.

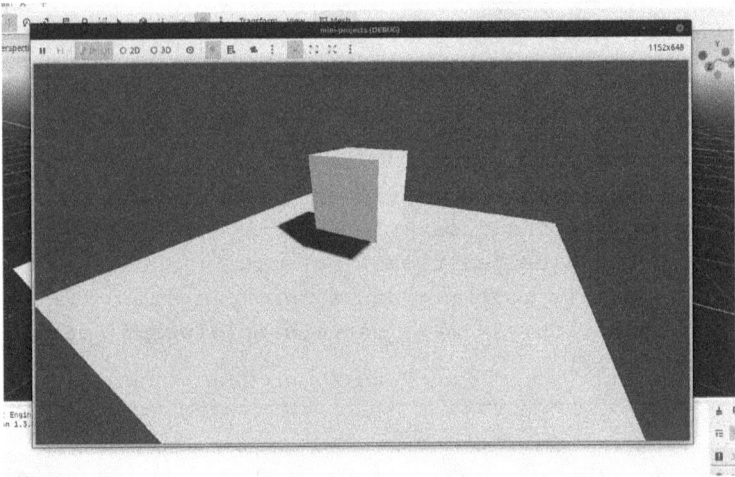

FIGURE 9.23   Creating the interpolation curve.

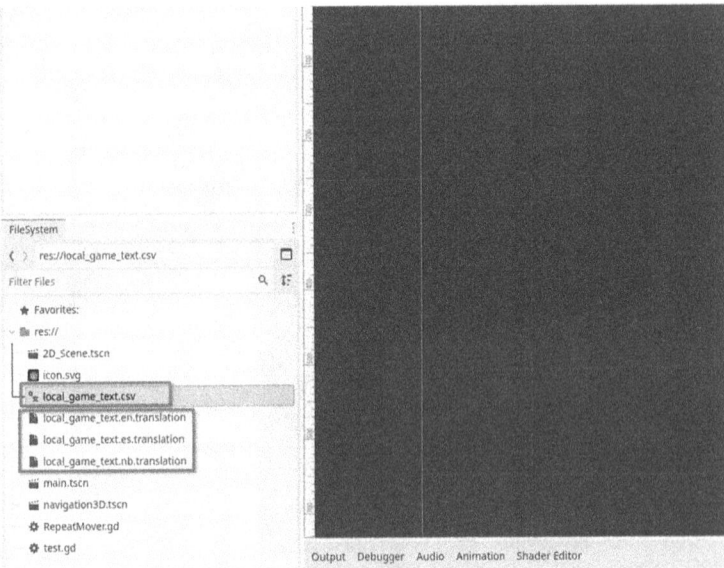

FIGURE 9.24   Interpolating mesh, up and down.

9.5 LOCALIZATION – TRANSLATING YOUR GAMES

You'll probably want to translate your game into other languages, such as Spanish, French, Norwegian, or many others. Or, at least, you'll want to have the potential to do so without facing the tedious prospect of scanning through your entire project for every element of text and translating it separately for each and every language. This is especially important for games featuring a lot of text, such as RPG games with quest descriptions and details or narrative games with closed captions. Godot offers a range of useful features for localizing your games, and I recommend that you build localization into your games at the earliest opportunity. Let's see how it works. First, you'll need to create a Comma Separated Value (CSV) file, which contains all text data in all languages for your game. This file will be structured into key-value pairs. The *Key* defines the kind of text being specified (e.g., *GameTitle, PlayButtonText, OptionMenu1Text*, and so on). And the *Value* field defines all the variations for this element in each language, in a structured order. Let's see an example in Code Sample 9.5.

CODE SAMPLE 9.5

```
KEYS,en,es,no
GREETING,Hello!,Hola!,hallo
NEW_GAME,New Game,nuevo juego,nytt spill
QUIT,Exit,salida,gå
LOAD_GAME,Load,cargar juego,laste spillet
```

The first line defines all the named columns for the file, and it also defines the order in which data will be presented. The remaining lines are all records in a single database, one record per line. Each line expresses a unique element in the game, such as the text for a button, the text for a HUD element, or a single caption within a narrative sequence. The key (which is the first column) is the global name across the project for referring to the element, and all subsequent values are the localized versions of that field. To import this data, you should drag and drop it as a single CSV file into the *FileSystem* Tab. See Figure 9.25. As the file is imported, Godot will automatically generate separate *.translation* files, one for each language.

Next, you'll need to add the generated localization files to the Godot Project Settings. To do this, choose *Project > Project Settings* from the application menu. Then select the *Localization* tab. See Figure 9.26.

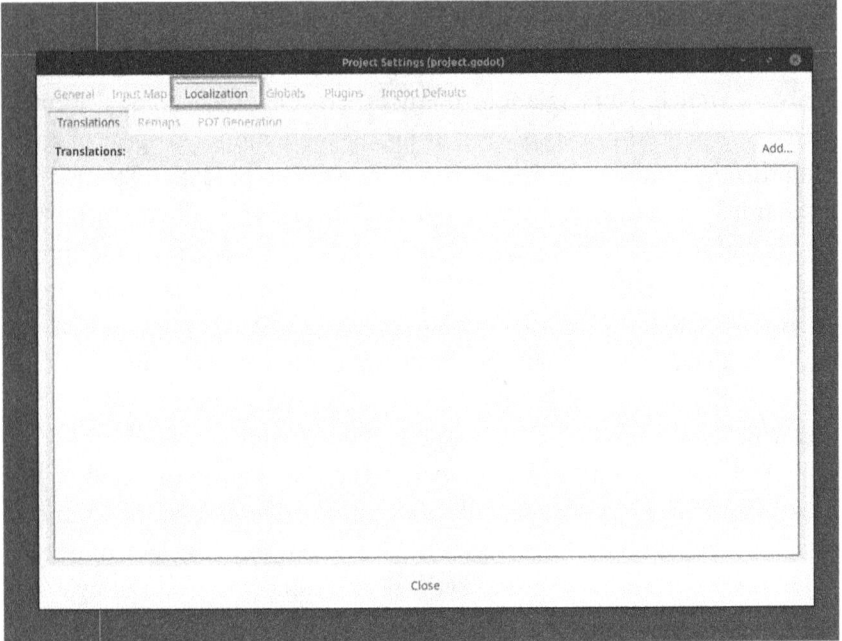

FIGURE 9.25   Importing localization data.

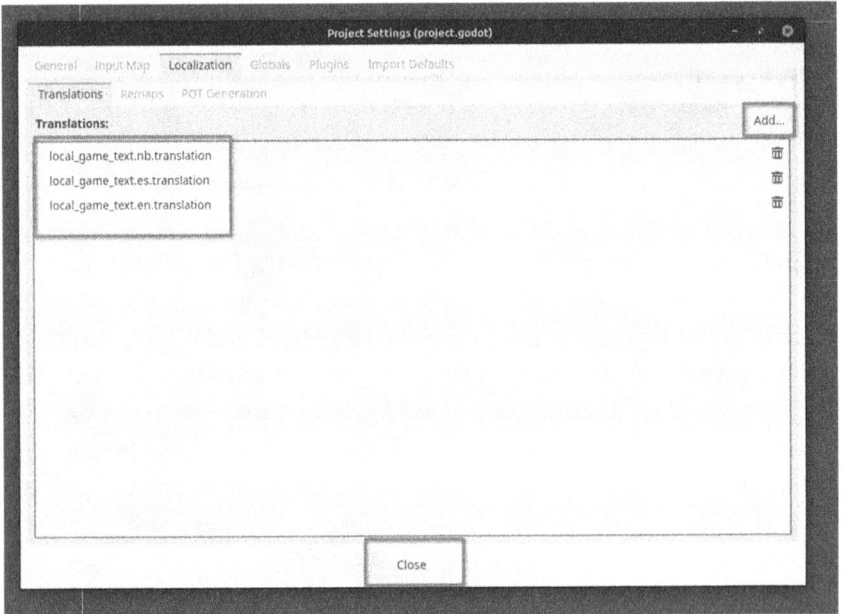

FIGURE 9.26   Access localization data.

Now choose *Add*, and select all the translation files to add them. Godot will recognize each as a separate language localization. See Figure 9.27.

You're now ready to localize your game through *GDScript*. To start, if you need to determine which language your OS is currently in, you can run the following code in Sample 9.6:

CODE SAMPLE 9.6

```
var OS_Language:String = OS.get_locale_language()
```

The *get_locale_language* will return a string in a domain code. For example, 'en' means English, 'fr' is French, and 'es' is Spanish. For a full list of domain codes, you can visit the following page at the Godot online documentation: https://docs.godotengine.org/en/stable/tutorials/i18n/locales. html#doc-locales.

You can set the game language using the following code in Sample 9.7.

CODE SAMPLE 9.7

```
//'en' can be replaced for any domain code
TranslationServer.set_locale("en")
```

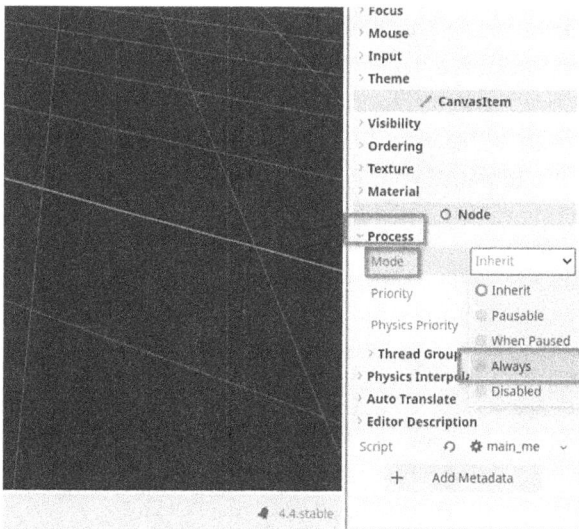

FIGURE 9.27 Adding all languages to the project.

After you've set the language, you can always retrieve the correct, localized string for each string element, using the following code in Sample 9.8.

CODE SAMPLE 9.8

```
var translated_string:String = tr("GREETING")
```

The *tr* function will return the translated string for any named key.

NOTE. More information on translating your games can be found at the Godot online documentation here: https://docs.godotengine.org/en/stable/tutorials/assets_pipeline/importing_translations.html#games-and-internationalization.

9.6 PAUSING GAMES

Pausing games is an interesting but often complicated process, primarily because most indie developers don't really consider pausing a game until much further along the development process. Pause behavior can be implemented in one of two main ways: one is through an entirely artificial process whereby you code all your functions and classes to recognize and adapt to an established pause system that you identify and plan in advance. This is about building your classes so that each object knows if and when the game is paused and then responds as needed. The second method, shown here, is a 'true pause' in that it causes the game tree, physics, and all your nodes to actually pause. Consider the code in Sample 9.9. This code should be an auto-load object, and it will become a singleton that you can use to pause your game as and when needed.

CODE SAMPLE 9.9

```
extends Node
#-------------------------------------------
#Use a properties system
var pause:bool: get = _get_pause, set = _set_pause
#Can the game be unpaused manually
var _pause_manual_restore:bool = false
#Can the game be paused at all?
```

```
var can_pause:bool = false
#Can the game be paused or unpaused by change in
Window focus
@export var pause_deactivate:bool = true
#Event to fire when pause status changes
signal on_pause_changed
#----------------------------------------
func _set_pause(_new_value):
if !can_pause: return
_pause_manual_restore = _new_value
pause = _new_value
get_tree().paused = _new_value
emit_signal("on_pause_changed")


#----------------------------------------
func _get_pause(): return pause
#----------------------------------------
func _notification(_source):
if !pause_deactivate or _pause_manual_restore:
return
if _source == MainLoop.
NOTIFICATION_APPLICATION_FOCUS_IN:
   pause = false
   get_tree().paused = false
elif _source == MainLoop.
NOTIFICATION_APPLICATION_FOCUS_OUT:
   pause = true
   get_tree().paused = true


#----------------------------------------
```

You may not want every node to pause during a 'Pause'. For example, when the game is paused, you may wish to display a UI menu showing a *Resume* button, which can be clicked to restart gameplay. This button, which needs to detect and respond to the click, should not be truly paused, as it needs to be 'alert'. Godot offers us a powerful setting for controlling whether a node is affected by a pause. This is the *Process Mode*. To ensure that an object is not affected by a pause, be sure to set the *Process Mode* to *Always*. See Figure 9.28.

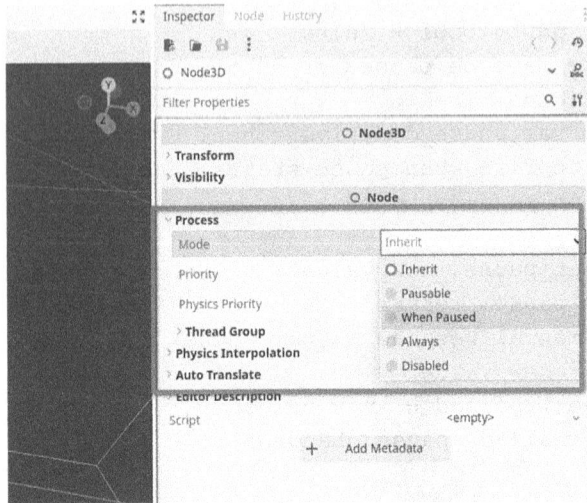

FIGURE 9.28   Changing the pause mode of an object.

NOTE. More information on Pausing Games can be found at the Godot online documentation here: https://docs.godotengine.org/en/latest/tutorials/scripting/pausing_games.html.

9.7 DEFERRED CALLS

Imagine this scenario in *GDScript*: you're iterating through a fixed loop of 100 items, and then, suddenly, someone removes one of the items during the loop. You expected 100 items, but now there are only 99. This is a problem. The loop could extend too far. Sometimes in Godot, this kind of problem can happen during the *_ready*, *_process*, and *_physics_process* calls. During these events, scene changes or the addition or removal of nodes to the tree can cause problems. To protect against this, Godot offers the *call_deferred* function. This function queues up your function call until the next *Idle Time*. That is, when the current frame completes, the engine can take a 'breather' to prepare for the next frame. This ensures that your selected code only executes outside of critical system loops. Consider Code Sample 9.10, which calls a function named *end_level*.

CODE SAMPLE 9.10

```
call_deferred("end_level")
```

9.8 PROCESSING RESOURCES

Each resource in Godot can be automated and customized through *GDScript* at import time. Consider the following example: we have a single *GLTF* mesh file exported from Blender and imported into Godot. This file contains many meshes, and we want to separate each mesh into a separate mesh resource file, one mesh per resource file. This is useful because we can access each mesh as a separate entity. Now, we could export the meshes separately and manually from Blender, one at a time. But this would be tedious. Instead, we could write a custom GDScript to automate the process inside Godot. Here, we'll consider how to achieve this. First, Figure 9.29 shows the mesh file to be imported, which contains many meshes.

Once imported, create the following script in Sample 9.11, named *mesh_modifier.gd*.

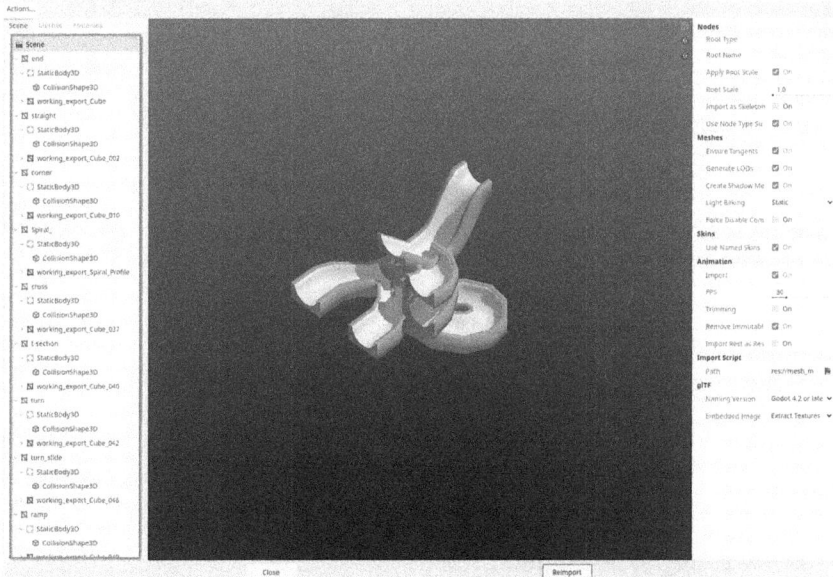

FIGURE 9.29   Importing a file with many meshes inside.

CODE SAMPLE 9.11

```
@tool #tool to cycle through all meshes in an
imported file and separate them into individual
resources extends EditorScenePostImport
class_name MeshSeparator
var _dir var _root:Node
var _mesh_inst:MeshInstance3D = null
#run when the resource is imported

func _post_import(scene: Node):
    _dir = DirAccess.open("res://meshes") #opens
folder
    _root = scene _loop_meshes(scene)
    return scene

#separates each mesh
func _loop_meshes(node):
    if node is MeshInstance3D:
        var path_str :=
_get_parent_folder_recursive(node)
        DirAccess.make_dir_recursive_
absolute("res://meshes/" + path_str)
    _mesh_inst = node.duplicate()
    _set_owner(_mesh_inst, _mesh_inst)
    _process_second_UV()

var packed_scene := PackedScene.new()
    packed_scene.pack(_mesh_inst)
    ResourceSaver.save(packed_scene,"res://
meshes/" + path_str + "/" + _mesh_inst.name +
".tscn") #save to file

    for child in node.get_children():
        _loop_meshes(child)

func _get_parent_folder_recursive(n:Node,
s:String="") -> String:
    var parent_node:Node = n.get_parent()

if parent_node == null:
        return s
```

```
        var _modified_string = parent_node.name + "/"
+ s
        return _get_parent_folder_recursive(parent_
node, _modified_string)

func _set_owner(n:Node, p:Node):
        if not n == p: n.set_owner(p)
for child in n.get_children():
                _set_owner(child,p)

func _process_second_UV():
        #store the original mesh
        var orig_mesh = _mesh_inst.mesh as Mesh
        #make a new version
        _mesh_inst.mesh = ArrayMesh.new()

for _id in range(orig_mesh.get_surface_count()):
    _mesh_inst.mesh.add_surface_from_
arrays(Mesh.PRIMITIVE_TRIANGLES, orig_mesh.
surface_get_arrays(_id))

        var old_mat = orig_mesh.
surface_get_material(_id)
_mesh_inst.mesh.surface_set_material(_id, old_mat)

        _mesh_inst.mesh.lightmap_unwrap(_mesh_inst.
transform, ProjectSettings.get_setting("rendering/
lightmapping/primitive_meshes/texel_size"))

        _mesh_inst.use_in_baked_light = true
```

On its own, the above code has no effect, but it can be selected and applied to an imported resource. To use this code, select the imported mesh file in the *FileSystem* dock, which contains many meshes, and then view the *Import* tab. This displays file-specific properties for the imported mesh. See Figure 9.30.

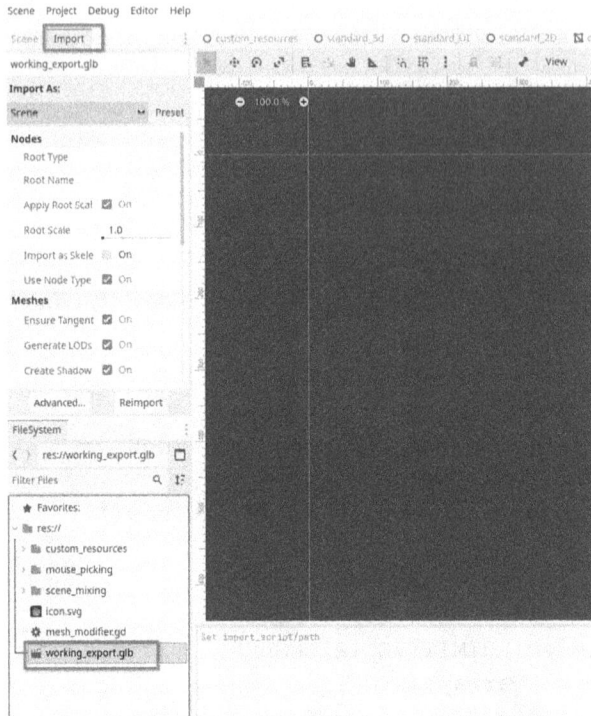

FIGURE 9.30   Importing a file with many meshes inside.

From the *Import* menu, scroll close to the bottom, to the *Import* Script section, and in the *Path* field, enter the fully qualified path name to your script file. See Figure 9.31.

Finally, click the Reimport button. When you do this, the script will execute, running for the selected resource. See Figure 9.32.

All the meshes in the selected mesh file will then be extracted as separate resources. Consider Figure 9.33.

9.9 EXPORTING PROJECTS

Exporting a project is often known, in other engines, as *Building* or *Compiling*. It refers to the process of converting a project into a standalone form that can run 'by itself' as an application, outside of the game engine. Each *Export* has a *Target* or *Platform*, which refers to the operating system that you're making the export for. This can be Windows, Linux, Mac, Web, Android, iOS, and others. It can also include consoles under

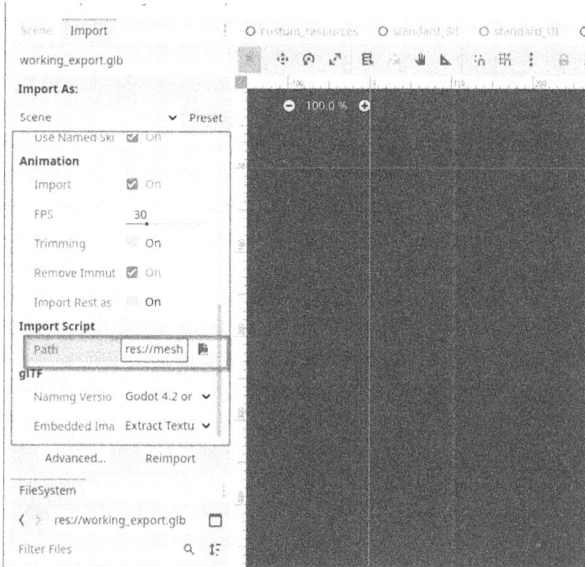

FIGURE 9.31   Selecting the script to attach.

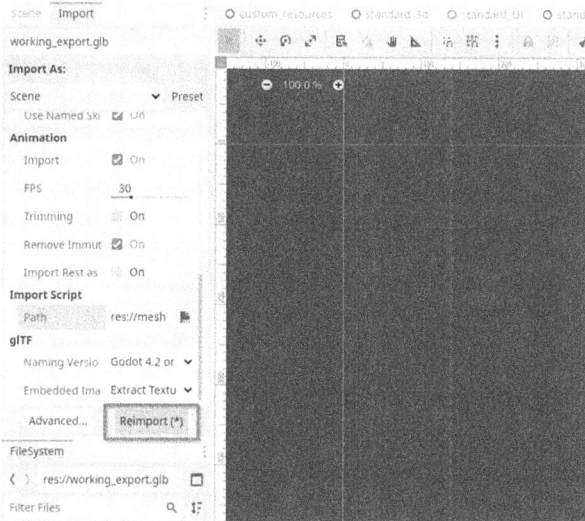

FIGURE 9.32   Run for the selected resource.

specific conditions. The dream scenario for most game developers is that the export process is simply a one-click process for any platform and that the export will always work flawlessly whatever the operating system. I call this a dream scenario because the reality is nothing like that. In practice, exporting is complex. Every platform requires setup and platform-specific configuration before the build can be made at all, and even after the build has been created, you may still have further steps to pursue for the game to run properly or optimally. Rather than go through every platform and every setting for every case, I will focus here on how to make a Windows build. This is the place to start if you're building for the first time. So, let's get started. First, select *Editor > Manage Export Templates* from the application menu. This displays the Export Template menu, as shown in Figure 9.34.

Next, click the button *Download and Install*. This downloads all the necessary functionality into the Godot Editor to create builds. See Figure 9.35.

Once installed, you can then make a build of your game. To do this, select *Project > Export* from the application menu. See Figure 9.36. This displays the Export dialog.

From the Export Dialog, click the *Add* button and choose the *Windows* platform. Here, you can add potentially as many platforms as you want to build. See Figure 9.37.

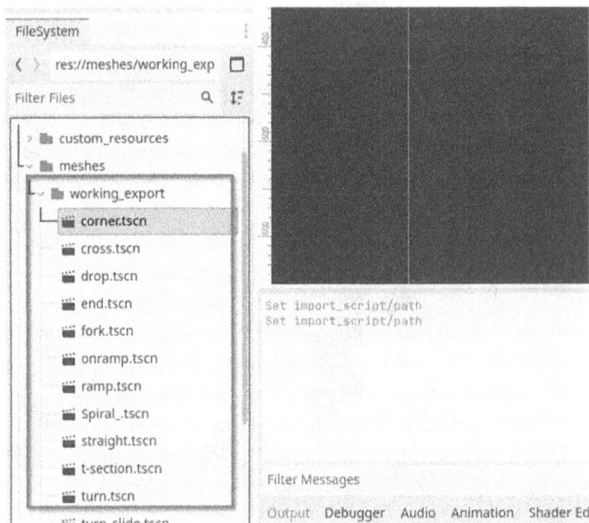

FIGURE 9.33   Separating a file into multiple meshes.

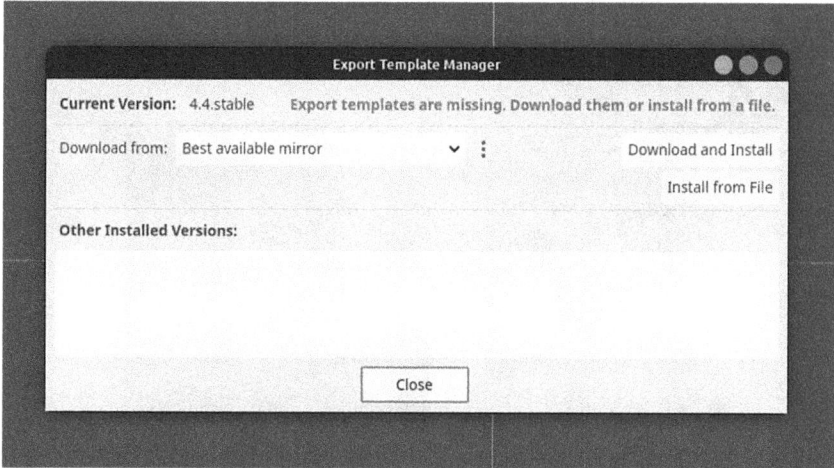

FIGURE 9.34   Viewing the installed build templates.

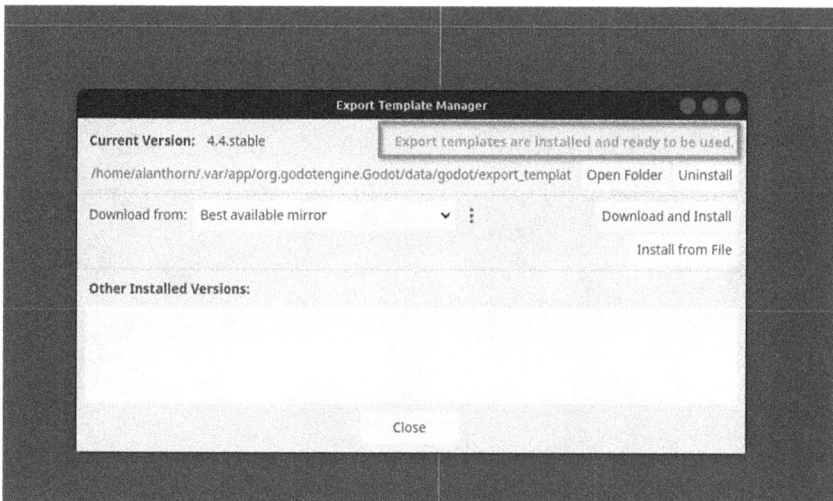

FIGURE 9.35   Confirming that the export templates are installed.

Next, select the CPU architecture that you're building for, which varies depending on the age of the computer and the hardware. Then scroll to the bottom and click Export Project. Choose a destination location, and then your application will be built, alongside any externally referenced files. If additional files are generated, in addition to the executable, then these should normally be shipped with the executable. See Figure 9.38.

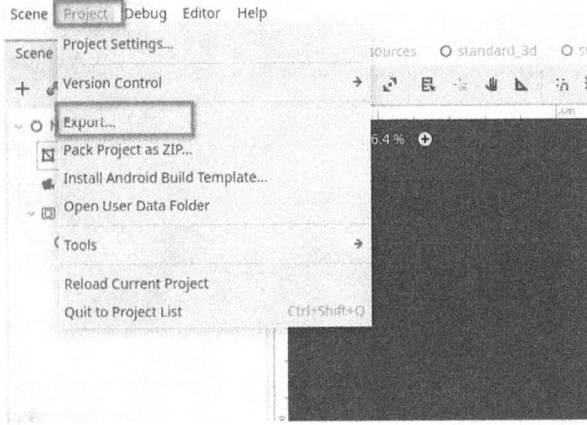

FIGURE 9.36   Confirming that the export templates are installed.

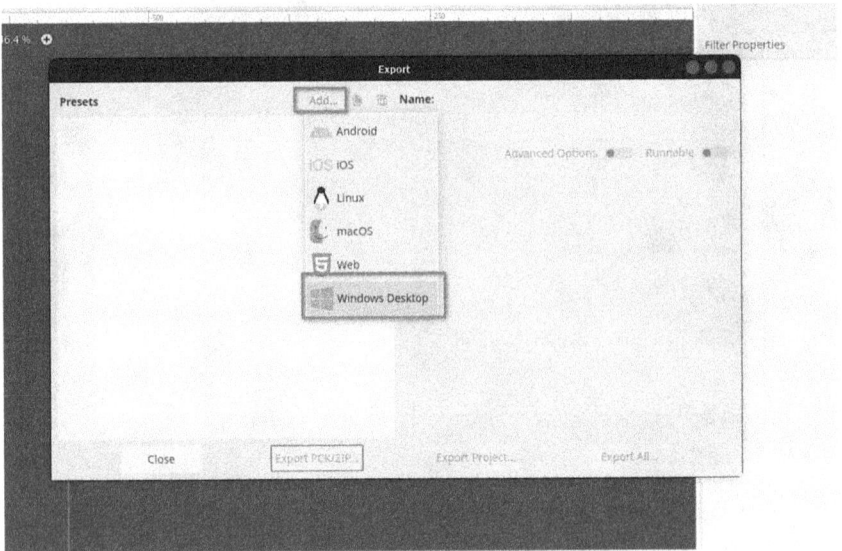

FIGURE 9.37   Choosing a build platform.

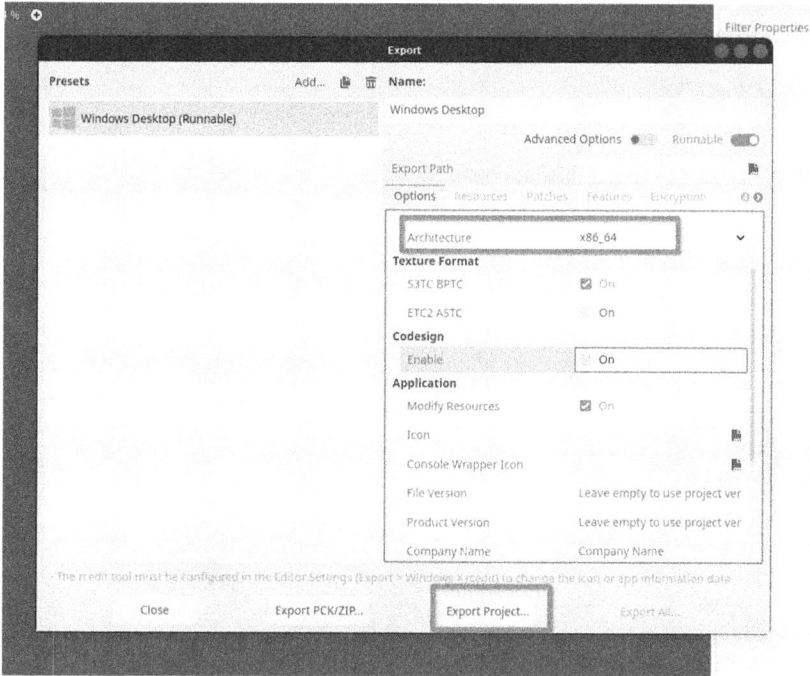

FIGURE 9.38   Building an executable.

9.10 CONCLUSION

This chapter considered a broad range of powerful tips and tricks for Godot. In reaching this point, you have explored the fundamentals of the engine, alongside many tools and features for more advanced use that can be deployed for a range of project types.

Index

Pages in *italics* refer to figures.

For Product Safety Concerns and Information please contact our EU
representative GPSR@taylorandfrancis.com
Taylor & Francis Verlag GmbH, Kaufingerstraße 24, 80331 München, Germany

www.ingramcontent.com/pod-product-compliance
Lightning Source LLC
Chambersburg PA
CBHW060757220326
41598CB00022B/2469

9 7 8 1 0 3 2 7 5 9 2 4 1